Braided Lives

Braided Lives

A 20th-Century Pursuit of Happiness

June Bingham

Straus Historical Society

PUBLISHED BY STRAUS HISTORICAL SOCIETY, INC.

EDITORIAL, PRODUCTION, AND DESIGN SERVICES
BY MTM PUBLISHING, INC.

President	Valerie Tomaselli
Developmental Editor	Carol Rial
Editorial Coordinator	Tim Anderson
Design and Layout	Annemarie Redmond
Copyediting	Carole Campbell
Proofreading	Zach Gajewski; Ingrid Wenzler
Indexing	Janet Mazefsky

The excerpt on pages 155–156 is from *Personal History* by Katharine
Graham, copyright ©1997 by Katharine Graham. Used by permission
of Alfred A. Knopf, a division of Random House, Inc.

Distributed by Syracuse University Press
ISBN # 978-0-9801250-2-3
Library of Congress Cataloging-in-Publication Data in progress.

Printed in the United States

With deep love to my living pulpiteer

"The past is a foreign country. They do things differently there."
—L. P. Hartley, *Go-Between*

Contents

Preface

THE 20TH CENTURY AND I HAVE waxed and waned together. I assumed that I would reach my end before it did, but in a phrase from my childhood, "By the grace of God and a long-handled spoon," I managed to outlast it. My fourteen great-grandchildren laugh when I use such terms as "ice box," nor can they believe that I knew nothing of radio or Pepsi. When I tell them no one knew of tomato juice until I was about eight, and we were forbidden to drink much of it because it was said to be too acidic, they are dumbfounded.

We didn't have pasteurized milk. There was no air travel. No telephone to Europe. I remember when transatlantic calls first became possible. My father phoned his mother, who had left New York and was living in Germany. Each minute cost $25, a vast sum at the time. When finally, after much shouting, he reached her, she was so thrilled to hear his voice that she began to cry—for the full three minutes.

What we did have, until antibiotics became available in mid-century, were diseases like mastoid (an infection of the bone behind the ear that nearly killed one of my two older brothers), polio and scarlet fever (which nearly killed my mother as a girl), diphtheria, and the puerperal fever that even in my own early adulthood was killing one out of 150 healthy women shortly after she had given birth. I was convinced that I would not survive beyond the age of thirty. Although I grew up in the New York area, and a girl I made friends with at Vassar grew up in California (four days and nights away by train), she had that identical conviction about herself. When she and I, by good luck and good medical attention, were closer to ninety than eighty, she phoned recently and said, "You and I are in danger as never before!"

She was referring to not the danger of death but to a prolonged, unattractive dying. Either could occur at any moment, as we both well knew but ordinarily forget about. We spoke about our hope to imitate the "one-hoss-shay" whose wheels all fell off at the same time or, failing that, to have one target organ whose collapse would rapidly do us in. In any event, she and I quickly moved along to her report about the trout fishing she had recently enjoyed with her eldest great-grandchild, and my report about the tennis my husband and I had enjoyed with ours.

My generation encompasses all the decades of the 20th century except for the first. We were thus lucky to be mere babes during the obscene carnage of the Great War (World War I). On the other hand, my generation was unlucky in that we were shaken, as a toy by a puppy, by the war's aftermaths. These included the stock market crash of 1929, the Great Depression of the 1930s, the death-dealing dictatorships of Stalin and Hitler, Mussolini and Franco, and the seemingly endless years of World War II. Small wonder that I, like every member of my generation whom I have queried, would not wish to live through it all again.

At the same time, if I had been born in any century previous to the twentieth, I would have died of physical ailments at ages 8, 27, 48, 74, and 82, and would have found my freedom of action radically curtailed because I was female and Jewish. Ruling the United States, not only governmentally but also socially, was the Protestant Establishment (the acronym "WASP" had not yet been coined). Even into my middle age, millions of Americans, as a matter of course, refused to sell their home to a Jew or hire a Jew. Yale University had small quotas for Jews (15 percent or less of under-graduates) and a zero quota for females. Amid the rich tapestry of the 20th century, therefore, I am particularly grateful for three inter-woven strands: improved health care, including emotional health; greater opportunities for women; and greater inclusion of minorities, whether Jewish or Catholic, African American or Latino, gay or lesbian, or the physically or mentally "challenged."

Preface

The most startling historic period in my lifetime was the 1960s. In large part because of the sixties' upheaval, my generation separated itself into two groups. One retains the post-Victorian values with which we were raised: that the man is head of the family, that the wife should stay at home and manage the household and children, and that the children should never "talk back" to their "elders and betters." Not without arduous effort, the second group has adapted itself to some of the trendsetting that started in the 1960s. By now, for example, these elders cordially welcome into their guestroom a family member accompanied by a significant other (what used to be called "living in sin"), or a baby born out of wedlock (what used to be called "a bastard").

At the same time, I am grateful that I don't have to try to explain to my parents what some of my four children and their ten children have been up to. In fact, this book is not intended to be an exhaustive autobiography of my life, but more an account of the public life I shared with my first husband, nine-term Congressman Jack Bingham, and my second husband Bob Birge, and also of my writing career. For this reason, my four children are largely left out in this book and only the moments with them that significantly changed my life and thinking are included. While my four children are little found in these pages, they were with me on every trip abroad, every political dinner, and each time my trusty old typewriter came to the end of a page. As I now write these pages, I now have my grandchildren and great-grandchildren to think of, too.

The passage of time has given two advantages to us in the older generation: we've been around for so long that we don't surprise easily, and everyone knows we won't be around much longer. Both of these enable us to say to a recalcitrant young person, "Here's what I think, but if you don't want to go along with it, then don't; at least I won't have to be around to help pick up the pieces."

When I spoke to the young actors in one of my plays, I found that they were yearning to know which things, in the long run, turn out to matter. As I look back on this tumultuous century, I can only report on what mattered to me and what now matters to me. Starting in the 1930s, it was the mate with whom my life and work became inextricably braided. Of course, some factors remain exclusively his, and some exclusively mine, but the majority, for better or for worse, were ours. (The living example of what we shared is our twenty-eight direct descendants.)

This image of the braiding of two lives is memorialized in my mind by a couple of trees I saw in Beijing. In the 1980s, Jack and I were on a congressional trip to China. One of the last things we saw before we left were the towering trees of Forbidden City that seemed as lifelike as us. Two trees in particular—locals call them "love trees"—have so thoroughly wrapped themselves around each other year after year, I can only think of Jack and me and our lives together when I remember them.

This braiding of two lives, while nothing new, has taken on a welcome new dimension now that many men also are willing to adapt their lives to their spouses' work. I still feel pleased when I hear stories that prove the worth of the adage, "Behind every successful man stands a woman," and today's updated version, "Behind every successful woman stands a man." (The version that the nine-term congressman from the Bronx, Jack Bingham, and I laughed over most was, "Behind every successful politician stands a surprised mother-in-law.")

Regardless of whose life's work takes prominence, the intertwining of lives is, I think, what matters most. In fact, I remain convinced that love, so indigenous to the human creature, will one day be found in our DNA.

PART ONE
The Thirties

Love in the open hand, no thing but that,
Ungemmed, unhidden, wishing not to hurt,
As one should bring you cowslips in a hat
Swung from the hand, or apples in her skirt,
I bring you, calling out as children do:
'Look what I have! — And these are all for you.'

—Edna St. Vincent Millay, Sonnet XI

CHAPTER 1

Romance

THE BAND WAS NOT A BIG ONE, but the woodwinds and saxophones invited us to foxtrot and waltz, or occasionally to charleston or tango. The Yale Law School boys were all in tuxedo or white tie, while we girls, mostly from nearby all-female colleges like Vassar and Smith, wore floor-length silk or velvet or taffeta dresses. February 9, 1939, was a freezing night. I would have been covered in goosebumps had I worn a sleeveless dress or one with a low-cut back. Dancing, of course, warmed us up, as did the fruit punch that, with Prohibition now repealed, was liberally spiked.

Aged nineteen, I arrived at the dance with a beau other than the one to whom I was unofficially engaged. My semi-fiancé, Fred—Frederic Hanes Lassiter—had recently been transferred by his employer, the United States Lines, a big shipping company, from New York where I lived to far-off Norfolk, Virginia. I had no inkling at the time that these two events—his being moved and my place of residence—might even remotely be connected. All I knew was that Fred and I hated being able to see each other only one weekend a month, and not even a full weekend at that, because he, like everyone else, worked on Saturday mornings. Needless to say, he and I spent few of our precious twenty-eight hours together other than wide awake, with every sense atingle.

During the rest of the month, we wrote each other every day, and on weekends I tried to keep myself busy rather than mope around my parents' apartment in New York or their house in suburban White Plains. I always reported to Fred on whatever my plans might be, and he had encouraged me to accept the Yale Law student's invitation to

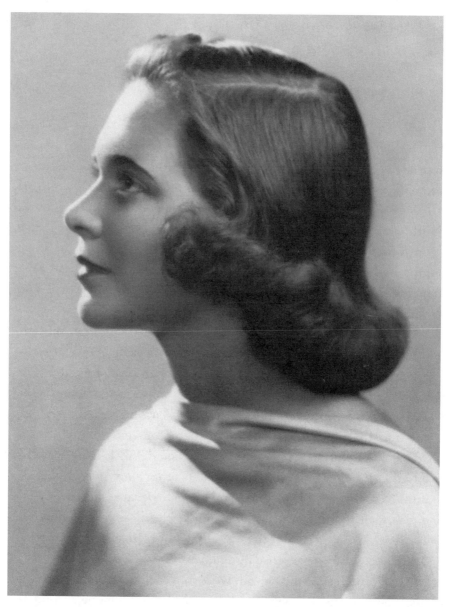

My high school graduation photo, taken at the end of my time at Rosemary Hall, the sister school to Choate (now combined into one school, Choate Rosemary Hall), located in Wallingford, Connecticut, close to New Haven.

their winter dance. At home in White Plains that morning, however, my oldest brother, Howard Rossbach, five-and-a-half years my senior, suddenly weighed in against my going to New Haven. He didn't like my escort's reputation as a "ladies' man." I saw no need to inform Howard that this same escort had already tried to get me drunk on "South Sides" (a deceptively potent combination of gin and lemon juice, fizzy water and mint), but instead of the drink's encouraging amorous feelings in me, it had merely caused nausea. Nor did I tell Howard about the time this escort took me to the Savoy Ballroom in Harlem, the garish nightclub whose brass band had a rhythm so infectious that the crowded wooden floor literally shook from the dancers' response to it. My escort had left me at our table for a few minutes and returned with two marijuana cigarettes (a dollar apiece, he said—the equivalent of ten dollars today). But when he and I later smoked them, it was clear that he'd been cheated. Absolutely nothing happened. We were forced to go back to our usual Camels without filters.

The morning of the Law School dance, my chic beautiful mother, perhaps encouraged by Howard's objections, also told me not to go. Her perfectly valid reason was that I was starting a cold. But I had given my word to the escort months in advance and I wasn't about to go back on it. Had I done so, my whole life would have been different.

That evening, as my escort and I were dancing, I caught sight of Jack Bingham, an erstwhile Yale College classmate of Fred Lassiter's and also of my second brother, Dick. Jack was tall, lean, hawklike, with a prominent nose, curving lips, and expressive brown eyes. He had a dazzling reputation as BMOC (big man on campus), having been chairman of the *Yale Daily News*, a member of Skull and Bones, the co-founder of the Yale Political Union, and a member of the Junior Prom Committee and the Debating Team, all of which had impressed my brothers to the point of causing them to mention his name in my presence enough times for me to remember it. I, on the other hand, had been trying all my life to impress my brothers, but with signal lack of success. They still called me "Shrimp" although by age fourteen I was five foot nine, and, as I was about to go off to Vassar, Howard told me not to come home and talk about what I was learning. "After all" he said, "I've been to college."

During my freshman year, I had been introduced to Jack Bingham by Fred one night at the speakeasy, the 21 Club. That afternoon, both Fred and Jack had been ushers at a big wedding of a classmate. After the newlyweds had departed, a group of ushers and bridesmaids decided to continue their partying at the 21. Fred detoured to pick me up at my family's apartment, and we joined the group at the three red-checked tables that had been pulled together to accommodate us all.

Though seated near Jack, I made no effort to talk to him. His reputation had elevated him to such a level that I couldn't imagine his being interested in anything I might say. Yet I knew that if Fred, as Jack's Yale classmate, had similarly yearned to be a big shot, he, too, could have succeeded. But in 1932, while Fred was a star on the Yale freshman football team and his brother Bob was captain of the varsity, a tragedy occurred in the game against the Army. I was sitting with my parents in the Yale Bowl when we watched a combination of hard tackling and bad luck result in a cadet being knocked unconscious. I remember the eerie silence, followed finally by nervous applause, as he was carried off the field on a stretcher. He died that night.

Fred promptly told Bob that he never wanted to play football again. Bob, a member of Skull and Bones, said, "Then you'll never be tapped for Bones." Fred said he didn't care. And by and large, I think he really didn't. In place of football, he played squash and attended literary teas at the Elizabethan Club. He, like Jack, got high marks. Had Fred stayed with football and become Jack's Skull and Bones colleague, Jack might have felt so much collegial loyalty to him that, again, the rest of my life might have been totally different.

After an hour at the 21, Fred signaled me that he wanted us to go off alone. As I rose from the table, Jack looked up. "Why do you always snub me, June?" he asked. I was so astounded that for once I couldn't think of a word to say; I merely threw around my shoulders the pale blue cavalry cape that my mother, the previous year, had spirited out of Mussolini's Italy for me, and, smiling, I fled.

The following spring, Fred escorted me to a party in New Haven at the huge Victorian stucco house owned by Jack Bingham's family. Jack and his four law school housemates were the hosts. As I walked across the marble floor of the front hall, I saw Jack coming down the stairs. I smiled up at him, but this time it was he who did the snubbing. (He told me later that the roulette wheel that he and the other hosts had hoped would pay for the party was unexpectedly running at a loss, so his mind was elsewhere.)

Fred and I didn't stay long at the party. Though the mint juleps were delicious, we didn't want to gamble, and the rooms cleared for dancing were crowded. Fred had recently given me a ring with seven tiny square jewels in a row, a diamond, emerald, amethyst, ruby, emerald, sapphire, and topaz. Although I thanked him, I was disappointed that it was not a traditional engagement ring. Whenever the subject of marriage came up, he always said he couldn't wait, and I, knowing his passionate nature, fully believed him. The problem, he said, was that his parents, lifelong residents of Charlotte, North Carolina, were reluctant to have him anchor himself so thoroughly to the North. I said—with the certitude of ignorance—that I could be equally happy in the South, although I was vaguely aware that overt segregation was still practiced. When I asked Fred about it, he assured me that "the Nigras and Whites" understood each other far better in the South than in the North because of their centuries of living in close proximity. Since I didn't know even one Negro, or even anyone who had a Negro servant, I was in no position to make an informed judgment—although

7

the subject of segregation continued at an unconscious level to plague me. What I also didn't know was that in the South the discrimination against Jews, too, was even greater than in the North. And heaven knew, there was plenty of it in New York. I can still point to the place on my solar plexus that felt punched when I or some member of my family was confronted by it.

My brother Dick, for example, a tall, blond, handsome, gray-eyed graduate of Hotchkiss and Yale, had fallen in love with a former Rosemary Hall classmate of mine. Her family lived in fashionable Greenwich, Connecticut, fifteen minutes from unfashionable White Plains. According to Dick, one day the young woman's father called him into his study, and said, in effect, that no daughter of his was ever going to marry a Jew. Dick said in that case this would be his own choice, and he marched out. For a while he was desolate without the girl. But he rose up again, so graceful a dancer and so merry a conversationalist that he kept being invited to debutante parties not only in Greenwich but in nearby, equally fashionable, Rye, New York.

The people I knew in Rye I had met at summer resorts. One was Bunnie Struthers who, like me, preferred playing tennis on the Bretton Woods courts to lunching in elegant fashion with our fellow guest, Oleg Cassini, later to become known as one of the great American fashion designers. It was at a party of Bunnie's in Rye that my brother Dick introduced me to his Yale classmate, Fred. Fred and I danced and danced. He said he would phone me the next morning. I said I'd probably be out riding with my father—and I was. But Fred persevered, and we ended up seeing each other almost every weekend, sometimes in White Plains but mostly at Vassar where I had just started freshman year.

On the weekends at Vassar, Fred's and my time together was happily uninterrupted (even though the door to a student's bedroom was expected to remain open if a male was visiting). He and I read poetry, took long walks, played squash, swam in the gymnasium pool, and talked as we had never talked to anyone before. He was patient and restrained as he led me through the steps of kissing to necking to petting. I couldn't believe the wild thrills that coursed through my body and caused a major reorganization in my mind, seemingly even in my soul. The innocence of a female teenager in those days is hard for subsequent generations to credit. It was a decade since radio had arrived in our homes and would be more than a decade before television did the same. Our ignorance, of course, was potentially dangerous in that birth control was not only unreliable but also illegal. In many states, both doctor and patient were sent to jail for provision or use of it, and back-alley abortion often led to the woman's sterility or death. Though my ignorance could thus have gotten me into trouble, I remain grateful for the privilege it gave of being able to discover sex as if it had only just been invented. I knew no names for relevant body parts in either boys or girls until after I took Physiology 110 at college, nor did I have an inkling of how irresistible a girl's urge to make love with the man she loved could be until I read a copy of the banned D. H. Lawrence novel, *Lady Chatterley's Lover* (a friend had smuggled it into the United States). In fact, the first time Fred kissed me goodnight, standing outside my family's front door, my first thought was why he needed a flashlight in his tuxedo pants pocket.

Around that time, my usually indulgent father saw fit to warn me that if I were ever to have a baby out of wedlock — Nice people didn't use the word "pregnant" except for animals — he would bar me from the house. My father was usually so indulgent that I was shocked. Here was I, his only daughter whom he adored — yet my virginity mattered so much to him that he would have cast me from his presence, perhaps forever, were I to "lose" it. For a moment, I had a fantasy about the glorious drama around such an event, but then my mother said, "If June goes, I'll go with her," thus taking the fun out of it.

Yet my father had encouraged both my brothers in their early teens to have sex when they felt like it. Dick actually won a silver cup at the Orpheum, a New York City dance hall, with such girls. The girls were "good time Charlies," and my brothers, I was informed, very much enjoyed going home with them.

At that time, Howard differed from Dick and me by not wanting to be part of the debutante circuit. Tall, slim, dark, with big brown eyes behind eyeglasses, he had fallen in love with a Jewish girl slightly older than himself. When he took her to the end of the dock one summer night in the Adirondacks, he was immobilized by fear. She, however, spoke up: "Faint heart ne'er won fair lady." He then kissed her, but not long afterward she announced her engagement to an older cousin of ours.

Whereas my ancestors in Germany had been ghettoized by the government—my maternal line in the towns of Rimpar and Limburg, my paternal line in the burgeoning city of Frankfurt—my parents' relatives and friends in Westchester County still wanted to live in groups. One such clump adjoined the Century Country Club in Purchase, New York, adjacent to White Plains. Its members were all Jewish, but my father chose not to join. "Why do you have to push a little white ball over the green grass?" he would ask when my brothers wanted to join in order to play golf. "After all, you have tennis and swimming and horseback riding right here at home."

The term "our crowd" was often used by my parents to refer to their relatives and friends, almost all of whom were married to fellow German Jews. Much later, Stephen Birmingham adopted the phrase as the title for his memorable portrayal of this lively group who looked down their not inconsiderable noses at Jews from Eastern Europe and Russia. His book, *Our Crowd*, starts with my great-aunt Hattie Lehman Goodhart saying, "There are some people we visit and some people we don't visit." Birmingham's sequel, drolly entitled *The Rest of Us*, is about the Eastern European Jews and includes a quote from another great-aunt of mine, Adele Lewisohn Lehman, wife of my great-uncle Arthur Lehman. When told that a young relative of hers was engaged to the son of a fabulously wealthy Eastern European family, Aunt Adele's response was, "But those people have just come down out of the trees."

My mother, Mabel Limburg Rossbach, was a member of the Lehman clan by way of her mother, Clara Lehman Limburg. Of my mother's thirteen first cousins, eleven married Jews and two married Christians. My mother and her two younger brothers married Jews. My father, Max J. H. Rossbach, and his two younger sisters also married Jews. In short, we rarely had guests for dinner or tennis or swimming who were not Jewish. This social matrix felt secure and comfortable, and my brother Howard remained rather absentmindedly within its confines, perhaps because his best friend was our cousin, Charles Altschul. Charles was in Howard's class both at Hotchkiss and Yale, and Charles's sister, Edith, was my close friend. On one of the first commercial flights in Arizona, in the early 1930s, however, the plane crashed, and among the dead was Charles. I don't think that Howard ever got over it. The funeral was impressive to me because Charles's father, the major financier, Frank Altschul, broke down in tears. It had never occurred to me that a grown man, one of those huge, seemingly omnipotent creatures, could cry.

Fortunately, the snobbery of the Lehman sisters, including my grandmother, was not shared by their brothers. Herbert, Irving, and Arthur went out of their way to be helpful to the Jewish newcomers by way of the Henry Street Settlement and other charitable endeavors. When time came to vote, those newcomers who had become American citizens returned the gesture. In 1928's New York gubernatorial election, the governor and lieutenant governor were still running separately. Out of more than four and a quarter million votes cast, Roosevelt won by only twenty-five thousand, and Lehman, by even less (fourteen thousand). Without help from the people scorned by his sisters, Herbert Lehman would likely not have become lieutenant governor and then governor.

My brother Dick and I, without ever mentioning the subject to each other, felt restive within the limits of this gilded ghetto. We wanted something more exciting, more challenging than just fooling around with the children of our parents' friends. At some level, too, we probably yearned to be part of the mainstream. In any event, none of the people whom either of us, as adolescents, happened to fall in love with were Jewish. (Much later, Dick, as well as Howard, did fall in love with a Jewish girl, marry her, and live quite happily ever after.)

The girls who were my earliest friends were daughters of the four couples my parents saw the most of. In addition to Edie Altschul, there was Marian Sulzberger, granddaughter of Adolph Ochs, publisher of the *New York Times*. Marian lived across from us on North Street, White Plains, as well as in a big townhouse in New York City. Another pal was Marjorie Lewisohn, granddaughter of Adolph Lewisohn, the copper magnate, who lived in a vast townhouse as well as on a Westchester estate ten minutes from us by car. Still another was Joan Untermyer, granddaughter of the prominent lawyer and civic leader Samuel Untermyer, who lived in a large apartment filled with antiques so valuable that we children were not allowed to place our behinds on any of the chairs decorated in petit point.

The two Jewish boys I had the most fun with while growing up were distant cousins of each other, both named Straus. One was Donny, with whom I rode horseback and sailed, played tennis and swam; the other was Billy (later the successful publisher known by his first name, Roger) with whom I went to Glen Island Casino (where Glenn Miller's band played). There we compared notes on who our latest love happened to be. As for my own loves, the first was Walter Birge, a Harvard senior whom I met at The Homestead Hotel in Hot Springs, Virginia, when he arrived as part of a Harvard Hasty Pudding show (as did Bobby Hepburn—brother of Katharine—with whom Walter and I played tennis). How strange that my first love's name would one day again play so big in my heart. Our young romance, however, was doomed when I finally had to admit to him my real age—which was only fourteen and the reason for my parents' refusal to let me go out with boys in the evening. Soon after his graduation, Walter got married, but he appeared back in my life many years later. Three years after I had met Walter at a dance, I went to Bunnie Struthers' coming out dinner dance—and that's where I met Fred.

The one time Fred's parents came from Charlotte to New York, the four of us had dinner at a restaurant. It was very polite all around, but there was an undercurrent of tension that I didn't understand and that Fred brushed off when I inquired about it. On another occasion, his older brother came and stayed at the Plaza Hotel with his wife. While I was using their bathroom, the sight of his blue cotton pajamas hanging next to her pink crepe de chine nightie made me cry I wanted so much to marry Fred.

Fred would set a distant date for the announcement of our engagement, but something would always interfere. My parents and my brothers liked him, but after two and a half years they began to wonder. I felt as if I were punching against a huge soft pillow. During one of Fred's and my inconclusive discussions about our future, I said that I wished I could fall out of love with him. He didn't seem unduly perturbed by this threat, but I couldn't imagine how any such an enormity could possibly take place.

From Europe, the news about Hitler's growing strength became worse each day. In 1938, when he marched into Austria, the people greeted him as a savior, but when he marched into Czechoslovakia, the Czechs, the Slovaks, and even many of the Sudeten Germans recognized him as their enemy. Before long, his Panzers had become so terrifying that the flow of people from Europe to America turned into a flood. My father qualified for inclusion in a category that I learned about much later, namely that of "foul-weather Jew." This meant a Jewish person who in ordinary times had no interest in his fellow Jews, as such, but in tough times did everything he could for them. My father signed so many affidavits (a legal promise that the refugee would never become a public charge, i.e., that my father would pay the person's bills if necessary) that he was known as Mr. Affidavitnik. Had all these refugees gone broke, he, too, would have been bankrupted, but not one ever did.

By the beginning of Fred's and my third year together, I was sleeping badly, gaining weight, and losing the ability to concentrate on my studies. With marriage vaguely planned for the following school year, I realized that I couldn't finish Vassar. My roommate, Adelaide Finkbine, blonde and gorgeous with a gray-green eyes and a firm chin, had already gone home to Pasadena, California, to prepare her trousseau for her upcoming marriage to Alec Hixon, who would be graduating in June from Yale. Our other roommate, Celia Coit, fey and glamorous, was leaving Vassar in order to travel. My parents were pressuring me to return to New York and become a day student at Barnard College. If Fred could succeed in pressuring U.S. Lines to reassign him to New York, then I could finish at Barnard as a married girl, a contingency that the Vassar administration flatly refused to consider. In those days, no certified nonvirgin was allowed to be part of the student body.

I transferred to Barnard where I studied the faces and demeanor of its three married students with far greater interest than I did my books. I did, however, pick up the useful knack of doing homework on the subway (from Columbus Circle to upper Broadway). Noisy, bumpy, jammed with people of every imaginable shape and color, the subway's hurtling motion reminded me of my fox hunting days at Rosemary Hall School. Having grown up under constant supervision by an ever-present nanny or governess, I loved the anonymity that the subway provided.

My parents still demanded my presence in White Plains on weekends. I rode with my father on Saturdays and Sundays, sometimes accompanied by my mother on her sidesaddle. In the city, on weekday evenings, I enjoyed being taken to plays and concerts and supper clubs by various boys. One evening, Jim Stokely from Tennessee insisted that we pay a visit to a friend of his at the Brevoort Hotel on Twelfth Street. The friend turned out to be Thomas Wolfe whose *Look Homeward, Angel* I had just read. As an incipient writer, I was so awed by Wolfe that I could hardly speak to him. He was even taller than I expected. His flesh seemed soft, but his words were penetrating. In his living room were several card tables piled with handwritten yellow foolscap. His manner was one of Southern courtliness, and by phone he summoned his mother and sister Mabel from their nearby room to join us for a drink. They, too, were very tall and extraordinarily polite. I began to wonder how much of Southern flattery could possibly be sincere.

As for anti-Semitism in my life, I have never not known that there was an Us and a Them. As the Delaney sisters in their nineties recalled about the South when water fountains were still marked "colored" and "white," "We may have been little children, but honey, we got the message loud and clear."

The message I got was that the Them, whether referred to by my parents as Gentiles or Christians or Goys, didn't want Us living near them or joining their places of work and play. Indeed, my parents, I realize only now, must have bought our place because White Plains, unlike the nearby fashionable Greenwich and Rye, did not have "covenants running with the land." These covenants were tacit agreements by homeowners not to sell to a minority person. Heaven forbid that the white, predominantly Protestant citizens of these areas should have to greet someone even remotely different from themselves. Only after World War II was this sub-rosa practice exposed by Laura Z. Hobson in her popular novel, *Gentleman's*

Agreement, later made into an even more popular movie. The resultant public outcry led to laws being passed against residential discrimination. But covertly this continued and still exists today in some areas. Formerly, it was directed primarily against Jews and Catholics; now the more likely targets are African Americans, Latinos, gays and lesbians, or people with serious disabilities.

In my youth, the top colleges so much preferred Protestants to Catholics and Jews that my brothers were fortunate to get into Yale from Hotchkiss, and I to get into Vassar from Rosemary Hall, even though, during the Depression, the number of paid applications to colleges had dropped. Nor might my brothers have been accepted by Yale if they hadn't had alumni cousins, like Frank Altschul, who went on to do well in life (and contribute generously to their alma mater).

What was true of Yale College was perhaps even truer of its law school: certainly very few Jews, of whom my brother Howard had been one, got in. And that night on the dance floor, at the fateful Law School dance, I didn't see either of the two I knew (one being Lloyd Cutler, who much later was a distinguished adviser to presidents Carter and Reagan).

The person I did see was Jack Bingham. I smiled at him, but he looked right through me. Why the arrogant son of a gun, I thought — but then I felt myself being cut in on.

It was he.

"Hello!" I said. "I just smiled at you and you cut me dead!"

"I never smile at a girl unless I'm going to dance with her."

This was the only time in almost half a century when a statement by Jack sounded totally illogical. But I refrained from saying, "Wait a minute, you *are* dancing with me."

What had happened, he confessed later, was that when I smiled, he knew I looked familiar but he couldn't place me. (He, too, had been enjoying the punch.) He had quickly asked another stag what my name was and when he heard it, he cut right in.

"Are you engaged to Fred?"

"Sort of."

"Then what are you doing here?"

"Having fun. Fred's stationed in Norfolk."

"Is that fair?"

"I can't stay home and twiddle my thumbs every Saturday night."

"Isn't that bitchy?"

"Isn't that none of your business?"

Before we knew it, we were in the midst of a terrible fight. As our voices rose, he suggested that we leave the dance floor and go to the nearby room of a friend of his. We went there only to find the friend passed out on the sofa. But we ignored him and shouted at each other some more. I suspect that both of us were trying to defend ourselves against a whirlwind attraction that might cause our future happiness to become dependent on a creature we scarcely knew and had no reason whatsoever to trust.

By the time the passed-out friend began to stir, Jack and I had simmered down enough to discover that we both hugely admired President Franklin Roosevelt, loved to play tennis and golf and attended plays and movies. He was so passionate about Greta Garbo that when he went for the fifth time to see her in *Camille*, he started crying as soon as the cast of characters was flashed on the screen. He suddenly asked me, "What are you doing next Saturday night?"

When I got over my surprise, we agreed to meet in New York and see *The Gentle People* with Franchot Tone and Sylvia Sidney. (Just as well for me that we didn't have to meet within Yale; in those days, if an unescorted girl crossed the campus, the boys threw open their windows and yelled, "Fire!")

Jack arrived to pick me up at the apartment of my paternal grandmother. Her name was Ida Kopp Rossbach Schwartzschild, and she was a hearty enjoyer of life. Following the premature death of her first husband Joseph Rossbach, in New York, she had taken my four-year-old father, Max, and his two-year-old sister, Carrie, back to Frankfurt, Germany. My father, therefore, though fluent in English (as well as German and French) spoke it with a slight German accent. After he had earned his Ph.D. in economics in Germany, he returned to New York to take his place in the family business, J. H. Rossbach and Brothers, which had been founded by his father, Joseph, and Joseph's two brothers. The company imported mostly hides and skins.

My father's mother, meanwhile, had remained in Frankfurt and married a sweet-natured magistrate, Ferdinand Schwartzschild, who was both younger and shorter than herself. They had a daughter, Grete. After Hitler was elected in 1932 and began his campaign against the Jews, my father arranged for his parents, whom we called "Oma" and "Ocky," to move to the Duchy of Lichtenstein, a tiny country that welcomed new citizens (for a fee). But by the mid-thirties, my father felt that even Lichtenstein was too dangerous. By then, Ocky was ill and Oma insisted on staying with him, which worried my father. But after Ocky died in the winter of 1938, Oma came to New York. My parents found for her a full-time companion named Miss Werthauer and a pleasant housekeeping apartment for the two of them at Hotel Delmonico, three blocks from our small Park Avenue Ritz Tower apartment.

It was at Oma's that Jack, in tuxedo, arrived bearing a red camellia which went well with my black velvet dress with white lace at the neckline. (People dressed up for the theatre then.) When Oma heard that Jack's real name was "Jonathan," she recalled a German play by the name of *Der Arme Jonathan*. Jack and I knew enough German to realize that this meant "Poor Jonathan." Since Jack was visibly anything but "poor," we all shared a laugh, and he proceeded to get along with her in a way that Fred never had even attempted. Oma, in her perennial black, was old and homely with heavy glasses and a heavy German accent; Jack was young and handsome, well-spoken and well-born. She was a recent immigrant; his family on both sides stemmed from Elder William Brewster who came on the *Mayflower*. Despite their differences, Jack appreciated her worldly savvy and she appreciated his charm.

Jack took me to dinner at Armando's, and after the play we went to the Stork Club to dance. In the wee hours we drove to White Plains, and the next afternoon I took him to Stamford, Connecticut, to catch a train back to New Haven.

I told Fred all about the weekend. He wasn't happy, but neither was he ready to counter by having our engagement announced.

On my next date with Jack, he kissed me. The same incredible thrill I had assumed could be provided only by Fred made me return the kiss with enthusiasm. This, in turn, he told me later, gave him an unprecedented thrill. He had long ago decided that he would not fall in love till after law school, but in his pocket diary he kept a short list of girls who might be worth looking up. I, unbeknownst to myself, had made this list, not for any real accomplishment, but simply for having been elected vice president of my freshman class at Vassar, a position without any duties worth mentioning but with enough prestige to make Jack think that I was more politically minded than, in truth, I was.

The more dates Jack and I had, the more torn I became, and the more complaints Fred was writing. Finally he said he couldn't stand it any longer and asked me to stop seeing Jack. When I wrote to Jack to tell him this ultimatum, he asked if Fred would permit us one last date. Somehow Jack had procured two tickets for the opening night of *The Philadelphia Story* with Katharine Hepburn. White tie. I had never been to an opening night before. Fred acquiesced.

Jack and I were enchanted by the play but felt the weight of the knowledge that this would be our last evening. Instead of talking about our early lives as we often did, we got stuck arguing about how the labor movement should be organized. The next afternoon when I drove him to the Stamford station, I said, just as his train steamed in, "The girl you marry some day will be very lucky."

He swung onto the train step and blew me a kiss. I assumed that I would never see him again.

Fred was pleased. Three weeks later, as he and I were driving across the Henry Hudson Bridge into the city (the toll was ten cents), I mentioned that the following day was Jack's birthday. Should Fred and I send him a joint telegram, since Jack had been such a good sport about writing a note to Fred wishing him and me all happiness? Fred shrugged. "If you want." So I sent Jack a silly rhyme about the limits of his future being the moon, with best regards from Fred and June.

Hitler, or no Hitler, in the spring of 1939 my mother was planning one of her annual trips to Europe to resupply her wardrobe in Paris and take in some plays in London. I felt so restless and conflicted that I asked if I could come along. She said no. Over the years, she had many beaus—not necessarily men with whom she was sexually intimate, but something akin to a best girlfriend, only male. My mother said she was planning to meet her closest beau, Arthur Sulzberger, publisher of the *New York Times*, in London, as well as a long-time not-so-serious beau, Amajit, rajah of Kapurthala, in Paris. So the last thing she needed was a mopey teenage daughter as de facto chaperone. My father never objected to these trips of hers nor, as far as my brothers and I could judge, to the beaus. Indeed, our parents seemed more affectionate with each other after their travel-based separations than during their ordinary lives together.

My father, during my mother's absence, would invite one of his adoring lady friends, usually Louise Untermeyer, Joan's mother, to ride with him and me on weekends. After lunch, he would take his usual nap on the living room sofa, with his head on Louise's lap. Though he snored loudly, she looked happy.

20

The evening before my mother's scheduled departure, I returned to White Plains from Barnard to find an envelope in Jack's handwriting on the hall table. All that the note said was, "Where do we go from here?"

I ran out of the house and into the woods. A storm was brewing. Dark scudding clouds, gusts of high wind, the rumble of thunder, short flashes of lightning, and then the rain. By the time I decided that I could not, in all fairness, marry Fred while feeling as I did about Jack, I was drenched. My mother was waiting in the front hall. "Get packed," she said. "You're going to Europe."

"Not for anything in this world!"

Later she would claim that I had ruined her trip because she worried about me. My father, it turned out, did what he could to reassure her. Long after both had died, I found a letter he had written to her on May 23, 1939:

> I left June at home this morning studying hard for her exams. Fred came out for dinner last night and spent the night with us but left at 7 o'clock this morning . . . I am trying to keep as close to the situation as possible and I must say that June has been quite open and frank about everything. She is in very good spirits and so are the boys [Howard and Dick].

Jack had a pilot's license, and while my mother was away he chartered a plane and flew to Armonk from New Haven. I drove from White Plains to the tiny Armonk airport to meet him. Helmeted and glamorous, he took me up in the open two-seater and off we flew over my parental home, which its previous owners, perhaps Scandinavian, had named Thirlsmere. The flying was fun. Though I felt some fear, I don't think I showed it. For a girl to be able to keep up with a boy and not act like what was then called a "pantywaist" was, I suspected, an important prerequisite in Jack's eyes. (The pantywaist was a cotton undershirt worn by little girls, including myself early on; at the waist it had buttons onto which she attached her underpants.) He had six older brothers but no sister and therefore knew little about how worn out a girl could get in her effort to match paces with him.

In July, I spent four days with Jack at the Camp, his family's country place in Salem, Connecticut. The one-storey Japanese-roofed house overlooked a lovely small valley with a pond and a meadow with classic New England barns and several wooded hills in the distance. The weather, alas, was perfect, which meant that every single day Jack wanted to play tennis all morning and golf all afternoon. In the evening, my indefatigable host took me out dancing. No chance for me to sleep late because family breakfast was promptly at eight. His small, white-haired, fine-featured mother would come to the guest room where I lay under mosquito netting and announce that it was 7:30. Her voice was gentle but the message was clear: don't be late. We would be served fruit or juice, hot or cold cereal (Jack rather revoltingly combined the two), eggs with sausage or bacon, toast or muffins. How all the Binghams stayed so thin I never figured out.

One day, Jack in white ducks and a polo shirt, and I in plaid shorts and a polo shirt, hiked through the woods and fields to the site of a cabin he had built as a teenager. I was only mildly interested in seeing it, but he was keen to discover if any part of it had survived the vicious hurricane of 1938 the previous autumn (in which a Vassar classmate of mine, Barbara Byrne, and her mother and sister had perished when they stepped down from their house in Watch Hill, Rhode Island, to see the wildly churning waves). Brambles badly scratched my legs as we walked, and the midday sun was parching. Finally we reached the spot. Nothing in sight but a stone chimney and more brambles. Exhausted, I sat down on the only rock without poison ivy on it. Jack started rummaging around the chimney. To my amazement, out came a bottle of sherry. He had built into his chimney a hiding place for booze because of his mother's opposition to it.

Jack had no corkscrew but managed to ram the cork down into the bottle. We alternated swigs. I didn't feel the brambles at all on the way home, and our golf strokes that afternoon were even more off line than usual. While Jack could beat me at tennis, I could occasionally win at golf. He didn't adore my victories but seemed to respect me for them. I felt that no matter what fame or fortune I could ever manage to achieve, he would never feel threatened by it.

As we learned more about each other's childhoods, we were astounded by how many experiences we'd had in common.

Neither family had been beset by desperate money worries during the Depression, although later on it turned out that some financial problems had arisen in each family. My father had a crisis in his business at the depth of the Depression. He went to borrow money to his wife's Lehman uncles, Irving, chief judge of New York's highest court, and Herbert, New York's governor, who gave him a loan, probably interest-free, which he paid back with alacrity. Around that same time, Jack's father had maneuvered his wife into advancing $30,000, which he subsequently did not feel needed to be repaid. Her non-Bingham heirs did not agree with him on this matter nor did some of his sons, including Jack, according to Alfred M. Bingham's book, *The Tiffany Fortune*.

Jack and I also both greatly preferred our country places to our city homes. We also both had older brothers (I had two; he had six), and nary a sister between us. He and I were the youngest children and, as a result, were a bit spoiled by our parents and resented by at least some of our brothers. We had both been sent to Episcopal prep schools, he to Groton and I to Rosemary, where the stiff upper lip was a prerequisite at all times. (One of my school's songs about the typical Rosemarian ended with, "She has learned to dry her tears before they fall.")

23

Both Jack and I had worked hard to earn top grades. His record was one of the best at Groton during his time there. (Despite his predecessors having included such luminaries as FDR and Averell Harriman, Jack's eminence lasted for only two years, though, when McGeorge Bundy came along to surpass his record.) I had won Rosemary's "high standard prize" for best marks during my last three years, as well as at graduation the Optima Prize, voted on by students and faculty for the girl most qualified in the three-way combination of studies, sports, and citizenship. As I later discovered, the secret written votes had been unanimous, except for one. That one had been my own. Rosemary girls were expected to demonstrate modesty about their accomplishments. I was hugely relieved that while it had been hard for me to write in the name of my arch-rival, Jane Knapp, I had forced myself to do so. But then, Jane must have similarly forced herself to write in my name. (My Rosemary diaries are full of resolutions to stop being so jealous of Jane, and I shall ever be in her debt because at Vassar she was the classmate who nominated me for vice president of the freshman class, which in turn landed me on Jack's short list of girls.)

Jack and I were also alike in the drudgery we put into achieving varsity status in sports, he, in football, I, in field hockey. We had further both fallen passionately in love for the first time at age fourteen, he with a Southern girl whose family undermined the romance by serving him hominy grits and cottage cheese for breakfast, and I with Walter Birge.

Both Jack's and my childhoods were influenced less by the values of F. Scott Fitzgerald than by the prim remnants of Queen Victoria's. In both homes, small children were expected to be "seen and not heard"—and not even seen too often. Both of us were frequently warned by parents and brothers not to be "so full of ourselves," and were rarely complimented lest praise attract disaster. We both were trained to "knock on wood" whenever we said something that might be interpreted as boastful, and we never stopped doing so. We had both been told that in China in order to ward off the evil eye parents would loudly refer to their child as ugly or worthless or stupid. At least Jack's and my parents didn't go quite that far in their constant critiquing. We had also both been repeatedly reminded of "the starving Armenians" whenever we neglected to finish all the food on our plate, and because we had seen firsthand the shantytowns spawned by the Great Depression and the men in threadbare Chesterfield coats selling apples for five cents apiece on the street, we knew how privileged a life we had been born into.

Privileged or not, our childhoods were characterized by the biblical injunction, "Spare the rod and spoil the child." I, despite being Daddy's little darling, had been spanked hard on the bare bottom, and Jack had been spanked not only by his strong stern father, Hiram Bingham, but also on occasion by his gentle mother who had armed herself with a hairbrush.

Jack and I were also alike in having had a full-time nurse or governess. His earliest years were spent in the company of his diminutive French mademoiselle on whose lap he would sit and teasingly say, "*Tu ne m'aime plus*" (You don't love me any more), only to be hugged and reassured, "*Mais si, je t'aime.*" I, similarly, had spent my first four years with my Scottish, white-uniformed Nanny Morrison who slept in the same room. During those years, I was subsequently told, I spoke with a Scottish accent, and much later, on a trip to Scotland, I startled my hosts by singing, "A Wee Doch'n Dorris" at the top of my malt-lubricated lungs.

After my nanny left, I, like Jack, had a French mademoiselle, except for the times when I was stuck with a German fraulein. Even as late as my thirteenth year, a governess was in residence in White Plains because my parents stayed in the city for the evening so often during the week and didn't want me alone with just the "servants." Little did they suspect that I much preferred my early supper in the kitchen with our young German cook, Carla, and her husband, the butler-houseman, Erich Thieme, to the fancy late dinner in the dining room with my parents who on occasion were not even speaking to each other, only to me. I hated having Erich and our Belgian waitress, Helene, witness this breakdown of family solidarity, and as a result I probably became the blabbermouth at mealtime that I still can be.

Jack's parents, too, went through a time when they weren't speaking to each other. In Washington in the latter 1920s, Hiram Bingham, famous since 1912 for having discovered Machu Picchu, would come home from the Senate (he was a Republican from Connecticut) and greet the dog but not his wife. She was Alfreda Mitchell Bingham, granddaughter of Charles Tiffany, the jeweler. A few years later, Hiram and Alfreda got divorced. He married Suzanne Carroll Hill, the woman he'd been "seeing" for some time, and Alfreda married Henry Gregor, a professional pianist and composer who had been accompanying her on the violin.

What Carla, our cook, had been to me, the Binghams' Scottish gardener, Albert, had been to Jack. In Salem, little Jack followed Albert around as he tended the large vegetable garden, the chicken house, and the ponies and donkeys for the boys to ride. Albert also filled Jack in on the ghastliness of trench warfare during the Great War. Carla, however, had only been a child in Germany during the war, so I didn't hear much about it. She came to the United States as a young woman and met Erich when she answered an ad he had put in a German-English New York newspaper. They met at the 86th Street subway station. When the train pulled out, only two people were left on the platform, both wearing white boutonnieres. It was love at first sight. But Carla was also practical. She lobbied me to marry my chum, Donny Straus, rather than Fred, because Don was so much richer. And she was horrified when Jack came to Thirlsmere for the first time wearing a brown herringbone jacket with chamois reinforcement of the elbows, a non-beguiling garment that he happily sported for several more years.

Neither Jack nor I ever had to live in a dogless house. As a boy, he had a white terrier whom he taught to jump to remarkable heights. I, starting at age four, had my own black Scottie. He was named "Bobby," after Baron Robert von Hirsch, a school friend of my father's and long-term beau of my mother's, who had presented him to me. Later I could easily identify which gentlemen were in love with my mother because so many of them gave me dogs. Poor Bobby had to be shot because of rabies (my father, brothers, and I were given twenty-one days of horrible abdominal injections to ward off the disease). Robert then gave me a wire-haired fox terrier that I named Ace, and later, New York Port Authority commissioner Howard Cullman gave me a Scottie that I named Commish, and Arthur Sulzberger gave me a Welsh Terrier that I named NYT-Wit (with prescience as to his low IQ). It was just as well that my mother's other beaus, including George Hellman, the poet, and Irwin Untermyer, the judge, refrained from that particular way of flirting or our place would have resembled a pound.

From early childhood on, both Jack and I were thoroughly exposed to classical music, which we loved. Jack took violin lessons; I took piano lessons. His mother played the violin; my mother played our player-piano, and, after 1926, our new big brown radio with its cathedral-type top. Every Saturday afternoon she would listen to the Metropolitan Opera, and I, out of choice, often joined her. Jack, who continued violin lessons through his six years at Groton, often joined his mother in playing duets, or, together with his pianist brother Alf or, later, Henry Gregor, in trios.

In early childhood, Jack and I both had explosive tempers that we learned to curb, less as a result of punitive action by our parents (whom we saw little of) than by our brothers. When teased by his, he would run after them and try to kick them. But, of course, this never worked, and as they ran further, they continued to turn and taunt him until he learned to stop it. I had a similar experience when my brothers teased me to the point that I hurled my favorite porcelain-headed doll down onto Park Avenue at 49th Street and they danced around me singing, "Don't you wish you hadn't broken meeee?"

Jack and I also went throughout childhood naïve about sex. Jack later told me about a visit to his Granny, his mother's mother, Annie Olivia Tiffany Mitchell, at her place in Coral Gables, Florida, when Granny's brother, the artist, Louis Comfort Tiffany, appeared. "Uncle Louis" was seated in the back of a huge open touring car, with a pretty young lady swathed in yellow chiffon. She, little Jack was told and fully believed, was "Miss Hanley, Uncle Louis's nurse."

Yet both Jack and I—this we did not reveal to each other until much later—had not been quite as innocent as we pretended. He found something to do with the trunk of a thin tree which he hugged, while I discovered that if I rolled over on my tummy in bed, with my pajama bottoms riding up as far as possible, I achieved an experience even more desirable than vanilla ice cream with chocolate sprinkles. On one of the few nights my mother came to kiss me goodnight she told me to keep my hands at all times above the covers. I thought this an odd request and didn't immediately connect it to my pajamas. I then figured that there was no way she could enforce her will. Defying her in this way became my first memorable secret and, as a result of my ability to keep it, I developed a new confidence in myself. Eighty years later, Harvard professor of psychology Daniel M. Wegner said that "In a very deep sense, you don't have a self unless you have a secret. . . . We all have moments when we need to re-assert our identity as somebody apart."

Jack and I were both also introduced to politics at an early age. His tall, imposing, white-haired father had served as Connecticut's lieutenant governor and, for a day, as its governor before going to the U.S. Senate. My mother's uncle, Herbert Lehman, short, bald, transparently honest, had been New York's lieutenant governor while Franklin D. Roosevelt was governor and was currently serving as governor. A decade later, he, too, became a U.S. senator.

Our families' party loyalties, however, were opposites. Jack's was Republican although Jack himself, during college, switched to the Democrats because of FDR. Mine, because of Uncle Herbert, was Democratic, although my father, a businessman, retained traditional Republican values. Jack explained that he had chosen law school not because he wanted to practice law but because he needed a fallback career for such periods as he would not be elected to political office.

For both Jack's and my families, the main financial grounding had been laid by our respective maternal great-grandfathers. Jack's great-grandfather, Charles Tiffany, two decades earlier, had established Tiffany & Co., the ever-more-successful jewelry store. My great-grandfather, Mayer Lehman, had come to New York from Montgomery, Alabama, after the Civil War, to run the New York branch of Lehman Brothers, the family brokerage house. In fact, while in Montgomery, the Mayer Lehmans owned seven slaves. When the Lehmans moved to New York, they brought with them the children's "Mammy," who was by then free and was paid as a nanny to the four younger children, the eldest of whom was my grandmother.

There is even an off-chance that Charles Tiffany might have met Mayer Lehman, especially if Tiffany's had needed a loan from Lehman Brothers, but there was no place where Harriet Young Tiffany would have met Babette Neugass Lehman. Christian and Jewish dwellings, private schools, banks, law firms, hospitals, charities were separate, and ladies did not escort their children to that effective melting pot, Central Park: that was what nurses and governesses were for. This thorough separation was often maintained in both directions. For example, when my grandmother, Clara Lehman, was young and had caught the eye of Edward White, a young non-Jewish lawyer up from the South, her family sent him away. He later became chief justice of the Supreme Court. Whether she had loved him or not was not the kind of thing that grandparents discussed with grandchildren in those days.

Jack and I both turned out to have had a vividly remembered childhood moment when we felt especially close to our respective fathers. At age seven, Jack had been determined to join his brothers in reading aloud to Hiram during the summer that Hiram was thought to have tuberculosis and lived apart in a small window-studded cottage in Salem. When Jack was brushed aside as too young to read aloud, he made such a fuss that his father agreed to give him one chance—but warned that Jack had better read rapidly and accurately. When Jack read out the word "chowse," his father stopped him: "There is no such word." Jack brought the book over and pointed. The word was "chaos." Jack feared the worst, but his father merely laughed and let him continue.

As my family and I returned, in August 1930 from our biannual trip to Europe, I could hardly wait for the *Berengaria* to dock so that I could be reunited with my dog and horse. But we were met with the news that infantile paralysis (polio) had spread through the New York City area. Consequently, without even a stop at Thirlsmere to repack, we were driven straight to the Adirondacks. There we stayed at Fish Rock Camp on Saranac Lake with Guta Seligman, grandmother of my friend and schoolmate, Marjorie Lewisohn. This, to be sure, was no hardship. I loved the sparkling blue lake surrounded by thickly wooded dark green hills. They were locally referred to as "mountains," but since I'd recently viewed the Alps, I considered this an exaggeration. Still, I loved treading the pine-needled paths punctuated by red-topped mushrooms and delicate, off-white "Indian pipe" flowers. From many of the tree trunks you could snap off a big palm-shaped fungus on which, with a sharp stick, you could create a drawing that would harden there for life. I also enjoyed our cool-off visits to the one-storey icehouse where huge squares of last winter's frozen lake lay in their sawdust coating, ready for use as the only available refrigeration for food and chilling for drinks.

What I did not like was the dictatorial manner of Miss Muller, the governess to Marjorie and her younger sisters. Not only were they awed by Miss Muller, but so was my own governess—a dreary woman who deferred to Miss Muller even on petty rules, such as making us fold our cloth napkins after each meal.

One evening for dessert we were served layer cake with a delicious thick fudge icing that I decided to save till last. But Miss Muller was in a hurry and rose from the table, followed by the Lewisohn girls. "I'm not finished," I cried. But my governess, intimidated by Miss Muller, snatched up my plate and handed it to the waitress. I suspect that my lifelong habit of eating too fast dated from that moment.

Miss Muller was also learning to dive, as was I. The only place to practice was the dock. Miss Muller took an endless amount of time walking to the far end, curling her toes over the edge, bending over, with arms forward and finally, finally, plopping headfirst into the lake. I would follow almost immediately, but even though I climbed back out of the water first, my governess made me wait for Miss Muller before I could dive again. One day I could stand it no longer and as Miss Muller stood and stood at the end of the dock I ran up and gave her a push.

After she had belly flopped into the lake, I followed with a dive, but there was no way I could hide out in the water forever. When at last I emerged, my governess marched me, dripping and shivering, to the cabin where my father worked before lunch.

He looked up from his desk to see a wet small daughter and an outraged governess. She told him what I had done. I knew it was wrong and dreaded his wrath.

Oh help, I thought, as I saw his face working. This must be even worse than I thought. My shivering increased.

"June pushed Miss Muller into the lake?"

"Yes! She iss a vicked girl."

It was then that I realized his facial gyrations came from his trying not to laugh. I edged over to him. Wet though I was, I felt his arm come around me. "You *are* a wicked girl," he said, shaking with laughter, "but I can't entirely blame you."

He was a warm-hearted sweet-natured balding man with an impressively thick mustache. In the city he dressed nattily, with spats (flannel in winter, linen in summer), a pearl stickpin, and a cane. His appetite for food was prodigious and his table manners terrible. He adored his three children and admired his child bride. My mother, Mabel Limburg Rossbach, was eleven years younger than he, just as he was eleven years younger than her mother, Clara. When he really wanted to rile my mother, he would gang up with my Granny. On the other hand, he was Prussian in his manner toward servants and dogs; they had to measure up or else, and he was reputed to be a dictator at the office.

Yet all my life, the memory of his unexpected and unmerited forgiveness has impelled me toward forgiving others more readily than I might otherwise have done. Some religious people might see the following event an example of grace at work, though my father would have answered any such suggestion with the German word, "Schtuss!" (Nonsense!) Jack would have been even more dumbfounded than I was by the experience that the Sulzbergers—Arthur H., Iphigene, and Marian—together with the Rossbachs—Max, Mabel, and June—had while motoring on Cape Cod in August, 1932. The sun was about to set when we reached our destination, a big white hotel in Chatham. The two men went in to claim our reservations. When they emerged, Arthur's face was ashen and my father's was beet red with rage; no room at the inn, at least not for the likes of us. Instead we drove to a second-rate hotel, which Marian and I much preferred because we didn't have to dress for dinner. But I never forgot the chagrin and helplessness on the faces of those two otherwise powerful men.

32

Chapter 2

Decision

BECAUSE REFORM JUDAISM WASN'T established until the 19th century, all my earlier ancestors must have been Orthodox, but there is no mention of anyone's ever having been a rabbi. The portrait we have of my father's great-grandfather is of a young fellow dressed like a courtier, perhaps for a visit to a local *schloss*. Otherwise, I assume that they were middle-class merchants, with an occasional bon vivant among the no-nonsense money-makers.

On the paternal side of the family, the Rossbachs got their name at the beginning of the 19th century in a somewhat fluky way. Napoleon had sent out word to the captured areas, including today's Germany, that for convenience in taxation, Jews would have to take a last name. Up to then, a Jew would be known as, say, Ben-Joseph, or simply, Son of Joseph. Now many Jews chose either floral names they liked, such as Rose, or other aspects of nature, such as Berg (mountain) or Thal (valley), or precious materials, such as Gold or Diamond, or they were assigned names by derisive officials, such as Katzenellenbogen (cat's elbow).

My father's great-grandfather, a businessman in Frankfurt, had become friends with a Christian miller named Rossbach. After Napoleon's edict became known, my ancestor went to the miller and asked if he could assume his name. Herr Rossbach said he would be pleased. Thus my family, the Rossbachs, obtained a name that is sometimes borne by Christians and sometimes by Jews. On my father's mother's side, the names were Koppel and Kopp. Their most famous member, Leopold Kopp, my grandmother's brother, went to Bogota, Columbia, in the late 19th century and founded the successful

Bavaria Beer Company—which continues today, although no longer in the hands of the family. He was such a benefactor of the poor that his bronze statue has a shiny foot from being rubbed for luck.

As for the paternal side of Jack's family, in 1819 Hiram Bingham was the first Protestant missionary to be sent by the Congregational Board of Missions to the Sandwich Islands (Hawaii). He sailed together with an expert farmer and a doctor. Hiram Bingham was the prototype for the idealistic but at times obnoxious minister, Abner Hale, in James Michener's colorful novel, *Hawaii*.

Later, Hiram's son, Hiram II, was similarly sent forth to the Gilbert Islands. Both men translated the Bible into their adopted country's native language and devised its first local language–English dictionary.

On the maternal side of my family, my great-grandparents, Mayer and Babette Neugass Lehman, attended services at the Reform Temple Emanu-El when they came to New York City from Montgomery, Alabama, in the mid-1860s (and in time Mayer Lehman became chairman of its board of trustees). So as not to flag their difference from other Americans, the Lehmans stopped serving solely kosher food or expressing in any outward way, such as wearing a yarmulke or a wig, that they were Jewish. Yet they never denied their Jewishness. I remember the scorn with which my parents spoke of Jews who had deliberately changed their name to a famous Christian one (Chabotinsky to Cabot, for example). On the other hand, they didn't blame the Katzenellenbogens for shortening theirs to Kellen, and they smiled about our close friends, the Hemings, whose name had been Heimerdinger. One day Charlie Heimerdinger had visited a Christian boy whose grandmother was deaf. The boy tried to introduce Charlie, but she kept saying, "What?" Finally she said, "I give up; I can only hear Heimerdinger and no one could be called *that*."

Among Mayer and Babette Lehman's seven children, only one, the sixth, Irving, was devout. He and his wife, Sissie Straus Lehman, went regularly to Temple Emanu-El, newly built and Moorish on Fifth Avenue and 65th Street. I was never invited to accompany them although my grandmother, Clara, when she had nothing better to do on a Friday evening (we by then would be off to White Plains), occasionally did. My parents, to my knowledge, never set foot in the temple except for funerals. I never heard the term "bar mitzvah," and "bat mitzvahs" didn't exist. Yet, secular as my parents were, they and almost all their relatives had married Jews. In short, if I were to wed Fred or Jack, I'd be breaking with family tradition.

Jack's parents appeared to be scarcely more devout than mine. His father, though descended from missionaries, rarely went to church, and Jack's mother never did, but Jack, like his brothers, had been sent to Congregational Sunday School in New Haven. At least he got a smidgin of biblical knowledge, which was more than I had, although I pled with my parents to allow me to attend the Friday afternoon Bible sessions that Iphigene Sulzberger, Arthur's wife, set up for their eldest daughter Marian and some of Marian's friends. But my parents refused because it would interfere with our commute by car to White Plains for the weekend. The only Jewish contact I therefore had on Friday afternoons was with Mr. Huckster, a butcher in the Bronx, a jolly sort with a mustache even wider than my father's, who called me "Sonny Jim" for reasons that escaped me then and still do. While our chauffeur waited, my mother would regularly stop off to inspect and pick up the four-rib beef roast, legs of lamb, or capon for our dining room and the stew meat or hamburger for the servants. We would then drive up the "Grand Concourse" which in those days was truly grand, a mini–Champs Elysée, with a wide green area between the north- and southbound roadways. It was relief for us when the first of the parkways, the Bronx River Parkway, was built in 1925, followed shortly thereafter by the Hutchinson River Parkway. These shortened our commute to an hour from its previous hour and a half.

In addition to the religious difference between Jack's family and mine was the difference in the handling of privacy. Privacy was punctiliously honored in the Bingham household and sometimes shockingly breached in mine. Few personal questions were ever asked of young Jack by his parents, whereas my father was forever demanding to know whether I was happy, and my mother, as I eventually discovered, was reading my diary. When I confronted her with this, to me, intolerable invasion, she said it was her duty as a mother to know what her children were thinking. I never wrote anything of substance in the diary again.

On the other hand, my mother was my savior in regard to schooling. She, as a bright eighteen-year-old, had been forbidden to go to college and was not even allowed to take extension courses at Columbia. She was determined that I be able to continue my education. My father wanted me to stay at home. "Don't you want to be with me?" he kept pleading; "You know all you need to know" (for a girl).

My mother put an end to that. "June is going to Vassar," she announced. I, of course, was never asked whether Vassar was my choice; I was simply informed that that was where I was headed, mainly because two of my mother's first cousins, Elinor Fatman Morgenthau and Frances (Peter) Lehman Loeb, had gone there. (Half a century later, Peter gave the college a large gift for its modern art gallery.)

Jack's mother, as well as his father, would have agreed with my father that men are superior to women. I once asked Jack's mother (who was addressed as "Mothe" by her sons and daughters-in-law) if she hadn't ever wished for a daughter. She said that by the time her fifth son was born, she had so much equipment for boys that she would hardly have known what to do with a girl. Yet her favorite among the twenty-nine Bingham grandchildren was a girl, Alfreda, Mothe's namesake, a daughter of Mothe's son, Alfred.

Another difference between Jack and me was the way our academic achievements were treated at home. My father, to my knowledge, never once looked at a report card of mine, and my mother appeared indifferent to them. Jack's father, on the other hand, kept elaborate records of all his seven sons' marks, as well as their respective heights at specific ages, and how many feet they could high-jump and broad-jump and shot-put. Jack's older brothers were thus repeatedly made aware of him as competitor, while my brothers loftily appeared to pay no attention to the boring accomplishments of "a mere girl."

My brothers and my father were also not as impressed as I was by the occasional brief reviews of first novels that my mother, thanks in part to her great friendship with Arthur Sulzberger, had been hired by the *New York Times* to write for the Sunday section.

A more dramatic difference between Jack and me was the emotional style of our respective parents. His finally got divorced, a rare and scandalous occurrence in those days. Mine stayed together, but I often wondered if my brothers and I wouldn't have been better off if we had been able to live with each parent separately. Jack's parents' fighting was icy; my parents' was fiery. My father once slammed a big vase down on the edge of the grand piano, thus breaking both, while my mother indulged in a loud rhythmic laughing-and-crying that we cringed at having the servants hear. Mercifully, it ceased after our house in White Plains was enlarged enough to provide her with a separate bedroom.

Another difference between our two families was that his parents caused their grown offsprings' visits to feel special because so few of these were expected, whereas my parents demanded such visits so frequently that I, at least, never had time to build up an appetite for them. If we children lived in the neighborhood, we were expected for lunch every weekend; if we lived several hundred miles away, we were expected to stay over Saturday night at least once a month. Jack went along with this schedule because he thought it would make life easier for me; only much later did we both realize that we should have spoken up at the beginning and laid down firmer ground rules. It's not easy to build one's own happiness when it causes others distress.

A difference between Jack and me that at first was difficult to speak about was that, from the point of view of social status, his family had a superiority complex, while mine had an inferiority complex. Because he had been brought up to think of himself as an aristocrat, Jack remained forever embarrassed by the memory of the day he acted as if he were a superior being. It was a snowy afternoon in New Haven when he, aged five, was sledding down a hill near his family's big house. An ill-dressed little boy from the town cut across in front of him. Infuriated, young Jack marched over to him and said, "My mother told me never to play with common little boys like you."

Fortunately, his older brothers' tutor overheard him, took him by the ear, and marched him up to the house in disgrace. I suspect that part of the thrill Jack later got from his proven popularity with the ordinary Bronx voters was connected to a dilution of the shame he still felt about his earlier snobbishness.

Because Jack was so forthright in telling me about some of the unattractive aspects of his earlier life, I eventually confided in him some deep embarrassments of my own.

One was the way that my parents, feeling looked down on by Christian society, also looked down on certain fellow Jews. This snobbery prevented me from visiting friends I had made at the Lincoln School in New York—which I had attended through seventh grade. One friend was my classmate, Tommy Goldberg, son of the great cartoonist, Rube Goldberg; another was Tessim Zorach, four years ahead of us, son of the famous sculptor, William Zorach. Both boys invited me for home visits, but my parents told me it was simply out of the question. Tom, whom I ran into during World War II when he was in uniform, made it clear that he still resented my refusal. I told him he was absolutely right.

Decision

What I was most reluctant to reveal to Jack was the night, during my thirteenth year, when a married cousin of my mother's came to dinner and, to my delighted amazement, asked if he could take me to the movies. My parents agreed and off he and I went. We saw Katharine Hepburn in *A Bill of Divorcement*. On the way home, he parked the car on a deserted road and put his lips on mine and pawed me. I didn't know what to do, so I just wept. Eventually he must have gotten tired of kissing a sopping wet face and he drove me home. I ran a bath and scrubbed myself all over. My governess came in and asked what I was doing. Had that man done something to me? I shook my head. This was not the kind of thing, I felt, that one should discuss with a hired hand. Nor did I tell any family member until my nightmares became intolerable. Finally, when my mother and I were off alone together in a hotel room in Toronto, about to take the Canadian Pacific train to Banff, I told her. She turned white. "Did he touch you down there?"

I said no and puzzled over why anyone would have any interest in this least attractive part of me. My mother phoned my father whose yells were audible to me from across the room. He, apparently, went off to buy a gun, but because he first had to apply for a permit, this provided several days in which, fortunately, he was able to cool down.

My parents never invited the cousin again, but my brothers continued to go off on fishing trips with him. They appeared to blame me more for having tattled than him for having given me something to tattle about. Or perhaps they just loved fishing and didn't want to miss a major occasion for it because of a stupid kid sister.

Similarly, it took me a while to tell Jack about a distressing experience that took place when I was twelve. It was during my first months at Rosemary Hall, which had more day students than boarders. The only other Jews in the school were the Gimbel twins, Hope and Caral, but they graduated the next year. (Caral went on to marry Hank Greenberg, the first Jew in major league

39

baseball.) My uncle and aunt, knowing that I knew no one in my class, were kind enough to suggest that I invite a classmate for a Saturday night on the town. The four of us would have dinner at a speakeasy and take in a Broadway show!

Greenwich had, and still has, mansions set so far back from the street that one can hardly glimpse the vastness of their proportions. The classmate I invited lived in one of these. She was thrilled at the invitation but said that of course she'd first have to ask her parents. The next day she came to school looking glum.

"I can't come."

"Why not?"

"Mummy says that if I'm seen out with Jews, I won't get danced with when I'm a debutante."

The only thing I could think of to say was "Oh." The only thing I could think to do was prevent my uncle and aunt from finding out.

"Don't invite anyone else," she begged. "I'll work on Mummy and Dad." Since I had no intention of asking anyone else ever, I nodded.

A few days later she turned up smiling. "They said I'm still so young that no one will remember it by the time I come out."

So the evening took place as planned. Although I chattered and giggled, I was, for the first time, looking down at myself chattering and giggling. If growing up involves expanding one's perspective, then I'd been thrust forward fast. If growing up also includes discovering a purpose for one's life, then I'd been forced a ratchet forward in that direction as well. For now I experienced myself as part of a group, not just as part of a family. Whatever I might accomplish would redound to my group's credit, while any failure on my part would increase the disrespect to which my group was being subject. Irony was not a concept I yet understood, but I did eventually marvel that my effort to fit in with the Christian majority was what had led me to discover my bond with the Jewish minority. I also felt a secret—and somewhat spiteful—pleasure that my

Decision

Protestant classmates, being born into the reigning class, could not share my newfound sense of purpose.

But how could I become enough of a success to achieve my goal? Good marks would not impress "them" because they expected "us" to be smart, even sly. But what if I forced myself to become an athlete? That would blast their preconceptions. So, after our required daily sports, while my pals went to our only permitted tearoom to relish its marshmallow and peanut butter sandwiches on French bread, I kept myself running around the track. It took five years but I won my varsity letter in field hockey (as left fullback). I also, with pounding heart and clammy hands, joined my schoolmates who fox-hunted. I won my hunt colors (a yellow velvet collar banded with red on the regulation black tweed coat), but on the way to that honor, I took some damaging spills.

One day a friend and I were "schooling" our horses for the pair-jumping class in the school's upcoming horseshow. Our horses took off simultaneously but, for some equine reason, disagreed in mid-air and tried to bite each other. My horse, not watching where he was landing, stumbled, and I was thrown under the other horse. All I remember is a barrage of hooves, akin to the chariot scenes in the movie, *Ben Hur*. The next thing I knew was the sound of a repeated whimpering. It took me a while to realize that it was coming from me. Teddy Wall, our handsome, stern riding master, was standing over me, tapping his riding crop against the side of his full length leather boot.

"All right, Rossbach. Get up."

I would have done anything for Teddy, but nothing happened.

"Up!"

"Can't."

"What do you mean?"

"My legs won't move."

"Do they hurt?"

41

"No. In fact, I can't feel them at all."

He yelled for one of the grooms. Together they carried me out. An ambulance appeared and I was delighted to lie on its gurney, with a hastily summoned headmistress, Miss Caroline Ruutz-Rees, sitting alongside, as the siren wailed and we hurtled toward the Greenwich Hospital.

Miss Ruutz-Rees, an imposing, blue-eyed lady, tried to divert me by asking which edition of the *Iliad* and *Odyssey* I was reading. She succeeded better than she knew, for in order to take the school's mandatory pass-fail exam on this subject, I had sneaked over to the Lower School Library and borrowed a children's version. I was literally accurate when I said I couldn't remember the name of the edition, but I was also, at best, being disingenuous, or, at worst, a deceiver. I closed my eyes and hoped she'd let me rest. Thanks to youthful resilience, I regained the use of my legs, but the ligaments of my back had been stretched or torn, which necessitated two painful, debilitating spinal operations later on.

Having ridden horseback since early childhood, I knew that as soon as I recovered, I would have to mount that same horse and take him back over that same jump, together with my friend and her horse. Sometime later, holding my breath, I was able to do it.

Jack, too, had experienced many spills off ponies and donkeys when he was small and off horses when he was wrangling cattle one summer in Wyoming. But he never sustained any serious injury; indeed, he was in splendid health—and by nature much more courageous than I—even to the point of recklessness. When full of drink of an evening, he sometimes drove absurdly fast, with tires squealing at every turn. And, when sober, he looked for every excuse to pilot a small chartered plane. While I was in Salem, we dropped off one car in the meadow below the Camp and drove another car to New Haven to pick up a plane. I recall that the sky was abloom with big white cumulus clouds against its clear cerulean background. Inside a cloud over Salem, Jack cut the motor. My heart, too, stopped. We were dropping fast before he started the motor again, and we emerged from the bottom of the cloud to make a fine landing on the designated meadow. My hands were visibly shaking as I emerged from the plane. I drove the car to the Camp to pick up his mother and stepfather so that they could come and admire the plane — and its benighted pilot whom I would have been happy to throttle. On our flight back to New Haven, however, he did behave himself.

Learning about all that we had in common only drew us closer. At night, Jack and I stayed up late, talking nonstop, except when silencing each other's lips by passion. Jack was surprised to learn that I was still a virgin, and his pleasure at this news was pleasing to me. Yet how could my body be responding with such joyous surrender to two men at once? What kind of a person had I become? Was I some kind of whore? Somewhere I had heard that the biblical word for intercourse was to "know" the other person. Jack and I had been baring our souls to each other; why not, at least in part, our bodies? The section of the 16th-century Anglican prayerbook that I most liked was, "With my body, I thee worship." My feeling of physical surrender combined with love held no connotation of subservience or defeat, only a path to joint exultation. Was that kind of surrender related to the one that can be imbedded in prayer, or in receiving visits from the Muse, or in childbirth, or even, if one lived long enough, in acquiescence to death?

Jack's response to such musings was that I reminded him of Gumdrop Sal.

"Who?"

He proceeded to sing to me the ditty he had learned when working the previous summer as a busboy on a Mississippi River boat:

Way up yonder in the frozen North
In the land of the Eskimo

The Thirties

I got stranded from the Mary Jane
And I don't care if I never get home again
For the Queen's some gal
Her name is Gumdrop Sal
And for me, she's very strong.
For the King's in wrong and I'm in right
And the King goes out most every night
And the nights. . .are…six…months…long.

Jack and I still had two more days and one more precious night together at the Camp before my four-day visit was scheduled to end. But then Fred telephoned.

His voice was hardly recognizable, it was so choked. He said he couldn't bear my being in Salem one minute longer. He was planning to fly to New York that night and would take the train to New Haven the next morning. Would I please bring my car and meet him at the Taft Hotel at eleven o'clock? When I told Jack about this plan, he said he would drive me as far as New Haven and then go back to Salem by train and bus.

When Jack stopped the car at the entrance to the Taft Hotel where Fred was, I headed for the revolving door. I could see Fred coming toward me. Perhaps because I had spent the previous days gazing at a scimitar-like profile, perhaps because my long-ago wish to fall out of love with him had, without my knowledge, unconsciously germinated, I suddenly saw Fred's face as different, as weak: the same features, of course, but their configuration was no longer crisp. He didn't appear like a man I could look up to for the rest of my life.

The three of us went to Mory's and had South Sides. But nothing could make the occasion other than misery. Fred drove me back to White Plains and promised that we would be married within three months, if that was what I wanted.

44

He also confessed that the cause of all the previous delays had been his parents' anti-Semitism. Not that they didn't consider me "a lovely girl," but in their view I would "never fit in." It was they who had arranged, through John Hanes, brother of Fred's mother, for Fred to be transferred to Norfolk, away from that Semitic siren, me. Fred had done everything he could to alter their attitude, but now he was ready to proceed despite it. I thanked him and said I needed more time. He was surprised that I, who for so long had been pressing for marriage, was now the one to delay it, but I was so hurt at his not having been honest with me that I didn't know what to do.

After Fred went back to Norfolk, I continued seeing Jack. He and I, together with both his close friend, Dick Moore (who would become an assistant to President Nixon and subsequently his ambassador to Ireland) and their Yale classmate, Brendan Gill (already at work at *The New Yorker*), had a hilarious evening at the 1939 World's Fair in Flushing Meadow. We visited the Futurama, which included the startling sight of toy cars racing up to bridges on figure-eight approaches (the kind taken completely for granted a decade later), and we ourselves yelled through roller coaster rides. The fair's trylon and perisphere seemed magical icons, symbolizing what people were still daring to hope for, the co-existence of all nations, not excluding Germany or Russia, which would vie peacefully through their exhibits at a World's Fair rather than bloodily with their armaments in a second world war.

Among several interests that Jack and I shared, but Fred did not, was travel. Jack had gone to Europe many times, first with his parents (his mother spoke fluent German as well as good French), and subsequently on bike trips with fellow students. Every other summer I had been taken abroad. ("Abroad" meant only Europe to my parents who had little interest in other continents or even in America west of the Hudson.) Jack, however, had been taken as a boy as far west as Hawaii (where his father was born and at age eleven had tried

to run away from his stern missionary parents and grandparents).
Jack had spent a college summer hitchhiking west to California, taking jobs wherever he was dropped off until he accumulated enough
money to venture further. He departed from Salem with $25 in
his pocket and returned there six weeks later with $25, which he
proceeded to blow on a taxi from New London to the Camp.

In 1931, as on many previous trips, my mother and I visited
Baron Robert von Hirsch at his museum-like house in Frankfurt,
Germany. He was a lifelong bachelor, with gray eyes and a neat little
mustache over thin, rather red, lips. On his walls hung big Cranach
portrayals of Adam and Eve; on a nearby antique table stood a
Dürer etching of a semi-dressed woman holding a globe. I thought
the pictures ugly; I didn't like fat ladies with too few clothes on.
Robert also had two Renoir oil paintings (my thought at the time: the
ladies are fat and uncovered but at least these are colorful) as well as
some Sisley and Pisarro landscapes that I loved.

Until Frankfurt's picturesque old city (Altschtadt) was obliter-
ated by Allied bombing in World War II, its streets were so narrow
that a house's second (top) storey jutted out so far it nearly touched
the one across the way. My father and I used to walk about munch-
ing Frankfurter Wurstel (the model for the American "frankfurter")
that were sold from sidewalk carts. Another time, he bought my
brothers and me some Bavarian beer at a Hofbrau Haus at noon. All
four of us got tiddly. Afterward, he hired a horse-drawn carriage,
a *droschke,* out of which he leaped, ran alongside, and then leaped
back in again. We laughed so hard I wet my pants. When we arrived
back, my mother was enraged and sent us children to bed. We slept
right through lunch.

But there was no laughter on the evening of my mother's and my
departure from Frankfurt in 1931. As Robert's chauffeur drove us
to the station, we passed a torchlight procession of young men in
brown shirts, marching with their legs stuck out straight ahead.

Decision

Robert, I noted in my diary, registered more alarm than I had ever witnessed in an adult:

> I love Germany but I don't know when I'll see it again, as, though everything seems peaceful enough, there is a sense of impending danger and suspense. The atmosphere is charged with it—like a lull before the storm. I hope nothing will happen—but everybody is scared stiff, and even Robert, the calm and cool, is shipping most of his valuables out of the country. . . . I certainly hope nothing happens—but as Germany is really my ancestor country, I feel more than the American casual feeling—and I can do nothing, though, but hope for the best.

A year later, the German people elected Hitler to power, and Robert soon followed his art collection out of the country to Basel, Switzerland. The Cranachs and the Dürer, because they were by German artists, were held back. After the war, they were returned to him. On the back of each was a label saying, "Property of Hermann Goering." Today, Robert's Basel house at Engelgasse 55 is a museum.

Russia was a place that both Jack and I had visited as young adults. At age seventeen, I had gone with my parents, and he, the following year, was on assignment from the *New York Herald Tribune*. Before going to Russia both of us had heard that some people considered it "the workers' paradise," but neither of us was all that much impressed. True, there seemed to be no unemployment, and true, women could work at some jobs that in the West were held only by men, such as street cleaning, but the people, to me, seemed furtive, the new buildings looked sleazy and drab, and our rooms in the fiercely hot Hotel Metropole being bugged was unnerving. Also, rumors circulated that Stalin's reorganization of agriculture had caused the starvation deaths of three million Kulaks (land-owning farmers). Still, Red Square was breathtaking, with such a glorious contrast between the brightly colored onion-shaped spires of St. Basil's Cathedral and the high, windowless walls of the mysterious Kremlin. My parents and I dutifully visited the squat square tomb where Lenin's corpse lay on display. Rumor had it that his hair and nails still grew and had to be trimmed. Though all day long docile crowds of Russians waited to view him, I found him unimpressive. But then, I'd never seen a corpse before.

By the latter 1930s, both Jack and I were cheering for the Loyalist side in Spain's Civil War. The Fascists were led by Generalissimo Francisco Franco and supported by Nazi Germany and Mussolini's Italy. Neither Jack nor I knew any young Americans who had joined the International Brigades and gone to Spain to fight. Few of us at the time knew that the Comintern, the foreign affairs branch of Stalin's Communist Party, was directing the "Loyalists" or "Republicans" with as much brutality as the Nazis were directing the Fascists. Both parties were more interested in testing weapons for an expected second world war than in Spain itself. Even after Ernest Hemingway's *For Whom the Bell Tolls* was followed by the movie, many Americans remained naïve.

In 1935, my parents and I took the train from Moscow to Warsaw. There, too, it was unbearably hot. One day we were driven by taxi through the ghetto. I couldn't believe how awful it smelled, an unremitting combination of garlic, garbage, and sweat, or how awful the people looked. Despite the heat, the bearded men wore long black coats and black felt hats under which hung their long, curly black sideburns. My father privately referred to such hair as "Kinim-Schaukel" (a swing for fleas). The women also wore full-length, heavy dark clothing with big scarves over their mandatory wigs. We heard that Orthodox Jewish married woman had to have their heads shaved lest they appear attractive to a man other than their husband. Even the children looked indoorsy and solemn. Back at our hotel for lunch, we were served a typical Polish dish, pounded chicken breast sewn around a blob of butter and then baked. As I punctured the meat with my fork, the melted butter spewed forth. I excused myself. Whether it was the shock of smelling and seeing the ghetto or the greasiness of the food, something was making me feel sick at heart as well as in body.

Who could have known that in three years, the Nazis would be invading Poland and ruthlessly murdering those innocent men, women, and children? Or that from those people would rise the magnificent and ingenious heroes who managed to survive and harass the Nazis for the next seven years?

Jack and I, independently, had been chagrined that the United States, following World War I, had refused to join the League of Nations. Yet, in 1935, my first published article reflected what was becoming an increasing hope that the United States could keep its young men out of what appeared to be Europe's perennial civil wars. The article appeared in the *Greenwich Daily News-Graphic*, which had offered a prize for the best student essay on public affairs. Jack, at the same time, was writing similar editorials in the *Yale Daily News*. When he showed me his huge book of clippings, I was awed by how much he had produced, starting with the *Third Form Weekly* at Groton and culminating in a 1938 series commissioned by the *New York Herald Tribune* that compared youth groups in Nazi Germany, Communist Russia, and Fascist Italy.

Back in the United States, I visited the World's Fair with my great-uncle, Irving Lehman, and his wife, Aunt Sissie. She was the niece of Isador Straus whose wife, Ida had refused to get into a lifeboat on the *Titanic*. She'd said, "I have lived with Mr. Straus for fifty years, and I am not going to leave him now." Just as those Strauses served as Aunt Sissie's model for marriage, so did she and Uncle Irving serve as mine. For them each day together was a treat.

When they swam, they did the sidestroke so as to be able to keep looking at each other. They refused to be separated for any reason other than the demands of his work or some major interference like hospitalization. They had no children of their own and informally adopted Howard, Dick, and me as surrogate grandchildren after Irving's beloved older sister, my grandmother, Clara, died.

Uncle Irving, like Herbert, for reasons that fully escaped me, always retained a bit of a crush on Clara. Indeed, Uncle Herbert after his evening martini, would occasionally bemoan the fact that I didn't look more like her. Since I remembered her as a fat, tightly corseted, crabby old lady with marceled iron gray hair who openly preferred my brothers to me, I was delighted at this non-resemblance.

Only decades after that evening with Uncle Irving and Aunt Sissie at the fair did it occur to me that they might have had a hidden agenda. For after our delicious dinner with wine at the French Pavilion, they hired a horse-drawn carriage. They sat hand in hand in the backseat, while I faced them on the jumpseat. They brought up the subject of Fred and what a nice, polite, attractive young man he seemed to be, but what was he planning to do to improve the world?

Silence at my end, for Fred had no plan beyond making as much money as he could. "I'm a Republican because I'm rich," he used to say with a smile, "and I want to stay that way." In desperation for some kind of answer, I told the Lehmans they would enjoy meeting another boy I was seeing, Jack Bingham, who planned to help the world by going into public life.

They said they would be glad to meet him, and we spoke of other things. But their question remained with me.

A week or so later, my brother Dick invited me to Wall Street where he had a job in the banking firm of Lazard Frères. He even bought me lunch, something he had never done before. During the meal, he warned me not to let myself get too involved with Jack Bingham—that he, Dick, suspected Jack of having simply made a bet with his buddy Dick Moore that Jack could win me away from Fred and then, once he had succeeded, he would dump me. It seemed virtually impossible, Dick said, that Jack would want to marry me, since Jack could have any girl in New York or elsewhere. I told Dick he didn't know what he was talking about and that if I ever trusted anyone's integrity, it was Jack's.

The next time Jack came to New York, we danced the night away and drove to White Plains as dawn was breaking. He had what he thought was a brilliant idea:

"Let's play tennis?"

"Are you serious?"

We changed into tennis clothes and started to play. My father appeared for his usual pre-breakfast swim in the pool and was startled at the sight of us. He summoned me off the court. Oh help, I thought, here it comes. But all he said was, "Now, that's the kind of young man I approve of: he gets you up in the morning."

My mother, however, was furious. She knew that my bed had not been slept in.

Drowsily, Jack and I lay by the pool that afternoon. He was regaling me with examples of how absentminded his charming little mother could be. On one occasion, when the bank notified her that her account was overdrawn, she said, "Oh dear," and immediately sent them a check. As I laughed, Jack said, "You remember the way Mothe talks to the servants about my brothers as 'Mr. and Mrs. Alfred' or 'Dr. and Mrs. Charles'?"

"Yes."

"Well, the final day you were in Salem, I overheard her telling the cook that 'Mr. and Mrs. Jack' would be out for lunch."

I rolled over on my stomach and quietly wept. Mothe's casual assumption that I was a fully eligible daughter-in-law stood in such stark contrast to the attitude of Fred's parents. Only then did I allow myself to recognize how deeply hurt by them I was.

The following Saturday night, Jack invited Douglas Auchincloss, his old Groton and Yale friend, to meet me. Doug assumed that this meant that Jack and I were engaged. He therefore arrived at Oma's hotel with a large, handmade celebratory placard. We thanked him but told him it was premature. In the course of our dinner near the bar of the 21, Jack asked Doug if he'd excuse us for a short time. Jack asked me if I'd like to drive around Central Park. I thought he meant in a horse-drawn carriage, but he only flagged a taxi. In its backseat, he turned to me and said, "Will you marry me?"

I couldn't answer. I had always been told that a girl should not accept a man's first proposal. Sensitive as Jack was to subtle cues from me, he surmised this possible reason for my hesitation and asked for the second time, "Will you marry me?"

Suddenly, explosively, and with utter certainty, I said, "Sure!"

He burst out laughing and, after a second, so did I. I'm not even sure that the taxi driver didn't join in. In any event, he drove us around the park not once but twice, with Jack and me entwined in the backseat. My decision felt entirely right. Later, after we'd rejoined Doug and then abandoned him again in order to go off to dance at the Stork Club, a stranger sent over a bottle of Champagne with a note, "You two look so happy, I can't resist. May you feel this way all your lives."

Our theme song became, "This can't be love/Because I feel so well/No sobs, no sorrows, no sighs. . . . Still I love/To look in your eyes."

The next day Jack went to my father to ask formally for my hand. My father was thoroughly bewildered. All he could think of to say was, "Is there any insanity in your family?"

Jack, not being able to foresee a development in that regard, honestly answered, "No!" My father then proceeded to call him "Fred" for the next several days.

For almost half a century thereafter, my brother Dick, who had so badly misjudged Jack would send us an amusing "mea culpa" message on our wedding anniversary. Even after Dick's death, his widow told me, "Dick adored Jack, and why wouldn't he? Jack was the most elegant man I've ever met."

Before long Jack became fond of both my brothers and their eventual wives, Susan Goodman for Dick, and Eleanor Frank for Howard. I also liked all six of his brothers and their wives: Woodbridge, a university professor, who was married to Ursula Griswold; Hiram (Harry), a diplomat, who was married to Rose Morrison; Alfred, a writer and magazine publisher, who was married to Sylvia Knox; Charles, a doctor, who was married to Kathleen Howell; Brewster, a minister, who was married to Frances Beach; and Mitchell, an artist and farmer, who was married to Norris Nevins. All the couples except Bruce (Brewster) and Fran had children, and in Harry and Rose's case, eleven of them.

On the Monday following our Saturday night engagement, I went into the city to have lunch with Fred. He sat waiting, holding a huge stuffed panda. I had to break the news. I was scheduled to meet Jack two hours later at the then most famous place for a rendezvous, "Under the clock at the Biltmore." Fred put up so many arguments and counter-plans that I soon realized I would never be on time to meet Jack. So I summoned a Western Union boy and sent Jack a telegram, "Your date will be an hour late, but your mate, never."

But Jack didn't receive the message. When I ran in, breathless, to the Biltmore lobby an hour late, I found a white-faced fiancé pacing in front of the clock that, of course, was ticking off every second of his girl's apparent disloyalty or desertion.

Fred had accompanied me and he shook Jack's hand. His only request was that he be permitted to give me a stuffed animal on special occasions. To this, Jack graciously acquiesced. But Fred never again gave me one. Just as Jack and I bid Fred good-bye, my telegram to Jack was delivered.

Jack and I checked the panda and went uptown to Tiffany's to order my engagement ring. Because the store had been founded by his great-grandfather, Jack was given a discount. But when he chose a smallish rectangular diamond, I reminded him of my mother's demanding and critical eye. So he threw his budget to the winds and ordered *two* such diamonds to be set in platinum, one catty-corner from the other, with a horizontal baguette along the side of each. "The big stones are for thee and me," he said, "and the little ones for our babies."

"You only want two?

"Heavens, no. But later we'll add more stones. Right now I'm broke."

Chapter 3

Marriage

It was discomfiting to me that my fiancé's family always seemed to top even the best things mine could accomplish. While my family's shingled Thirlsmere house dated from Revolutionary days, with its small square-paned windows and wide floorboards, two of his family's houses in Salem dated from well before the Revolution and had been built by his direct ancestors, the Mumfords and the Woodbridges, some of whom lay in the family cemetery adjacent to the Camp. Similarly, my family had a tennis court (which had been presented to us by Robert von Hirsch shortly before the 1929 Crash), yet the Binghams had two tennis courts: with seven boys born within twelve years, one court was deemed insufficient. How could I live up to Bingham standards for what a daughter-in-law should be?

Fortunately, what mattered most to Jack's family also mattered immeasurably to mine, namely, that we would be happy with each other and in time produce several children. Now that we were engaged, Jack confessed that he had previously been worried about my children because they would be doomed to suffer from anti-Semitism. But as his love for me had grown, he realized that he wanted to be right there in the house to provide those kids with all the support he possibly could.

An instance of anti-Semitism directed against him—together with his and my future children—was brought to our attention the following year. His name was dropped by *The New York Social Register* because of his marriage to a Jew. Since Jack did not even own a copy of this little black book, we had a good laugh at their expense.

Shortly after our engagement on July 20, 1939, Jack was scheduled to drive to San Francisco to go off on a backpacking trip in the Rockies with Dick Moore, Bill Orrick (later a federal judge), Potter Stewart (later a Supreme Court justice), and Louis Stone (later a CBS executive). Jack didn't want to leave me, but my mother insisted. We both, she wisely pointed out, needed some time to catch our emotional breaths.

He drove west in his old blue Chevrolet sedan named "Ralph." For both of us the separation was even worse than our dread of it had been. The first night, he got as far as Albany and telegraphed, "The beauty and awe of the Hudson River in the light of your love makes me wonder if I am not wrong about God."

I drove my little black Ford roadster to Easthampton to visit the old Rosemary friend whose parents had feared for her to be seen with my uncle and aunt in New York. But despite her and my daily tennis games on the local club's grass courts and our daily swims in the bracing Atlantic, I felt like a puppy with its tail a-droop, ears down, and nose close to the ground. When parcel post brought the engagement ring from Tiffany, I put it on and ran out alone onto the beach. Waves in the Atlantic were distantly connected to waves in the Pacific where Jack was. The atoms of his life and mine were thus not wholly separated—and never would be. As the sun was setting and the stars became visible, I took comfort in the concept that the whole universe is interconnected and that even at its furthest reaches, in some inchoate form, the preconditions for love exist.

As departure time for the backpacking trip approached, Jack found that he couldn't bear the prospect of being out of touch with me by phone and letter for a whole week. He bribed Potter, Louis, and Dick to drive "Ralph" back East in due time, and he himself took a train to New York. When it reached Penn Station, I was there, in a new navy-blue polka-dot dress with a white collar. We clung to each other and swore never to be separated again if we could possibly avoid it.

We then had a whole week together in Salem, including a meal at each of the houses of his three brothers and sisters-in-law who lived there, and a large, lighthearted, joint picnic at the family beach in New London. One day Jack and I were scheduled to go for lunch to Wood and Urs's so that I could be introduced to Jack's father, now married to his second wife, Suzanne Carroll (of Carrollton, Maryland) Hill Bingham. I was a bit nervous about it, but Jack quoted the French phrase: *Courage, mon ami, le diable est mort* (Courage, my friend, the Devil is dead). What Jack couldn't reassure me about was my lack of a suitably dressy garment. He had assured me before I came that I would not need any fancy clothes, so the best I could muster was a dark blue cotton dress with a white sweater. Not chic.

Jack's father, the senator, turned out to be even taller than Jack, with a wide forehead, high cheekbones, shrewd hazel eyes, and thick, pure-white hair. Suzanne was thin, dark-haired, dark-eyed, narrow-mouthed, fashionably attired, with a lot of jewelry for Salem. When I was introduced, she didn't seem to look at me. I thought little about it. At lunch she was seated on Wood's right, I on his left. She was reporting to him about the youngest of her three daughters, Kitty Hill.

"Oh, Mrs. Bingham," I asked, "Where does Kitty go to school?" Mrs. Bingham didn't answer. I asked again. Again no answer. Heavens, I thought, the poor lady must be deaf. I tried a third time. Her lips scarcely budged as they ejected the word "Madeira."

The instant that lunch was over, they took their leave. This time I didn't try to shake hands with her but still had no idea what her problem was. Only when Wood, the staidest of the seven brothers, slammed the door and said, "That bitch," did I gather that anti-Semitism had again raised its ugly head.

The next day Jack went to call on his father. His father said that if Jack insisted on marrying me, he and I would never be welcome at his and Suzanne's house. Jack said, "So be it," and walked out. To my knowledge, Jack was never seriously perturbed by this rift. He knew exactly what he wanted, and if his father had the ill judgment to try to stand in the way of it, then that was just tough.

One reason for this, to me amazing, emotional detachment of Jack's, was that ten years earlier, his respect for his father had been seriously undermined. At breakfast in Washington one morning, the senator had informed Jack's mother, within Jack's hearing, that he planned to dine that evening at the Metropolitan Club and play bridge. That night, fifteen-year-old Jack went to Washington's only legitimate theater, the National, with a friend whose family had a box. On arrival there, whom should Jack see in the orchestra section but his father with a dark-haired lady? At intermission the two Bingham males did not acknowledge each other's presence. Nor was the subject ever raised between them. But, to a degree, Hiram lost a son that night.

Another factor that may have insulated Jack against his father was Hiram's frequent absences from home while Jack was young. Jack, the baby of the family, became very close to his mother. She, a serious amateur violinist, encouraged him to learn the violin, which he enjoyed, and the two spent hours playing duets. When pianist Henry Gregor entered her life, they moved on to trios. Henry, a cultured man of Russian and German parentage, had taught music at a junior college near Washington. He was eleven years younger than Alfreda Mitchell Bingham and, at the time of their marriage, her doctor-son Charles warned her that she should be prepared for her new husband's masculine vigor. "After what I went through with your father," she had said, "that won't bother me." In fact, it had the opposite effect. She and Henry, both around 5' 4", used to walk hand in hand ahead of Jack and me down the family beach, and I consequently was faced with an entirely different mother-in-law from the hard-to-please one whom several of my sisters-in-law complained about. When they had been newly married, Mothe would give them no peace. If their baby's window was open, she would shut it. If it was shut, she would open it. She considered herself *the* authority on childrearing.

In a light moment regarding her sons, each of whom had grown to be at least six foot tall, she boasted that she had "forty-two feet of sons."

By the time I came along, Mothe was concerned with far more important things than a seventh daughter-in-law. Also, because she was so unspoiled, I had a happy time sending her dainty gifts, such as a baby pillow with embroidered cases or a bed jacket. For these, she was inordinately grateful, in contrast to my mother who almost never seemed to think that anything I found or, when young, made, was good enough for her to use. Nor had Mothe ever before been the recipient of a valentine! I reveled in spoiling her, but in time two of my eldest sisters-in-law scolded me for becoming so close to the lady who had badly offended them when they were my age. I didn't blame them for resenting the way she had treated them, but Jack had early on set my priorities.

"Do you want to do me the greatest favor in the world?"

"Of course."

"Somehow manage to get along with my mother."

"Is that all?"

"Isn't that enough?"

"It can't be that hard."

Nor was it hard from then to the day she died aged ninety-two, a quarter century later. But what I didn't fully realize, and therefore couldn't share with Jack, was how thoroughly the demands constantly made on me by my own mother were undermining my emotional balance. In those days almost no one felt free to reveal, or even so much as inwardly to recognize, the negative feelings a parent could arouse in oneself. One simply responded as respectfully as one could. A quarter of a century later, Jack and I and our children invented and the phrase, "controlled disloyalty."

During our engagement, Jack and I spent a few days with Aunt Sissie and Uncle Irving on Cape Cod. Two minor catastrophes

The Thirties

occurred. One was that I developed impetigo, a wildly contagious, repulsive, gooey skin-eruption, on my face. Aunt Sissie was a fanatic about cleanliness, and here was a houseguest with a "dirty" disease, contracted, perhaps, from a hand insufficiently scrubbed after hanging onto a subway strap. Aunt Sissie was petrified that Uncle Irving might catch it; it was far worse for men because of their whiskers. I was petrified that I might give it to Jack. I felt like a leper. The only treatment was Gentian Violet, a dark-purple ointment, or Mercurochrome, a poison-pink liquid. The dermatologist put one on one side of my face, and the other on the other. Neither seemed to do much good, and I had visions of marching down the aisle in my dazzling white dress with my purple and pink face heavily veiled. No subsequent uglification by age, whether wrinkles or wattles, has ever been so hard to bear as that impetigo. If Jack had wanted to break our engagement, I wouldn't have blamed him. But, in fact, he was more attentive than ever, though in a more cautious mode. I began to have an inkling about what the phrase "in sickness and in health" could involve.

The second blow came on the morning when the list of New York candidates who passed the bar exam was published in the *New York Times*. Instead of the name of that former editor of the *Yale Law Review*, Jonathan Brewster Bingham, leading the list, it wasn't to be found. No matter how often Jack read the list, the fact was that he had flunked. And being a houseguest of the chief judge of the New York Court of Appeals didn't make his humiliation any easier. He promptly borrowed my car and drove to Albany to find out what he'd done wrong. He returned exhausted but relieved. His pattern of failure was confined to the True/False section: he had typically reasoned one step too far. Instead of writing down the obvious answers, Mr. Smarty Pants had figured that they were too obvious.

A bar exam was scheduled again for shortly after we were to return from our honeymoon. Jack would need to bring along some law books. Having never failed or even received a mediocre mark on a test before, he was chagrined, but later admitted that it had probably been good for him. He had, as he could see, been "above himself." Certainly when he phoned Dick Moore to tell him, Dick couldn't stop laughing—and proceeded to remind Jack of the pleasure Jack was thus providing to various competitors whom he had consistently beaten out for academic honors, including, of course, Moore himself.

As my complexion began to clear and the shock of Jack's failure began to wane, we were able to concentrate on wedding plans. Jack wanted us to be married by Endicott Peabody, the rector of Groton, whom Jack loved and admired. Toward the end of Jack's sixth form year after taking the rector's course in "Sacred Studies," Jack had gone to him to ask to be confirmed in the school chapel where he had served both as bell ringer and choir member.

"All right, Jack," Mr. Peabody said, "Why do you want to be confirmed?"

"I love the school, sir, and I love the chapel."

"That's not good enough."

The result was that Jack, a great-grandson and grandson of missionaries, remained unbaptized and unconfirmed. But both he and I respected the rector's decision. Jack's reasons had been insufficiently profound.

I, naturally, was also unbaptized and unconfirmed. Nor was I an appropriately educated Jew. I had never even entered a Jewish house of worship until the funeral of my maternal grandmother, Clara Lehman Limburg, at Temple Emanu-El in 1932. And, at the time, I was more impressed by the screaming motorcycle escort for the governor-elect, Granny's brother Herbert, than by the service. A week later, I was dismayed when my mother forbade me to go to a tea dance in Greenwich. "How could you even *want* to?" she asked in horror. But I did want to and therefore felt guilty for my thoughts as well as for my words. I didn't honestly mourn my grandmother. Later, when Granny's will was probated, she had left $25,000 to each of my brothers, but only $10,000 to me. This was explained as reflecting the fact that a man would need money to establish a business, while a lady would only need it for some frippery that her husband might not be able or willing to pay for. None of this came as any surprise to me, and I thought little about it.

Both at the time of Jack's and my engagement and our marriage, a big photo of me appeared in the *New York Times* with a headline to the effect that the New York governor's grand-niece would be linked to the son of the former senator from Connecticut. One would almost have thought that Uncle Herbert and Hiram Bingham were marrying each other. Even Elder Brewster was mentioned because both of Jack's parents were descended from him. I told Jack that one would have been enough. Actually, it was my father, rather than Jack, who thought this ancestral item should be mentioned, and clearly the *New York Times* society editor agreed.

After the announcements, Jack, more than I, received hate letters from total strangers berating us for deserting the faith of our fathers. Some letters were signed, some not. Either way, we pitched them out and went off cheerfully to have the Wasserman blood test for syphilis, a prerequisite for a marriage license back then.

Though it was natural for us to choose for our wedding the Rosemary Hall Chapel, which I loved, problems arose because of the date. The only midweek day that would not coincide with one of the many Jewish holidays in September was Wednesday the 20th. This, alas, was also the day Groton was scheduled to open, which meant that the Rector could not marry us. We had to content ourselves with the Episcopal priest from Greenwich, who was rigid about including every single one of the optional prayers although we begged him not to.

From the Rosemary Hall Chapel, the guests drove to the Port Chester Elizabethan-style house of Uncle Irving and Aunt Sissie. (Thirlsmere at that time was too small to accommodate 150 people.) In ten minutes,

Jack and I emerge as man and wife from the Rosemary Hall Chapel on our wedding day, September 20, 1939.

our guests traveled from a very visible cross at the altar to a very visible menorah on the mantel in the Lehmans' living room.

Several lively parties had been given before the wedding. Jack threw a bachelor dinner in Salem and I had a bridesmaids' luncheon at Thirlsmere. His ushers included my two brothers and three of his, Alf, Charley, and Mitch, plus five of his friends, Dick Moore, the best man; John Hersey, later the famous writer; Louis Walker, uncle of two subsequent Republican Bush presidents; Doug Auchincloss, later a writer for *Time*, and Dick Barr, an architect. My bridesmaids were Bunnie Struthers, my maid of honor; my favorite cousin, Edith Altschul; my friend Marian Sulzberger; my Rosemary friend, Elaine Oakley; and one of my Vassar roommates, Sue Bontecou. (Another roommate, Adelaide, was off on her yearlong honeymoon with Alec Hixon.)

The ushers presented Jack with a martini-filled solid silver cocktail shaker engraved with their signatures; my bridesmaids presented me with a solid silver cigarette box engraved with theirs. Since Jack and I both drank and smoked, these gifts were far more useful at the time than later. And, as we soon realized, silver needs to be polished.

On the Saturday evening before our wedding, Arthur and Iphigene Sulzberger gave a large, elegant dinner dance at Hillandale across North Street from Thirlsmere. Jack Bingham and Dick Moore, as former editors of the *Yale Daily News*, took it upon their tipsy selves to set "Mister S." straight about how the *Times* could be improved. One of their ideas would be to run two articles side by side on the same page to cover both sides of a current controversial issue. Mister S., I thought, was remarkably patient with them. Later he told my mother that he preferred to see young men caring too much about the coverage of current events than not enough.

For our wedding, Jack and the ushers wore cutaways, with striped pants, gray vest, and ascot. The bridesmaids wore rose taffeta dresses with heart-shaped necklines and small bustles that my mother had chosen at the Salon Moderne at Saks Fifth Avenue. I begged her for something less expensive and more useful for later, but she was adamant: "Their parents can afford it." I continued to feel embarrassed, but there was no point in arguing with my mother about clothing, including my own. She had marched me into the Salon Moderne and made me stand for hours while a gorgeous dress of white slipper satin with white velvet horizontal "frogs" on either side of the front zipper were fitted to my buxom form. The bra I wore was as tight as could be, as was the "merry widow" cinching my waist. While my petticoat boasted great-grandmother's lace, my veil was of fresh white tulle.

September 20th dawned chilly and overcast, with light rain predicted. I had breakfast in bed and stayed put, writing thank you notes for some of the hundred presents that had already arrived. Like someone on death row, I'd been allowed to choose the menu for my final meal as a maiden. We had lamb chops and French-cut string beans from the garden. Almost never does anything impede my appetite.

I was seated in my white dress at my mother's dressing table while a seamstress from the Salon Moderne was arranging my veil when my brother Dick, in his cutaway, entered the room. His lips were working and his eyes overly bright. "Good-bye, Miss Rossbach," he said.

My father also started to get tearful and was chewing his mustache as he walked me to the door of the Rosemary Hall Chapel, but I whispered the punch line of an off-color joke that he liked, which elicited from him a tremulous smile.

By five in the afternoon the sun was out, and guests were served Champagne and dinner outdoors on the Lehmans' terrace. Indoors, people were dancing. Even after the wedding party's separate dinner in the dining room, punctuated by happy toasts, Jack and I were having such a good time on the dance floor that my mother had to interrupt us and say that Aunt Sissie was tired and we should depart.

Jack and I during our wedding reception at Uncle Irving Lehman and Aunt Sissie's home in Port Chester. The pleasure we took in each other's company is evident even in this posed photo.

After we left, my brothers had to pile a case of Champagne into the back of Howard's black Buick roadster, The Black Bullet. This served, like the Pied Piper's music, to lure the remaining merrymakers over to the nearby estate of Whitelaw and Helen Reid, publishers of the *New York Herald Tribune*, where a cottage had been turned over to friends of their eldest son, Jack's classmate, Whitie. Meanwhile, the Lehmans' chauffeur drove Jack and me into the city to the Pierre Hotel. Many years later, Fred, who had agreed to keep away from the wedding, told me that he'd spent the whole night pacing the sidewalk outside the Pierre. I'm glad I hadn't known.

Marriage

The next morning, the Pierre's chief portiere had to phone Penn Station to hold the overnight train to Miami for a few minutes because a pair of stupid honeymooners had forgotten their golf clubs. This was but the first of many suspenseful train, ship, and plane departures masterminded by Jack Bingham who enjoyed the kind of adrenaline-surge, that I, and later our children and grandchildren, did not.

Originally, Jack and I had planned to go to Europe for our honeymoon. Because of Hitler and Stalin's recent nonaggression pact, the advent of war seemed less imminent. But on September 1st, three weeks before our wedding, Hitler marched into Poland, and the Allies declared war.

I'm ashamed to say that my first reaction to this horrendous news was "Damn! Now Jack and I can't go to Europe."

Instead, we spent our second night on the train, and our third, together with hundreds of mosquitoes, at his mother's place in Coral Gables, Florida. The next morning, we flew by pontoon plane to Cuba. After a brief time of sightseeing in Havana, we drove an hour and a half to Varadero, a beautiful simple resort right on the water. Our one-room cabin at the Cavama Beach Club was the furthest from the main building, and thus offered privacy enough for midnight swims in the nude. In the mornings, we played tennis on the club court and in the afternoon, golf on the nearby Rockefeller-built course. Evenings we dressed up and drank Cuba libres (rum, Coca Cola, and fresh lime) at the main building. I had never before tasted papaya or red snapper, nor had I slept to the accompanying rattle of palm trees right over my head. When the night came for me to wash my hair, however, I was frightened. Jack, with no sister, had likely never seen a girl with her hair curled up in bobby pins. What if he were to be repelled? Shyly I peeked around the corner of our tiny bathroom. He looked up from his law book and shouted with joy: "Oh, could you wear it like that all the time?"

But after four or five days, the pace he set was too much for me, and one morning on the tennis court, I started to faint. That earned me an afternoon off and served as the first of many warnings to him that my endurance was far from equal to his.

A week later at seven in the morning when our overnight train from Florida rolled into Penn Station, my father had come all the way from White Plains to greet us.

As I stepped onto the platform he took my elbows in his hands and looked deep into my eyes: "How are you?"

"Hungry."

The word was greeted with a guffaw by him and also by Jack.

PART TWO

The Forties

CHAPTER 4

Parenthood

DURING THE FIRST FIFTEEN MONTHS of our marriage, Jack and I, together with most other Americans, were deeply torn about what role our government should take in regard to Hitler. The Luftwaffe was pounding England and the Wehrmacht was overrunning the Lowlands. One group of Americans, the Isolationists, did not want the United States to become involved in any way. Another group, the Interventionists, wanted the United States to send an expeditionary force as soon as possible. A third group, the Noninterventionists, wanted the United States to do everything possible to aid the Allies, including the convoying of supplies to beleaguered Britain, but to stop short of sending American boys into what appeared, in effect, to be just one more of Europe's bloody, perennial wars.

Jack and I had long been admirers of Great Britain. His ancestors came from England and Scotland. (When informed of this, an Irish travel agent once said, "What a horr-rrible combination.") Jack, as a young boy, had traveled through England with his parents and had taken pictures with his Brownie camera of more cathedrals than I knew existed.

My own admiration for Great Britain also derived from childhood, not because of blood, but because of the many English novels I had read, ranging from sufferings of the poor in *Oliver Twist* to the dramatic accomplishments of *The Scottish Chiefs*. In fact, the latter had inspired me to name my two Scotties Bruce and Wallace. I also read all novels by Hugh Walpole as soon they came out, my favorite being *Fortitude*. I, too, had been taken to England as a youngster by my mother. My diary as a twelve-year-old waxed lyrical in regard to the train trip to London after the docking of our ship, the *Aquitania*, in Southhampton:

> We had high tea and we looked out the window. Oh it was divine—fields, brooks, forests, trees, cattle, and everything—but oh those flowers. Every little house, no matter how small and poorly, had its little garden in the rear. It was perfect—and nearly made me wish I was English—which is really sinful—and that made me so unhappy. The ruddy children, the huge haystacks, even the blooming flowers seemed to mock me; and after all, I have not seen the most beautiful parts of America—just the dingy countryside, and grimy New York—even the [Adirondack] mountains—There is no comparison!

Now I've grown calmer and my feelings less agitated—but when I reread that passage, I can keenly remember how sad I felt.

During that trip, I noticed that most of the people on the street had discolored or crooked or missing teeth, but this was not true of the upper-crust people we met. Among the latter were my British second cousins, the Goodharts. My mother's first cousin, Arthur Goodhart, was the first American to have been a don both at Cambridge and Oxford. Later, when he was offered a knighthood, he turned it down in order to retain his American citizenship, but his British-born wife, Cecily, was addressed thereafter as "Lady Goodhart." Arthur subsequently became head of University College, Oxford; their two elder sons went into English politics. Philip was knighted for being a long-term Conservative member of the House of Commons, serving also in Prime Minister Margaret Thatcher's sub-Cabinet. William was made a lord for having cofounded the Liberal Democratic Party, as well as being a distinguished member of the bar.

Parenthood

In 1940, President Roosevelt, long an Anglophile, was sashaying skillfully between the various sections of American opinion. His reelection campaign was based on his ability to "keep us out of war," but, at the same time, he was taking steps—all of which Jack and I fully endorsed—to be able legally to supply the Allies with all military aid "short of war."

In New York City, the Federation of Jewish Philanthropies, headed by German Jews, including the Lehmans, set up the Joint Distribution Committee to help impoverished refugees from Europe. Some of the stories these refugees told were impossible for Jack and me to believe. The Nazis decreed that Jewish judges must be defrocked; Jewish teachers and civil servants would be dismissed; Jewish doctors, musicians, and actors would no longer be paid for their skills; theatres and concert halls must no longer sell tickets to Jews; food stores would only serve Jews between four and five in the afternoon (after the best items had been sold); and Jews of all ages must not own pets. Even harder to believe were the beginnings of unprecedented atrocities that later became included in the newly coined term, "genocide" and, later, by the capitalizing of an old word, "holocaust." How could any such thing be going on in the country of Mozart and Goethe? Nor were Jews the only victims of the Nazi regime. At Uncle Irving and Aunt Sissie's, Jack and I heard mention of political liberals, Gypsies, and what were then called "sexual deviants" (homosexuals) being forced to drink castor oil until their insides literally came out, but who could believe that either?

Jack and I had greatly enjoyed our childhood visits to Germany. Now we were confounded by trying to mesh what we were told about it with what we had seen firsthand. Also, in principle, we were reluctant to be taken in by atrocity stories because our teachers at school had assured us that similar stories had been deliberately manufactured by British propagandists and American armament makers in order to gull the United States into entering World War I. For example, the famous photo of a Belgian child with its hand cut off by the brutal Hun was later proved to have been a fake produced by British Intelligence. Nor did Jack's and my daily "bible," the *New York Times*, do much to counter our youthful suspiciousness. More than half a century later, the *Times* was accused of having played down its war coverage of the atrocities before American entrance into World War II because the paper's founder, Adolph Ochs, and his son-in-law, our family friend, Arthur H. Sulzberger, wanted to prevent the paper from being condemned for shrillness or hysteria, two qualities associated with being Jewish.

Jack and I were further deceived, as were many Americans, by the diabolical means by which the Nazis were hiding their atrocities. One example was their model "Camp" in Theresienstadt where a foreigner could see for himself how clean and well-fed the Jewish prisoners were, and how, in the evenings they could even enjoy concerts by fellow prisoners. The famous fake villages set up by Catherine the Great's favorite administrator, Potemkin, were child's play compared with the masking of official barbarity by Hitler's minions.

Philosophically, too, it was hard for Jack and me in 1940 to make room in our worldview for the depths of evil attributed to Hitler as well as to Stalin, Mussolini, and Franco. During our formative years in the twenties, most Americans had assumed, together with Professor John Dewey of Columbia University, that human nature, by way of education and social betterment, was on its way to improvement and that, as a result of a better life for everyone, the evils of poverty and war would in time be eliminated. My father wore a thin, circular gold ornament on the gold watch chain that spanned his ample belly. On the ornament were the words of the French philosopher, Émile Coué: "Every day in every way I'm getting better and better." This theory, also formally known as the "perfectibility of man," was widely believed at least until the American stock market crash and the worldwide Depression that followed.

Parenthood

At last, on June 20, 1940, I became 21, old enough to vote in November. Of course I chose FDR, whose mellifluous voice was soothing the American people into assuming that we would never become militarily ensnarled in Europe: "I know war; I hate war." On behalf of him, I also did my first, very minor, campaigning, both as a student interviewee on the radio, and then as a contributor to the letters column in *Common Sense*, the magazine copublished by Jack's brother Alf.

Jack and I, from the noninterventionist position, agreed with Roosevelt's exchange of overage Navy destroyers for British overseas bases, as well as his announcement that America would now be "the arsenal of democracy." After Congress voted for the peacetime draft, Jack signed up. But the high number he drew meant that he and I did not need to worry for the moment. (A few of his Yale classmates, whom I did not then know, were pacifists who refused to register for the draft and were jailed.)

Still, even the off-chance that Jack might be called up by the military made the two of us cherish each day and night in our fourth-floor walk-up at the corner of 58th Street and Sutton Place. We paid $85 per month for a small bedroom, living-dining room, kitchen, and bath. From one window we could just make out the East River with its barges and hooting tugs and occasional sailboats. At first, the only food I knew how to cook was scrambled eggs; the only food my mother knew how to cook was fudge. Another aspect of my ignorance was somewhat cured by *Ideal Marriage*, by Dr. van der Velde. My first reaction to its description of the various positions of love-making was, "Heavens to Betsy, what will they think of next?"

Jack had informed the prestigious Wall Street law firm of Cravath, deGersdorff, Swaine and Wood that he would stay with them only for one year. The managing partner just smiled, and said to come ahead. The morning Jack started work, I hung as far as I could from our 58th Street window and watched him stride down the sidewalk, his arms swinging more sideways than forward. I cried. How could I face a whole day without him?

One of the many ways I tried to please him was to take piano lessons—something I had gleefully stopped doing when I went to Rosemary—so that he and I could play violin-piano duets. Subsequently, he would also teach himself the viola and the cello. With most subjects I've tried to master, I have had a reasonable degree of success, but not with tempo. If I see black notes bunched on a music page, I automatically speed up and when white space appears between the notes, I tend to slow down. For Jack, whose mind was part metronome, my inability to give proper value to a sixteenth note was inexplicable. Luckily, once I had learned a piece of music by heart, I could handle its rhythms correctly, but in the early stages of learning, I was sometimes reduced to tears of frustration and he to outspoken impatience. But we kept going, and our repertory, and our enjoyment of it, began to mount. He preferred Bach, Haydn, and Mozart; I preferred Beethoven, Brahms, and Wagner. But in time, by dint of attending concerts at Carnegie Hall and operas at the Met and listening to our classical records with their red labels on our new Capehart machine, we each broadened our appreciation of the other's favorites.

We continued to be enchanted with each other and if we could escape having to spend the weekend at Thirlsmere (both my parents kept heavy pressure on us in this regard), our routine was to hold what Jack called a "party" on Saturday night. This meant collecting a full ice bucket, two glasses, and a bottle of Dewar's Scotch, and having in the oven some food that could wait.

One evening as we sat together on the sofa, he made a statement I disagreed with and said so. He was furious.

"Why do you always contradict me?"

"I don't!"

"You just did."

A pause. Then he pushed his point one step further. "At least, if you disagree, you should be polite enough to say, 'I beg your pardon . . .'"

"All right. I beg your pardon, but your original statement was a lot of baloney."

"Oh it was, was it?" And there followed a pillow fight.

On another occasion, we got into a disagreement about the value of philosophy. I insisted that much can be learned from studying it, yet when he, in lawyerly fashion, pressed me for specific evidence, I had trouble coming up with good examples. He claimed that ontology and epistemology were little more than what his family called "spinning," i.e., pompous palaver about vague concepts. His years of debating enabled him to argue me into the ground, but he could not dull my enthusiasm for philosophy. This time it was I who became furious. I rose.

"What's the point of winning an argument if all it does is make the other person want to get away from you?"

He too rose. "I don't ever want you to get away from me."

I couldn't think what to say.

"Please." He took me in his arms.

I didn't know how to respond. But eventually I figured it out. There are times, childbirth being another example, when our body knows so much more than our mind does that we might as well give up and let it lead us.

More than a decade later, Jack brought up the subject of philosophy again: "You know, I've decided you were right. I wish now that I'd taken some courses in it in college."

That time it was I who held out my arms.

Much as Jack and I loved dining at home, we also enjoyed evenings at private parties. One night, Helen Rogers Reid, of *New York Herald Tribune* fame, threw a dance for her two grown sons, Whitie and Brownie (Ogden). Jack and I had never before gussied ourselves up in each other's company. I didn't realize how complicated the boiled shirt of the "white tie" outfit is, and he had never seen a "merry widow" waist cincher being struggled into. My dress was my former wedding dress, but with its white velvet "frogs" converted back to the model's original black. (Little did I know—or even imagine—that some twenty-odd years later, I would be berated by grown daughters for not having saved the dress for them and their weddings.)

When Jack and I arrived at the party, we found we had less interest than we had anticipated in talking with our friends. All we really wanted to do was to dance with each other. When the orchestra took a break, Mrs. Reid marched over to us. She was clearly not pleased. "How do you two think your dancing makes the other young people feel, the ones who are not in love?"

Chagrined, we did our best to act in a more seemly manner, but by then, all we wanted to do was go home. How, I wondered, could any institution as delicious as marriage be permitted, let alone sanctioned, by society? The kind of exultation we sometimes felt in each other's company had formerly derived only from forbidden actions.

Fred was living around the corner with two male roommates, and he phoned me every month or two. Because Jack recognized that for almost three years Fred and I had been each other's closest friend, these phone calls didn't bother him. He trusted me to be fully honest when I reported to him on what was said, and I was. He also trusted me to be fully loyal to him, which I also was. Jack was confident enough—and wise enough—to play out his frisky filly on a long lead rather than try to hold her in on a tight rein. Nor was he an exemplar of 100 percent fidelity, himself, at least in his mind.

One summer evening when the sun's rays came on reddish and low from the city's West Side and the shadows were stark, I strolled down 57th Street to meet him at the 3rd Avenue El. (That structure was soon torn down and its steel shipped to the Japanese—or so we Americans later came to think.)

I could see Jack coming half a block away, striding along, his fedora at the back of his head. As he came closer, I noticed that he was appraising each woman he approached, starting with her feet and moving upward to waist to bosom to face. I stayed in the shadow until he was almost abreast of me. Then I stepped out into the sunlight. He appraised me in the same fashion from foot to waist to bosom to face and his expression of shock was worth a thousand words.

We both laughed so hard we had to lean against the nearest building. Later we came across a definition of marriage we fully approved: "Marriage is two people with a secret."

Hand in hand, we returned to our fourth floor eyrie where Essie Green, a plump open-hearted resident of Harlem who had once worked for Alf and Sylvia Bingham had a three-course supper waiting for us.

Essie was the second Negro I had ever met. There were none at Vassar and only one at Barnard. I had tried to talk to the latter who was tall and elegant with straightened hair and married to one of the Paris Cartiers, but she made it clear she had no interest in me.

Essie, too, had straightened hair, and a sweet, pretty face. For $12 a week she came weekdays at two o'clock and served us dinner at seven, having cleaned the apartment, done the shopping, plus done a bit of laundry and ironing (our sheets and Jack's shirts were sent out). One day I blinked hard when she changed from her street clothes to her self-chosen uniform, thus revealing a frizzy dark bush under each arm. I was also startled by the violence of her reaction when in a joking manner my father referred to my black toy lamb as a "little pickaninny." Essie pulled me aside and announced that she was quitting. I was appalled: "But why? What have I done?" She blamed my father. I immediately spoke to him—and he made an apology sufficiently abject to keep her with us.

My main complaint about Essie was that she was too good a cook. Jack and I both gained weight. On him this was becoming; on me it was not. Another mild complaint concerned Essie's single-minded attachment to the Jehovah's Witnesses. Not only did she follow its edicts about not utilizing my new aluminum pots, but she inserted copies of *The Watch Tower* in our suitcase when Jack and I went off for the weekend.

One such trip came during the spring following our autumn wedding. We drove to Woodbury, Connecticut, to visit Jack's former Yale classmate, Hugh Chisholm, a poet and bon vivant. Jack and I were dazzled to find black sheets on our double bed, and even more dazzled to find that our fellow guest in Hugh's beautiful old Revolutionary-era house was Stephen Spender, already established as one of England's major poets. On Sunday morning Hughie took Stephen and us to call on Hugh's neighbor Alexander Calder whom we found in his barn-studio working on a giant mobile. I had never seen a mobile before and was delighted at the way art keeps coming up with new forms. Both Stephen and Alexander were big, blond, impressive-looking men who were clearly enthralled by their work. What I still remember is the final lines of a poem by Hugh who was then trying to bear up under fierce disapproval from his parents because of his refusal to go into the family business, the Oxford Paper Company:

> *The old man staring at the wall*
> *Knows that the world is square*
> *Knows that the prodigal never returns*
> *Always is there.*

Another weekend trip involved an overnight train to Fred's birthplace, Charlotte, North Carolina, the city to which I was not invited while single. The occasion was the marriage of our erstwhile usher, John Hersey, to the handsome and brilliant local girl, Frances Ann Cannon. I was determined to look my best and asked my mother's doctor, Dr. Leopold Stieglitz, brother of the great photographer,

Alfred Stieglitz, for some diet pills. He gave me an open-ended prescription for dexedrine, which killed both my appetite and my ability to sleep. (Today it would be called speed.) I lost the pounds I wanted to and bought a full-length pale blue silk dress for the black-tie wedding in the Cannons' vast mansion, which had been built by James B. Duke for his daughter, Doris. While Jack was to be one of John's ushers, John's best man was Fred.

At the evening wedding, as the ushers marched in, it was clear that too many preprandial drinks had been served. Robert (Choochoo) Train, Yale's 1936 football hero and Fred's former roommate, was swaying badly as he lurched up to the spot where he was supposed to stand—in front of one of the giant candelabras that provided the only light for the vast marble hall. In front of him stood bridesmaids in their pale green bouffant chiffon dresses that would have gone up instantly in flames had he knocked over a candelabrum. I was so worried, I didn't take in a word of the service.

Afterward, Train was spirited away, and Jack and I found ourselves standing near Daisy Hanes Lassiter, the formidable mother of Fred. Jack, too, had had his share of drinks, and when I introduced him to her, he said, "Mrs. Lassiter, you've made the worst mistake of your life . . ."

"Oh, indeed?"

" . . . by not letting Fred marry June."

There was a long pause. "Perhaps you're right," she said and turned away. We never saw her again.

But most of the time when Jack and I were packing our suitcases, it was for yet one more compulsory weekend in White Plains. We hated having to give up our time alone in town, but my parents were so deeply hurt if we didn't come—"You mean you don't want to see your own mother and father?"—that it didn't seem fair to indulge ourselves. Also, we liked the chance to see my brothers and play tennis if weather permitted. Another advantage was financial (our food budget being $10 a week). For in addition to all the free meals over the weekend, we would return laden with fruits, vegetables, and flowers from the Thirlsmere gardens.

The first party we gave was for Jack's brightest lawyer friends, Dick Moore, Harold Steinberg, and Lloyd Cutler. The admitted agenda was to help me with the homework I'd been assigned by the head of Barnard's English department, Professor Minor Latham, who taught the course on playwriting. She was the best teacher I ever had, but some of her assignments were close to impossible. This one was to write a scene in which the captain would be the *first* to leave his sinking ship—with the full consent of the audience.

To no one's surprise and everyone's amusement, the solutions offered by these young men were even more bizarre than the assignment—and of no use to me at all. I finally ended up portraying the captain as a wartime intelligence officer who was the only person to know by heart the key to the enemy's secret code. His survival, therefore, was essential to his country. Little did Jack or I suspect that, within a little more than a year, he himself would be made privy to the results of a similar "key" to an enemy's code. Had Jack or any of the few Army personnel assigned to teasing out the significance of these decoded messages ever leaked that secret, the number of Americans lost in the Pacific would have been even more gruesome than it was. Because he did defy orders and let me in on what he was doing, our definition of marriage as "two people with a secret" was given a new and far broader dimension.

During 1940, Hitler, emboldened by his successful invasion of Poland in September, 1939, had turned his blitzkrieg westward. In the summer, his Panzers conquered first the Low Countries and then France. One of the inspiring events of the war was the way hundreds of British civilians ferried their private boats back and forth across the English Channel to rescue the three hundred thousand British, French, and Belgian troops from the Belgian beaches.

Despite all the matériel the United States was risking our sailors' lives to convoy across the Atlantic, plus the eloquence of Britain's newly appointed prime minister, Winston Churchill, and the heroism of RAF pilots, Britain's survival remained terrifyingly in doubt.

At that same time, unbeknownst to Jack and me, his brother Harry, a vice consul at the American consulate in Marseilles, France, was secretly, against the express orders of his superiors, aiding in the heroic rescue work of Varian Fry by issuing hundreds of visas, valid and faked, for prominent refugees from Hitler so that they could escape from France into Spain and Portugal, and from there across the Atlantic. Among the escapees Harry helped were Marc Chagall, Lion Feuchtwanger, and Max Ernst, and "Aryans," including the brother of Thomas Mann. Harry's own wife, Rose, and their four children had been ordered home by the State Department because Europe was considered too hazardous for American dependents. Had Harry's activities been discovered, he would have been summarily dismissed.

Harry's hope was that, although Hitler had openly targeted the famous refugees for extinction, Hitler would not bother about the thousands of non-famous ones. These people, Harry assumed, could blend in with the general populace of southern France, which was not yet under German occupation. But Harry, as it turned out, had underestimated not only the Nazis' anti-Semitism but also that of the French. So much in danger were even native French Jews that after the Germans occupied all of France, a cousin of mine, Edmond Kahn, divorced his Christian wife, Jeannine, so that she would not be persecuted. She went, with their children, to live with her Christian family, while he fled to Latin America. After the war, he returned to France and the couple remarried and lived happily ever after.

My brother Dick, while at Yale, had joined Army ROTC. By the time he graduated in 1936 he was a second lieutenant in the Field Artillery Reserves. In the middle of 1940, he volunteered for active duty. Originally he had hoped to be assigned to the cavalry. While at Yale he had deliberately played polo. But our cavalry became so mechanized that his equestrian skills were no longer of use. Instead, he joined the Second Armored Division under the command of General George S. Patton, "Old Blood and Guts." Patton, as Dick observed him, "always wore riding britches with black boots so well polished that you could have shaved in their reflection." By the following summer of 1941, my brother Howard, whose eyesight had always been poor, managed to memorize the Army eye chart and thus get admitted as a private. After basic training he was sent to OCS (officers' training school) in antiaircraft at Camp Stewart near Savannah. Fortunately for him and the nation, he was permitted to wear his eyeglasses while on duty, or the planes that flew within range of his unit's guns might not have been correctly identified. Later his unit was shipped to a country south of the border; he could surmise in which direction they were headed by the tropical uniforms being issued. In a postcard to my parents, he announced his safe arrival in "a city very aptly named." After considerable research with a map, we figured out that he must mean Colon in Panama. There he remained for the duration of the war, helping to guard the Canal, and in his free time teaching English to some of his local troops, and practicing his sculpting. He had taken applied art at Yale although he knew that he could not get a good mark, and he needed good marks to get into law school. But he wanted to learn how to sculpt and by gum, he learned it and proceeded to practice it for his own enjoyment. But the years in Panama must have been hard for him, especially when Dick, by then a multi-medaled war hero in North Africa, was reported missing in action in Europe. We tried not to worry, but we did.

Jack and I, unheroically, continued to applaud all of Roosevelt's steps to aid the Allies although we knew that some of these, like the freezing of German and Italian assets in the United States, might

My family during the war years. I am seated (on the left) with my oldest, Sherrell, on my lap. Sitting next to me are my mother and father. My brother Howard is standing behind us at the far left. Next to him (left to right) are my brother Dick's wife, Susan; Dick; and Jack.

well draw America into the fighting. We also briefly joined the America First Committee, along with Herbert Hoover and Theodore Roosevelt, Jr., and others less famous at the time, including Kingman Brewster, a distant cousin of Jack's who later became president of Yale; Sargent Shriver, who later became the first head of the Peace Corps and a Democratic candidate for vice president; Chester Bowles, who later was elected governor of Connecticut and twice appointed U.S. ambassador to India; and Chester Kerr who later headed *The Yale Press*. High on the America First Committee masthead was my childhood hero, Charles Lindbergh.

But then, in September 1941, Lindbergh made a speech in Des Moines, Iowa, that caused Jack, me, Sarge Shriver, Chet Bowles, Chet Kerr, and many others to resign immediately from the committee. Half a century later, Charles Lindbergh's daughter, Reeve, listened to a tape of that speech. When she heard her father say one of the "greatest dangers" to the United States was the influence of Jews, she wrote, "I was transfixed and horrified, ablaze with shame and fury. 'Not you!' I cried out silently to myself and to him, 'No! You never said such things.'"

But, alas, he did say them, and Jack and I cut all ties with his committee. I also threw out the signed photo of him that Arthur Sulzberger had given me many years before.

Arthur Sulzberger, or "Mr. S" as my brothers and I called him, never stopped his generosity to me. He wrote me funny poems on my birthdays and in 1940, when I was about to graduate from Barnard, he offered me a job as a reporter on the *New York Times*. But while I pondered this tempting step, something even more important in my life was going on.

While Vassar had forbidden me to remain as a student because I was about to commit the sin of matrimony, Barnard now threatened to withhold my degree because I could no longer take part in compulsory athletics. When I went to the head of phys ed to tell her I couldn't play volleyball that winter, she was horrified: "Well, you won't get your diploma."

"Well, at least I'll have my baby," I said.

Never before had the college had to cope with a pregnant, full-time student. Professor Latham was so unnerved by news of my condition that even before I "showed," she would rush up during playwriting rehearsals and try to help me down from the stage. "Honest to God," said a classmate, "one would think you were pregnant."

Later, when I was just short of giving birth and trying to concentrate during the six hours of my English comprehensive exam, Miss Latham kept interrupting to ask if I was all right. Between her, and the baby who kicked whenever I started to answer a question wrong—and also whenever I started to answer it right—I marvel that I passed the exam at all, especially the compulsory section about Middle English and "the vowel shift" that accompanies the evolution of the English language but whose details were incredibly boring to have to memorize.

The baby, due early in March, delayed its arrival. On March 15, my mother's birthday, a Saturday, Jack and I were planning to arrive at Thirlsmere in time for dinner. Early that morning, I phoned to congratulate my mother and tell her how much we were looking forward to her birthday festivities (untrue). Icily she said she had expected us there by lunchtime. I explained that Jack had to drive to the Rockaways on Long Island for an aspect of his brand-new job at the New York State Labor Board. (He had resigned from Cravath's after a year, just as he had warned them he would and as they had visibly doubted.) "Let him go," my mother said. "You can come out on the train, and he can meet you here later." I explained that I wanted to go to the Rockaways with him; that his and my exploring this unfamiliar territory would turn a chore for him into a pleasant adventure for us both. He entered our bedroom just as she told me that I had ruined her birthday and then hung up on me. "What's the matter?" he asked, but I was too stricken to speak. I flung out of the room, slamming the door behind me.

He came after me, shouting, "Don't you ever do that again."

To his total surprise, I turned and flung myself into his arms, crying and crying. He drew me over to the sofa and comforted me. We ended up having a lovely day in the Rockaways, driving in the rain to visit a number of bakeries whose workers had just voted on whether or not to join the local union. We arrived in White Plains in plenty of time for dinner, but my mother was barely civil to our faces or about the expensive (for us) birthday present we had brought.

Two week's later, on the eve of April Fool's Day, Jack took me to dinner at Asti's, an Italian restaurant on 12th Street where the waiters sang opera. We drank chianti and ate spaghetti and sang along. The next morning I woke up feeling peculiar and assumed it was a mild hangover. But hangovers don't include pains in one's lower back at regular intervals.

After twenty-two hours of labor, our daughter Sherry (Sherrell) was born at Presbyterian Hospital to a fully anaesthetized mother. I returned to consciousness following what I was later told had been a dangerous birth: only the obstetrician's manual intervention had saved the baby's life—and mine. (The amniotic sac had adhered to the cervix; the doctor had fortunately seen one instance of this before and finally reached in and forcefully ripped the two apart, thus allowing the cervix to dilate, as it had been trying vainly to do.)

When Sherry was wheeled in in her bassinette, she was, in Keats's phrase, "a joy forever."

Though I was given zero encouragement from my doctor, my mother, or the hospital nurses for my plan to breastfeed the baby, the baby herself was enthusiastic, and that was all that mattered. As I lay in bed during her six a.m. feeding (in those days babies were fed at six, ten, two, six, ten, and two o'clock, regardless of how hungry they were), I knew I was doing what I was put on earth to do.

Parenthood

From my Harkness Pavilion window, I could see the ever-changing Hudson River, sometimes gun-metal with sparklers when the sun caught the tip of a wave, sometimes like "the great gray-green greasy Limpopo River," sometimes an almost tropical turquoise under a cloudless sky, sometimes flecked with whitecaps, sometimes glassily calm. Its tidal flow was connected to the same lunar events that cause women's bodies to undergo their predictable twenty-eight-day cycle. Browning's "God's in his heaven /All's right with the world," echoed in my mind (which had recently been crammed with literary quotes for that English exam). My yearning to offer thanks for this new tiny person created by way of my body made me resonate more to God's presence than ever. For how could I express my over-whelming gratitude for being alive, for the baby's being alive, for Jack's being alive, unless God, in some fashion beyond the wildest stretches of my mind, was also alive?

On my tenth evening in the hospital, I had a mounting fever. I wanted Jack to leave peacefully for home before I summoned the nurse — no point in his worrying all night — but when he kissed me good-bye he felt how hot my face was and rang for the nurse. She phoned the doctor who appeared literally at a run. In those pre-antibiotic days, puerperal fever was still a major killer of new mothers. He yanked my bedcovers away in an unceremonious and, to me, embarrassing, manner. But the infection was not in that area. Instead it was in one breast, an "engorgement" treatable only by icepacks and no more nursing. When I pleaded to have Sherry con-tinue on my other side, the doctor sternly told me that my variety of engorgement might lead to cancer later in life. This, of course, seemed nonsense to me at the time.

Fortunately, Sherry didn't mind switching to formula. "That baby must have Scotch blood," said a nurse; "She won't give up a drop."

At long last, on the eighteenth day, Jack was allowed to bring his two ladies home. (Two generations earlier, ph Ochs had exultantly boasted in a letter about his daughter Iphigene who had recently given birth to her fourth child, "She is coming home after only twenty days in the hospital!")

Aunt Sissie lent us her car and chauffeur. Jack held Sherry in her overly warm receiving blanket. "Look!" he suddenly exclaimed, "She can sweat!" Sure enough, above the tip of her nose was a tiny drop. (As a child I'd been taught to say that animals "sweat," men "perspire," and ladies "dew.") Sherry then proceeded to show off other skills, such as yawning, sneezing, then stretching. "How does she know how to do these things?" he marveled.

Actually, Jack was far ahead of his time in being a hands-on father. He quickly picked up the few tricks I had learned at the Well Baby Clinic at Bellevue Hospital where I worked as a volunteer before Sherry's birth in order to gain some much needed experience in handling infants. Jack and I also fired the soon-to-be famous Benjamin Spock, M.D., as Sherry's pediatrician. Ben, a classmate of Harry Bingham's, had taken care of Alf and Sylvia's children, but by the time Sherry was about to be born, he was apparently busy writing what would become his classic, *Baby and Child Care*. I phoned his office to ask what items to have ready when the baby came home. After several weeks, I received a sheet of paper on which was (badly) typed, "diapers, zinc salve, and a sterilizer." (Baby bottles were of glass and had to be boiled every night in a sterilizer.) I found us another pediatrician.

My mother was horrified when I said I planned to take care of the baby myself, and she proceeded to refer to Sherry as "that poor child." After all, as my mother kept reminding me, a contemporary of mine, married to one of my cousins, not only had a full-time starched English nanny, but a relief-nurse for Nanny's day off.

Sherry was adored by all her Rossbach relatives. Before Howard was sent to Panama, he was granted "compassionate leave" to come to New York to view her in the hospital and Dick, newly married to bright and attractive Sue Goodman, saw Sherry before he was sent overseas. On the Bingham side, however, she was merely grandchild #19, welcomed by all, but in no way special.

Jack volunteered to give her the six a.m. bottle. I don't know of any sound more gratifying to an exhausted new mother than a hungry baby's cry from the next room, quickly followed by a deep male crooning and then an abrupt happy silence. The rest of the time, Essie and I took turns with her. Though Sherry was still supposed to be on the rigid four-hour schedule set by the then-popular behaviorist, Dr. John Watson, I couldn't force myself to stick to it. Neither could Essie. Whenever Sherry worked herself into a prolonged screaming fit, we were quicker with the bottle than Dr. Watson would have liked.

I did leave her with Essie one afternoon in order to go to my own graduation. No family member bothered to come and, as things worked out, this was just as well because the Barnard proceedings were but a small segment of a huge program on the Columbia University campus.

I also found that standing up for any length of time was difficult, for the muscles of my back, originally injured by the fall from the horse, often went into such violent spasm that one leg became shorter than the other. I was reduced to painkillers and hot water bottles and massage by an osteopath. My back's ligaments had been stretched by pregnancy; they needed time to be reinforced by exercises to strengthen the belly muscles that support those of the back. I did these exercises daily the rest of my life, with interruptions only for the two spinal operations I eventually had to undergo after our three subsequent children were born. Had it not been for the 20th century's X-rays and new surgical techniques, I might have ended up like Ethan Frome's lady love, in a wheelchair suffering from chronic severe pain and making everyone else's life miserable as well.

Jack, meanwhile, was enjoying his law work for the New York State Labor Relations Board. His colleagues there were from far less "shoe" backgrounds than the well-connected WASPs at Cravath's. In fact, two of them turned out to be "fellow travelers," that is, people who agreed with the sentiments of the Communist Party of the U.S.A. but did not actually join it. In June 1941, Jack was baffled by their overnight switch from isolationism to interventionism. This switch was the result of Hitler's betrayal of his nonaggression pact with Stalin in order to invade Russia. Party liners, like Communist members, automatically based their opinions on what appeared best for the Soviets. When Jack tried to argue with them about Stalin's ruthless cruelty revealed at the recent Moscow trials, the rote answer was, "You can't make an omelet without breaking eggs." (Sixty-three years later Shimon Perez reversed this adage in favor of withdrawing Israel's settlements in Gaza: "You can't make eggs from an omelet.")

Jack and I had trouble comprehending how such citizens of a democracy could so completely delegate their freedom of choice to a political party that, in turn, blindly delegated their freedom of choice to a foreign government. At the same time, we continued seriously to question our own choices in regard to what we thought America should do about the war. Which of our convictions were objectively based and which were unconsciously determined by our private reluctance to be separated from each other? Jack wrote an article called, "Men Prefer War," which laid out the macho reasons for males having encouraged bloodshed throughout history, but no one would publish it.

My own reasoning for our position on U.S. involvement in the war was that as long as Jack, as a civilian, was free to come home at night, I wanted to be with him. I therefore turned down the job at the *Times*. From what I know about newspapers in the 1940s, I may not have missed much because female reporters were largely restricted to society news and the decorative arts. Also, I was happy taking care of baby Sherry and fitting my freelance writing around her needs. Before long I found a literary agent willing to peddle my short stories, but she was not able to sell them. And my parents, rather than reducing their demands on me now that they had a grandchild to love, seemed even more insatiable.

One hot Sunday evening in July 1941, Jack and I were getting ready to drive back from Thirlsmere to our new two-bedroom walk-up apartment on 55th Street. My mother was insisting that it would be much better for "that poor child," who had developed prickly heat, to stay in the country until the weather improved. When I reported how much I hated to be separated from her, my mother said, then I, too, should stay. But little as I wanted to be parted from Sherry, I wanted even less to be parted from Jack. We finally compromised on my leaving the baby in the country overnight to see how it went.

The next morning I was frantic. I finally extricated our car from its garage in the basement of a nearby small house — not easy because our arrangement with the non-English-speaking owner was that we would need the car only on weekends. When I arrived at Thirlsmere I was ridiculed by my mother for my possessiveness, but in time I was able to escape with my baby, prickly heat and all. Together with the urge to breathe, eat, and have sex, the yearning to be in physical contact with my baby was so potent that I could hardly recognize myself.

When Sherry was a few months old, I was sitting in the park with her in her carriage and a pad of yellow foolscap on my knee. With almost no conscious forethought, I wrote a letter to my father-in-law. The gist was that the rhododendrons were blooming and he had a fine new grandchild.

By return mail, I received a self-typed letter offering congratulations. I don't think that Jack would have made the first move toward a reconciliation any more than his father would, but both seemed relieved that the move had been made. From then on, Father Bingham and I continued to correspond cheerfully in a haphazard fashion.

Much to the family's relief, Harry Bingham was ordered back from Marseilles. He cabled his wife, Rose, who was living with their five children at her parents' house in Waycross, Georgia. She quickly weaned the fifth baby, David, and came to New York to meet Harry's ship.

The only bed Jack and I could offer her was in Sherry's room. In the morning, Rose looked ravaged. It turned out that all night long, every time our baby squeaked or huffed, Rose's milk would spurt.

By mid-morning, Rose was in such a state that I decided I had better chaperone her to the Hudson River dock where Harry's ship was expected. As the tugboats nudged the great liner alongside the pier, Rose suddenly cried out, "There he is! But his hair's gone all white." She pointed out to me the brother-in-law I had not yet met, and after he raced down the gangplank to embrace her, she introduced him. But he had eyes only for her, and as the two of them embraced again, I tiptoed away.

Later we learned that when Harry and Rose went to the Plaza for the night, they were interrupted by a frantic phone call from Waycross. Their second son, Thomas, had developed polio. They hurried home, and he recovered adequately (though in his late middle age his painful leg symptoms returned with a vengeance).

Not long thereafter, Harry was posted to Buenos Aires to which Rose and the children would accompany him. Occasionally he would mail Jack long analyses of the world economy and claims that Nazi gold was being hidden in Argentina. The documents, we felt, were far from compelling, and we feared that their undiplomatic vehemence might injure Harry's career. Forty-odd years later, his views about the Nazi gold proved to have been right.

In August 1941, the extension of the draft passed Congress by only one vote. Like many young civilians at the time, Jack was increasingly restless. Though he didn't want America to plunge into the bloodshed, he personally wanted to share in the war effort. He went to Washington to reconnoiter. He was promptly hired by the Office of Price Administration (OPA), which needed lawyers to battle the inflation that would seriously harm the economy if the shrinking supply of civilian goods were allowed to elicit much higher prices. Producers of goods and services were therefore ordered by OPA to keep their prices stable or rationing would have to be instituted, which, in many fields, it eventually was.

My parents went into a state of acute desolation over our move to Washington, but I was overjoyed. Also, with both my brothers in uniform, my parents could scarcely argue too hard against Jack's insistence on going to work for the government.

Though Jack had lived in Washington as a boy, I knew little about the city. My mother helped me to house hunt, and we found a red brick colonial for rent in the leafy suburb, Chevy Chase, Maryland. But though the area would be cooler for the baby than the city was, all our neighbors turned out to be middle-aged or actually old and extremely conservative. No babies for Sherry, no young mothers for me, no Democrats for Jack. The only contemporaries we knew were my Rosemary Hall friend and rival, tall, athletic Jane Knapp, and her bright, jolly husband, Godfrey Kauffmann, whose family owned the *Washington Star*. Jane invited us for dinner at the Chevy Chase Club, the nearby fashionable enclave that included my father-in-law and Suzanne among its members. But the anti-minority views casually expressed by the Kauffmanns' other guests, in their soft sweet Southern accents, combined with the palatial formality of the clubhouse, made me feel faint. I went to the ladies' room and slumped down with my head between my knees. Finally, I recovered well enough to get through the rest of the evening, but we were the first to take our leave.

When, surprisingly, the dizziness did not wholly go away, I consulted a doctor. He became so alarmed that he ordered tests for a brain tumor. These turned out to be negative. Finally he ordered a basal metabolism, the hour-long breathing test that measures a patient's thyroid. For years I'd been taking the thyroid extract that Dr. Stieglitz had recommended when I was fifteen. But after Sherry's birth, my obstetrician had told me to skip it because pregnancy might well have corrected the deficiency. This basal metabolism test, however, revealed that my thyroid output was so minimal as to be almost below the chart. So back I went on the pills. (Forty years later, that dosage turned out to be too high, and I was rushed to the emergency room of Presbyterian Hospital with atrial fibrillation; the dosage was then halved.) Without these pills, which were unknown before the 20th century, I would have been "swooning" all over the place. As it was, I had enough episodes of fainting for that naughty Jack Bingham to admit that when he saw my cheeks turn ashen and my brow bead with sweat, he was tempted to shout, "Timber!"

I kept seeing Jane—her daughter was Sherry's age—but I didn't see the other guests again. Such entertaining as Jack and I did was rare and likely to be centered on friends or family members from out of town. A simple dinner was cooked and served by our Negro maid, Mildred Neal, a homely, energetic, middle-aged woman with a deep throaty laugh. After she'd been with us for over a year she confided to me that she had been physically beaten by her previous employer. I could hardly believe such a thing, but Millie was a fully honest person, and the pain on her face as she spoke made it clear that I had to believe it.

Millie stayed with us for years, coming along on visits to White Plains and Salem, and when we left Washington after the war, I made sure that she had a job with people who would treat her well: our friends, Jack's Yale classmate, the poetic and witty John Ferguson, and his artistic wife, Peggy. They kept Millie with them for decades until she retired. In their house, as in ours, she was not just respected but loved. In the 1950s, when Jack was summoned back to Washington, I didn't think it fair to try to extricate Millie from her permanent post, and I had to look elsewhere for a domestic helper for ourselves.

By the first Sunday in December 1941, Washington was starting to put up its lavish Christmas decorations. Jack and I decided to take Sherry for an afternoon "airing" in our Plymouth roadster. The New York Philharmonic, conducted by Artur Rodzinski, was on the radio. The music was gorgeous but suddenly, as we drove along Western Avenue, it was interrupted. I could show you the exact spot where we were when the announcer said that the Japanese had bombed Pearl Harbor.

Jack made a U-turn and we drove home. The immensity of the disaster became clearer as the hours passed. How could it have been allowed to happen? Jack could visualize the naval base, for he had spent time as a child in Honolulu.

The war that so many Americans had been dreading was now upon us. Yet Jack and I couldn't help feeling some relief that the decision about our country's role had finally been made. Roosevelt's ringing tones as he went to Congress the next day for an official declaration of war sent shivers down our backs. Almost all the former noninterventionists hurried to support the war effort, and Jack and I were inspirited by feeling ourselves part of so vast and essential an endeavor. Despite the horrors of that first year of war, 1942, when the American forces kept being defeated in the Pacific in bloody, humiliating battles, and our convoys in the Atlantic were being sunk to a ghastly degree, home front morale remained buoyant. In retrospect, it seems clear that the Allies would eventually prevail in the two-front war, but at the time this was far from evident and for more than a year, many people, including myself, had moments of nightmare panic for the nation's future as well as for our babies' and our own.

CHAPTER 5

Wartime

FOLLOWING PEARL HARBOR, one of the first things I did was get pregnant.

One of the first things Jack did was to go to work at the Pentagon.

One of the first things the United States did was to institute a searing investigation into how the Navy and Army could have been caught so lethally by surprise. The conclusion was that if only a small group of trained people had been analyzing the American intercepts of Japanese cables every day, the Pearl Harbor attack could have been averted. Amidst the considerable Japanese cable "chatter" at all levels of security had been enough information to have forewarned us.

A new military outfit was promptly set up in the Pentagon. The Special Branch of MIS (Military Intelligence Service) was headed by a top lawyer from New York's Cravath, deGersdorff, Swaine, and Wood. His name was Alfred McCormack and among the lawyers he recruited was Jack, who had impressed him despite Jack's having spent only one year in the firm. Jack, therefore, promptly resigned from OPA and went to work six days a week for McCormack's "Special Branch" in its windowless chamber under twenty-four-hour armed guard. One of America's most important secrets was that our cryptographers had finally succeeded in breaking Japan's top secret code, an activity referred to as "Magic."

The British, for their part, were having spectacular code-breaking success in regard to the German "traffic." So essential to their war effort did they consider this activity, referred to as "Ultra," that no action was permitted that might arouse the enemy's suspicion about it.

At MIS Jack learned that British intercepts had revealed a Nazi plan to shoot down the plane on which several English notables, including the actor Leslie Howard, would be traveling. But no change of flight plan was allowed, and these men went down to their deaths.

Partly because of Jack's editing experience at *Yale Daily News* and *Yale Law Journal*, he was appointed coeditor of the daily digest of intercepts of intra-Japanese communication. This digest was taken, under armed guard seven days a week, to the president, the secretary of state, and the secretaries of Army, Navy, and Air Force. (There was no Department of Defense as such nor any CIA as yet.) Al McCormack was commissioned a colonel in the Army, but he demanded that rank be completely ignored in the preparation of the digest. Thus Jack, a civilian, was free to blue-pencil or send back for revision any document, regardless of whether its author was a colonel or even a general. Fully in support of this unprecedented handling of military business was Al McCormack's professional military cohead of the Special Branch, General Carter Clark, a career officer whom Jack grew to admire for his forthrightness expressed with Southern courtesy. Their admiration was mutual.

While Jack was working twelve hours a day, six days a week, I was troubled as to what my own wartime role should be. Now pregnant, I was continuing to take care of Sherry and do some writing, but that didn't seem like half enough. Women, even if married, even if they had young children, were being welcomed into the workplace as never before. My mother was putting heavy pressure on me to come to New York for the birth of our second baby. I kept reminding her that it was Jack's baby, too, and that his job would not permit him to be away from the Pentagon on any day other than a Sunday. Of course, I couldn't tell her what exactly he was doing. My mother became incensed that I wasn't choosing, at all costs, to be with her, and accused me of having "a symbiotic relationship" with Jack. I wasn't altogether certain of what that meant, but a rose by any other name would smell as sweet, and his and my relationship was such that I didn't want to change a thing.

One day my obstetrician, who had examined me the previous week, phoned to say that a bed had just become available at Garfield Hospital. Would I please come there right away and let him induce the baby? After some eighteen hours of labor, our daughter Micki (June Mitchell Bingham) was born. Although the cord had been around her neck, the doctor had saved her. She was beautiful. I was nursing her happily when he marched into my room.

"What the hell are you doing?"

"What does it look like I'm doing?"

"You had an engorgement last time. You can't nurse."

"Why not?"

"It might bring on cancer."

Reluctantly I handed over the baby, and by the time we got her home, she had colic. She also had an enraged one-and-a-half-year old sister who kept trying to put the baby's eyes out. Finally we got Micki stabilized on a formula difficult to prepare (the necessary lactic acid tended to curdle the milk)—and hired a young Negro nursemaid to help with her and her archfiend sister. A pacifist friend from my Lincoln School days spent an afternoon on the back lawn with me when Micki was old enough to be mobile and Sherry was, if anything, even more infuriated by her. By the end of his visit, he was sadly shaking his head: "Now I've seen original sin."

Sherry's acute case of sibling rivalry was probably attributable, at least in part, to the severe post-birth back pain that prevented me from picking her up or even roughhousing in bed with her as she had been accustomed to. Nor could I start my back exercises until the painful inflammation had subsided. I was, therefore, a helpless blob, and my mother turned out to be a blessing for us when she came to Washington for a week. She adored Sherry and continued showing favoritism toward her with the lack of self-consciousness of her generation. That,

101

apparently, was just what Sherry needed, and Micki's eyes were safe from Sherry's probing fingers, at least for a while. Micki grew up far less fond of my mother than Sherry was.

On her next Washington visit, my mother got in touch with her first cousin, Elinor Morgenthau, whose husband, Henry Morgenthau, Jr., was secretary of the Treasury in FDR's Cabinet. Cousin Ellie had a droll sense of humor, and Cousin Henry's solemnity at times set it off, to the delight of their dinner guests who, on rare occasion, included Jack and me. Ellie regaled us with tales of her daily early morning horseback rides with Eleanor Roosevelt. What Jack and I didn't know—though Ellie probably did—was that the first lady's mother-in-law, Sara Roosevelt, shared the anti-Semitism typical of the upper Protestant classes. Decades later, in Joseph P. Lash's *Eleanor and Franklin*, I came across evidence of Sara Roosevelt's condescension toward my family. In a letter of 1918 after her first visit from my cousins, she wrote: "Young Morgenthau was easy and yet modest and serious and intelligent. The wife is very Jewish but appeared very well."

So taken-for-granted was anti-Semitism in those days that Eleanor Roosevelt, herself, had shared in it. In a letter to Sara (also quoted by Joseph Lash), she mentioned a party for Bernard Baruch "which I'd rather be hung than seen at . . . mostly Jews." Two days later she added, "The Jew party [was] appalling. I never wish to hear money, jewels and . . . sables mentioned again."

Ironically, author Joseph Lash was a Jew, yet despite being a generation younger than Eleanor Roosevelt, he became a trusted friend about whom she once said that she felt closer than to any of her four sons. A somewhat comparable friendship later developed between her and her much younger doctor, David Gurevitsch. As her grandson Curtis Roosevelt once mentioned to me, many of her closest friendships were with people of a lower socioeconomic group, including New York state trooper, Earl Miller, and the journalist

Lorena Hickock. Curtis conjectured that one reason might have been her old feelings of insecurity aroused by male social peers. Certainly well before World War II, Mrs. Roosevelt had extirpated the slightest anti-Semitism in herself and was active in helping Jews escape from Hitler—an effort, as Jack and I discovered decades later, that included funds for the visa-writing efforts of Harry Bingham in Marseilles and the political speeches all over the United States by Protestant leader Reinhold Niebuhr.

Shortly after Micki was born, Cousin Ellie phoned to congratulate and ask if I would come work as a volunteer at the Office of Civilian Defense (OCD), which she was helping Eleanor Roosevelt and New York City's mayor Fiorello LaGuardia to run. By that time, some German U-boats had dropped off saboteurs on America's Atlantic Coast and a Japanese submarine had shelled an oil refinery on our Pacific Coast. The American people clearly needed guidance in putting up blackout curtains, laying in emergency supplies, and similar civil defense measures about which the British populace had much to teach us.

In the big OCD office near Dupont Circle, an attractive young Negro woman had a desk near mine. One day I asked her to have lunch, but she brusquely turned me down. Shocked and hurt, I asked an older woman if I had said something wrong. She only shook her head. "There isn't a restaurant within miles that would admit her and you together."

Washington was Southern in other ways, too. Ladies were expected to wear mid-calf skirts, preferably with hats and gloves, and never to take issue with a gentleman except in a deferential way. Among the limits that I, a Northern, relatively independent-minded female, objected to was the boring unimportance of the work assigned to volunteers by the OCD. Mine was to clip from newspapers whatever stories appeared about civil defense and file them. I soon asked Cousin Ellie if I could be transferred. Because Cousin Henry was secretary of the Treasury, she was able to move me over to its new war bond sales division. This meant that I went daily to the many-columned old Treasury building where I worked with two intelligent women scarcely older than myself, Judy (Mrs. Harold) Graves and Laura (Mrs. Carl) Auerbach. Together, every two weeks, we turned out a sixteen-page illustrated journal, *The Minute Man*, which provided news, know-how, and morale-building to war bond offices throughout the country.

One of the chief aims of the division was the same as that of Jack's former OPA, namely, to fend off inflation. The OPA did it by holding down prices of consumer goods; the Treasury did it by siphoning off some of the war-workers' purchasing power by persuading them to invest their earnings in bonds to finance the war. I found myself grateful for skills I had learned at college, both in classrooms and on the *Vassar Miscellany News*. For *The Minute Man*, I not only wrote and edited articles but also composed photo captions, designated fonts for headlines, and helped with layout. A photo of a very young Sherry and Micki Bingham was featured on one cover as they played on the stoop of a house being visited by a war bond volunteer (myself). I also wrote several short plays for children, dramatizing the importance of saving money during wartime. These went out to local offices, which disseminated them to schools and clubs.

As a result of this job, like millions of Americans, I awakened each morning excited about the prospect of making at least a small contribution to the war effort. Certainly many of us were working harder and longer and getting more tired than we ever had before, or perhaps ever would again, but our morale was high. Norman Rockwell's 1943 *Saturday Evening Post* cover depicted an impressive-looking Rosie the Riveter with her foot firmly placed on a copy of Hitler's *Mein Kampf.*

The Treasury official to whom *The Minute Man*'s editor reported was an easygoing woman who was suddenly replaced by Harold

Mager, a high-ranking economist, who came from New York to tighten up the war bond organization.

He turned out to be a tough intellectual in his early forties with a broad brow, a boxer's nose, and dark, unsmiling eyes. As an editor, he was demanding and his knowledge of economics was impressive. At his recommendation, I began reading books on Marxism and grew to understand that while Karl Marx himself had belittled the bourgeoisie in favor of the proletariat, some of his followers were stressing the importance of a healthy middle class for the optimal functioning of a democracy. Another thinker whose work Harold introduced me to was John Maynard Keynes. Because of my genuine fascination with Harold's specialty, he began to thaw and occasionally took me to lunch. I developed a bit of a crush on him and was sure that Jack, who had majored in economics at Yale, would be fascinated by his ideas. I therefore invited Harold and his wife, Naomi, for a Saturday night dinner.

Naomi Mager was a former teacher, with a merrier outlook than her husband's. Their little boy, Ezra, was Sherry's age. After some months, Naomi mentioned that she wanted Ezra to have the experience of seeing a little girl undressed. I figured that the obverse was true for Sherry. One summer afternoon in my backyard, Naomi and I removed the children's clothes. Unselfconsciously they played in the sandbox and then sat together at the edge of our little square canvas wading pool. Sherry looked down. "Ezra!" she exclaimed. "What's on your wee-wee place?"

He glanced down. "Sand."

It was the beginning of two great sets of friendships.

In the Treasury office one day during lunch break, I was lying on the floor, demonstrating my new back exercises to Judy and Laura. A knock on the door. I was scrambling to my feet as a pleasant and familiar-looking middle-aged lady with bangs entered. "I love this war bond poster you have of General Eisenhower," she said. "Where could I get one?"

It was Mamie Eisenhower and, after an informal chat, we gave her ours.

Jack's and my arrival in Washington had put Father Bingham into a quandary, for though he could comfortably correspond with us without alerting his wife, Suzanne, he could scarcely have dinner with us without her finding out. Eventually he solved the problem of reintroducing us into their life by inviting us to the wedding reception of her youngest daughter, Kitty Hill. For us to go through the receiving line meant that Jack and his father would finally be face to face. Their mouths similarly tight, their eyes similarly blinking, they shook hands. Suzanne was frosty, but Kitty was welcoming. Among the guests, we found some people we knew and had a good enough time, but within the hour we thanked our hosts and fled.

Subsequently, on rare occasions, we were invited to Father and Suzanne's house for dinner. They had a haughty butler who glared when I tried smiling at him as he was serving the peas. I was so unnerved that I spilled a few peas, whereupon he glared even more. On even rarer occasions, Father and Suzanne came to us for a meal when other members of the family were in town. One such occasion was when Harry and Rose and their seven children came back from Argentina. Father Bingham hired a Capital Transit bus to take us all sightseeing. At the Shoreham Hotel where the Harry Binghams were staying, the bus got stuck under the porte cochere. There was much honking and grinding of gears, which the kids, including mine, seemed to enjoy even more than the Lincoln and Jefferson memorials. Our last scheduled stop was the Washington Zoo. By that time a drizzle had started and Suzanne announced that she would stay aboard the bus while the rest of us trooped out to view the animals. Rose then asked Suzanne if she would mind keeping an eye on infant Abigail asleep in her carrier. Suzanne could hardly refuse, so this unlikely pair remained alone together for what turned out to be too long an interval. For Abby awakened and started to howl. When Suzanne lifted her out of the carrier, Abby tried to nurse through Suzanne's elegant suede jacket, which left drool marks that incensed Suzanne. Jack and I didn't dare look at each other for fear of laughing.

On to our small house for lunch. Platters of sandwiches, fruit, and cookies awaited the children. When they were through eating, the grown-ups sat down and were served tuna fish salad with all the trimmings, rolls, and dessert. Suzanne complimented me on my arrangements, but I gave all credit to Milly who, while competent, was far from polished, especially when compared with Suzanne's butler.

In August, 1942, Washington's heat was at its sultriest. If you went out to dinner, you had to bring a handkerchief to swab the sweat as it ran down the sides of your face. Jack and I were more than ready for the short vacation he was granted. After dropping the children and Millie off at Thirlsmere, we drove to a New London boatyard where we parked our car and took over the twenty-eight-foot sloop that he had chartered. Our goal was Nantucket, with overnight anchorings at little-known islands like Cuddyhunk and Naushon. I wasn't at all confident about my sailing skills, but Jack was fully confident about his, having spent the year before he went to Groton at the Adirondack Florida School where the boys raced each other daily in sailing canoes on Tupper Lake and in sailing dinghies in Miami Bay.

Our cruise was part heaven and part hell.

The heavenly part comprised glittering days on the open ocean, no vessel in sight except an occasional submarine sleekly surfacing or a destroyer-escort heading for convoy duty to England. It also comprised peaceful evenings, with drinks and supper on deck (I still wasn't much of a cook, but could combine canned goods with panache, such as corned beef hash with baked beans and condiments). It also comprised nights in the cabin, with waves lapping against the hull, and bunks that appeared too narrow for one person being fine for two.

The hellish part comprised Captain Jack's missing of a crucial buoy en route from Woods Hole to Nantucket, which caused us to sail across shallow flats, with me on my stomach at the prow, screaming whenever I caught sight of an underwater rock. How we avoided going aground, I will never know. Several nights later our sloop was slapped about, together with the other boats anchored in the Edgartown harbor, by a serious storm. The following morning Jack judged it safe for us to head down the craggy coastline of Martha's Vineyard to Menemsha Bite. As the wind continued, my job was to hold the tiller against the waves, pushing us ever closer to the shore. Jack, meanwhile, was desperately trying to drop the mainsail in order to take a reef in it, and by the time he came to retrieve the tiller, I was sobbing with exhaustion and fear.

When we finally and somewhat miraculously got our intact boat back to New London, we found that our car was almost out of gas. We stopped at the first gas station. They asked for our ration card. Our what?

It seemed that while we were out of communication, gasoline rationing had been instituted. Four gallons per car per week. We explained our dilemma to the attendant. He sighed and allowed us to buy one gallon. We went on to the next gas station and did the same. And still another. Fortunately our youth and red peeling noses must have persuaded the attendants that we were telling the truth. Finally, we managed to get our car back to Thirlsmere to retrieve our children and return to Washington.

It was there, in October of 1942, that we said farewell to my brother Dick, by then a captain in the artillery, who was heading overseas. His wife Susan was pregnant with their first child. Dick's unit soon took part in the Allied landing in Casablanca. They moved on to Tunisia and the battle against General Rommel, the "Desert Fox" who managed to destroy half our First Armored Division. Dick was awarded the Silver Star for "gallantry in action." (Decades later when interviewed by a teenage grandchild of mine for a school assignment, he demurred, "I wasn't so damn gallant.") Subsequently, he led several commando raids on Sicily in support of the projected Allied invasion of Italy. For these, he was awarded two Bronze Stars. Three times he was captured by Italian troops, but managed to escape. The fourth time he was taken to a large camp in central Italy. There he made friends with a fellow-captive, Joseph S. Frelinghuysen, Princeton, '34, who had been commissioned an Army captain only a few weeks after Dick. While Dick could speak German and French, Joe could speak Italian. This made them an auspicious pair for the joint escape they were carefully planning.

In late autumn of 1943, the Nazis took over that camp and put the Allied prisoners onto a train headed for Germany. As the train chugged up the rugged Apennine Mountains, it was forced to slow down for the track's sharp curves and its steep grade. At their designated moment, Dick and Joe jumped off the train and rolled down a steep embankment. Despite the pain in his knee, Dick managed to hobble, together with Joe, back toward the Allied lines. For weeks they suffered severe hunger and cold as they barely managed to evade Italian and German patrols. Some of the peasants they encountered were generous with their sparse supplies of food and blankets, but other peasants were terrified. The Italians had been warned by the Nazis that anyone caught helping an Allied prisoner of war would be shot on sight, his possessions burned, and his well poisoned.

Dick's knee was growing worse. He told Joe that if they were ever apprehended, Joe should abandon him and find his way back to the Allied lines. Joe very reluctantly agreed. As he later wrote in his book, *Passages to Freedom*:

> Two German soldiers burst from the woods at a dead
> run. A third came at me from behind the hut. Another

screamed in German, "Halt! Halt! Or I shoot." Two of them fanned out on either side of Dick until we were surrounded. . . . Dick stared stubbornly at the noncom and said in German, "Now listen! . . . I'm crippled. I cannot and will not go with you."

. . . The corporal rattled off a string of orders to the other two men, then took off. . . . Still clutching their rifles, the [remaining] two soldiers looked on in astonishment as Dick . . . made sandwiches. . . . The private took the clip out of his rifle and dried it on a rag. With a bow, Dick passed around the four sandwiches and started to munch his with great gusto. When the two Germans stood their rifles against the wall . . . Dick murmured to me, barely audibly, "Now, you go!" . . .

I whirled around, wrenched the double doors inward, and jumped out, yanking them shut behind me. As they slammed, Dick's body crashed against them from the inside, and they banged and shook with the violence of the struggle. . . . Racing for the steep bank, I dove over the edge just as rifle fire cracked behind me. . . . Shots ricocheted and whistled off the trees, but by then I was a poor target. . . .

A poor target, but a great friend. Joe got back to the Allied lines and later to the States. He promptly went to see my parents. No one knew whether Dick was alive or dead or, if alive, where. The Red Cross had not been able to locate him. But my parents, seeing how much guilt Joe was suffering, assured him that he had done precisely what Dick had wanted, and he should stop blaming himself.

A month later, the Red Cross reported that Dick had been located in Offlag 64, a German prison camp for Allied officers in

Posen, Poland. We promptly sent off the first of the few food parcels the Red Cross was permitted to deliver to American prisoners of war. Robert von Hirsch did the same from Switzerland. But despite these, Dick, like many prisoners, lost more than thirty pounds. In their constant hunger, the officers boiled and ate grass and, during the warm months, they saved their urine in order to water the vegetables for which we and Robert were sending seeds. Dick, in turn, was elated to hear that his daughter had been safely born and was thriving.

We were also allowed to send Dick a form-postcard every two months. When my turn came to write, I found it surprisingly difficult. If I conveyed good news, the contrast between Jack's and my easy lives and his hard one might be too awful, yet if I conveyed bad news, he might think I was comparing our very minor woes with his major, life-and-death variety. His wife, Sue, admitted that the same was true for her.

Near the end of the war, the Russians swept westward and took over Poland, including Offlag 64. Again, Dick managed to escape. He worked his way south and east to Odessa and was able to send a message home that he was finally free.

When Uncle Herbert Lehman was notified, he cabled the American ambassador in Moscow, W. Averell Harriman, that Dick might have information about the Russian countryside that could be useful. Harriman immediately summoned Dick to Moscow, to stay at Spasso House, the American residence. On his first night, Harriman asked Dick if he needed to borrow some pajamas.

"No, thank you, Mr. Ambassador."

"Do you have any?"

"Well, no, sir."

"Then you must borrow a pair of mine."

Harriman sent the footman for some red silk pajamas, which he handed to Dick.

"I'm sorry, sir, I can't take these."

"For God's sake, Dick, why not?"

A pause. "I have lice."

By the time Dick got back to America, Joe Frelinghuysen had been sent to the Pacific for two more years of fighting. After the war, he and Dick got together, but as Joe later wrote, "We were both tense and having trouble adjusting to civilian life. Besides, I felt we each had a sense of frustration at the time wasted in prison, unable to serve in the ways for which we had trained so hard."

Today their symptoms would probably be called post-traumatic stress disorder, but this condition had not yet been identified, except, to a degree, in terms of World War I's "shell-shock" and World War II's "nervous breakdown." As it was, Dick's boss, General Patton, had been so disgusted by a young soldier hospitalized for this poorly recognized ailment that the general struck him. To many Americans like Patton, it was inconceivable that some potent emotions could be totally beyond the reach of the patient's willpower. Dr. Freud's ideas about the human unconscious only began to spread in the United States after the war.

As for Dick, he remained almost entirely mute about the horrors he had witnessed and participated in. Yet, as Sue said decades later, the war remained the central event of his life. Nothing that happened before or after mattered so much to him. She also reported on the typical kind of schism that arose between a returning soldier's expectations and the habits of ordinary civilian life. Dick's daughter had had time to grow to be a toddler before she met this big, bossy, hairy man who preempted so much of her mother's attention that, up to then, had been centered on herself. One evening, Dick and Sue were dressed for a fancy evening. The toddler in her crib started screaming at the prospect of her mother's departure. Dick, accustomed to commanding men, told her to stop screaming or he'd wash her mouth out with soap. She kept on screaming. He grabbed her and washed out her mouth whereupon she threw up all over his pristine starched shirt.

On the homefront, by 1942 the shortages were extreme: we had to keep our home temperature below sixty-five degrees and buy only the small amount of meat and sugar, as well as gasoline, that our ration coupons allowed. If we had too few coupons to feed guests, I could shop around for so-called "organ meats," such as beef liver or tongue, which were not rationed. Butter was gone, but something white called margarine, to which you added powdered yellow coloring, was available. We spent hours mixing the two.

Dinner parties were rare and took place only on weekends. People were working harder and also drinking more than ever before. Conversations often grew hilarious or contentious or both. Among the Washingtonians with whom Jack and I became friends was Katharine Meyer Graham, daughter of the owner of the *Washington Post,* and Eugene Meyer, who was an acquaintance of my parents. (Eugene's brother, Walter, had been an usher in their wedding.) Kay was a bright, lively, attractive young woman, with snapping dark eyes and naturally curly dark hair. She and I occasionally met for lunch at a small downtown French restaurant and were treated regally by the maitre d'—until the day we both turned up vastly pregnant. Instead of his escorting us to our usual front table, he shunted us off to one in the rear, where the swinging door from the kitchen banged against its corner. We went into a fit of giggles and decided to meet elsewhere until our babies were born.

Although I loved my work, Jack was dissatisfied, not with his work as such—the material from the intercepts was often fascinating and demanded all his skill to organize and condense. But he hated being a civilian when so many contemporaries were out there fighting. Also, with his characteristic frankness, he admitted to me that he couldn't any longer afford to be indifferent to the way his war service would look later if he were to survive and go into politics.

113

At age twenty-nine and as a father of two, he would not have been drafted. Available at the time was a naval officers' V-12 training program that he could have joined, but he preferred the Army. Colonel McCormack offered him an immediate commission as a second lieutenant if only Jack would stay put, but Jack refused.

I was torn. I desperately wanted him to do what he felt was right, but I was naturally terrified of his being killed or severely maimed. Even the prospect of our being separated from each other for months at a time while he was safely in this country was almost more than I could bear.

He finally made up his mind and enlisted as a private in the Army. By the spring of 1943, he was ordered to Fort Dix, New Jersey. We let our rented house go, put our furniture in storage, and the week previous to his induction he and I drove with two-year-old Sherry and six-month-old Micki to White Plains.

Within a few days, to my utter dismay, I discovered that I was pregnant yet again. I couldn't imagine how I could cope, physically or emotionally, with three babies under the age of three, nor was I willing to give up what little time the Army might allow Jack and me to have together. With the chances high of his being sent overseas, our time together had become almost unbearably precious. With deep reluctance, therefore, we decided on an abortion. Because the procedure was illegal, it was generally performed by a "doctor" with dubious credentials and under far from sanitary conditions. The patient underwent real danger of death or subsequent infertility.

Jack consulted with his brother who was a doctor. The brother put pressure on an obstetrician friend who finally agreed, as a huge personal favor to Jack's brother, to perform a legal D&C in their local hospital. The reason given for this procedure was a miscarriage that I was reported to have suffered. On the day Jack went off to Army camp, I went off to the hospital. The surgery was done under anesthesia, but the pain following it was considerable. My brother and sister-in-law welcomed me into their home, but I couldn't stop crying. Here I was, separated from my husband and from my babies — the ones who got to live. The following day, I had to dry my tears and return to Thirlsmere and somehow get on with things.

After several weeks at Fort Dix, Jack was granted a weekend pass. We met at the 21. Many of the men there were in uniform, all officers, some of top rank. Jack was the only private, and in his heavy khaki flannel shirt, his B.O. was noticeable. For me, this was irrelevant, but the people on the banquette to the other side of him seemed to keep edging away.

Oddly, by the time Jack returned to Fort Dix, all the G.I.s with whom he had arrived had been given their assignments. But nothing was on the docket for him. After more weeks, he was summoned by the sergeant.

"Say, Bingham, you lucky son of a bitch . . ."

"Sir?"

"Your assignment. Only guys over six feet, with an IQ of over 110."

"What for?"

"Guarding the White House."

"Oh . . . Well, no, but thank you anyway."

"Whaddayamean?"

"I don't want to be a guard at the White House."

"But you wouldn't have to go overseas."

"That's not the point. Please put my name back in the hopper."

"You're outta your fuckin' mind."

"Yes, sir."

After several more weeks of waiting, Jack was assigned to basic training in the Air Force. At first he hoped they might use his piloting skills, but his vision was no longer up to their stringent requirements. Still, he was out of Fort Dix and assigned to a location where I could follow, namely, and of all places, Atlantic City!

I left Micki at Thirlsmere with the wonderful European "Nana" my mother had found, and drove Sherry to Atlantic City, thus using up our gas coupons for the month. In the back of the car was my bike with its baby seat, which would be her and my means of transportation. I found a tiny one-bedroom apartment on the second floor of a dentist's house. No phone, however, and no chance of getting one. Sherry and I took to hanging around the boardwalk at five every afternoon, in hope of catching a glimpse of "Dadda." Some days he was allowed off "base" for a few hours. One day Jack felt ill and reported to the post's doctor. But because Private Bingham's fever was not quite 101 degrees, he was ordered to go out and drill. By the next morning his fever was 104 and his lungs were making strange sounds. Diagnosis was pneumonia. He was sent to the military hospital where his trays contained only the usual meat and potatoes; no fruit juice or ginger ale or broth. When I finally got in to visit him, his lips were cracked and peeling and his reddened eyes could hardly focus. I visited as often as I could find someone to take care of Sherry. But with most civilians doing war work, this was not easy. Finally, by word of mouth, I heard of a woman who sold saltwater taffy but would also keep a casual eye on a youngster. By this time, I myself had a roaring sore throat. I was told to go see an Army doctor at the hospital. He ordered me to take off my blouse and bra. "But my problem is my *throat*," I said naïvely. Since he was a full lieutenant and my husband only a private, there was nothing I could do but clench my teeth and obey. No great harm came of it; indeed, in retrospect, I can see that it taught me what most other people are forced to learn far earlier in life, namely, how denigrating it is to feel oneself within the total power of a stranger. This lesson was also one that Jack was having to learn.

With antibiotics still years in the future, both Jack's pneumonia and my (presumably) strep throat were potentially lethal, involving as they did, a week of raging fever. I bought as much food for Sherry as I could carry in my bike-basket, pedaled us back to our apartment, and took to my bed. I arose only to feed her and keep her clean. Then she, too, became ill. I don't know which of us was the more miserable. She cried a lot, but my throat hurt too much for me to comfort her the way I wanted to. Worst of all, I didn't know if Jack was alive, and I had no way to get in touch with him.

Two days later, a lady in a Red Cross uniform appeared at my door.

"Your husband put in a request for us to find out how you are."

"How is *he*?"

"I don't know. Do you need any money?"

"No, but I desperately need someone to take care of my baby."

"Sorry. All I'm authorized to do is give you some money." And off she went.

In time, I regained enough strength to clothe myself and totter down the stairs and outside to a pay phone. My pride was gone. After ascertaining that Jack was alive and improving, I called my parents. The next day, the Nana hired to take care of Micki arrived by train in Atlantic City. She was a godsend. Within a week, a wan, thin Jack was allowed out of the hospital on a two-hour pass. We clung to each other and thanked heaven that we and Sherry, too, had made it.

When Jack's basic training was completed, he was told that the Air Force had a premium assignment for him. He was to go to Denver, Colorado, dress in civilian clothes, and hover around bars in hopes of catching a Nazi spy. At this point, his pride, too, was gone, and he answered the several letters he had received from our friend and his MIS coeditor, Lou Stone. It seemed that the Special Branch had not been able to find a wordsmith as thorough and speedy as Jack. Would he therefore stop being a horse's ass and agree to let the Special Branch order the Air Force to transfer him back to his old job?

Louis, by then, was my close friend as well as Jack's; in fact, we had chosen him for Sherry's godfather. He was 6'7", homely, brilliant, wildly funny at times, shrewd almost to the point of clair-voyance about some people and utterly dense about others. He was, I've thought since, in some ways, not unlike Abraham Lincoln, a lawyer who was both ambitious and literarily gifted but subject to deep depressions that he tried to hide. (With their big features and huge hands, both of these men may have suffered from Marfan's Syndrome.) Both also had a deep inner sweetness and an irrepressible sense of humor. When Sherry as a toddler was sent to school at The National Child Research Center in Washington, its report cards were extremely detailed: She got an A for appetite and sociability, manual dexterity and language skills, but an F for "interest in moving large objects around." When this was relayed to her godfather, he said, "That's the first sign of intelligence I've seen in the child."

When Jack sent back word to Louis that he was willing to return to MIS, he requested the orders to be cut so that he did not have to appear for duty in Washington until the following Monday morning. This would enable him and me to spend the weekend together. MIS obliged, but the Air Force sergeant in Atlantic City nonetheless insisted that Jack go forthwith to Washington (and thus be out of the sergeant's area of responsibility). He summoned a military police escort to make sure that Jack would get onto the appropriate train. At the railroad station, Sherry and I bid Jack farewell. He stepped aboard the train. The escort remained on the platform until the train gathered momentum. I took Sherry as fast as I reasonably could to our car. She and I drove to the next scheduled train stop and parked in the underpass. The rumble of a train overhead. We waited. And waited. Then, blessed sight, Jack, carrying his bag, sneaking toward us. He was AWOL—and laughing.

We had a blissful weekend, even taking the risk on Sunday of going to the beach with the baby, on the theory that in a bathing suit he wouldn't be spotted by the Air Force military police. Sunday night, he went off to Washington to report for duty, as ordered, on Monday morning. The military was never the wiser.

118

Because some generals don't bother to pin their stars on the shoulders of their uniform, and because there were few, if any, other privates in the Pentagon, Jack found himself being respectfully saluted by many colonels and majors. Fortunately, Jack's commission came through before long, and he could at least sport the bars of a second lieutenant. He was doing the identical job he had done as a civilian, at a quarter of the pay, but at least his New England conscience felt clearer.

I house hunted in Washington—not easy in wartime. Finally, I found for sale a small, almost square, red brick colonial on Nebraska Avenue in northwest D.C. Alec Hixon, Adelaide's husband, accurately christened it, "The house the third piggy built." The Hixons, too, had been assigned by the Army to Washington and also had a baby, eight months younger than Sherry. Their Lex was blond, chunky, beautiful, and willful, and in later years became an extraordinary spiritual leader who wrote a number of ecumenical books and was a close friend of our children.

In time, Jack, too, was given orders for the Pacific. For reasons as irresistible at the time as they are hard to comprehend now, he and I went to work on starting a third child. But a few months later, the Military, in its so-called wisdom, cancelled Jack's orders. Some muckety-muck apparently decided that Jack was privy to too many military secrets for him to be sent into an area where he might be captured and tortured by the "Japs." Jack's feelings were mixed. Mine were pure elation though by then I was "left holding the bag" from the amniotic point of view. When Tim, our third baby was born, I resigned from the war bond division.

While I was still a bedridden mother in Garfield Hospital, I rang for a bedpan. To my surprise, and embarrassment, the bedpan was brought by a volunteer nurse's aide, Nancy Kefauver, wife of Senator Estes Kefauver (who later became Adlai Stevenson's vice-presidential running mate). I had met the red-haired Nancy socially and cringed at the idea that she would have to handle my body wastes, but my body was not to be argued with. She made light of the situation but after she had departed with the smelly pan, I dove under the covers to hide.

The day the new baby and I got home from the hospital, my brother Dick, home at last from Europe, came to see us in Washington. "The baby's name is Mabel," I told him. "Would you like to see her?" We went upstairs. The baby was wet so I removed the diaper. Dick gasped. There on the changing table lay no niece but a nephew. His name was Timothy Woodbridge Bingham and he had, on but the first of many occasions, made his Uncle Dick laugh.

A few months later, in April 1945, Jack and I, together with millions of people all over the world, were stunned by the death of President Roosevelt. Jack and I felt so privileged to have seen him at least once in the flesh. In 1936, Jack had been invited by his friend Barbara Cushing to her New Haven house one day. FDR, an old friend of her father (the famed surgeon Harvey Cushing), was coming for a drink after having received a Yale honorary degree. Jack was stunned by the contrast between the power of FDR's chest and shoulders and the punyness of his legs. The two men had a brief, friendly exchange about their mutual alma mater, Groton, and Jack came away feeling that he had been in the presence of greatness. My own encounter was not personal, but nonetheless gratifying. After FDR had won his fourth term as president in November, 1944, he was scheduled to return to the White House by driving up Pennsylvania avenue from Union Station. I was standing in the crowd on the street when the rain began. But then the motorcycles came roaring up the avenue followed by an open touring car with FDR in the backseat, smiling that inimitable smile and waving. His fedora was shapeless from the rain but his face was alight. We all screamed our welcome and he seemed pleased.

His death came five months later, only a few short weeks before the war in Europe was finally won. All kinds of international plans were soon proposed, like the one named for General George Marshall, focused on rebuilding the whole continent of Europe for the future. Meanwhile, Japan's forces still opted for suicide rather than surrender, and the carnage in the Pacific was horrific. An American invasion of the Japanese islands was predicted for the near future. The published estimate, hard to take in and even harder to live with, was that this would cost at least a million American casualties.

CHAPTER 6

Peacetime

FOLLOWING TIM'S BIRTH IN FEBRUARY 1945, it was clear that our nation, still at war with Japan, would continue to need its women in the workforce. That included those with three babies. I was lucky enough, through Kay Graham, to be given the job she had once held on the *Washington Post*. This was as editorial assistant. My duties were to handle the Letters to the Editor column and devise titles for some of the Op Ed pieces. My privilege was to be assigned, on occasion, a non-momentous subject about which to write an editorial and thus be able to learn from the top-level professional blue-penciling that it would receive.

My ultimate boss was Kay's father, Eugene Meyer, referred to behind his back as "Butch." Almost daily, I saw bald, jaunty, decisive Butch when he came to the editorial area to confer about policy with my immediate boss, Herbert Elliston, the humane, imaginative, and beguilingly homely chief of the editorial page. Herbert, a former Yorkshireman, was a brilliant editor. I promptly developed a crush on him, and he, like Fritz Redlich and Harold Mager before him, enjoyed my adulation. Occasionally, he would take me to lunch at the rooftop restaurant of the next-door Willard Hotel or I would prepare a picnic for two that we would eat in nearby Lafayette Park. (He had never before tasted smoked salmon and cream cheese on rye, a delicacy that I didn't know at the time was quintessentially Jewish.)

Herbert Elliston was an accomplished flirt even though married to Joanne, a beautiful, well-born, much younger American. She preferred playing cowgirl at her beloved ranch in Arizona to playing hostess in Washington. The Ellistons' huge Georgetown house was next door to its almost twin bought by Kay and Phil Graham after Phil's return from the Pacific when he was anointed Meyer's successor at the *Post*. Nor did Joanne Elliston have much interest in Herbert's literary endeavors. I, on the other hand, was avid to pick up every bit of writing skill I could. In his office, Herbert handed me an editorial written by the *Post*'s poetic editor Joseph Lalley. "It's too long," Herbert said. "Cut it."

The editorial was superb and not, I felt, subject to having even small cuts. When I handed it back in total frustration, Herbert reached into his desk drawer and pulled out a pair of scissors. With a flourish, he simply cut the editorial in half. And thus, on two consecutive days, it was published, with hardly a word needing to be changed.

A fellow new-arrival at the *Post* whom I saw each day when he came to clear his cartoon suggestions with Elliston was Herbert Block, who would later become the legendary cartoonist Herblock. After the war, he and I would play golf together on the public course at Haines Point, accompanied by my brown miniature "Yankee Poodle." One chilly day, after I'd narrowly won our competitive match, I drove Herb home. Yankee was on the front seat between us, cuddled into Herb's woolen scarf. When Herb got out and retrieved his scarf, he found that Yankee had chewed a hole in it. "Imagine," he said, "what she would have done if I'd won!"

Kay, during the war, did not do much entertaining, but she did include us in a dinner party that she described fifty years later in her Pulitzer Prize–winning autobiography, *Personal History*:

> Jonathan and June Bingham . . . were visiting for the weekend, and I decided to have a few friends over, including [Ed] Prich[ard] and Isaiah Berlin, a relatively new but close friend who was in Washington . . . as an information officer in the British Embassy. The other couple . . . was Donald

and Melinda Maclean. Donald was something like third secretary at the British Embassy . . . None of us could remotely have suspected that Donald would later emerge as a communist spy. Even now it's hard for me to comprehend that both Donald and Melinda were Soviet agents. . . .

No sooner had we settled down [after dinner] than the conversation got edgy. Prich and Donald began to tease Isaiah about his social life, which they portrayed as being too conciliatory of right-wing or isolationist people. Everyone teased hard in those days, but that night the teasing gradually slid into acrimony and became unpleasant, exacerbated no doubt by Prich and Donald's alcohol consumption.

Out of the blue, Donald said to Isaiah, "The trouble with you is you hunt with the hounds and run with the hares. You know people like Alice Longworth; that's disgusting. One shouldn't know people like that. If I thought you knew her out of curiosity, I wouldn't mind so much. But I'm told you actually like her company. That is dreadful."

Isaiah asked why Donald thought it was dreadful.

"Because she's fascist and right-wing. She's everything that's awful," Donald spat out.

Isaiah, totally taken aback . . . replied, "Well, you know, we're supposed to be fighting for civilization. Civilization entails that we're allowed to know anybody we wish. It's true that in wartime or during the revolution one may be prepared to shoot them, that I concede, but so long as one doesn't have to. . . . Of course, one must be judged by one's friends, I don't deny that either. That is my defense." Donald immediately pounced, saying, "That's wrong. What you say is absolutely false. Life is a battle. We must know which side we're on. We must stick to our side through thick and thin. I know at the last moment, the twelfth hour, you'll be on our side. But until then, you'll go about with these dreadful people."

Isaiah claims that I then said, "He's absolutely right." . . .

The poor Binghams were flabbergasted. They didn't know what it was all about and shuffled around nervously.

How right Kay was. Jack and I were horrified by Maclean's attack on Isaiah, which Prich was abetting, and were baffled by its subtext. Russia then was America's ally against Hitler and would not ultimately have been victorious without all the matériel the United States sent, plus our diversion of Hitler by the Normandy invasion. Similarly, the free world might not ultimately have been victorious without the brave resistance by Russian civilians as well as military forces when the Nazis forced their way to the very outskirts of Stalingrad. But why, from even a far left point of view, should Isaiah's having dinner with Mrs. Alice Longworth be viewed as a political betrayal? Jack and I could see no significance in it, other than providing one more example of Washington's famed ability to blur the line between work and pleasure, especially in the evening. (MacLean, indeed, later turned out to be a full-fledged Communist and fled to Russia.)

Except for the few lawyers Jack had known at the New York State Labor Relations Board, he and I had no contact with Communists. Much later it was publicly revealed that our Washington friend Michael Straight had had a short fling with the Communist Party while a prewar student in England. Also, it was rumored that my Vassar student adviser, Agnes Reynolds, remained close to the party line. Of course, the media kept issuing warnings against Soviet espionage, and we had no doubt that the Russians were trying to learn as much about America as we were trying to learn about the Soviet Union. Some of our friends had joined American sleuthing efforts by way of the newly established Office of Strategic Services (OSS), the precursor to the Central Intelligence Agency (CIA). But Jack and I had no great faith in American intelligence organizations after the early June day in 1944, when, because of physical repairs in the Pentagon, the phones in Jack's Special Branch of MIS were temporarily disconnected. Jack and his colleagues, therefore, thus became probably the *last* Americans to learn about our D-Day invasion of Normandy.

Casualties among the people we knew kept mounting. Although Jack's and my families were far luckier than many, ours also had their heartbreaks and heroisms. In addition to my aviator cousin, Peter Lehman, killed early in the war and leaving a young widow with two small children, my Navy cousin, Bob Morgenthau, subsequently Manhattan's distinguished district attorney, almost drowned on two occasions when the destroyer on which he was serving was sunk by German torpedoes, and my Army cousin, Orin Lehman, subsequently New York state's parks commissioner, lost a leg while heroically partaking in the Allied invasion of Europe. When Orin was sent back to Walter Reed Hospital in Washington, I took Sherry and Micki, ages three-and-a-half and two, to visit him. They wore matching red bonnets, coats, and leggings (gifts from my mother), and I warned them not to say a word about his leg.

No sooner had we entered the big noisy amputation ward than they ran over to Orin's bed.

"Hi, Cousin Orin."

"Hi, girls."

"Where's your leg?"

"Under the bed."

As the little girls dropped onto their stomachs to search for it, the men in the nearby beds roared with laughter. Although our visit wasn't proceeding in the manner I had intended, it became a happy one, with Orin's spirits lifted by the kids, and myself impressed by the gallows humor used by the young soldiers to cope with their mutilations. "Deal faster," shouted one bridge player to a colleague who was missing an arm.

Usually the drama of a watershed year is manifest only in retrospect, but 1945 was so filled with tectonic shifts that Jack and I, together with most other people, could recognize at the time how historic our era was in the process of becoming.

The sudden death of President Roosevelt on April 12 was followed in a matter of weeks by Germany's surrender. On June 26, a second dream of Roosevelt's was realized: fifty nations signed the U.N. Charter, including the United States. On July 16, the world's first nuclear device was detonated in Alamagordo. On August 6, we dropped one of our two atom bombs on Hiroshima and three days later the other on Nagasaki.

For the first time, humans had invented a force so destructive that it could obliterate not just America's enemies, or, reciprocally, ourselves, but human history itself. For my generation, brought up with Dr. Coué's dictum about everyone getting better and better, to grasp the enormity of this possibility was like trying to pick up a marble with tweezers—you couldn't hold it for more than a second, and your hand would tremble afterward. What on earth remained worth doing, if everyone and everything—past, present, and future— might, without warning, go up in mushroom-shaped smoke?

A similarly stunning shift had occurred shortly before VE Day. This applied not only to an outer event but also an inner one, our view of human nature. That was when the American public was first exposed to the shattering photographs of the stacked skeletal bodies, alive and dead, in the Nazi camps. What on earth remained worth doing if a land of high culture, long famous for its education and social justice, could, with the apparent acquiescence of many, if not most, of its citizens, murder millions of its own people?

What should I teach my children? To trust their fellow humans, or not? A world without trust might be a world without love, yet seven million Europeans, not all of them Jews, had been willing to trust — and had been mortally betrayed, together with their trusting children.

Compounding Jack's and my bewilderment was the rumored plan for our Army, Navy, and Air Force to invade Japan. A letter of mine to my parents on June 29, 1945, when I was twenty-six, gives a small sense of the era:

> Jack's [second] application for Pacific duty has been accepted — and if he gets the job he wants he will be Security Officer for one of the armies out there. . . . This time, judging from [Colonel] McCormack's reaction, I think Jack will definitely go and am making plans accordingly, i.e. keeping Patrick [our retriever] as I think I'd feel safer, and telling *The Post* that I will, after all, be able to handle the one night a week make-up job. So, don't even say anything to "the family.". . . There are two kinds of pain, we figure — one a dull unlocalized, sort of rheumatic pain; the other a sharp bloody pain like a cut. Separation is the latter, his staying here and being restless is the former. The latter is curable, the former is not, unless exchanged for the latter. So although it isn't our idea of a beer picnic to be separated for a year or more, it is something we'll be glad we did after the time is over, As you know, one can't play any game, even Life, with the cards held too close to the chest.

When President Truman made the world-altering decision to drop the bomb, I, like every young American I knew, cheered, for—despite the hideous result for hundreds of thousands of Japanese—it meant that the Pacific war was, in effect, over. Jack could remain alive, and he and I could proceed with our precious time together. In retrospect, I cannot bring myself to regret that first bomb dropped on Hiroshima, though I continue inwardly to cringe about the second one dropped on Nagasaki.

Another watershed event, at least for Jack and me, was the newly established United Nations. To us who had grown up both enraged and embarrassed by America's earlier refusal to join the League of Nations, this fledgling organization offered the exhilarating hope that peace, when finally declared, could last for much longer than it did following the Versailles Treaty (the twenty-year interval between the world wars was later termed "the weekend between the wars").

With the United States joining the United Nations and a peace treaty having been signed with Japan five days after the second bomb, Jack and I, like most Americans, felt a surge of hope about the future—our own, the nation's, the world's. Under the new G.I. Bill, millions of veterans who would otherwise not have had a chance at college education were able to go. Even Jack took advantage of the bill in order to study Spanish. At the same time, however, the demobilization of the veterans meant that millions of women like me were expected to withdraw from our jobs to free them up for the G.I.s. This pressure to return to our homes, however, was gradual, and I was grateful to be able to stay on at the *Washington Post* for a further year. Jack by then had the rank of captain (with a departmental citation) and was glad to retire from the Army, but he still wanted to be of use to the country. He, therefore, took on a short-term assignment at the State Department as head of a tiny improvised unit called the Enemy Alien Control Section. Its purpose was to make restitution to the thousands of Japanese Americans and German Americans who, because of some Latin American connection in their past, had summarily, and often inappropriately, been deported to Latin America for the duration of the war. Helping Jack were two fellow lawyers. One was an old friend, Daniel Tenney, Yale '35; the other was a younger man who quickly became a friend, Louis Henkin. It was from Lou that Jack began to learn about Jewish customs, a subject about which I was almost as ignorant as he. One day when Jack and Lou took a bus together to a restaurant for lunch, Lou asked Jack to pay his fare because he had no change; Jack, of course, obliged. But on the way home, the same thing happened, though Jack had seen Lou receive some change at the restaurant. When Jack inquired, Lou explained that even on a minor Jewish holiday, which this day happened to be, Orthodox Jews were not supposed to pay the cost of transportation. Little did Jack and I foresee that awareness of such customs would end up being of signal importance in our lives.

Among returning veterans, one we had especially looked forward to meeting was Phil Graham. Soon after he got back, we invited him and Kay to dinner. Phil turned out to be tall and lean and craggy with a brilliant mind, a sharp sense of humor, and a charming smile. Unfortunately, however, that evening he got so drunk that he spent most of the time laying supine in our backyard. Kay and I never saw fit to say much to each other about the evening or our husbands, but it seemed to me that Phil and Jack behaved a bit like two competitive dogs with their hackles up, sniffing and circling each other. Perhaps if they had met in boyhood, they might have become friends. For both did have male friends who were as bright and competitive as themselves. In any event, the two husbands' edginess with each other did not extend to the other man's wife. Jack continued to be cozy with Kay, as Phil did with me (whom he addressed as "Junathan"). The four of us proceeded to enjoy running into each other at large dinner parties and also occasionally battling on the tennis court in Washington or at the Meyers' place in Mt. Kisco, not far from Thirlsmere.

Perhaps Phil's drinking, reminiscent in my brother Dick's tension with his wife, were attributable to the horrors they had witnessed during the war. Certainly it was not unusual among my female friends to find the return of their husbands, so joyously anticipated, triggering grave distress. One example was of two sisters who had had a wartime double wedding. After a year of marriage, each young woman gave birth to a child. The Navy husband of one sister perished in the war; the Air Force husband of the other survived but returned with his violence simmering not far below the surface. He shouted vulgarities at his wife, blamed her for whatever imperfections arose with the child, and finally hit her. For the sake of her own and the baby's safety, she got a divorce. One day when I was sympathizing with her, she said that during the war she had considered herself far luckier than her sister who had lost her adored husband, but her own husband's behavior had forced her to revise her thinking. She now realized that her sister, though deprived of the love of her life, had been able to retain her own sense of self, while my friend had been deprived of hers, at least for a time. Several years later, both young women married again and happily and each went on to have three more children.

Jack's brother Charles came home altered in a way that baffled his wife and children as well as ourselves. He had been a successful doctor at the time he enlisted in the Navy and was sent to the Pacific. But after several years of trying, often unsuccessfully, to help wounded sailors back to health, he concluded that no ailment is ever entirely physical and that therefore doctors should apply spiritual measures. This was the time when the relationship between mind and body was first termed "psychosomatic" and this soon became an extremely controversial subject among doctors. Dr. Franz Alexander's book, *Psychosomatic Medicine*, was my introduction to it in the late 1940s. But Charlie took the psychosomatic concept one step further and insisted on basing treatment on Christ's teachings rather than on medication or surgery. This approach got him fired from the hospital where he had been a star. He then took a lesser job with an antialcohol treatment center but in time was also fired from it. These experiences turned this beguiling and outgoing man into something of a hermit. Although she disagreed with most of Charlie's ideas, his wife stayed loyal for the rest of their long lives together. Fortunately, as he aged, he regained flashes of his earlier humor and we and our children had brief, friendly encounters with him every summer in Salem.

Jack's brother Harry and his wife, Rose, had different difficulties: he decided to resign from the Foreign Service, despite her pleading to the contrary. He took their ever-growing family back to Salem. By then he was a passionate follower of Rudolph Steiner, the anthroposophist, but Rose was unable to share that enthusiasm. She remained a devout, churchgoing Episcopalian and bore four more children. I asked her why so many. She smiled benignly and said that after she'd had five, the kids kept taking her diaphragm to the sandbox.

Shortly after the war, to Jack's and my surprise and sorrow, the best marriage we knew, that of Uncle Irving and Aunt Sissie, was broken by death. At age seventy, Irving had been in good health when he was knocked to the ground by one of their two dogs, a boxer. Irving's leg was broken and while he was stuck in bed his leg developed the kind of clots that had recently killed his brother Arthur. (Blood thinners were not yet in use.) One of the clots, presumably, went to Irving's heart and stopped it.

Aunt Sissie was totally devastated. I had never seen such despair in human eyes as emanated from hers while she sat near the head of his coffin, as we all stepped up, one at a time, to lay a single rose on it.

When Uncle Irving's will became known, I was flabbergasted. It seems that he, the judge, had long intended to rectify the injustice, as he saw it, of my grandmother's having left only ten thousand dollars to me while each of my brothers got twenty-five. He, therefore, left me fifty thousand dollars! Though the will also bequeathed his large law library to my brother Howard, I suspect that Howard viewed the books as but minor compensation. After all, Howard was the descendant of Irving's who had followed him into the law and was similarly on track for a judgeship. Thus, through no action of mine, I attracted further antagonism from my brother—which I believe he remained unaware of.

In the 1990s, half a century after Uncle Irving's death, I was called upon to make a speech at the Columbia Law School, his alma mater, at the time of its inauguration of a scholarship in his honor. This scholarship had been my idea, and I managed to raise seventy thousand dollars for it from family members. I ended my speech by noting how influential Uncle Irving had been on my brothers and me: Howard had become a judge, Dick had become a trout fisherman, and I had married a man with a big nose.

By 1946, Jack, nose and all, was anxious to enter elective politics. Yet for that dream to be realized, we would have to leave the District of Columbia—whose citizens were voteless. Where should we go? Not to Connecticut because his brother Alf was already running for its State Senate and Jack didn't want to jump into direct competition with him. Also, Connecticut had so few electoral votes that even if Jack were to become as successful as he sometimes wildly dreamed, a tiny state would not be a promising launching pad for someone seeking national office. New York, which then had more electoral votes than any other state, was an obvious place for us to settle, but we did not want our babies growing up on concrete sidewalks with sunlight filtered between skyscrapers. Nor did I think I could retain my sanity if we lived too near, or even on the way to, Thirlsmere. For there would be no way we could tactfully prevent my parents from dropping in to see their grandchildren on Friday late afternoons or Sunday evenings or both, thus depriving Jack and me of the dwindling amount of joint privacy, which we both still treasured above almost everything else.

A friend I had made while at the U.S. Treasury, a dapper, jovial, big fellow named Pete (Julian) Street, kept talking up Scarborough-on-Hudson, a village in Westchester County where he and his wife, Narcissa Vanderlip, had built a modern house. They offered to scout out a place suitable for our pocketbook, which they promptly succeeded in doing. It was an Elizabethan stucco with beams across the front, on an acre of land with just enough bedrooms. Compared with our "house the third piggy built," which we had bought for twelve thousand and sold for fifteen thousand, it seemed palatial, though Sherry and Micki still had to share a bedroom. Best of all, it was a good half hour west of Thirlsmere, and from the second floor we had a narrow view of the ever-changing Hudson.

I hated giving up my job on the *Washington Post*, but clearly Jack's need to put down political roots was the dominant factor in our plans. He would be commuting (an hour by train) to Manhattan to practice law by day, and then, on evenings and weekends, would put himself at the disposal of the local and state Democratic leaders. Although Westchester County was then heavily Republican, its Democratic Party was growing, thanks to the influx of families with children from the city and returning veterans.

For me to get our household well settled in Scarborough was not easy. I hired a couple, in part because the young man was a German Jewish refugee. He and his wife, an American-born Protestant, had a little girl who, I thought, might be fun for our kids to play with—but they thought otherwise. The wife was an adequate cook but the man was barely adequate as a cleaner. She kept begging me to make allowances for him because of his wartime traumas, which I was willing to do. Sherry and Micki enrolled in the Scarborough School, which was but a short walk down a country lane. This freed me to take a part-time job as a reporter on the nearby *Tarrytown Daily News*. But the only subjects the male editor would assign to a new female employee were items for the society page. After several months I handed him one, all typed up in appropriate journalese (who, what, when, and where, covered in the first paragraph). It announced that Mrs. Jonathan Brewster Bingham of River Road, Scarborough, was resigning her job at the *News* because she was expecting a baby, whose name would be made public at a later date.

On February 22, 1947, the worst blizzard in decades hit the metropolitan area. All parkways were blocked, all trains immobilized. By the grace of God, my unborn baby, though not expected for weeks, had begun signaling arrival two days before. Thus, Jack was able to drive me safely from Scarborough to New York's Presbyterian Hospital, a trip that would have been totally impossible two days later. At the hospital, I was in the hands of the same obstetrician who had delivered Sherry less than six years before. This time I refused anesthesia. All I could think of during the contractions was the image of a huge wave mounting, mounting, and then crashing down on the beach. No one had coached me on how to breathe, and the pain was intense. I was about to give up and ask for a knock-out drop when our daughter emerged. The doctor held her up from between my legs. Claudia was peaceful and wet and perfect.

"Hello, darling," I said, and then bedlam erupted.

"For Christ's sake, get some ergot! Press down on that damn uterus!" The terror in my doctor's voice sent the masked attendants spraying off in all directions. As he explained later, the muscles of my uterus had neglected to clamp down, as nature intended, on the interspersed blood vessels leading to and from the placenta. I was therefore painlessly and rapidly bleeding to death, like Hemingway's Catherine in *A Farewell to Arms*.

I felt no fear, only a profound gratitude for the baby's safe arrival. Whatever happened next was up to God and the doctor. Then, without warning, someone, for reasons I was never able to ascertain, rammed an ether cone over my face.

When I came to, I was lying in a sunny cubicle, with both arms immobilized. Blood was flowing into one, plasma into the other. No one was in sight, and my main feeling was hunger.

I yelled and yelled. Finally a nurse came. She told me about the previous night's drama and how lucky I was to be alive. Yes, baby Claudia was fine, and I could see her when I was wheeled back to my room. I begged for some breakfast, and she said it was waiting for me there.

Eventually an attendant was located to do the wheeling and I arrived in my room. Jack was there and we embraced hard. But I was so ravenous, I said, "Where's my breakfast?"

He looked stricken. He had been assured that I would be fed upstairs, so he'd eaten it!

Claudia Rossbach Bingham was a good baby who, before long, was vastly entertained by the antics of her siblings. But my back, once again, became a source of anguish. This time, I could hardly walk. Peggy Rockefeller, David's wife, came over from nearby Pocantico Hills to bring a new-baby present. When our doorbell rang, I had to crawl to the front door to unlatch it. Peggy was very nearsighted and didn't think to look downward. As she peered vaguely about at the face-level, she had no idea how the door had been opened.

"Hi, Peggy."

"Oh, *there* you are."

We burst out laughing.

The chief orthopedic surgeon at New York's Presbyterian Hospital, Frank Stinchfield, wanted to ease my acute pain by operating to fuse my lower two vertebrae that apparently (there were no CT or PET scans or MRIs in those days) were pinching the nerves. But the operation was still fairly hazardous, with only one-third of the patients improved, one-third unchanged, and one-third worse off. Of the final third, one-third were dead. I decided that if I could struggle along with painkillers, a steel-ribbed brace, and eventually some back exercises, I would not risk half-orphaning my four children. I wore the brace for six months, and for a year after that I had to lie down on the backseat of the car if we traveled for any distance. I hated having to keep reminding the three older children—often at the level of an unpremeditated yelp—that they must not bounce on my bed or even bump it. This may have caused them to be even more resentful of the new baby than they probably would have been anyway.

When Claudia was six weeks old, Jack said he thought our habit of staying home every night should now be outgrown. He wanted to go to a movie and very much hoped I'd accompany him. I said I couldn't bear to leave the baby. He said that although umbilical cords were essential for a time, they could also become damaging if kept intact too long. In short, he was going to the movie with or without me. After much inner debate, I decided that the best present I could give to my precious infant was a sturdy relationship between her mother and father, so I went to the movie and enjoyed it, though sitting for that long made my back hurt.

The back pain also severely limited the muscle-rebuilding exercises. As a result, I took longer than usual to get my figure back. I was made only too aware of the ungainliness of my body when I tried to squeeze into an old evening dress for a spring dance that Pete and Narcissa Street were giving. There, a lissome creature in her early twenties made an unsubtle play for Jack. He didn't seem to mind at all as he danced with her again and again. When I suggested to him that it was time to go home, he showed no interest. I was feeling more and more exhausted, more and more miserable, until finally I became desperate. Only then did I recall that inside my evening purse was a duplicate key to our car. I thanked Pete and Nar for the lovely time, took our car, and drove home.

I never found out who gave Jack a ride nor at what hour. He had a hangover the next morning, so I thought it wise to let the subject drop. We did, on occasion, run into the young lady again, but fortunately, by then, she had become engaged. Her fiancé, I was pleased to note, was, like herself, some fifteen years younger than Jack.

Still, even the most distressful problems of private life were dwarfed by the alarming developments in the wider world, especially Stalin's breaking of his promise at Yalta to allow democracy to flourish in Eastern Europe. Thus Russia, our former ally in the war, was becoming our enemy in what was later called the Cold War. So hostile was the Soviet leadership toward the United States that Stalin self-destructively brushed aside Russia's putative share of what later came to be called the Marshall Plan. This landmark form of American financial aid helped Europe, including our former enemy, Germany, to rebuild itself. At least, Jack and I thought, the Marshall Plan was proof that Americans had learned something from the mistakes made after World War I.

That Americans had learned another crucial lesson was demonstrated on Long Island by the enthusiastic welcome given to the delegates to the first General Assembly meeting of the United Nations. As men and women of every color and background converged on New York, Jack and I were enraptured. Around that time, we also applauded the Dodgers' welcoming of Jackie Robinson. (Like Hank Greenberg, the first Jew in the major leagues, Robinson, the first Negro, became a big success.) Years later, on minor matters, Jack did some legal work for Jackie and Rachel Robinson.

Abroad, too, millions of blacks found cause for hope, as former African colonies were organizing movements that would eventually lead to their independence. The word "Negro" began replacing "colored" as the polite term and Leopold Senghor, the poet and glamorous president of Senegal, hoisted "Negritude" as a flag of self-pride. As for the Jews, Jack and I were so exhilarated by the prospect of their having their own nation in Palestine after almost two thousand years of wandering that we both donated our blood as well as our dollars to the Haganah, the moderate arm of Zionism's underground. My father, on the other hand, gave money to the Irgun, the violent arm, led by Menachim Begin, which caused the deaths of many British soldiers on occupation duty. It was the Irgun that bombed the King David Hotel in Jerusalem. Yet people in public life like Uncle Herbert Lehman worried that American Jews would be further distrusted because of fear that we had divided loyalties. Certainly anti-Semitism continued undiminished. Pete and Nar Street, aware that Jack and I loved tennis, proposed us as members at the sole country club in the area. They were stunned and appalled when the Sleepy Hollow Club refused to consider us. No room at *that* inn for a Jewish woman even if married to a Christian man. Jack and I had zero interest in the social side of the club, but we hated to give up our favorite sport. Scarborough was too small to afford public courts and our children's school had none. Then Jack had a bright but expensive idea. Why not build our own hard-surface court? It would provide a safe fenced-in playground for the kids on their tricycles, roller skates, and scooters, as well as year-round tennis for us. Also, as an improvement to the property, it might perhaps pay for itself when the time came to sell the house. Thus, although we did not think of it at the time, we were, to a degree, duplicating the facilities of Thirlsmere.

Where to swim provided no problem. Again, there were no public pools, but Nar Street's mother, Narcissa Vanderlip, the grande dame of Scarborough, had a pool on her estate, Beechwood. She also had fascinating tenants in the various cottages she owned. One couple was Jack (E. J.) Kahn, writer for the *The New Yorker,* and his actress-wife Ginny. When I wrote a full-length play for a neighborhood theatre group, Ginny played the heroine. Nearby, an even more famous actress, Dorothy Maguire, was living with her husband, Gerard Swope. Jack and I were dazzled to meet her as well as such nearby writers as John Cheever, with his wife, Mary, and such artists as George Biddle, with his wife Helene. On rare occasions, we would run into them at Mrs. Vanderlip's pool.

I was counting the years now. By far the worst birthday I would ever have was looming, the thirtieth. I had set myself the goal of being published by that time, but this didn't seem within my power to

Jack and I with our full complement of children at our home in Scarborough. From left to right, Claudia (on my lap), Sherry, Micki, and Tim (on Jack's lap).

accomplish. My school and college teachers had stressed the criminality of girls not putting their education to good use. I was writing daily but without success. Even though I had a wonderful husband and four fine children, I felt I was betraying my teachers' expectations.

Of course, in self-extenuation, I had to admit that there were weeks—even months—when I had no time for writing at all. Like when the children all got mumps and looked like hamsters with cheeks full of seeds. Or when they all got measles—alarming because of the then-serious hazard to their sight and hearing. When they all got German measles, it wasn't so bad for them but awful for me because I, too, came down with it (one can catch it more than once). When they all got chicken pox, I kept a bathtub full of water with bicarbonate of soda in it so that I could dunk them when their itchiness became too intense (no antihistamines, as yet). They loved the splashing, and I would get soaked when I had two, even three, spotted urchins in the tub together.

Jack had always wanted to be an involved father, but his time with the children was limited by his long commute by day and his political engagements by night. Over a couple of weekends, however, he organized us into making a home movie, with Tim as Hansel, Claudia as Gretel, Sherry as the father, and Micki as the stepmother. The wicked witch was myself, with a long nose made of paper. Claudia was so frightened when she first caught sight of me that I had to take the nose off and hold her until she was calm. Jack acted the part of the woodsman who pointed the children to the witch's house, and did all the directing and filming. The result wasn't bad and the children adored watching it (as, in time, did their children and *their* children).

One summer evening I bundled my freshly bathed and pajama'd young into the Plymouth with its top down and we drove the mile to the Scarborough station to pick up their daddy. His train pulled in. We could even see him at a window. But he made no move to get off. The children were screaming "Daddy!" as the train pulled out, with him still on it. I speeded on to Ossining, the next station up the line, where a sheepish Daddy emerged to hug his tear-stained babies and apologize for having been sound asleep.

We owned a cocker spaniel and a cat that were both loved and mauled by the children. But one Christmas Eve, the spaniel got loose, and also, unbeknown to us, so did a mastiff owned by some neighbors. As far as we and the police could later tell, the mastiff had killed and eaten poor Paddy. Those neighbors gave—or put—away their mastiff, but that was small comfort to our bereaved children.

Still, death is something that children can't forever be protected from, and ours appeared somewhat comforted by the thought that God loves everyone, including small dogs, dead or alive. One noontime I had brought a favorite lunch (hamburger, peas, and mashed potato) to Timmy in his high chair. The sun was slanting across his blond head and his smile was beatific. "You know," he announced, "Goddie is my friend."

Later Jack and I surmised that because Tim liked the diminutive of his own name, he thought that God would feel the same about his. I saw no reason to interfere with Timmy's reasoning.

Sherry's reasoning tended more toward the legal, although at that time very few women became lawyers. (One was my cousin, Helen Lehman Buttenwieser.) It had been raining for several days and Sherry complained more each day. "Really, dear," I snapped, "there is very little I can do about the weather." Her eyes lit up. "What little can you do?"

One day I received a phone call from an older woman, Clifford Henderson, a Vassar graduate whose husband, Ralph, was a top executive at the nearby *Reader's Digest*. Mrs. Henderson sounded pleasant but no-nonsense.

"I'm told you're a writer."

"Well, yes."

"Well, I'm chairman of the Westchester Mental Hygiene Association. We need someone to write a booklet that explains to laypeople what the difference is between normal, neurotic, and psychotic."

"But I don't know a thing about it."

"You're a good Vassar girl. Go find out."

The challenge was irresistible, and I began reading books and interviewing psychiatrists and psychologists. Several of our neighbors were professionals in the field and all were remarkably generous with their time, especially Eunice Armstrong, a lay psychoanalyst,

143

and Bus (Bernard) Glueck, Jr., a psychiatrist who owned and ran a small mental hospital, Stony Lodge, in Ossining.

During one of my visits there, Bus asked me to assist at the electroshock treatment of a schizophrenic patient. I was holding down the man's legs while a male attendant held down his shoulders. When Bus applied the electricity, I could hardly keep my hold on the legs, so powerful was their jerking. Afterward, Bus told his wife, Dutch, that I had registered more shock than the patient had. That poor man endured several more zaps, but by that time he was fully unconscious. Nowadays, the procedure has been vastly improved by the administering of a muscle relaxant beforehand and a mild anesthesia. The cure rate for patients with schizophrenia has also much improved, and for patients with clinical depression the success of electro-convulsive therapy (ECT) has risen to over 90 percent. But people still fear the procedure, partly because of the book and movie, *One Flew Over the Cuckoo's Nest*, and partly because ECT is usually accompanied by a loss of memory (which returns within six months in most patients). Of course, there can be other side effects, but that, to a degree, is true of every form of treatment.

I named the booklet I wrote for the Westchester Mental Hygiene Association, *Do Cows Have Neuroses?* Its cover showed a goofy-looking cow, and, as one turned to the first page, one was informed that, no, cows don't get neuroses, but sensitive, intelligent human beings may.

I subsequently received irate letters from dairy farmers who insisted that cows do, indeed, get neuroses and that their output of milk is thereby reduced. For the next edition, I changed the first word from a flat "no" to a "no, in general," cows don't get neuroses.

The *Cows* pamphlet was featured at the first meeting of the World Federation for Mental Health in London and was later translated into many languages, including Japanese, Hebrew, Hindi, Marathi, and Gujarati. It remained in print for thirty years. Later, partly as a result of having to deal with my own children and their friends, I wrote a sequel, *Do Babies Have Worries?* Following that, I wrote, with the help of my semi-grown children, *Do Teenagers Have Wisdom?*

But some of the mental health professionals I interviewed struck me as inordinately ready to denigrate any person who didn't agree with their theories. I, therefore, wrote a short essay titled, "The Worm Turns: The Layman Looks at the Psychiatrists." Bus Glueck chortled at the impertinence of my observations and urged me to submit the piece to the *American Journal of Psychiatry*. The APA printed it and went on to invite me to address their annual convention that year, 1949, in Detroit. Jack couldn't get away from work, but both Gluecks were going. The three of us took the overnight train together. I was in a high state of nerves.

Shortly before the trip, I had written another grumpy missive, this time, a letter to the *New York Times*:

> Being one of the "millions" of laymen to whom you referred in your editorial "Paychiatry for Millions," on May 27, I was delighted with your statement that "none of our medical men and none of our scientists are better trained than psychiatrists." This is a valuable statement for a distinguished newspaper to make because many of your readers—my fellow-laymen—seem to be alarmed by psychiatrists, referring to them as "witch-doctors" or laughing inordinately when one of them happens to have trouble in his [sic] personal life.

To my surprise, the printed letter elicited a letter to me from Harold Strauss, editor in chief of Alfred A. Knopf, Publishers. Strauss flattered me by saying that I wrote "like a writer" and asked if I would consider collaborating with a psychiatrist who had a challenging idea for a book but whose first language was not English.

The Forties

At the dinner meeting in Detroit where I was to make my speech, my seatmate was Fritz Redlich, M.D., a psychoanalyst with a Viennese accent. A decade older than myself, he had deep-set blue eyes under heavy dark brows and a ready laugh. The title of his speech was "Humor and Psychiatry." Its thesis was that we can spot a great deal about people by what makes them laugh and what does not (Queen Victoria's haughty response to anything even slightly off-color was, "We are not amused."). Dr. Redlich had collected thirty thousand cartoons from which he selected twenty for a new "Mirth Response Test" that he had devised. Its results were as reliable as the Rorschach, but no better. Among his chosen cartoons was Charles Addams's skier looking back at the hillside where a tree has a single ski-mark descending on either side of it. Some schizophrenics see nothing odd—and certainly nothing funny—about being able to ski on both sides of a tree at the same time.

Fritz and I were so involved in conversation that we each ignored our other dinner partner. Nor did it take us long to figure out that Fritz was the doctor about whom Harold Strauss had written me.

My speech went off all right, but I was astounded afterward to have several psychiatrists come up and inquire who my analyst was. When I said no one, they refused to believe that someone as outspoken as I was had not been analyzed. This struck me as so narrow-minded that I wrote a follow-up essay that the *American Journal of Psychiatry* also published. Its conclusion was that not everyone needs braces for their teeth to happen to grow in straight. I was not invited back to speak. Many years later I met the editor of the *Journal*, a bright and charming man who, however, in private saw fit to make several anti-Semitic remarks. One never knows when this particular weed is going to force its way up amidst the most attractive flowers.

Fritz was brought up as a Catholic, but when he was twenty-one his father informed him he was half-Jewish. Fritz and his psychiatrist-wife therefore fled Austria shortly before Hitler annexed it.

146

Although the young pair knew little English, they worked at a state mental hospital and further educated themselves. By the time I met him, his wife Elsa was working in New Haven as a child psychiatrist and he was chief of psychiatry at the Yale Medical School. He and I worked for several years on our joint book — New Haven being but an hour and a quarter by car from Scarborough. I finally became so bleary from poring over his boxes of cartoons that I could no longer laugh at any of them. He and I developed a bit of a crush on each other, which Jack was able to handle with aplomb but that caused Elsa to act somewhat edgy. She, however, was quite attracted to Jack, so the four of us had pleasant enough times together. One such evening was at Thirlsmere, and afterward Elsa referred to my mother as "die Frau Generalin," ("Madame General"). I was grateful to her for that characterization, which lifted from me some of the guilt I felt for my resentment of my mother's frequent criticisms of me and her attempts to direct my life.

At first Fritz and I foundered in regard to what the book should cover, but gradually we came to an agreement. If a decision concerned the content, Fritz would have the final word, whereas if it concerned the manner in which the content was presented, I would have the final word. We utilized about a hundred cartoons and drawings but never referred to them in the text. The idea was for them to appear alongside our discussion of the primal emotion, whether love or fear, aggression or dependence, that underlay the cartoon's appeal and thus perhaps enable the reader to resonate to it at an unconscious as well as conscious level.

Fritz had high respect for the common sense of ordinary people (as well as for the uncommon sense of psychiatry). He, therefore, asked me to take part in an experiment. He gave me a long white coat and introduced me as Dr. Bingham to one new patient at a time in a room with a one-way mirror. Outside the room, he and some faculty members observed my attempts to elicit from the patient what his basic problem was. They then watched other professional job applicants do the same. Apparently my amateur skills, developed at the knee of the "Frau Generalin," worked as well as their professional techniques. The faculty voted to hire me and were somewhat chagrined when Fritz confessed that I had no medical qualifications.

After several years of hard work on the manuscript, we submitted it to Harold Strauss. Then we waited and waited. At last, Harold summoned us to his office. He was a brilliant, dark-haired, dark-eyed, somewhat serpentine man, with great literary skills and an impressive knowledge of Japanese culture, but on that day he repeatedly refused to come to the point. He raised all manner of interesting subjects but would not tell us whether or not he was going to publish our book. Somehow, without looking at each other, Fritz and I jointly determined to refuse to beg for the verdict. So we nodded and smiled as Harold talked on and on. He must finally have decided that we were never going to accommodate him. Abruptly he rose from his chair, came around the desk, and congratulated us on a fine job. We thanked him and departed. Over our celebratory drink, we shared some opinions about his unconscious that would not have delighted him.

The Inside Story: Psychiatry and Everyday Life stayed in print for twenty-five years, first as a Knopf hardcover and then as a Vintage paperback. Following its reviews (the one in the *Sunday New York Times* was by Dr. Karl Menninger), Fritz and I appeared on *The Today Show* and some other television and radio programs. At first I found this great fun, but soon it palled. For me, to win respect from faceless strangers turned out to be much less meaningful than receiving approval from Jack and family members and friends. After a while getting up at dawn, having make-up applied, and being asked difficult questions hardly seemed to me to be worth the inconvenience. Also, with our crushes as well as the writing of the book having run their course, Fritz and I were both ready to move on to other projects.

He remained a sophisticated, older friend from whom I was grateful to have learned a tremendous amount, but, in the end, the insights offered by psychiatry left me yearning for something more profound or ethical or perhaps more spiritual. Adequate health, after all, despite its crucial role in our functioning and our moods, did not strike me as a goal worthy of being placed at the very center of a person's life. But what did?

Jack, meanwhile, had been learning a lot as a partner in his small midtown law firm, Cohen, Bingham, and Stone. The Cohen was Henry, nephew of Morris Raphael Cohen, the philosopher. Martin Stone was a Yale Law School classmate of Jack's whose contacts in the entertainment world led to the firm's having occasional clients like Bob Smith, the puppeteer of Howdie Doodie. (Our children were thrilled.) Jack worked for several years on a Dickensian law case for the Bata Shoe Company, but legal practice never really grabbed him, and, perhaps for that reason, he was not as successful at attracting new business as he had hoped. What interested him was politics, but there, too, he felt frustrated.

Mornings, after he left, usually on foot, for the train station and I had dispatched the older children to school, I could sometimes fit in an hour or two for writing. But the household was not running smoothly and the houseman appeared more antagonistic by the day. "I dun't take no orders from no vommen," he shouted at me one time. Finally, I grew so alarmed by the venom in his expression that I asked Bus Glueck to drop by for an informal diagnosis. Bus came over within the hour and told me to fire the man immediately. The wife didn't seem too surprised by this and begged only to be allowed to stay on with their little girl. She promised that her husband would never return to our house. But after a month, I came home unexpectedly and found him there. So I had to fire her, too. This was almost as difficult for me as it must have been for her. Nor was it possible for me to locate a replacement immediately who was both trustworthy and loved children. But after several false starts, we were lucky enough to attract the Nana who had taken care of Sherry and me in Atlantic City. She was now married to a Mr. Cosner and agreed to work for us if her husband, too, could come live in our downstairs bedroom. Despite the fact that he turned out to be an alcoholic, the arrangement worked well. The children called him "Connie" and he adored them. They dubbed the shot glass he filled for his first whiskey of the evening, "Connie's juice."

A happy occasion for the pouring of "juice," this time Mumm's Cordon Bleu, was the wedding of my brother Howard to Eleanor Frank, a lovely, civic-minded graduate of Smith College whose nickname had been "Savannah" in honor of her birthplace and her Southern accent, which was untouched by her many years in the North. Because a Jewish settler in 17th-century Savannah had been a doctor who saved the lives of many civic leaders, Ellie was able to grow up experiencing far less anti-Semitism than I encountered in New York. She, for example, had been accepted without question in the best school for girls in Savannah, while, as I later was told, I had been turned down at age five by The Brearley School in New York because, as the headmistress said privately to my mother, "We already have a Jewess in that class." (The Jewess turned out to be my cousin and pal, Edie Altschul.) In fact, Ellie's first experience of anti-Semitism was at Smith College where her housemother tried to segregate the Jewish girls in the basement. This arrangement, for Ellie, did not last long, for she was so attractive and intelligent that shortly thereafter she was invited to room with one of the class leaders, and thus she moved upstairs in both senses of the word. (I am grateful to historian Kenneth Libo for the insight that there was so little anti-Semitism in the American South because the WASPs viewed Jews as fellow whites, against the Negroes. Similarly, there was little anti-Semitism in 17th-century Manhattan because the Dutch viewed Jews as fellow whites, against the Indians.)

In Scarborough, Jack's reputation as an accomplished amateur violinist, as well as an acceptable violist and cellist, brought invitations for him to play quartets with all manner of people. One evening, we went to the house of a stranger so that he could play the viola in the Mozart clarinet quintet—my favorite piece of music. The clarinetist was superb, and as we were departing, he offered us a few hot licks in farewell. He was, of all things, the minister of the Briarcliff Congregational Church. His name was Dick Beebe and he assured us that we would be welcome any time with the children at his Sunday service.

On our way to Thirlsmere for Sunday lunch, therefore, we began stopping off at his church, armed with plenty of pads and crayons to keep the children quiet. They preferred to remain with us rather than attend the Sunday School. Jack, as a boy, had disliked Sunday School and agreed with this plan. The church with its high clear windows provided an almost shocking architectural contrast to Notre Dame, or even to the Rosemary chapel, but its atmosphere of simplicity and clarity I found appealing in its own way. Dick's sermons were similarly simple and clear, yet also thought provoking. One that I remember explained why it does no good to pray about the weather. For weather, as he said, is the result of measurable, predictable physical events, and the God who created a universe that follows the laws of cause and effect "is not a God of whim." God offers us "the everlasting arms," but if we jump off a high building, God is not going to breach the laws of gravity to save us. (Besides, for each bride who prays for sunshine on her wedding, there may be ten farmers praying for rain.)

Though Jack Bingham reveled in his role as paterfamilias, he refused to let it prevent him from taking risks in life. He had given up flying, but in the summer of 1948 he decided to devote his two-week vacation to hitchhiking with me across the country. I was intrigued with the idea, but my parents were horrified.

"How can we get in touch with you?" my mother asked him.

"You can't."

"You have to take a gun," my father said.

When Jack hesitated, I spoke up. "I'd rather be raped than shot in the foot." My attempt at humor was far from successful in reassuring them.

Jack explained that he had hitchhiked across the continent ten years earlier, earning his way as he went, and had met with nothing remotely alarming. He compromised with them by saying that we would bed down at night, not in barns or fields as he had when he was young, but in motels or rooming houses, and that we would never accept a new ride after dark.

Reluctantly, my parents agreed, mostly, I surmise, because they so wanted to have the children, plus Nana (but not Connie) at Thirlsmere.

Jack and I talked to Lester Markel, the redoubtable editor of the *Sunday New York Times Magazine* about our possibly writing an article based on the trip. Markel suggested that we stop off to interview some of the newly settled displaced persons (DPs) from Europe to see how they were faring. We thought this a fine idea and got the appropriate names and addresses from Protestant, Catholic, and Jewish refugee organizations. Off we went by thumb, Jack wearing a straw hat and a backpack with our very few extra clothes, and I carrying only a large purse. Ahead of us by rail, addressed to the elegant St. Francis Hotel in San Francisco, went our suitcases and golf bags.

We averaged three hundred miles a day and never had to wait longer than fifteen minutes for a ride until we reached the West Coast.

On our way, we stopped off in Sayner, Wisconsin, where the Hixon family has a batch of well-built cabins on a lake. Adelaide and Alec were tickled by our chosen means of transportation, and when time came for us to leave, they waited in their car across the road until our first ride of the day slowed and then stopped for us.

But on the West Coast the drivers not only didn't slow to take a look at us but actually speeded up, and we had to wait as long as an hour. One ride we took was in a hearse; another was in a huge empty trailer truck. As we clambered up into its high cab, I asked the driver what he usually transported. "Cats," he said.

"Cats!?!"

Somehow he and Jack sensed that I had small furry creatures in mind, and they shouted with laughter at my ignorance that caterpillar tractors go by that name.

The gist of our article was that a young couple of respectable appearance could easily and safely hitchhike across the country and that the newly arrived DPs we interviewed were all adapting relatively well. In short, the trip was delightful but not newsworthy. Just as "No news is good news," so, often, "Good news is no news."

Another form of hitchhiking took place in August 1948 when Jack was driving our four children, Nana, and me to La Guardia Airport. From there he planned to fly to Philadelphia for the 1948 Democratic National Convention, while the rest of us flew to the Adirondacks to visit Aunt Sissie, who was still in deep mourning. On the way, we had a flat tire. The only chance for the children and me to catch our plane would be to hitchhike. Jack and Nana and the kids moved back from the road behind some bushes while I stood at the curb with thumb outstretched. A nice young man in a station wagon stopped. I asked if he could take us to the airport. "Hop in, Girlie."

"Thank you," I said, "but I also have some friends."

To his open-mouthed astonishment, out came the kids and Nana, followed by Jack. But the man was a good enough sport to laugh, and he allowed the kids, Nana, and me to pile into his car, complete with luggage. We just made our plane. It was a small, two-engine propeller plane, and the winds were fierce. The four children and Nana became airsick, and by the time we put down at Lake Placid, I was worn out. To my further dismay, after our luggage was unloaded on the tarmac, I found that Jack's bag had been included with ours. I ran out onto the airfield, waving wildly at the departing pilot. He put on the brakes, wheeled back to where I could hand him the bag and took it aboard. Somehow it got to Philadelphia and Jack was able to be photographed in a clean shirt when he stood next to Hubert Humphrey, the newly elected mayor of Minneapolis, who was leading the fight in support of President Truman's courageous civil rights plank. (Hubert, whom we knew slightly at the time, made at the convention what I've been told was the best—and shortest—speech of his long, loquacious political life.)

The civil rights plank, when finally approved by the Democratic delegates, triggered the defection from the party by many conservative Southerners led by Strom Thurmond. They proceeded to form their own party, the Dixiecrats, and seriously undermined Truman's chances of reelection against Republican Governor Thomas E. Dewey of New York by drawing away votes that would otherwise have been Democratic. But in November, to the surprise of the pollsters and everyone else except Harry Truman and perhaps his daughter Margaret, Truman won.

Jack and I were elated by Truman's victory, and also, a few months later, by his inaugural address. In it, the president promised to support the United Nations, the North Atlantic Treaty Organization (NATO), the Marshall Plan, and to establish a "bold new program" to help the underdeveloped countries help themselves. Because the last point was the fourth on his list, the program came to be known as Point Four. Jack and I had, of course, no inkling that one day Jack would become its acting director or be greeted in Iran during our official trip to the Arab world and Southeast Asia as "Master of the 4th Spot."

Point Four had three main emphases, namely: education, agriculture, and health. What neither Jack nor I foresaw in the late 1940s was that a by-product of Point Four, namely, the forging of friendships abroad for democracy and America, would cause the program to be condemned in some circles as a deliberate weapon in the rapidly chilling Cold War between the Soviet Communists and the United States. When mainland China became Communist in 1949, America's relationship with it also froze solid. In hindsight, Jack and I were naïve, but at the time our focus was on how well Point Four was working, not on how it might appear to America's political critics. Our education in this regard came by way of Jack's membership in the American Veterans Committee (AVC). This was the liberal alternative to the conservative American Legion and also the Veterans of Foreign Wars. At one of the AVC's national meetings, the far left-wing members offered so many obfuscating amendments to a plank they disliked that by two in the morning most of the other members were groggy with fatigue and straggled off to bed. By staying awake, the far left-wingers thus became a rump majority. They then passed a substitute that they knew the true majority would never have approved. The majority woke up in the morning to find that some aims of their organization had thus been subverted.

Partly because non-Communist liberals, like Jack and me, were thus forced to become less politically naïve, and partly because by 1948 Truman was being challenged for the presidency by Henry Wallace, the candidate of the Communist-influenced Progressive Citizens of America, a call had gone out the previous year to found a new organization, liberal in persuasion but refusing membership to any Communist or fellow-traveler. This was the ADA—Americans for Democratic Action. It was headed by Mrs. Franklin D. Roosevelt, Reinhold Niebuhr, several union officials such as Walter Reuther of the United Auto Workers, political figures and economists, such as J. Kenneth Galbraith, and others, including writers Arthur M. Schlesinger, Jr., James Wechsler, and Lillian Smith, author of "Strange Fruit," and Negro leader Walter White of the NAACP. Jack and I went to the ADA's first meeting at Washington's Willard Hotel and were excited by the group. Elmer Davis ran the gathering with ease and humor and welcomed us all as "The New Deal government in exile."

Two years later, Jack and I took the overnight train to Chicago for the ADA's 1949 national convention. Saturday evening's banquet featured several powerful speakers, but, like most political people, they talked too long. I was verbally saturated and suggested to Jack that we sneak out and go to bed, but he said there was only one more speech to go. The following is the opening of my book, *Courage to Change: An Introduction to the Life and Thought of Reinhold Niebuhr*:

> The speaker straightened his tie, ran a big-knuckled hand over his shiny pate, pulled his long nose further downward, and spoke out rapidly in a deep voice. By the end of one sentence, he had every person's full attention; by the end of one hour, he had several hundred people on their feet, clapping, stamping, shouting their approval.
>
> Few speeches can have rivaled this one for profundity, for range, for electromagnetism. . . . One minute the deep voice would boom out; the next it would drop to a whisper—and then boom again. The blue eyes would fly open as he presented a nugget of thought; then squint in diabolic conspiracy as he demolished it. Yet wait—a long index finger would rise—there may be a phoenix stirring in those ashes. With both arms in motion, like an orchestra conductor, he swept his listeners into the soaring of that phoenix, and the "unpredictable," "incongruous," and "ironic" results which in turn could lead to. . . .
>
> The suspense he built by these verbal, facial, and gestural dynamics became close to unbearable. And the depth of his own caring was so profound that the listener's intellect was finally accompanied by a racing pulse: the whole of the self was involved as well as the mind.

As the applause thundered, and finally slackened, a young wife turned to her husband. "Who is this man?"

"Famous, but I'm not sure what for."

"What do you suppose his job is?"

"Minister."

"A *minister*?"

The completeness of her incredulity made him smile. "Why not? They've got to have *some* good ones."

The next day at lunch Jack and I met him and were amazed by the delighted way he accepted the irreverent, often impertinent, comments by our three secular lunchmates: Arthur Schlesinger, Jimmy Wechsler, and Jimmy Loeb. (Loeb had been executive director of UDA, the Union for Democratic Action—which was ADA's predecessor.) On the train going home from Chicago to New York, Niebuhr joined Jack and me for dinner and set our minds afire.

During that same year, to the surprise of many Americans, the Soviets detonated their first atom bomb. Like some other people I sank, for a while, into black gloom. With this nuclear threat, how could Jack and I prevent our children and ourselves from being blown apart, literally or figuratively? Our older ones were being trained at school to hide under their desks at the first siren alert, while we adults were instructed to load our basement with bottled water and cans of food. Yet these measures seemed absurd and pathetic as measured against the incredible destructiveness of the new weapons. Would it ever be possible for humanity to develop sufficient wisdom to manage the results of its own inventiveness? Indeed, where in the contemporary world could one even begin to look for wisdom? The only person I could imagine knowing enough both about the visible world of political action and the invisible world of religious and ethical values was Reinhold Niebuhr. I began to read his books with avidity—and to dream of seeing him in person again.

PART THREE

The Fifties

CHAPTER 7

Publication

THE 1950S ARE GENERALLY PICTURED as the stodgiest decade of the 20th century. As in the early 1920s, when return to "normalcy" had been the Republican Party's slogan following World War I, so in the early 1950s the Republican administration of President Dwight David Eisenhower promoted normalcy following World War II. This meant, in effect, that Mother would go back to the kitchen and Father would work hard to earn enough to provide her and their numerous children with the car, refrigerator, and other consumer items that factories began producing in large quantities.

Still, Jack and I found our wartime fears hard to erase. A formal peace had been established, but its fragility was becoming increasingly apparent. In Eastern Europe, Stalin was repeatedly proving himself to be a treaty-breaker, and in Asia, in June 1950, Communist North Korea crossed the 38th parallel to invade democratic South Korea. The United Nations, with the United States in the lead, moved to defend South Korea, but Communist China was supporting the North Koreans. As the situation grew more bloody, many people like Jack grew more restless. He felt that he should be, if not in the thick of battle, then at least a part of our government's efforts to stem the aggressive spread of communism.

During the five years we lived in Scarborough, Jack had become acquainted with Truman's secretary of state, Dean Acheson. Their meeting was a totally unforeseen by-product of Jack's long-ago status as big man on campus at Yale. A group of young alumni, unbeknownst to Jack, got together to promote a representative of their generation to Yale's ruling board, the "Corporation." When a vacancy for alumni

161

trustee opened up, these Yalies organized a national write-in vote to nominate Jack. To the surprise of everyone, including Jack, he was elected. Not many liberals had ever served on the Corporation, though the liberal governor of Connecticut, Chester Bowles, was an ex-officio member. The Ohio Republican senator, Robert A. Taft, was the leading conservative. Yet there were also some middle-of-the-road members, like Dean Acheson, the Yale professor, Wilmarth Sheldon (Lefty) Lewis, and the Episcopal Church's bishop, Henry Sherrill. After Jack's election, he was invited to caucus with these three, plus Bowles on occasion, in the lobby of the Taft Hotel before the monthly Friday evening meeting of the full membership. This was a crucial period for Yale because the Corporation was searching for a new president. At one point, Jack asked me to sound out Niebuhr as to whether he would be interested in the job. For a week, Niebuhr considered it, but then concluded that he should stay at Union Theological Seminary to teach and write, rather than go to Yale to administer and raise money. Also, as he pointed out realistically, someone as liberal as himself was unlikely to be chosen by the Corporation.

Finally, after a number of candidates had been seriously considered, the small group that included Jack succeeded in attracting enough swing votes to elect Yale's young, thoughtful, witty professor of history, Whitney Griswold. Jack and I exulted, and after Whit was duly installed in office, we occasionally stayed with him and his educator-wife, Mary, in the President's House on Hillhouse Avenue for the Friday night between the Corporation's first meeting and the subsequent one on Saturday morning.

I also enjoyed accompanying Jack to New Haven because it gave me time to work directly with Fritz Redlich on our psychiatry book. Besides, it was fun to meet Jack's illustrious new colleagues and their wives. Dean Acheson was tall, very handsome, often convivial, with a waxed mustache and slightly protuberant big blue eyes. His wife, Alice, rarely came to New Haven, but she too was a most impressive personage, being beautiful, artistic, and reserved. Later, when I saw some of the watercolors she had painted, I was even more impressed, and Jack and I bought one that still hangs in the house. Still later, in Washington, Alice and I became friends.

At the time, I didn't at all want to uproot the children to move back to Washington, but with Secretary Acheson encouraging Jack to come down there for a job interview, I couldn't stand in Jack's way. Besides, the private practice of the law did not really satisfy him, and the political prospects for a Democrat in largely Republican Westchester County still looked unpromising.

Jack finally sent a telegraph to the secretary of state: "Barkis is willin'."

The next thing I knew, I was surrounded by boxes, excelsior, crying children, a discombobulated dog and cat, and a real estate agent escorting prospective buyers through our Scarborough house.

Each time we moved, Jack and I had to decide what kind of schools our children would attend. In principle, as liberals, we preferred public schools, but in practice, as parents, we wanted our children exposed to a better education than was offered in the typically huge classes of Washington's public schools. I went to see the headmistress of the private, innovative Potomac School in Virginia, across the bridge from Georgetown. Could she take four new pupils for the fall term? "I don't even have room for one," she said, "so I might as well take four."

Jack and I had decided to settle in Georgetown so that he would have only a short commute to the State Department. We knew from experience that if he were to see anything of the children, our home would have to be nearer to his place of work than our previous houses had been. We also decided to rent rather than buy because we had no idea how long the Korean War would last.

One day the real estate agent who was driving me around Georgetown pointed to a large stucco house set back from Wisconsin Avenue where the trolley tracks were still in use.

"It's for rent—but of course only to the right people."

"What do you mean?"

"Oh, you know. No Jews."

"But I'm Jewish."

She stopped the car and turned to stare at me. "Surely, only . . . half . . . at most."

"I am full-blooded!"

We found a different—but almost as roomy—red brick with a bay window on each of its three floors. It was at the corner of R Street and 32nd, and was locally known as "El Dumpo" because its owners were visibly doing little to keep it up, but we were content with its crabgrass "lawn" and antediluvian garage.

Jack's first job in the State Department concerned "national security affairs." His boss was Thomas Cabot, a newly arrived Bostonian. Tom kept his big beautiful sloop, the *Avelinda*, in Chesapeake Bay, and took Jack and me for sailing weekends on several occasions. The first time, he neglected to study the tide chart sufficiently and ran us aground on a mudbank where we spent a prolonged and giggly cocktail hour until the tide floated us off. Another time, he included our four children in the invitation.

Later, Jack moved to the Technical Cooperation Administration (TCA), far better known as Point Four. Thirty years later, Jack received a frantic phone call from the Truman Library in Independence, Missouri. Former President Truman had a speech to make that night and needed to know what were the first three points in his 1949 Inaugural Address. Fortunately, Jack remembered: support for NATO, the United Nations, and the Marshall Plan.

By the early 1950s, the Marshall Plan was succeeding to a major degree in rebuilding war-shattered Europe, thus defanging the

Communist parties that were vying for power within some of our erstwhile allies and as well as our former enemies. But this American accomplishment in no way succeeded in silencing Senator Joseph McCarthy, the Wisconsin Republican who was making a national reputation by accusing American public servants, especially those in the State Department, of being Communists. While campaigning in his home state of Wisconsin in 1952, he even saw fit to impugn the patriotism of the heroic General George C. Marshall in the presence of Marshall's long-term friend and one-time protegé, General Dwight D. Eisenhower. "Ike," then running for president, was apparently so fearful of McCarthy's power during this period of anti-Communist hysteria that he spoke not one word in defense of his old friend.

More loyal than Ike, but politically less cautious, was Dean Acheson. He, apparently, was unable even to imagine the possibility that a long-term colleague of his, Alger Hiss, could have been a Communist or, God save the mark, might actually have spied for the Soviet Union. When Hiss was accused of these actions, first by Whittaker Chambers and then loudly by McCarthy, Acheson flatly stated, "I do not intend to turn my back on Alger Hiss." This remark, Jack and I felt, was laudable in the private sphere but perhaps hazardous in the public one. And, indeed, as more and more damaging evidence surfaced against Hiss, the easier it became for McCarthy and his slick-haired minions, Roy Cohn and David Schine, to smear not just Acheson for being "soft on Communism" but, by association, President Truman and, after a time, all Democrats. Cohn and Schine were especially loathsome to me because they were Jewish.

Jack and I summoned our social courage and invited the Achesons to dinner, reciprocating for a dinner invitation earlier extended to us. To handle the cooking, I had found Roberta Lee, a tall, regal black woman who had originally been sent to us by the U.S. Employment Service as a once-a-week laundress. But, as Roberta and I became friends, I asked if she would like to try her hand as cook. She ended up cooking for us five days a week. Also in our employ was Mademoiselle Elizabeth Heiden, a White Russian countess, whose father had been the tsar's chief admiral before the Bolsheviks took over in 1917. Mademoiselle had simply appeared at our front door one day and said that a mutual acquaintance suggested that she come work for us. She had fled Russia as a child and spoke French and German. She was also a devout member of the Russian Orthodox Church. With Jack and me out in the evening as much as his job demanded, it was important to have an educated person living in. It also struck me that the children could benefit from Mademoiselle's devoutness as a counterbalance to Jack's and my casual attitude about religion. She was an inefficient housekeeper, but a warm and loving person and got along swimmingly with Roberta (whom she called "Bertie"). They were an unusual pair of friends, the "Negress" whom society relegated to a level far below ours, and the countess whom it would have raised far above ours if she had had the money to be socially visible. Between the two, they handled all domestic duties for which I had neither the time nor skill, and served in loco parentis to the kids when Jack and I traveled.

Georgetown at that time was like a village, with someone we knew—or at least knew something about—living on many of its tree-shaded streets with their brick sidewalks humped by the roots of those venerable trees. A few African Americans still owned shacks, one but a few blocks from the Dumbarton Oaks estate. On a side street near us lived Senator and Mrs. Robert A. Taft. One summer afternoon I was walking our big, obstreperous male poodle, Figaro, when a taxi stopped outside the Tafts' house. Out of the cab leapt Senator Joseph McCarthy. I was tempted to unleash Figaro and "sic" him on McCarthy. As I stood on the sidewalk stunned to inaction, McCarthy reached the top step of the porch. The front door was thrown open and there, grinning broadly in welcome, stood Senator Taft.

When Jack had been an undergraduate at Yale, he knew Bill Taft, one of the senator's sons. Now Jack and Bill were both working in the State Department. The next day, Jack went to Bill in dismay about his father being so welcoming to McCarthy. Bill said, "If you have anything to say to my father, why don't you and June come to the house for supper next Sunday?" The senator's wife, Martha, invited us. She was a model of maternal solicitude and hospitality; the senator talked, rather nonstop, mostly about Yale. He also told us how much he admired Jack's father and said a few tactful words about his new senatorial colleague, my Uncle Herbert Lehman (who violently disagreed with Taft on the subject of McCarthy and much else). Jack and I felt paralyzed by the ancient rules of hospitality. How could you eat someone's salt and then attack him over his choice of a previous guest? Also, realistically, what could we possibly say about McCarthy that Taft hadn't heard before? We left early, our stomachs filled but our emotions roiled; we felt like cowards but were not sure that our silence had been wrong.

Jack and I continued to be convinced that the means used by some of the government officials against Communism did more harm to our own country than to the Communists. Worst was the barrage of accusations—usually false—against American professionals concerned with foreign affairs. These accusations had started in the House with the Un-American Activities Committee.

Through Jack's brother, Woodbridge, a tenured professor of Far Eastern history at Berkeley, Jack and I had met some of the "Old China Hands" in the State Department who came under suspicion by the witch-hunters. What was their crime? Having learned Chinese and spent their lives trying to understand China and improve American relations with it, whether under Chiang Kai-shek or Mao Tse-tung. The pair we got to know best were Oliver and Marian Clubb. We were appalled to see how injured they—and his career—were because of McCarthy's false accusations of their being Communists.

McCarthy's continuing defamation of loyal diplomats and other government employees so distressed President Truman that in early 1951 he established a Civil Service Loyalty Review Board to study the most questionable cases. To give it credibility, he appointed a conservative Republican to be its chairman. This was Hiram Bingham, Jack's father. Father Bingham, by then in his seventies, was delighted with the job. Jokingly, he told us that he had asked to review the FBI files on those of his sons who had merited such attention. Thus, he had learned about an escapade by Jack—a brief arrest for disorderly conduct while an undergraduate. On matters of serious import, Father Bingham was, of course, professionally discreet.

Our relationship with him and Suzanne had evolved in a mutually acceptable but thoroughly hypocritical fashion after this latest move of ours to Washington. He would phone me and ask, "Are you and Jack doing anything next Tuesday evening?"

"No, Father, we're free. How about you and Suzanne coming here for dinner?"

"Well, unfortunately, Suzanne will be out of town."

"I see. Well, that's too bad. But why don't you come along anyway?"

"Why, thank you. That's a lovely idea. What time?"

He would arrive on the dot of the appointed hour. (He told us that for diplomatic dinners, he and Suzanne always arrived five minutes early and sat in their parked car until the exact time.) Our children thus had a chance to be with him during the cocktail hour and then he, Jack, and I would have a quiet dinner together. The first evening he asked where the bread was. The menu included potatoes, which I had thought would be enough in the way of starch. (When I was growing up, our cooks were all German; they rarely included bread with dinner—or perhaps this was a German Jewish custom.) I quickly rang the bell for Roberta, who fished out whatever bread was available. His pronouncement was that a meal without bread was not a true meal. From then on, of course, we made a point of having rolls or muffins whenever he came to dine.

We were able to provide him with great pleasure, showing him the photographs Jack took on our trip to Machu Picchu. They were the first color photos Father Bingham had ever seen of the ruins—he had discovered them three years before Jack was born. Because color photography was relatively new, the pictures were dazzling in the contrast they revealed between the bright green of the grass, the gray of the impressive stone structures, and the dark green verging on black of the mountain that shadows the plateau. The road we had taken from the plateau down to the Urubamba River was named the Carratera Hiram Bingham and was the worst road I've ever been on: nothing but narrow hairpin turns from which I was certain our bus's rear would slip. The river itself was the fastest moving stream I'd ever seen—faster than the train that had brought us there from Cuzco. We had been able to include this one-day detour during a Point Four inspection trip by Jack that included visits to Argentina, Brazil, Uruguay, and Costa Rica, as well as Peru. My first sight of the Andes, from the plane's window at dawn, was of an unforgettable white montage, with peaks dwarfing even my memory of the European Alps.

In Washington on one occasion, Father Bingham was clearly upset when he arrived. Jack quickly fetched him a big Scotch and I quickly sent the children out to play. He told Jack and me that during the afternoon he felt he had to deny the reinstatement in the State Department of John Carter Vincent, a skilled China hand and old friend of Woodbridge's. Mrs. Vincent had dropped to her knees before Father Bingham, but to no avail. He had tears in his eyes when he reported the event.

"Wood," being both a dutiful eldest son to his father and a loyal friend to his long-term colleagues in Far Eastern affairs, was torn by some of Father Bingham's decisions. Many years later, in a privately printed, posthumous biography of his father, Wood reported that in their correspondence, "I defended the China experts and said that the Senate investigations were unfair. HB maintained . . . that the Senate investigators were simply getting at the facts. He also upheld the concept that a person's reputation might be based on his associates. . . . I am dismayed to mention that my father did participate in the decision against my friend John Carter Vincent."

Father Bingham was conservative both politically and socially. Suzanne was even more so. This was, after all, the pre-Pill era when premarital sex, especially by girls, was looked upon as a serious disgrace. One of our grown nieces went to stay with Father and Suzanne over a summer weekend. During that time, the news came through that her older sister "had to get married," that is, was slightly pregnant by her fiancé. Suzanne told the visiting girl to depart immediately, since she was no longer welcome in their home. The girl did so, but Jack and I never forgot this example of the Hiram Binghams' imputing guilt by association.

Shortly thereafter, my parents—and Jack's—planned an extended Mediterranean cruise. When each couple heard about the other's plans, there was talk of canceling, but both proudly refused to do so. The two ladies spent a month afloat not speaking to each other, but the men occasionally found themselves in the top deck bar at sunset. As far as I could tell, they had a pleasant time, each boasting about his child (and probably not listening to the other).

At the time of the ship's fancy dress ball (with prizes), Suzanne appeared in an elegant Egyptian costume newly purchased in Cairo. Unluckily for her, one of the three judges happened to be Max Rossbach. She was visibly furious when she got passed over.

One of the few senators who had the courage to speak out, first against Pat McCarran (Nevada Senator) and then against McCarthy was Senator Herbert Lehman. On one occasion, I was invited by Aunt Edith to accompany her to the Senate Visitors' Gallery because Uncle Herbert was scheduled to make a speech. If she hadn't kept an iron grip on my knee, I would have been on my feet yelling "hurray" at Uncle Herbert (visitors to the House and Senate galleries are adjured to remain mute at all times, on pain of immediate eviction).

But Uncle Herbert's denouncing of McCarthy's unscrupulous attacks on innocent people didn't begin to faze the Wisconsin senator. As Uncle Herbert later told an oral history interviewer:

> McCarthy was the most insensitive man I ever knew. You couldn't insult him. I would assail him in the most scathing terms, and after the debate he would come up grinning, throw his arm around my shoulder, and inquire, "How are you, Herb?" He seemed to have no sense . . . that right and wrong were involved. His activities were all part of a political game. If anyone got hurt, it was too bad, but it was part of the game.

Uncle Herbert had reached the Senate in 1949 by way of a special election. He won partly because of his record as a popular governor and partly because he had recently done such a good a job as director of UNRRA, the U.N. Relief and Rehabilitation Agency that saved the lives of millions of displaced persons after the war. He was also inadvertently helped by his opponent, the Republican John Foster Dulles, whose record in foreign affairs was so impressive that it had earned him the endorsement for the Senate by the *New York Times* as well as such highly respected columnists as Walter Lippmann. But Dulles was less skilled on the domestic political side and, while campaigning in upstate New York, he said to his white, Christian conservative audience, "If you could just see the people in New York City [who will be] voting for my opponent, if you could see them with your own eyes, I know that you would be out, every last man and woman of you, on Election Day."

This comment was thoroughly publicized by the Lehman campaign throughout the hot dusty streets of the Bronx and Brooklyn, Queens, and lower Manhattan. In November, the city dwellers came to the polls in such large numbers that Lehman's majority swamped Dulles's sizeable lead from upstate. Dulles never ran for elective office again, though he was appointed by Eisenhower to be secretary of state.

So indiscriminate were McCarthy's accusations against people for being secret Communists that no one we knew took him seriously. Even when one or two accusations appeared to contain a modicum of truth, Jack and I had trouble giving it credence. I had never met Alger Hiss but Jack had, and we liked his brother Donald who was a close friend of Kay and Phil Graham's (whose son Donald was named for him). Also, in regard to Alger, we had heard so many awful things about his prime accuser, *Time's* Whittaker Chambers, that it was hard for us to believe anything Chambers said. (He had, however, written a brilliant *Time* cover story on Reinhold Niebuhr.) Among those criticizing Chambers was our New York friend, Dr. Carl Binger, one of the psychiatrists who had helped me prepare my *Cows* pamphlet. When I heard that Carl was going to testify against Chambers, I went by subway to New York's downtown federal courthouse to show solidarity with him. Actually, he had been reluctant to appear in court, but his wife, Clorinda (Chloe) Garrison, a close friend of Priscilla Hiss, Alger's wife, had prevailed on him to do so, if not for the sake of friendship, then at least as a public duty. But his ambivalence appeared to me to be undermining his persuasiveness, and I was wrenching about in acute discomfort when he claimed that Chambers's unreliability was proved by the way Chambers raised his eyes to the ceiling each time he was confronted with a difficult question. Chambers's lawyer promptly objected and went on to accuse Carl of having raised *his* eyes to the ceiling with similar frequency. So eye-raising became an instant non-issue, and Carl—together with many people, including myself—came away from court chagrined by his performance.

Although Alger Hiss was eventually sent to jail for a short term, his punishment for supposed involvement with the Soviet Union remained controversial. Jack and I felt that though, of course, the nation's right to defend itself against spies is paramount, still, in regard to Hiss, crucial facts had been, and perhaps always would be, unknown by the public. On the one hand, Hiss's name did turn up in secret Kremlin files after the official break-up of the Soviet Union in 1991. On the other hand, his son Tony Hiss has written voluminously about his father's innocence.

To be accused of being a liberal, as people like ourselves, the Chet Bowleses, Arthur Schlesingers, and Alfred Binghams often were, could be pejorative but was far from frightening. To be labeled a Communist or even a fellow traveler, however, could cause people to lose their jobs and the prospect of ever finding a comparable one. Ironically, because the Foreign Service had itself, for so long, been anti-Semitic, the State Department had only a few Jews in its employ at the time McCarthy focused on it; his victims, therefore, were mostly Christians. Later, we were told by some talented young people, Christian as well as Jewish, that the witch-hunts of the 1950s had caused them to abandon their plans to join the Foreign Service.

In Washington, Jack and I were invited to diplomatic dinners given by several embassies. One evening at the Portuguese embassy we ran into Father and Suzanne Bingham. "What are *you* doing here?" was how my nondiplomatic father-in-law greeted us.

We also attended parties at which Dean and Alice Acheson were fellow guests. The secretary of state was a bit of a flirt, and when he danced with me at the Chevy Chase Club where I had once almost fainted, I felt the very opposite of faint. "I could have danced all night," I felt.

My flirting with Jack's boss or my own, or some other distinguished older man, like Walter Lippmann who at a cocktail party looked taken by my wide-brimmed purple hat, was just plain fun. But I certainly didn't want flirting to become the center of my life as it had for my mother. She provided me with what scientists call a "negative experiment." Her constant emphasis on the beau of the moment didn't, in the end, lead to her happiness.

For me, there was zero chance of any involvement with these gentlemen. The emotions they aroused in me from time to time were compelling enough to wonder about undermining Jack's and my marriage, but he had handled each situation with aplomb, partly as a result of his own alpha-male-type inner security. At a profound level, he did not feel threatened and neither was he overly possessive or prone to jealousy. He simply took it for granted that, in time, I would confide in him whatever went on and continue to be his loyal and loving wife. He knew that it would do no harm to his career if she were a charming dinner partner to his boss or other power-wielder. I always did whatever homework I could on the specialty of the coming evening's big shot. I, on the other hand, being inwardly far less secure, was apt to get frantic on the rare occasion when Jack flirted with some glamorous female of my age or younger.

One night in Washington, Jane and George Wheeler gave a dance at their large house on fashionable Foxhall Road. French Champagne was quaffed and at two in the morning Jane, in a full-length, one-shouldered, white Grecian tunic, ostensibly escaped from the attentions of her male guests, including Jack, by climbing a tree in her front yard. He was all for following her, but I forcefully made the point that, 1) it was time for us to go home, and 2) he should please hand over the car keys because he had had a lot to drink. This car-key-protocol was something he and I had fully discussed when sober, and he had promised not to balk if I reminded him of it. Reluctantly, therefore, he handed over the keys and we shouted our thank you's and good nights up the tree to Jane.

When we got home, I laid the keys in their usual spot on the mantel over the fireplace in the front hall. To my surprise, Jack swept me into his arms for a passionate kiss. Fortunately, there were tiny mirrors imbedded in the carving over the mantel. Something made me open my eyes in the midst of the embrace. There, behind my back, sneaking toward the keys, were Jack's fingers. "Oh no, you don't!" I shouted and grabbed the keys. Sheepishly, he gave up the effort to return to the party and came along to bed. Nor did he receive any sympathy for his hangover in the morning. Yet those hangovers turned out to be a disguised blessing because after this one, he decided—with my full agreement—that we should stop drinking as much as we had become accustomed to during the war years.

Even more important for Jack's and my mutual fidelity was our intimate version of MAD. "Mutually Assured Destruction" dominated the Cold War relationship between the United States and the Soviet Union. On Jack's and my literal home front, the possibility that our mate might make love to someone else held a mini-nuclear dimension, too dreadful to contemplate. It included a preventive aspect, in that each of us knew that if the other thus indulged, the partner would follow suit. This personal MAD resulted in enough self-control to keep the marriage intact even during our rare periods of severe disagreement. Decades later, when President Jimmy Carter admitted to the nation that he had lusted "in his heart" for someone other than his spouse, Jack and I looked at each other "with wild surmise" and a dollop of rueful empathy. For we, like the Carters, were lucky enough to have remained in love—and in lust—with each other, even though Jack and I, from a New Testament point of view, had certainly committed adultery in our hearts. In fact, it was likely no coincidence that the two men I adored enough to spend years of my life doing research for their respective biographies, namely, Reinhold

Niebuhr and U Thant, were themselves such pillars of rectitude that neither one would have laid a finger on me even if I had thrown myself at them. Yet, had I not been so dazzled by each of them, I doubt if I could have summoned the long-term energy to do the arduous research, writing, and checking that each biography entailed. Reinie sometimes teased me for being "indefatigable," a term he did not mean, nor did I take, to be a total compliment. Of all the unconscious defenses I had studied while working with Fritz Redlich, the two I'm most grateful for are "denial" and "sublimation." Writing those biographies was, in part, sublimation.

Before I wrote any of the books, however, one object of my crush had been far from rectitudinous. In 1946, my mother-in-law and her husband were visiting Jack and me in Scarborough when Herbert Elliston, my former boss on the *Washington Post*, phoned to invite me to a black-tie journalism dinner in New York. Knowing that Jack would be playing trios with his mother and Henry all evening, I told Herbert that I'd be delighted to drive into the city and join him. Jack was aware that these home evenings of trio-playing were not as beloved by me as were his and my times alone together, so he told me to go ahead. His mother was shocked and said so. I tried to explain that this journalism event would enhance my career, but she had no interest in my career nor, for that matter, the career of any woman, especially one who was also a wife and mother.

Herbert and I had such a merry time at the dinner with his old friend Alistair Cooke that we were inspired to go dancing at La Rue, a glamorous nightclub. When I finally chauffeured him to the Ritz Tower where he was to spend the night in my parents' empty apartment (they were in White Plains for the weekend), he begged me to come on upstairs. I said that I had an hour's drive ahead of me and that Jack would be waiting up (the first was true; the second, not). Herbert accepted the rejection in good spirit, and after his quick goodnight kiss, I drove off. Once home, I grabbed a dish of cold zucchini from the fridge and went upstairs to report to Jack on the evening. He was asleep but grunted a vague welcome. As I started to reveal all, he mumbled "Can't it wait till morning?" So I ate my vegetable in silence.

In the morning, I received a phone call from my mother. "What kind of a man is that former boss of yours?" It turned out that because she and my father had had a fight, she decided to spend the night in town. She was therefore in the apartment when Herbert appeared. (Just as well that I had not gone upstairs with him!) They had a nightcap and enjoyed each other's company so much that he invited her to share his bedroom. She and I had a conspiratorial laugh at anyone with enough brass to proposition a daughter and her mother on the same evening.

Five months later, I sent Herbert an announcement of the birth of Claudia Rossbach Bingham and a note ostensibly from her, thanking him for the evening he and she had spent dancing together in New York. Thus Herbert, unbeknownst to himself, had stimulated not just two generations of females in my family that night, but three. He wrote a chagrined and amusing response, and we remained in touch. But even before Jack and I moved back to Washington in 1951, he had a stroke and was partially paralyzed. Jack and I went to call on him and he was valiant about his predicament, but his life and career—plus his marriage—had been wrecked. In time, he married his nurse, a warm no-nonsense woman who saw to it that he lacked for nothing she could possibly provide. He died not long thereafter.

Before the days of air conditioning, the Washington summers were brutal. When we moved back in June 1951, having left the children at Thirlsmere, I would sit at my desk, dressed only in shorts and a sleeveless shirt, with the electric fan on high. Nonetheless, the sweat running down my arms would moisten my fingers to the point where they slipped off the typewriter keys. At night, if I arose from my bed, I could see my silhouette in sweat on the bottom sheet.

Not long after Jack had joined Point Four, Dr. Henry Bennett, the agency's director, was killed in the course of duty in an airplane crash in Tehran. Jack was appointed acting director. He was not a likely candidate to become its permanent one because he lacked the necessary agricultural background. He needed to see what was going on in the field, so he and I set forth on an eleven-week tour of the Middle East, Asia, and Africa. The trip confronted us with a shattering view of abysmal poverty, yet we also witnessed moments of elation on the part of some villagers aided by American experts in improving their lives. In a field once, a barefoot farmer limped rapidly toward Jack, shouting and waving a jug from which drops of water were spilling. His words were translated for us: "We were dead; now we are alive." The Point Four technical expert who had helped the villagers dig a deep well had enabled them to decrease dramatically their rate of illness and death, especially for children, and to increase their harvests.

Our trip started with a short visit to beautiful Beirut—where I first heard the mesmerizing call to prayer from the mosques. From there we flew to Iraq. Baghdad was the hottest place I had ever been, with temperatures of 110 in the shade. The foreign minister, Muhammad Fadhel al-Jamali, gave a lavish late afternoon garden party in honor of Jack. While we were standing in the receiving line, I felt so dizzy that I excused myself, walked down to the end of the garden, dropped to my knees, and put my forehead to the ground. Gradually the blood returned to my head, and I was able to resume my place in line. Jack was enchanted to hear praise for me from one of the notables who assumed that I was a devout Muslim attending to my evening prayer.

Fadhel Jamali was not a Muslim but a Christian, and had been educated in Britain and the United States. When we visited him at his imposing house in Baghdad, we were amazed to see shelf after shelf of books about Judaism. Indeed, he boasted of having the greatest collection of

Judaica in the whole Middle East. But its purpose, we soon discovered, was not to encourage mutual understanding between Muslim and Jew, but how best to "drive Israel into the sea." Jack and I could easily foretell how counterproductive, perhaps dangerous, it would be for us even to hint at my background.

One morning I got to spend several hours with an Iraqi lady and several of her friends. The women were unanimous in their opinion that arranged marriage is a wonderful institution. My hostess, typically, had never met her husband until his and her families agreed that the marriage should take place. After the wedding, the two young people fell in love, and had seven children. She mentioned the high rate of divorce in America. I was asked what was so good about young people being free to choose their own mate. I said what I could to defend our system but I had to admit that marriage can be like the little girl with the little curl: when it is good it is very very good, and when it is bad, it is horrid.

By the time I returned to the Hotel Semiramis on the bank of the malodorous Tigris River, the temperature in both of our rooms as well as my body were well over a hundred. Fluid loss from the heat and the fearsome diarrhea that struck me were more than my body could make up for, no matter how much water I drank. The ceiling fan circled lazily as I grew weaker and more dehydrated. Jack and I were scheduled to go next to Iran, but during my days of illness, he received a cable from Washington warning that the recent overthrow of Iran's Prime Minister Mossadegh made it too hazardous for me to accompany Jack there. Because Jack and I were sharing one diplomatic passport, Jack's departure for Iran would have left me stranded, without official American documentation, in the heart of Arab anti-Jewish sentiment. I was too sick to give a damn, but Jack cabled the State Department that instead of his going on to Iran, he would like permission to continue with me to Pakistan and India, which were already on our itinerary.

Then, on our way back, we would include Iran if, by then, its political situation had calmed down.

Luckily for me, two Point Four doctors happened to come into Baghdad from the countryside, and Jack asked them to pay me a visit. They gave me some generic pills to control the symptoms but advised against my being carted to the too-primitive local hospital for the intravenous fluids I clearly needed. A few days later, the pills made me well enough to travel. Jack and I flew to Basra on the Gulf, unbelievably hotter than Baghdad, and, after a long wait, we stepped aboard a KLM plane. I have no idea what heaven comprises, but it can't be much better than the cool of that plane and the chocolates we were given.

In Pakistan, we stayed first in Karachi (with its ever-present flocks of very vocal crows) and then north to the beautiful city of Lahore. Jack cabled the State Department for permission to drive on through the nearby Khyber Pass to Afghanistan's capital, Kabul, but the department responded that too many Afghan tribesmen were shooting at each other. From the Pakistan border, therefore, we were merely able to peer longingly down the harsh mountain pass. Later in the day, we visited a Pakistani village where we participated in a ceremony celebrating the planting of trees as a windbreak. Jack politely handed me a villager's wooden shovel to break the first ground, and I made a mighty stab at the dry, packed earth—and broke the shovel.

We stayed with Ambassador Chet Bowles and his wife Steb in New Delhi. Typically, they had opted to remain in their own comfortable but modest bungalow rather than move into the imposing U.S. Embassy residence. Also in typical fashion, they were not just employers to their Indian servants but also friends. (Household help in India in those days was mostly male.) This gave Jack and me our first, though severely limited, opportunity to talk to Indians other than the high- or middle- class officials who attended the social functions in our honor. The Bowles' chauffeur was an imposing Sikh from the Punjab who kept his big black beard under control with bobby pins.

The official we saw most of in India was S.K. Dey, director of India's Community Development Projects Administration. He was a dark-skinned, articulate, middle-aged man with a fine sense of humor. I had the impression that my very mild flirting with him, as Jack, he, and I trudged together around the countryside in the broiling sun (the monsoon was late that year), was appreciated by him at a basic level. At one point, the three of us reached a stream we had to cross. Look, Ma, no bridge. Jack and S.K. were able to swing themselves over the water by way of a rope attached to an overhanging branch, but I had no confidence that this maneuver would work for me. So I took off my shoes and peds and waded across the river, thus risking water-borne schistomasiasis but at least not making a total wet fool of myself. S.K. Dey teased me unmercifully about my cowardice, but I sensed that it rather appealed to him. Jack and I spent that night in Nilokeri, near the headquarters of the local office of the Community Development Projects Administration. In the primitive country inn, our room was so stifling that we decided to sleep out of doors on charpoys (cots with braided webbing). I was awakened at predawn by an unusual huffing sound I was unable to identify. When I opened my eyes, I wished I hadn't, for there, peering right into my mosquito net was a huge slobbering water buffalo. A bit later, I heard many guttural sounds; these turned out to come from a devout Muslim clearing his nasal passages by sniffing up water and then emitting it, as the appropriate cleansing before chanting the melodious morning prayer.

In Delhi, Steb Bowles, dressed in a sari, took me to the Gandhi Ghat, a memorial to the recently assassinated Mahatma who, in effect, had been India's George Washington. Out of respect for him, she said we should remove our shoes. But the marble floor in the sun was so blistering that the soles of our feet couldn't bear it. Therefore,

Jack and I pay a courtesy call on Indian Prime Minister Nehru (far left) and Ambassador Jha during our Point Four trip to the Middle East and South Asia.

instead of our planned decorous approach to the statue, we raced along helter-skelter until we reached a shady spot. Later in the day, dressed in formal garb, Chet Bowles escorted Jack and me on our courtesy call to Prime Minister Jawaharlal Nehru. Nehru exuded intelligence and boredom (he was famous for hating courtesy calls), offering but one word answers to the substantive questions raised by Chet and Jack. Silence fell. I plucked up my courage and reported to Nehru on Steb's and my undignified skitting across the Gandhi Ghat. At last a flicker of interest, even the precursor to a smile, and from then on the conversation flowed.

Toward the end of our visit to India, Jack and I decided that we desperately needed a few days off. We flew from Delhi to Jammu where we caught the tiny plane that skirts the mountain peaks in order to drop you off in Srinagar, the capital of Kashmir. The city was drab and terribly run down; for years virtually no tourists had come because of the continuing unrest and occasional violence between Hindus and Muslims.

One day Jack and I went on horseback through the Kashmir forest to a neighboring town. The town turned out to be even more poverty-stricken than Srinagar. When our time came to leave Kashmir, we both felt relieved, but then came a transportation nightmare. We were scheduled to be back in New Delhi for a party the Bowleses were giving in Jack's honor that evening. But because of storm clouds, the commercial plane could not get back to Srinigar to pick us up. Our sole option was to hire a car to drive us down the mountains to Jammu. We and another prospective passenger found a rattletrap vehicle with a maniacal driver. He kept his hand on the horn as we careened around the many hairpin turns (with no protective road barrier to be seen) to hear the warning horn of a vehicle coming toward us. Finally, we reached Jammu and were told that the train leaving for Delhi from the neighboring town was our only possibility of getting back in time. Jack grabbed our bags and off we went on a wildly overcrowded bus. But the bus broke down in the middle of the countryside, and Jack said we'd better try to hitchhike. Mule carts and donkey carts went by, as did an occasional camel, a rare elephant, bicycles, pedicabs, and overloaded trucks.

Finally, a well-off young Indian in a fancy car stopped to ask what on earth we were doing. He was undone with laughter (and delight) at our predicament, and invited us into his car. But he absolutely refused to hurry. We told him our train's hour of departure, but because his car was new, he refused to drive it above the recommended thirty miles per hour. When we finally arrived at the station, the train was visible, but its steam was up and we feared it would pull out. While Jack raced into the station building to buy tickets, I ran out onto the platform waving my arms and asking for the first-class car. Fortunately, that day, there was a paucity of first-class passengers, and the conductor signaled to the engineer to wait for Jack and our bags to appear. Even Jack with his enjoyment of split-second departures agreed that this occasion had carried it too far. Exhausted and feeling ill, I went to the bathroom connected to our stateroom. On top of the toilet cover was a large human turd. The porter was summoned and was equally appalled. In an embarrassed way, he explained that it might be a form of economic protest by some low-caste cleaning person who hated the often arrogant people who could afford to travel first class. He cleaned it up and our train arrived in Delhi just in time for us to dress for the reception.

Shortly before we were scheduled to leave India, the State Department cabled that it was now safe to go to Iran. By then, Mossadegh was back in power and relative peace had been reestablished (a peace that did not last long: Mossadegh was soon ousted again and jailed for treason). In and near Tehran, we visited schools and clinics, and then flew to Isfahan where the mosques are among the most beautiful in the world. In a nearby village, we sat one evening on the ground with a large group of farmer families to watch a Point Four movie about washing hands before preparing or eating food. But the concept of germs was so foreign to the villagers that they shouted with laughter at the magnified photos of a microbe. How could such a weird cockroach-like creature be on their hands without their knowing it?

Our Iranian escort, Ardeshir Zahedi, a young American-educated assistant in the Point Four office, drove us around. Years later, this tall, handsome youth, son of the prominent general who replaced Mossadegh as prime minister, married the shah's daughter and was appointed ambassador to Washington, and then foreign minister. In

Jack and I (on the right), with Ardeshir Zahedi (next to Jack). Our relationship with the prominent Iranian diplomat began in the early 1950s, when Jack was the acting director of the Point Four program and Zahedi was an assistant in Tehran's Point Four office. While serving as U.S. ambassador to Iran, Zahedi hosted this party in the mid-1970s in honor of William and Betty Fulbright (far left).

Tehran, he gave a black-tie dinner for us at his father's mansion—very elegant but with no chairs at the table. You stood in front of your place at which six plates had been piled. After each course, that plate was removed. I, at 5' 9" inches, had as my dinner partner Minister of State Ali, at 5' 2". I spoke no Persian; he spoke no English. French was not his language either, but finally we got to German and ended up having some substantive exchanges and several laughs. He was hopeful about the future of his country under the shah's new program of settling poor farmers on former government land. The next day, at the airport, Ardeshir presented us with a large tin of caviar. Because the temperature was over ninety degrees, we figured we'd better eat it during our plane trip, which we did, with soup spoons.

After Iran, we spent a few days in Saudi Arabia. Jidda, a bustling port city, is the equivalent of New York, while Riyadh, the quiet tree-lined capital, is the equivalent of Washington. I visited a brand-new hospital there that the royal family had built for their use and staffed with foreign doctors. The contrast between its state-of-the-art facilities and the medieval Bedouins on their donkeys passing by the hospital's entrance was an eye-opener.

When Jack and I met with various Saudi high officials, I was amazed at how Western they seemed. I had expected a more chauvinistic attitude on their part, but they appeared no more condescending than many American males could be. When I mentioned how frustrated the wives of Americans stationed there were because of the law against women drivers, they nodded and said that they hoped this law would soon be amended. This, however, had not happened by the end of the century, some fifty years later.

Finally, we went back to Beirut, which had been our entry to the Arab world. When we had first arrived there, I was impressed by how relatively Arabian the city seemed; now I was impressed by how relatively European it was.

Since no Arab country permitted its planes to go to Israel, Jack and I flew on to Cyprus to get to Israel. In addition to Jack's and my single fat diplomatic passport with all its Middle East and Asia visas, we also carried a skinny passport with just an Israeli visa because if that had been included in our fat one, the Arab countries would not have admitted us.

In Israel, we stayed for a few days in Ramat Aviv. Nearby Tel Aviv was a noisy modern city with lovely beaches on which hundreds of plump ladies, mostly in black bathing suits "took the sun" and splashed about in the warm water. We visited Ashdod and Ashkelon where Point Four projects were progressing, and also saw an "Absorption Center," which was readying newly arrived, mostly poverty-stricken, refugees from Eastern Europe and North Africa for life in Israel by teaching them Hebrew and a few simple skills. (In Ashkelon, there is now a retirement home named Beit Bingham that Jack dedicated.)

Then on to Jerusalem. The late afternoon drive, first through the lush orange groves at sea level and then up into the desert-like, mountainous terrain where the extraordinary clarity of sky recalled for me the words of the Bible, "I will lift up mine eyes unto the hills; whence cometh my help? My help cometh from the Lord." Maybe it was the dry air (Jerusalem is two thousand feet above sea level), but I had tears in my eyes. It may have been the most powerful part of the trip for me.

The next day Jack and I were granted a fact-filled private meeting with Minister of Finance Levi Eshkol. Because several American ships bearing desperately needed grain had recently arrived in Haifa's harbor, we received official Israeli gratitude to the United States. Eshkol had even been briefed on my connection to the Herbert Lehmans. When Eshkol heard that our schedule included no time for sight-seeing, he ordered his assistant to take us on a tour the next day, the Sabbath, when all government offices would be closed anyway.

Saturday morning our alarm clock woke us at six a.m. I suggested to Jack that we eat a hearty breakfast, for heaven knew when—or where—we would get any lunch. Still sleepy, I asked the waiter for bacon and eggs. He almost hit me. "Vee haff no bacon in Issroyyel." I blushed. How could I have forgotten that pork is forbidden, not only to Jews but to Muslims as well? Jack had trouble hiding his amusement, and we made do with plenty of cheese and olives, fruit, and unleavened bread.

Eshkol's young assistant arrived at 6:30. He was good-looking, with tousled hair and blue eyes, and spoke excellent English. He had been brought up in Vienna. His name was Teddy Kollek and he was one of the worst drivers I have ever known. When a cross-roads appeared in the landscape ahead of us, he would speed up.

Near Lake Tiberias (the Sea of Galilee), Teddy entered a small inn and emerged with the keys to a large, shabby powerboat owned by the kibbutz at the other side of the lake. During the 1948 war, his job had been to help defend that kibbutz from the Syrians on the Golan Heights—who kept lobbing shells down onto it or attempting invasion. Halfway across the lake in the blazing sun, he suddenly asked if we would like to stop for a swim. Having been forewarned to wear bathing suits under our clothes, we agreed. All three of us dove into the Sea of Galilee. The problem was that when time came to get back into the boat, there was only a rope with which to pull ourselves back aboard. Jack and Teddy managed it easily, but I couldn't. Every time I grasped the rope and tried to climb, Teddy would say something that made me laugh and I'd land back into the water. He finally threatened that if I didn't hurry and come aboard, he was going to continue the journey and leave me there. Jack dove back into the lake and pushed me from below while Teddy shut up long enough for me to stop laughing and be hauled up onto the deck.

Shortly before we arrived back in Ramat Aviv, Teddy mentioned that he had arranged for me to meet Dr. Chaim Sheba, chief psychiatrist of the nearby Tel Hashomer Hospital.

"Not tonight!"

"Of course, tonight. He'll be at your hotel at ten o'clock."

"You're kidding!"

"I never kid. Not about psychiatrists. Didn't you ask to see Sheba?"

"Yes, but not in the middle of the night."

"Middle? Why, the night has barely begun."

Dr. Chaim Sheba did indeed turn up at our hotel at ten p.m. He and I had an entertaining talk, a result of which was that my *Cows* pamphlet would be translated into Hebrew.

Our trip to Jerusalem was made quite special by Teddy Kollek, then assistant to the Israeli Minister of Finance Levi Eshkol. The energy Kollek exhibited showing us the sites later fueled him through his dynamic period as mayor of Jerusalem.

Teddy's energy remained prodigious all through his many decades as mayor of Jerusalem and further into his so-called retirement. He not only continued to beautify that already spectacular city but built clinics and schools and other needed facilities in the Arab sections as well as the Jewish ones. One of the many reasons he kept winning reelection was that Arabs and Jews both voted for him.

Our last stop was Paris for a much-needed three-day romantic interlude. What a relief to find that underneath our eleven-week stint as semi-diplomats, always on guard lest unintentionally we say or do something that might offend our foreign hosts, there had survived the irreverent rascal who originally attracted us to each other. Events that on the trip had caused us private chagrin or mutual reproach became the source of knee-buckling shared laughter. We slept late, walked along the Seine for miles peering at the wares of the vendors of books and art; we ate artichokes and omelettes for lunch, and three-course dinners with incomparable French vegetables plus wine. The linden trees were losing their leaves, and a pre-autumn mist sometimes embraced the Louvre, as we sat in the Tuilleries and expressed gratitude for the return of good health and the chance to revel together in the cultural and natural beauties surrounding us.

We didn't fly directly back to Washington because we had to retrieve our children from Thirlsmere. My parents were wonderful about taking in any number for any length of time, and the children reveled in being spoiled by them, their staff, and their equipment, including the newly purchased freezer from which they could extricate fruit-juice popsicles. In many ways, my parents, like many other people, turned out to be better grandparents than parents, though they did continue to play favorites among the young.

CHAPTER 8

Albany

IN 1952 THE NEW INVENTION, television, was something Jack and I were still resisting lest our children become addicted, but that autumn we ourselves succumbed to its wiles in order to keep up with the presidential campaign. To lessen television's appeal for our children, we placed the big ungainly brown machine in our laundry room where drying towels and clothing often interfered with sight lines. Jack and I were much impressed with Adlai Stevenson's eloquence, courage, and humor. At times he succeeded, we felt, in lifting American campaigning to a level approaching that of his—and our—hero, Lincoln.

But Stevenson went down in defeat. We were heartbroken. He, with characteristic grace, quoted Lincoln's comment about the boy who had badly stubbed his toe: "I'm too old to cry, but it hurts too much to smile."

In retrospect, I don't see how any person at that point could have won against the war hero Eisenhower, any more than a mere mortal could have won in the late 18th century against the war hero Washington. When I first caught sight of Ike on television, he was so beguiling a combination of the military and the grandfatherly that my stomach—and my hopes—sank. How could anyone defeat this medaled Santa Claus?

After Ike's inauguration in January 1953, Jack, like the other presidential appointees, tendered his resignation, to be picked up at the pleasure of the new administration. But before we dragged our family back to New York, Jack decided to let the children finish out the school year. He used the intervening months to write a book, *Shirtsleeve Diplomacy: Point Four in Action.* In one way it pinched me to

191

have him invade my turf of book-writing, but in another way I loved having him work at home and share my lunch hour and postprandial walks with Figaro. Also, Jack requested my editorial eye for his manuscript, just as I always needed his for mine. Thus, his book began to feel like one more joint child of ours. I was elated when the book was accepted by the John Day Company for publication. At one point, Jack and I drove up to the Pennsylvania farm where Richard Walsh, president of John Day, lived with his wife, Pearl Buck. She was plump and must once have been very attractive. Now, her hair was skinned straight back in an old-fashioned bun and she wore no make-up. I was awed by the natural way she spoke about her constant problem of fitting in time for her work between the needs of the Chinese and half-Chinese orphans she had adopted. Here she was, a Nobel winner in literature, speaking as if she and I, as writers, were on an equal plane.

Come the end of the school year, our family had to make the move. The children were even more upset—and rebellious—than usual at being wrenched away from their friends. Nor did I blame them. But Jack's yearning for elective politics was unabated and therefore he—and we—had to get back to where people had the vote.

As a small consolation, Jack arranged for the children to accompany him and me to the White House when he went to pay his courtesy farewell call on his former boss, President Truman. After a short wait, we were ushered into the Oval Office. The president was seated at the big desk in front of the window. He rose and gravely shook hands with each of us. Then abruptly, like a duck upending for a nibble, his upper body disappeared from view as he foraged in a bottom desk drawer. From it, he extricated four mechanical pencils, each covered with tiny photos of the White House, which he presented to the children. These mitigated, but only to a small extent, their woes connected with moving. It was then that I decided that moving is the one human endeavor that gets *harder* with practice!

For myself, when my nest gets disturbed, I sink into insomnia and facile irritability. Jack, on the other hand, having moved so often as a child, rather enjoyed the novelty. He and I decided that we didn't want to go back to Scarborough because his commute was too lengthy, but we had no idea where we should settle.

Meanwhile, my mother, in the course of reading the obituary page of the *New York Times*, came across the death of an acquaintance who lived in the tree-filled section of the Bronx along the Hudson called Riverdale. She promptly made a condolence phone call to the widow. In the course of it, the widow mentioned that she did not wish to stay on alone in her large house. My mother asked if, in due time, the Binghams could look at it. The widow liked the idea of a young couple with children moving in, and said yes. Jack and I flew up from Washington and immediately bought her utilitarian big stucco house with three Norwegian maples lining its front lawn and space enough for the children to play a modified form of soccer and baseball.

Next door to our new house was a Chinese family with twelve children. Beyond them was an Indonesian family with eleven children. For reasons we could never fathom, those two families were not on speaking terms, but both were welcoming to us.

Once again, Jack and I were faced with the public/private school dilemma, and once again we decided in favor of the private sector. All four of our children were accepted at the Riverdale Country School, which was within walking distance.

A few times a year throughout our lives, Jack and I would sneak off for a weekend alone together. The children objected, but we rationalized that maintaining our marriage in good order was the best thing we could do for them, as well as, of course, ourselves. One such weekend was in June 1954, at Sky Top, a golfing resort in Pennsylvania's Pocono Mountains. At midday, Jack and I, sweaty and hungry, trudged in off the golf course. In the pro shop, the television, to our surprise, was not showing a golf tournament but, rather, the Army-McCarthy hearings in Congress. As we entered, we could see and hear the formal, dignified Massachusetts attorney, Joseph N. Welch, in icy tones, interrogating a snarling Senator McCarthy: "Have you no sense of decency, sir?"

A few days later, Welch gave McCarthy's reputation a further downward shove: "Until this moment, senator," he said, "I think I had never gauged your cruelty or your recklessness."

Thanks to the combination of the free media and the basic decency of American voters, this dangerous demagogue was finally silenced. Jack and I felt an almost physical pleasure in his precipitous downfall. On the other hand, we also felt a mild embarrassment at his official censure by the Senate because his immediate predecessor in thus being dishonored had been Jack's father. Not that Senator Hiram Bingham had ever been a comparable danger to the republic. His censure, in October 1929, had resulted from his inviting a lobbyist for the Connecticut Manufacturers Association to sit in on Finance Committee meetings concerned with tariffs. Because some of Senator Bingham's colleagues considered this action improper, a motion for censure was introduced. A simple apology would have taken care of the problem, but Hiram was too stiff-necked to admit he might have been wrong. He ended up being censured—and, in the next election, presumably partly on that account, he lost. Ironically, during the two decades between his censure and McCarthy's, the admission of lobbyists to that kind of committee meeting became somewhat routine.

In Riverdale, our view of the Hudson was very limited, but every day I walked Figaro on the 28-acre estate across the street—which did offer panoramic views of it. The owner was Mrs. George Perkins, Sr., then in her late eighties. Jack had known her son, George, Jr., in the State Department, and she and I had many a cordial teatime together. Jack swore to me that no matter what happened, he would not ask us to move again for, at the minimum, two years. Idiot that I was, I believed him and took my time in getting curtains made for our house's high windows because I was so absorbed in the writing of my first novel. It was called "The Devoted" and centered on a love story between a New London scion and a New York girl whose father was a struggling artist and whose mother was a flirt. Objections to their marriage came not only from the boy's parents but also from a charismatic middle-aged man whose influence over the hero was both puzzling and upsetting to the heroine. In time, the reader discovered this man to be a Communist — and the hero was forced to choose between his mentor and his girl.

One day, Jack came into my study where I was typing with tears running down my cheeks.

"What's the matter?"

"Josiah died."

"Who?"

"You know. Josiah Starbuck, Peter's grandfather."

"Oh, you mean, in the book?"

"Yes."

"I'm so sorry."

But then we had to smile.

By that time, I was getting used to having my invented characters yell at me in my sleep, things like, "I never would have said such a thing," or "I'd surely have done the opposite." This aural invasion still continues for me from the characters in my plays, and I have never figured just where the line is between this kind of artistic endeavor and the "voices" that schizophrenics report hearing.

So intense was my concentration at the typewriter that the children began complaining that when they returned from school and came to the door of my study, I would look up as if I had never seen them before. I, therefore, stopped work half an hour before they were scheduled to arrive in order to return the "real" world. At a dinner given by David and Peggy Rockefeller, I met a Pocantico neighbor of theirs, Diarmuid Russell. He was a well-known New York literary agent, an Irish American whose father was the poet, A. E. I sent Diarmuid an outline of my novel and he agreed to take it on. He was also the agent for Eudora Welty, and I was enchanted when I met her in his office and got a chance to discuss with her some problems of novel writing. She was tall and plain, with a kindly, humorous expression. From then on, it surprised me to find in her fiction so many weird and sinister characters whom she vividly brought to life. Where would this ladylike person have ever met their counterparts in reality? Or were they truly just the products of her extraordinary imagination?

My novel's subject, the Communist scare of the early-1950s, was timely, but its completion kept being delayed by the duties of wife and mother and the obligations of being a daughter. My mother could not restrain herself enough to honor my writing time in the morning and kept phoning. She also kept pressing me to come into town to have lunch with her. If I did not truncate my workday to have lunch with her fairly often, I would receive a frantic phone call from my father complaining that she was making his life miserable, so would I please, for his sake, get into town and meet with her? My book had no deadline, so I felt I couldn't use time constraints as an excuse for not meeting her. When finally Diarmuid began peddling the completed manuscript, it received nice comments from publishers but no acceptance. With McCarthy's career in shreds, the subject of domestic Communism was receding from public interest.

I wrote some short stories, which Diarmuid also liked well enough to peddle, but they, too, did not sell. Perhaps, I began to think, I should turn to some other form of writing. Harold Strauss at Knopf was strongly recommending that I find the subject for another nonfiction book, but I'd had my fill of psychiatry for the time being. Also, I was more interested in individuals than in categories of people. Somewhere around that time the idea of writing a biography began to tickle at the edges of my consciousness. But who on earth would be worthy of such a huge investment of time and energy?

Albany

Jack and I had established a pleasant joint tradition with Arthur and Marian Schlesinger. Every November, when what we called the Yale-Harvard game, and they called the Harvard-Yale game, was played in Cambridge, Massachusetts, we would drive up and stay with them for Saturday night and Sunday lunch; if the game was held in New Haven, the Schlesingers would come back to Riverdale with us afterward. In 1953, I asked them for a short list of people they would like us to invite for Sunday lunch. The list was dazzling: Reinhold and Ursula Niebuhr, Robert Lowell and Elizabeth Hardwick, Jimmy and Nancy Wechsler.

After lunch, we wandered into the living room. I approached Reinhold and asked if I could join the line of people hoping to write his biography some day. His blue eyes opened wide in surprise.

"No one is lined up."

"Are you planning to write it yourself?"

"Never! Autobiographies are dishonest. They start with a conscious attempt at humility, but nothing can hide the fact that you think it worthwhile to tell your own little story."

"So I could try my hand . . ."

"Why would you want to?"

"Because you say such riveting things."

He smiled. "But people can read those in my books."

"Some laypeople don't understand your religious references."

"There aren't that many . . ."

"Besides, they want to know about your life."

"That part could be reduced to one page."

"What I propose is a sort of introduction to your life and thought. That way more people would read your books."

"My secretary's name is Mrs. Nola Meade. You could phone her at Union Theological Seminary and ask her to set up a time for us to talk about it."

Thus began for me a weekly series of one-hour interviews at Niebuhr's office on the fourth floor of Union Theological Seminary. His door was always open and occasionally a student or faculty member would drift in with a question. I would then busy myself with Reinie's files while listening to how he focused on whatever minutia the visitor had brought to his attention. At the same time, I could see that he had a low threshold for boredom, and woe unto any visitor who repeated himself or spelled out something that Niebuhr could have assumed.

His files were a disaster. Not one sermon had been written out. Only a few scribbled notes remained that even he, when I showed them to him, failed sometimes to decipher. And most of the letters from major figures in the past had been airmailed by him into the waste basket. After he left for the day, I would scrounge in the garbage for letters of interest or at least those with a worthwhile autograph (these papers, along with Reinie's letters to me, I later deposited in the Library of Congress).

Before each session, I would prepare a short list of questions. Some were triggered by his books and articles; others stemmed from events earlier in his life. Usually he answered the questions frankly and quickly—but not always. One time I asked whether, if he could live his life over, he would again be a theologian. He answered that first of all he was not a theologian because there was nothing "systematic" about his thought, and second, the question was cruel. Other times he deliberately withheld information I obviously needed. When I told him I was planning to fly to Chicago to interview his mother, Lydia, and his sister, Hulda, who lived there together at McCormick Theological Seminary, Reinie made no mention of the fact that his closest friend, William Scarlett, Episcopal bishop of Missouri, lived in nearby St. Louis. That information I had to pick up from Reinie's mother who, like me, was shocked that Reinie had been so inconsiderate as not to inform me in time for me to combine both interviews on the same trip.

When I returned to New York and confronted Niebuhr with his silence about the bishop, he shrugged: "You didn't ask about him."

Driving home on the Henry Hudson Parkway that afternoon, I was still so furious that I shot right past my exit.

Flying to St. Louis to interview the bishop was unnerving. I had never so much as laid eyes on a bishop, let alone talked to one in private. William Scarlett's baldish head had a tonsure like a medieval monk's, but his brown eyes twinkled. When I asked whether he was related to Robin Hood's friend, Will Scarlett, he raised his brows in mock disapproval: "How could I be? That Will Scarlett never married."

At the sight of my discomfiture, he laughed and after a split second, so did I. My scheduled hour with him extended to two—and beyond. An underling appeared to remind the bishop that the noon Lenten service at the cathedral was about to begin. After the fellow left, the bishop asked if I'd like to go. I swallowed hard and shook my head. "Let's play hooky," he said, and we did.

Jack soon became as enthusiastic about Will as I was, and Will became far closer to our children than Reinie ever did. Indeed, so much did they grow to love "Bishop Will" that in time the older three asked him to perform their weddings, which he did. Every summer Jack and I took the children for a week to Castine, Maine, where Will and his wife, Leah, had a house on Dyce's Head with ocean views on three sides.

Jack's and my relationship with Reinie's wife, Ursula, developed an entirely different set of problems. Beautiful, brilliant, and highly articulate, she taught religion at Barnard. But suddenly, for no reason she would explain, she announced that I should give up working on my book. One evening, she telephoned this decision to Jack, who had become her lawyer—just as my brother, Dick Rossbach, had become her broker. Ursula asked Jack to prevail on me to forget the whole project. Jack gently told her this was unlikely. Did she want to talk to me about it? No, she did not.

When I nervously appeared the following week for my regular hour at Union Theological Seminary, I asked Reinie what *he* wanted me to do. He sighed and said he didn't fully understand what lay behind Ursula's request except that she might want to write a book about him herself some day. I said that would be marvelous, that she could write what no one else could, but that my project—to get across Reinie's ideas to the lay world—would not be competitive with hers. I, therefore, continued my interviews with him and also his friends, colleagues, and a few enemies. It was now clear that I could never interview Ursula, but the Niebuhrs and we continued to see each other socially and even arranged to mate our Figaro with their female black poodle who was named Winnie in honor of Winston Churchill.

When the vet decided that Winnie was ripe, Jack and I drove Figaro to Union Theological Seminary on a Sunday afternoon. The instant we entered the Niebuhrs' apartment, Figaro had only one thing in mind. It was in their living room that the mating took place, right around the coffee table. Throughout the procedure, Reinie, extra pink in the cheek, kept up a rapid-fire conversation with Jack about politics. After "mission accomplished," the dogs remained joined at their nether ends for quite some time. Ursula and I ended up on the floor, she patting Winnie's head and consoling her, and I patting Figgy's head and congratulating him. Finally, the dogs separated themselves, and Jack and I took Figaro home. After the appropriate interval, the puppies were born at the Niebuhrs' summer place in Stockbridge, Massachusetts. We drove up there to take our pick. The male we chose turned out to have the world's lowest IQ for a poodle. We named him Randolph (after the son of Winston Churchill). Figaro was far from pleased to have a rival in the house, and as soon as Randolph was big enough to keep up, Figaro would beguile him forth and then manage to lose him. I would receive phone calls from local bars asking me please to come retrieve Randy, and once a man phoned from the Broadway subway, several miles away: "Hey, Lady, your dog is about to take the train to Brooklyn." The children adored him, especially

Claudia, who was happy to have someone younger than herself and the last to learn things.

Ursula remained edgy. One of her friends suggested to me that perhaps a tad of jealousy might be at work. My own suspicion was that she feared that my interviews tired him out. Yet the interviews seemed to stimulate him. Seminary students tend to be reverential and I was not. He wasn't accustomed to being asked questions like, "What's so great about Jesus anyway?" or "Why should anyone give a rap about eschatology (or ontology or epistemology or hermeneutics)?" He laughed out loud when I told him that one of our mutual friends, a liberal agnostic, had told me that Reinie was putting up the religious front he did solely to make his secular ideas more palatable to conservatives.

A major quality that had attracted Jack as well as me to both Niebuhrs was their unabashed Semitophilia. On occasion, I would have to remind Reinie that Jews are not always wonderful. We also chuckled together about the well-known, brief summation:

How odd of God/To choose the Jews.

In his course on Christian Ethics that I audited, Reinie pointed out how quintessentially Jewish Jesus had been—and Ursula in her Barnard classes often invited their friend, Will Herberg, a former Communist who had ended up teaching Old Testament at Drew University, to address her students. When Will's former loyalty to the Soviet Union had been undermined by Stalin's betrayals, he had frantically searched for a substitute form of faith:

"Reinie, I may have to become a Christian."

"Fine, Will, but why not a Jew?"

Will Herberg took Reinie's suggestion. He and his wife engaged in serious study and became devout Conservative Jews. The only time I ever attended a Conservative service was with them.

Reinie believed that religious people are so constituted as to need, in addition to their vertical relationship to God, a horizontal relationship to a group of fellow believers. Had I therefore ever considered joining a church?

Well, yes and no. I didn't ever want to be baptized because baptism had been forced on Jews by ruthless Christians over the ages, but if I didn't have to undergo that ritual, I would consider joining the Congregational Church. This "low" denomination, as it happened, had recently affiliated itself with the one in which Niebuhr had grown up, the Evangelical and Reformed. I told Reinie about our clarinetist friend Dick Beebe who had assured me that the only prerequisite for my joining would be a spoken agreement to try to pattern my life on the values espoused by Jesus. As for belief in an afterlife, Dick Beebe fully agreed with Niebuhr's statement that it is "futile to conjecture about the furniture of heaven or the temperature of hell." The next time new members would be admitted to Dick Beebe's Briarcliff Congregational Church was the following week, on Maundy Thursday, three days before Easter.

I talked to Jack, who said it was entirely up to me but since we'd had our children confirmed, it might be nice for them to feel that their mother was officially part of the same team. I talked to my parents who had only one question: "Do you have to be baptized?" When they heard there was no need, as my father described it, for me to be "gedunked," they had no objection.

Early Maundy Thursday afternoon, I had an interview with Reinie. Afterward, I got in my car to drive further downtown. Union Theological Seminary's elegant, aristocratic president was standing on the street corner, trying to flag a taxi. I offered him a lift and we had a fine talk until we emerged from Central Park just north of the Metropolitan Museum. He looked at the people crowding Fifth Avenue. "Wouldn't New York be wonderful if there weren't so many Jews?"

I stopped the car. "I am Jewish."

"No!"

"Yes."

He then mouthed all the clichés—"But you don't look . . . of course some of my best friends . . . " and so forth—by the time I dropped him at his destination.

I did not drive further but turned the car around and drove right back to the seminary. Reinie was still in his office when I steamed in:

"You can keep your blasted Christian Church."

He blinked. "Now what?"

When I finished telling him what had happened, he put his head down in his big hands. After a while he looked up, with those piercing blue eyes. "I wouldn't blame you one bit," he said, "if you refused to go to the service this evening. All I can say is that you have my humblest apology for the totally unacceptable behavior of a fellow Christian. We are all flawed vessels, but that doesn't mean that the message we convey isn't worth listening to, either alone or as part of a congregation."

If I hadn't been so devoted to him, I would never have gone to the service that evening. But I did go, and when the moment of joining the church came, I stood up and went forward as one of the new members. When I sat back down again next to Jack, I looked at my hands. They were lying on my lap, palms up, in an unprecedented state of total peace.

At the reception after the service, one of author John Hersey's older brothers came up to me and said:

"I thought you were Jewish."

"I am."

"Then how come you're joining our church?"

"I guess because there are all kinds of Jews, Jewish Jews and agnostic Jews and Christian Jews. I want to belong *some*where— and this church has made me feel at home. You can call me a Jewish Christian or a Christian Jew . . . "

"Do you care which?"

"Not the least."

He nodded, shrugged, and we toasted each other with grape juice. Decades later, on a visit to Moscow, Jack and I decided to elude our official U.S. embassy escorts and sneak off with a journalist friend, Alfred Friendly, Jr., to visit some of the heroic Russian Jewish refuseniks. These men and women, whether religious or secular, were subjected to severe and unremitting harassment by the Soviet authorities, including, for some of them, decades of imprisonment. They nonetheless continued to appeal to the Soviet government for exit visas to Israel and elsewhere, both for themselves and other Jews. The group we met with at the apartment of Alexander Lerner happened not to be religious. (At that time, Natan Sharanski, a devout Jew, was still in prison.) After several speeches by these heroic people (one of whom came there directly from the dread Lubyanka prison, where he had been interrogated for the nth time), the group broke into separate conversations. Judith Lerner asked me about Jack's and my backgrounds. I told her he was Protestant and I was Jewish and I was feeling bad for having, at least to the outward eye, left the Jewish fold. She patted my hand. "We always need a Queen Esther—and I'm sure you have been and will continue to be of help to us."

Another day in Moscow, Jack and I were taken by Al Friendly to the apartment of Andrei Sakharov. This white-haired, handsome Nobel-winning scientist had not been allowed out of the country to receive his prize because he had publicly objected to the Soviet dictatorship. What worried him far more than this missed occasion was the fact that his wife, Elena Bonner, who was Jewish, was not being allowed out of the country to receive treatment in Italy for the glaucoma that was gradually blinding her. The official Russian response to her request for a temporary exit visa was that she could only go to Italy if she was visiting a relative.

"Why don't I give her one of mine?" I asked. "I've got cousins in Italy."

"No," said Sakharov. "The authorities would never permit it."

"Why not try?" said Elena. "What do we have to lose?"

As soon as Jack and I left Russia, I wrote to one of my Italian cousins and asked if she would write a "Dear Cousin" letter to Elena Bonner, inviting her for a visit. Although this cousin was a doctor and knew how desperate Elena's need for treatment was, she declined. Her brother was in the Italian diplomatic service, and she did not want to do anything that might interfere with his rise (ultimately, like his father and uncle, he did become a successful Italian ambassador).

Back in Washington, I happened to tell this story to Jimmy and Ellen Loeb whose daughter Suzy, a sculptor, was married to an Italian. Jimmy, an agnostic Jew who claimed that "Reinie is my rabbi," immediately volunteered his daughter to be Elena's "cousin." After a number of letters back and forth, Elena's visit to Italy was arranged. The medical treatment was successful, and the by-product was that she and Suzy became friends.

Jimmy Loeb served for many years as top executive of Americans for Democratic Action (ADA). Tall, stooped, with blue eyes and a gentle manner, he could also be immoveable on matters of principle. His wife, Ellen, was a violinist with whom Jack enjoyed playing duets.

The four of us felt that one of the many bonanzas provided by ADA was the chance to make friends with people remote from one's usual circle. I had been brought up by parents prejudiced against blacks and had some serious internal homework to do. Subsequently, a high point in my life was when Jack and I were walking on either side of the labor union leader George Weaver, who was handsome, tall, sexy, and funny. Something I said caused George to lay an approving hand briefly on my shoulder. For me this was proof that I was at last inwardly clean, and I think he knew I wouldn't flinch at his touch. I gave him a smile and kept walking. Later he became assistant secretary of labor, and we continued seeing him and his wife, Mary, socially in Washington.

In 1954, New York state provided a dramatic battle in the primary for governor. One contender was the distinguished elder statesman William Averell Harriman, newly returned from Europe where he had headed the Marshall Plan; the other was Congressman Franklin Roosevelt, Jr., who had been at Groton a year behind Jack; he looked and sounded so much like his father that he gave voters goosebumps. Jack went to work for Roosevelt.

The State Democratic Convention was held at the 165th Infantry Armory in Manhattan. After the nominating speeches, Jack and I waved banners for FDR, Jr., and shouted ourselves hoarse, but what we did not know was that the decision on the candidate was being made in a back room by the boss of Tammany Hall, Carmine De Sapio, together with the boss of the Bronx, Charles Buckley, and a few other Democratic leaders. Franklin had told us he had been assured, or *thought* he had been assured, of De Sapio's support, but in the course of that tumultuous night, the delegates controlled by De Sapio and Buckley followed their bosses' orders and voted for Harriman. Harriman's autobiography, written with Rudy Abrahamson half a century later, adds to the story:

> When the stacked conclave opened . . . , it would
> have appeared to the uninitiated that Roosevelt
> owned it. His partisans drowned out Harriman sup-
> porters among the two thousand delegates and alter-
> nates on the floor . . . a brass band and a sea of
> streamers and banners gave the armory the air of a
> Roosevelt rally, as his managers launched a last-ditch
> attempt to stampede the convention. The show of force
> produced fistfights with Harriman supporters. . . .
> Raiders from each side stole the other's placards.
> Power to the elevators was shut off several times; the

public address system went dead; and the floor swarmed with boozy, argumentative Democrats . . .

At 1:10 in the morning, Harriman was voted the candidate, and we returned home angered and feeling betrayed. Although both candidates were "gentlemen," the battle had been far from gentlemanly. Did De Sapio lie to Franklin, or did Franklin merely hear what he wanted to hear when De Sapio told him, in effect, what a fine fellow he was and how lucky the state would be to have him as its governor? (Much later I was told by an intimate of Franklin's that Franklin later became convinced that the Kennedys had been involved in denying him the nomination.)

During the next four years, Jack and I ran into Carmine De Sapio at political functions and had to admit we were drawn to him. He was central casting's choice for the role of sinister politician, with his ever-present dark glasses (he suffered from iritis, a painful eye inflammation), shiny suits, slicked back dark hair, and tough way of talking with minimal motion of his lips. ("Howsdafam'bly" was his usual greeting to me.) He clearly loved his only child, Geraldine, and was enthusiastic in his reports on her doings. He also appeared to have respect for Jack. At that time, we became further acquainted with Carmine's colleague, Charles Buckley, the Bronx congressman, a less engaging man than Carmine. Buckley had succeeded Ed Flynn, the attractive man chosen by President Franklin Roosevelt. Flynn's son, Dick, with wife, Betsy, became not only our personal friends but also worked in all of Jack's campaigns. Later, Dick was one of the partners in the law firm, Pryor, Cashman, Sherman and Flynn, where Jack was "of counsel."

Jack's very first contact with Carmine had come a few years earlier when Jack vied for the Democratic designation for Congress against the incumbent, Vito Marcantonio, in the old Silk Stocking District of Manhattan. To fulfill the requirement of living within the district, we rented a small apartment way east on 96th Street. It had thin walls (we could hear everything going on in the neighboring rooms) and an ever-present smell of cabbage and onion in the halls. De Sapio advised Jack to try to win the support of the Democratic leader of that area, Johnny Merli. After a few visits from Jack to Merli's office at the edge of East Harlem, Merli asked to meet "da Missus." Jack took me there one night. During our easy three-way conversation, Merli decided to underline the seriousness of the point he was making by reaching into his desk drawer and hauling out a pistol. I was agog. Here were Jack and I, from our insulated backgrounds, finally out in the real world.

Tammany Hall, headed by De Sapio, included Jack on its list of five nominees offered to the Republican Party. The plan was for the two parties to agree on a fusion ticket against the American Labor Party's popular incumbent, Vito Marcantonio. Jack was the most liberal of the Democrats' five; Peter Hoguet, a nice contemporary whom we knew slightly, was the most conservative. The Republicans, not surprisingly, chose Peter, who, in the election, went on to be swamped by Marcantonio. I was relieved that Jack was no longer involved because the last thing I wanted was to have to move the family to Washington—or anywhere else—again.

Little did I know. The morning after Averell Harriman's victory at the 1954 convention, he phoned Frank Roosevelt to ask if he would release his former expert on state issues, Jack Bingham, to the Harriman campaign. Frank, not needing Jack's services at that point, agreed. Jack agreed to help Harriman against the Republican candidate, Senator Irving Ives. The election ended up unbelievably close, with Harriman winning with a margin of less than twelve thousand votes out of five million. Shortly thereafter, he asked Jack to be one of his two chief policy advisers, secretary to the governor (the other being counsel to the governor). "Dad," one of our children asked only half in fun, "do you have to sit at the edge of the governor's desk and take dictation?"

This offer resulted in the second worst fight Jack and I ever had (the first having been the night we met). Jack yearned to accept Harriman's offer because it was a step up the political ladder. I approved of his climbing that ladder but not in a way that would completely discombobulate the rest of us. I reminded him of his promise that we wouldn't have to move for a minimum of two years, and this was only a year and a half. Nor was it all that long since the children had adjusted to the Riverdale School, and Reinhold to my weekly interview. The sacrifice Jack was asking of us was simply too great.

He therefore offered to commute from Riverdale to Albany every week. It wasn't yet clear how much time the governor wanted to spend there, anyway. Perhaps the Harrimans would only want to live in the executive mansion during the legislative session, which lasted from January to around May, and would spend the rest of the year in the city.

We gave the commuting a good try, with Jack leaving Riverdale at dawn on Mondays and returning for a truncated weekend on Saturday afternoons. But he and I were thoroughly miserable. Being separated had always been hard, and it was even worse now. Even Reinie, who didn't always study his interlocutors with great care, could see that something was wrong.

"How does Jack like his job?"

"Okay, but that damn governor has decided to move to Albany full-time."

"What will Jack do?"

"Who knows. He's in love with the Bitch Goddess Success. So I'll just stay in New York and kick up my heels."

"No!"

"Why not?"

I was geared up to do battle against any biblical edict Reinie could throw at me, but I was stunned by his answer: "Because I don't want you to."

After a moment, I said, "But if I were to move to Albany, what about your and my meetings?"

"Write me your questions once a week and I'll answer them."

He had a point. A move to Albany looked closer.

Jack, meanwhile, had been given the grand total of two Albany jobs to employ people for. One was assistant for whom he chose a brilliant but somewhat wild young man from the Harriman campaign, Daniel Patrick Moynihan. The other was secretary, and he chose a bright young woman, also from the campaign, Elizabeth Brennan. After a few months in Albany, Pat and Liz Moynihan came to Jack with a silver dish engraved "To JBB without whom . . . " And they went on to have a lengthy marriage rich in diplomacy and politics.

As for ourselves, we summoned the children to the Riverdale living room and asked them if they would prefer to move to Albany within the next few weeks at the midwinter semester break or wait till the end of the school year. To our amazement, they unanimously agreed to make the move immediately. That way, they explained, when summer vacation came around, they would have friends, something they had missed when we moved to Riverdale. (As an adult, Sherry confessed to me that she, then thirteen, had caucused with the younger three and pointed out that Mom and Dad were doing so badly under the current arrangement that the kids had better agree to make the move before something worse happened.)

The following Monday morning, Jack and I drove the three hours to Albany. By the end of the week we had bought a big brown-shingle bungalow in Loudonville, an Albany suburb. The two younger children could walk to the excellent public elementary school, and the older two could go by bus to St. Agnes, a private Episcopal school for girls. Jack, whose job entitled him to a car and driver (he accepted the car), could reach the Capitol in ten minutes. A ski resort, Alpine Meadows, was only half an hour to the north, and in summer, we would have tennis and swimming at a club five minutes away. Jack and I were troubled about the club's lack of Jewish members but not enough to deprive our children of summer sport with their friends. Someone had to break the club's taboo, so why not myself? (Actually, a half-Jewish wife of a Christian athlete was already a member.)

The day we and the children, Mademoiselle, Roberta, Yankee Poodle, and all our possessions moved into the new house, the local paper announced that the Trojans had just defeated the Albanians. Wait a minute, I blurrily said to myself, what century are we in, what continent? Finally, I remembered that Troy, New York, is just across the Hudson from Albany. But when I stepped outside the door, I had another shock. The temperature had dropped to eighteen below zero and my nose whiskers immediately froze. My mother, horrified at our move, had been warning me against chilblains. I didn't know what a chilblain was, except that in novels like *Oliver Twist* poor children suffered from them. But I reassured her that I would remain on guard. At least, I consoled her, we no longer needed to worry about polio.

The previous evening in Albany we had all spent the night at the Hotel Ten Eyck. Roberta, as a black Southerner, couldn't believe that she was eating dinner with us in the dining room of a hotel for whites and spent most of the time shrinking back against the banquette wall. The children tried to kid her, and Jack, Mademoiselle, and I did our best to put her at ease, but nothing could free her from her terror of being evicted. She thus provided a lesson for the children—and ourselves—about the lasting effects of prejudice on an otherwise feisty American adult.

A few nights later, Jack and I were invited to the Executive Mansion for dinner. I was not exactly afraid of Averell Harriman, but he was an imposing figure—tall, impatient and brilliant in regard to numbers. I had heard that he had driven a former top assistant, the young but now bald Jim Lanigan, crazy with phone calls at dawn, to the effect of, "What do you think about that story on page forty-five of the *Times*?" After dinner, therefore, I said privately to Harriman that I hoped he would not make Jack as bald as Lanigan by phoning him too early in the morning. Harriman looked rather startled and mumbled something I couldn't decipher. What happened next, I don't know, but somehow gossip got around, even as far away as Washington, that I had laid down conditions on the governor. Before long, Kay Graham was delightedly telling people that when Harriman had phoned too early one morning and asked to speak to Jack, June had said, "Not at the moment, governor, we're making love." Even when I assured Kay that this story was wholly apocryphal, she found it too funny to relinquish. Forty years later, in Rudy Abrahamson's biography of Harriman, I am quoted as saying one morning that he couldn't speak to Jack because he and I "were having intercourse." Since "intercourse" was a word that no one in polite society would ever have used in that era except reluctantly during a visit to a doctor, the falsity of the story is thus underlined. Even at the time, I didn't really mind because I had achieved my hoped-for purpose — no early phone calls!

I never knew whether the story got back to Marie Harriman; if so, she would have thrown back her curly head and laughed. She was an elegant and worldly lady with a round face and big blue eyes who preferred laughter to almost anything else in the world. As a result, she tried to surround herself with people who could elicit it. Notable among them were Bill Walton, the artist, who came to Albany now and then for visits, and Philip Kaiser, who was Harriman's special assistant. We, together with Phil and Hannah Kaiser, and the counsel to the governor, Daniel Gutman, and his wife Ros, and Milton and Dottie Stewart had moved to Albany and were expected by both Harrimans to act as courtiers. This necessitated our being available for social occasions, as

Jack, second from left, standing next to Marie Harriman, seated with her mother next to her, on the floor of the New York State Assembly.

well as official ones, sometimes with very little notice, and cheerfully listening more than talking. When we did speak up, we were expected to be knowledgeable (by Harriman) and amusing (by Marie). Jack and I didn't engage in flattery, but our attentiveness must have registered with the Harrimans, with the result that we were included in all social events at the mansion as well as invited to vacation with them at Sands Point, Long Island, and Hobe Sound, Florida.

Marie wore designer clothes, and her hair was meticulously dyed a rich brown. I had to dress as fashionably as I could. Being the dinner partner of Averell Harriman was not easy because one was likely to be asked to comment on some person or event in that day's foreign or domestic news. If a person agreed totally with Harriman, he could seem a bit bored, but if the person argued with him, he could seem a bit irritated. For Jack and me, the Harrimans were a challenge because their interests were so different. Marie had a connoisseur's eye for art. She had run her own picture gallery during the Depression. She also appeared to know everyone of social importance in New York and Long Island. She had formerly been married to Cornelius Vanderbilt ("Sonny") Whitney and had a son, Harry, and daughter, Nancy, by him. Averell, for his part, had an incredible memory for facts and figures.

Marie's voice was the husky one of a heavy smoker, and when she spoke in an aside, you could hear her across the room. To her the quote from Scaramouche applied: " . . . born with the gift of laughter and a sense that the world was mad."

Although Marie was closer to my mother's age than to mine, she sometimes made me feel as if I were the older of us two. Especially was this the case when her characteristic tardiness made Averell so frantic that he would send me upstairs to get her to hurry (an impossible assignment). Around her neck she wore a small heart-shaped gold locket in which, she told me, were nitroglycerin tablets against her heart pain (angina pectoris). Were she to become dizzy or faint, I was to open the locket and put one of the tablets under her tongue. This never happened, and on many occasions, particularly late at night when she was still drinking, her energy far surpassed my own.

From the beginning, Marie told me to call her by her first name, but I was stumped about what to call the governor. "Averell" or, as she called him, "Ave," seemed insufficiently respectful, yet "Guv" which Jack used, seemed too work-oriented. Finally, I settled on "Guvvie," which he, himself, appeared to like.

One afternoon, Harriman, a brilliant antagonist who used to play bridge with General Eisenhower, bid a small slam in hearts. I doubled, praying that Jack would remember that the (Lightner) double of a slam commands your partner to "lead an unusual suit, usually the first one bid by dummy." Miracle of miracles, Jack did remember, and plunked down a spade, which I was able to trump. I then cashed my sole ace, thus setting the contract. Harriman, shocked at his defeat, leaned around the corner of the table to peer at my cards, to make certain that I hadn't been hiding a spade. Flushed with victory I said, "Guvvie darling, mind your manners." The four of us laughed and went on to the next hand. At the end of play, I had actually won back the dollar that Harriman had been owing me for months, ever since the day he and I had taken a taxi together in Washington and he, as usual, did not have a penny in the pockets of his double-breasted suit.

Fortunately for me in Albany, Marie liked to sleep late, thus freeing my morning hours for writing. For the next three and a half years, I wrote questions to Reinie and he wrote back. Decades later, when time came for me to turn over all my Niebuhr papers to the Library of Congress, those letters from him were far more valuable to future scholars than any notes of interviews by me would have been.

Often in the afternoons, Marie wanted me to accompany her to a new art show or a ribbon cutting or other official duty. She jokingly referred to her title for wife of the governor as "governess," but in actuality, she took her wifely responsibilities seriously both during campaigns and his four years in office.

She told me about their courtship, even when Averell was posted in London and the Soviet Union. Once he returned to the United States, he and Marie shared their outer lives. She went along when Truman sent him to Paris to help oversee the Marshall Plan and returned home with him when he decided to explore his chances of running for governor. Marie was unswervingly loyal to Harriman, furious at his enemies, and willing to put herself out for his friends. From her own point of view, the hugger-mugger of campaigning was a source of delight, and she spent long days and evenings beguiling every manner of voter. The fact that most people appeared more at ease with her than with Averell was not lost on him—and gradually the two evolved into a political team and an emotional one.

It was Marie's choice for them to move to Albany, and she promptly revived one of the customs my Aunt Edith had followed—holding weekly teas at the mansion for different groups of local ladies. We cabinet wives were expected to be on hand every Monday afternoon during the legislative session to act as co-hostesses. One of the teas was for a Jewish organization. Its leader, a woman with gray hair and a German name, was enumerating for me the events she had chosen to forgo in order be present. My jocular answer was, "Mann kann nicht, mitt ein Tochus, auf zwei Hochzeiten tanzen" (one cannot, with one fanny, dance at two weddings). The lady nearly spilled her tea onto Marie's Aubusson carpet. When she finally stopped laughing I asked what was so funny. She explained that "Tochus" is a Yiddish slang word for behind. What my naughty father had taught me, ostensibly as a German aphorism, was actually Yiddish and vulgar besides.

When I reported my gaffe, Marie was delighted. It turned out that she had had a Jewish grandfather, although his daughter, her mother, did not care to mention what in her view was a negative social attribute. Also half-Jewish was Pete Duchin, whom Marie and Averell had brought up from early boyhood, because his mother, a close friend of

Marie's, had died and his father, Eddie, was off on gigs so much of the time. Pete addressed Marie as "Ma" and Harriman as "Ave." He was a charming, gifted teenager and a bit on the chubby side. Marie thought that the Army would be the making of him. He agreed and enlisted for a few years before becoming the famous bandleader he still is.

Many years later, when I was writing a regular column for the syndicate, *One Woman's Voice*, I recalled an instance of Marie's ability to poke fun. She and I had been swimming in the Harrimans' Georgetown pool when Averell marched down from the house in a rage at something General de Gaulle had just done. "Oh Ave," Marie called out from the water, "de Gaulle doesn't know his ass from his elbow." Guvvie erupted with laughter and I simply sank to the bottom of the pool. Years after Marie had died, Pete Duchin made mention to me of "some idiotic column that quoted Marie as saying, 'De Gaulle doesn't know his arm from his elbow.'"

"Marie would never have said 'arm.'"

"Of course not, but I could hardly put 'ass' in a syndicated column."

"You mean, you wrote that damn thing?"

Pete and I shared a laugh that Marie, we felt certain, would also have enjoyed. But by then she had died and Averell had married Pamela Churchill, whose most recent husband, Leland Hayward, had also died.

When Jack and I escorted Marie to parties, unpredictable moments were likely to occur. At a jam-packed reception Perle Mesta was giving at the Democratic Convention in Chicago in 1956, Jack and I were following Marie down a few stairs and ogling all the celebrities. Suddenly, Marie turned back toward us. "This," she announced in her very audible deep voice, "is what I call a rat-fuck." Jack and I, having never before heard the expression, went into spasms of helpless laughter.

During the previous few days, we had also been sharing with the Harrimans a few moments of wild exultation. For, as Guvvie's official

New York state plane touched down at Chicago's O'Hare Airport, a phalanx of reporters and photographers converged on the stairway leading down from the plane.

"Governor Harriman, Governor Harriman, what do you think about President Truman's endorsement?"

"What endorsement?"

"For you! For president!"

While our plane had been in the air, Truman had publicly expressed his preference for Harriman over the other candidates, namely, Adlai Stevenson, Senator Estes Kefauver of Tennessee, and the young, not yet well known, Senator John F. Kennedy of Massachusetts. For the next forty-eight hours, all of us on the Harriman team found ourselves quite capable of imagining that we might end up in the White House.

The next day, Jack and I were invited by his former Groton and Yale classmate, journalist Stewart Alsop, to join him and his wife, Tish, for lunch. The only other guests were the John F. Kennedys. Jackie was hugely pregnant and Jack was the best listener I had ever met. The moment he learned that I knew something about mental health, he vacuum-cleaned my mind, while at the same time managing to exude charm. A few weeks after the convention, Jackie lost that baby—JFK was on the Mediterranean at the time—and I immediately wrote her a condolence letter—what on earth is worse than losing a child! I received back a note in girlish handwriting, signed, "Love, Jackie."

But Truman's endorsement of Harriman didn't have as great an impact as he—and Harriman— expected. Seeing this, Averell pulled out and threw his support to Adlai, whom Jack and I admired far more than Averell did (being a courtier also involved keeping some of our opinions strictly to ourselves).

Back in Albany, Jack enjoyed his work, although the Guv at times was a difficult and demanding boss. Yet the Guv also loved to ski, and on winter weekends he sometimes included our children and us on trips to Whiteface Mountain, whose ski center he had helped to found. On its opening day, Averell chose to go up on the chairlift's first official run. But the lift promptly got stuck. For almost an hour no one could make it move again because all the engineers had gone on its maiden voyage with the governor. So there Averell swung in the bitter wind, one hundred feet removed from New York state. Because the lieutenant governor, George deLuca, was basking in the Florida sun, Jack, as secretary to the governor, became the de facto governor until Averell, blue-lipped and flashing-eyed, was back on terra firma.

Skiing with our children had its high points and its low. A high point for me was the day I swooped in from the slopes earlier than the others and stood on the deck of the Alpine Meadows ski lodge with my father, who was visiting for the weekend. I could point out to him where Jack was traversing, followed in order of height by his four children. A really low point for me was at Bromley Mountain, Vermont, in a blizzard. Our daughter Micki was riding the J-bar when the point of one ski got caught in a drift, and she was spilled, screaming, onto the slope (no safety bindings in those days). I raced to reach her and just reached her side when a down-hill headed J-bar clonked me on the head. So there the two of us lay in the deep snow until Jack arrived with the ski patrol and a lit-ter onto which Micki was laid; her ankle turned out to have been broken, but all I had was a bump on the head and a sense of humil-iation. The children soon got to be better skiers than I was and would pass me on the slopes, calling back rude remarks about being a slowpoke. I explained that my role was to be the person whom everyone could be better than.

Marie was jolly with our kids, who in turn were delighted by her, but she also felt free to offer me advice about their upbringing. At lunch at our house one day, she insisted that I was letting Tim, age eleven, drink too much milk. I was consequently forced, when the Harrimans had meals with us, to choose between pleasing her or Tim.

Every Monday evening during the legislative session, Jack and I gave a buffet dinner party for a dozen state senators and assemblymen. The rule for our children was that they could eat any appetizer they liked but only after having passed the plate of it to the guests. When Tim came to Marie with his favorite Russian meat-filled pasties made by our Mademoiselle, Marie said, "Oh, Tim, I can't take another; I've already had three."

"No, Mrs. Harriman," he said, "Four." She shouted with laughter and promptly advised me to steer Tim away from the diplomatic service.

Jack and I were in the middle of our Albany years when news came from Washington that his father was dying of emphysema. Hiram Bingham was eighty years old and hospitalized. When Alf and Charlie went to visit him, they felt that Suzanne was trying to hurry his death along. She made it impossible for the other sons to see him, and Charlie, a physician, was appalled to find in his father's chart how many narcotics were being administered. Our nephew, Thomas Bingham, offered to donate blood for his grandfather, but Suzanne ruled that out. When Father Bingham asked to make some changes in his will, his lawyer refused to show it to Alf who, after all, was also a lawyer. Alf was wild. The existing will left most of Hiram's estate in trust to his "beloved" wife Suzanne, and, after her death, to his grandchildren. Said Alf in the book he later wrote about the family, "On our return to Connecticut, Charles and I were half inclined to charge the doctor and the lawyer and Suzanne with conspiracy to murder, if not murder itself."

But later, Alf modified this view, pointing out that "This was, to be sure, before the days of 'living wills' by which a dying person can be spared the horrors of a protracted death. . . . If Suzanne did in fact conspire with the doctor to give him a lethal dose . . . it was as much an act of love as of greed."

The funeral was a full military one at Arlington Cemetery, complete with horse and gun salutes. The previous day, there had been a "viewing" at Suzanne's house. I had never seen a corpse except for Lenin's, and Father Bingham's, too, looked wizened. None of us ever saw Suzanne again; within a few years she developed cancer and died. She was buried in Arlington Cemetery next to him. The brothers, led by Charles, had a plaque honoring Hiram placed on a rock in the family cemetery in Salem. Ironically, Charles is the only one of the seven brothers not buried there. His wife, Kathleen, hated Salem—calling it "Wombsville"—and they were buried in Farmington, Connecticut.

During that same year, another death was shattering to Jack and me, the suicide of our friend, Louis Stone. He had developed manic-depression and landed in a private mental hospital in New York City. As soon as we could, we had gone to visit him.

"Isn't this a helluva thing!" Lou said as we entered. We agreed that for him, of all people, to be in such a place was surreal. But although he seemed outwardly normal, Jack and I both sensed something new and odd about the expression in Louis' eyes. Because his state of mind seemed to be responding well to recently discovered psychotropic drugs, the hospital doctors began allowing him home on weekends.

Shortly after our visit, Louis was given a weekend pass. But instead of going home, he told his wife, Nancy, that he had to stay undisturbed at the hospital. On Saturday and Sunday, we found out later, he checked into three different hotels under the name of Potter Stewart. At each, he rang for the hotel physician and complained of being desperate for sleep. Each doctor gave him a sublethal dose of sleeping pills. Louis then swallowed all the pills at the same time, together with a lot of whiskey. By the time the hotel chambermaid found him on Monday morning, he was dead.

He had always wanted to be buried in the cemetery at Kent School, but because his death was a suicide the Episcopal Church refused permission for his body to rest in hallowed ground. It took the real Potter Stewart, by then a justice of the Supreme Court, plus some other highly placed people, to get Kent's headmaster to relent.

The whole incident with Lou Stone reminded me of the definition of friendship given by my childhood friend, Joan Untermyer, who also became manic-depressive and later hanged herself during a hospital pass: "If a friend appears at your door and says he has just committed murder, your answer should be, 'Have you had lunch?'"

CHAPTER 9

Washington

ON THE AMERICAN HOME FRONT, a number of couples we knew reminded us of the struggling suburbanites, Tom and Betsy Rath, described by Sloan Wilson in his 1955 best-selling novel, *The Man in the Grey Flannel Suit*. Betsy says, "Nothing seems to be much fun anymore; it's hard to be happy," to which Tom responds, "The important thing is to make money."

Some couples like us who were engaged in the country's political life were lucky enough to have an exciting time. On the national scene, the civil rights struggle was racheted several notches upward by the Supreme Court's 1954 decision in *Brown vs. Board of Education*. On the international scene, too, we had moments of exultant hope that the Iron Curtain might somehow be breached. One such moment was in 1956 when a group of Hungarian students rebelled against the Russian-dominated Communist dictatorship of their country. But then the Soviet Union sent tanks into Budapest and those students who were not killed had to flee. The United States accepted many of them, but had no plan for what to do with them. An appeal went out to ordinary citizens to open their homes to these valiant young refugees, most of whom wanted to continue their education. Jack and I discussed the situation with our children and Roberta and Mademoiselle. The result was that Jack and I drove from Albany to Camp Kilmer, New Jersey, where many of the Hungarians were being housed by Catholic, Jewish, and Protestant agencies. At the institution run by the Protestant Church World Service, the woman in charge recommended for us two girls, aged seventeen and eighteen, who were close friends. We tried to interview the girls, but their English was minimal. Both seemed very anxious to come along with us, and we returned with dark-haired and dark-eyed Maria and Iboya to Albany.

The girls' manners turned out to be a challenge. They stuffed themselves, while keeping their right elbows on the table, and left their room in even more of a mess than our own children did. I arranged for the girls to be admitted to St. Agnes School, bought them uniforms and books, and did my best to help them with their homework. They were totally uninterested. They loved our food but little else about us. Often I would come upon them dialing the phone blindly and plaintively asking, "Hungary boy?"

Our children, together with Roberta and Mademoiselle, did all they could to make Maria and Iboya feel at home, but none of us made much headway. A neighbor of ours who had taken in a "Hungary boy" was also upset about him but for a totally different reason. Laszlo Makk was a medical student, highly intelligent and passionately motivated to continue his career, but he had received word through the Hungarian underground that, after his escape, his parents had been taken in for questioning and were tortured. He couldn't stand being free while they were not, and therefore he decided he should go back and turn himself in so that his parents would not be further abused. Our neighbor wanted Jack, as a lawyer, to talk Laszlo out of this plan. On the evening Laszlo came to our house, the three of us talked far into the night. Jack and I were finally able to get him to admit that his continuing to stay in America and become a doctor was precisely what provided his parents with hope for the future, whereas if he were to return and be imprisoned (or worse), he would be destroying that hope. Jack was even able to extricate from him a promise to stay at the Albany Medical School until more hard facts about his parents' situation could be ascertained.

When Laszlo first arrived at our house, he had a brief conversation with our two girls. Later he revealed to us how appalled he had

224

been at the lies they had told about their past. They were not students at all; they were young factory workers who had escaped with their boyfriends for the sake of adventure. They were, in short, camp followers, and now all they wanted was to get to Passaic, New Jersey, where young Hungarians were beginning to congregate. There, the girls hoped, they would find jobs and have fun with the "Hungary boys."

Confronted by this evidence of our naiveté, Jack and I consulted the Church World Service. By that time, our experience sounded only too familiar to them. They advised us to give the girls a bit of money and buy them tickets to Passaic. The whole family, Bert and Mademoiselle included, were as relieved as Maria and Iboya when the two of them took off.

For several years, they stayed in touch with us. Then Iboya married a hard-working Hungarian man and moved up, in effect, into the middle class. She soon stopped having anything to do with Maria, who went on to have five babies with her irresponsible Hungarian husband. When he landed in jail, she divorced him and went on welfare. In time, we received a phone call from the Reverend Imre Bertalan, a Lutheran pastor in Passaic, begging Jack and me to come to his church to serve as godparents at the christening of Maria's four sons and one daughter. This we did, and for many more years we continued giving money to Maria and her children. But she wasn't through surprising us. When her ex-husband emerged from jail and started making an honest living, she remarried him. Together, they began managing a 7-Eleven store and later moved with the children to Texas. For almost fifty years, Maria occasionally got in touch with us by phone or with a Christmas card. Her children have all graduated from high school, gotten jobs, and married. She and her husband are proud Americans and grandparents.

Laszlo Makk became a successful pathologist in Louisville, Kentucky, and, as a hobby, he breeds race horses. His wife and four sons are all professionals, mostly in the health field. Two decades after Laszlo's and our long first night together, Jack and I were fêted in style by his parents, who survived after all, in their pleasant Budapest apartment. Since that time, the parents have visited Laszlo and his family in Louisville and vice versa.

In 1956, I was so involved with the problems of the Hungarian refugees that I wrote a script for television about an American family taking in two of them. I was elated when the script was accepted by the *U.S. Steel Hour*. But I was warned by Marshall Jamieson, the producer, that the program's usual advertisers would need to approve the drama's content before it could be aired. To my great chagrin, the McCarthy-spurred anti-Communist hysteria was still potent enough for these advertisers to refuse to allow their product to appear on a program portraying two refugees from Communism as other than admirable. The producer sent the script back regretfully, and it didn't sell elsewhere.

Marie and Ave Harriman had not the slightest interest in my writing, any more than my own father did. At best, it was viewed by them as a harmless hobby; at worst, an impediment to my devoting time to them when they needed me. Jack, on the other hand, was deeply involved in every project I engaged in, both as my sounding board and an incisive editor. Occasionally, he pointed out where my material had lost its focus and suggested that I clarify in my own mind what was most important. The best editors, we both felt, are question-askers, not people who suggest solutions, though having one's editor be disappointed in one's efforts is always painful.

Just as Marie impinged on my daytime hours, Averell sometimes impinged on Jack's nighttime ones, either by keeping him at the office very late or throwing a stag party at the mansion. But because of Marie, most dinners there were for both genders, and, through these dinners, we were given the chance to talk with various dignitaries. For me, the most memorable were the theologian Jacques

Maritain and Richard and Dorothy Rodgers. For Jack, the most memorable was Hubert Humphrey, who that evening revealed to us on the side his hopes for national office.

Other times, Jack and I would get gussied up and accompany the Harrimans to the New York state or City Democratic dinners. One such evening was held at the Glen Island Casino in Westchester County. To my surprise, Jack wasn't as eager to dance as usual. He finally admitted that he wasn't feeling so hot. We spent the night at Thirlsmere and by morning his belly was visibly swollen — and rising. After a few phone calls to doctors, I drove him to Presbyterian Hospital where he was diagnosed as having "classic appendicitis." My mother, at her best in an emergency, came to sit with me during the hour that the operation was predicted to take. She and I worked out bridge hands together, and the hour finally passed. But then came another hour, and the beginning of a third hour. I was frantic by the time the surgeon appeared, still in his green scrubs with the mask hanging below his chin. He explained that Jack had not had appendicitis at all, but diverticulitis. A big infected diverticulum was lying athwart the appendix. The surgeon had removed the appendix as a preventive measure but did not touch the diverticulum. Jack was now on intravenous antibiotics. If the diverticulum subsided, all would be well. But if it did not, the surgeon would have to operate again and excise it because it might be cancerous. We would know in a few days. I asked him what might have brought on the diverticulitis. He said that stress was often one of the factors. I wondered how I could keep Jack from being swallowed up by Guvvie.

Jack was too weak from the operation for me to share with him the news that he might be harboring cancer. For the first time, therefore, I was keeping a major secret from him, and I hated the process. Several days went by and his fever, blessedly, dropped to normal. But as he lay helpless in his bed, who should be scheduled to be admitted as a patient to Presbyterian Hospital but Averell! The gubernatorial prostate, it turned out, needed removal, and he, too, was to undergo surgery. I quickly summoned Jack's official car (plus, for once, its driver) and spirited Jack out of the hospital shortly before the governor was expected to arrive. If stress was to be avoided, I figured that a three-hour drive to Albany for my patient would be less onerous than a three-minute visit from his boss.

One of the best aspects of Jack's Albany job was our freedom to plan and actually take long summer vacations with the children (a privilege, as we later discovered, often not available to members of Congress). In 1956, we all went to the Diamond G Ranch in Colorado where we rode horseback every day, and the children were taken by guides on an overnight backpacking trip. The next year, we all went to Europe on the SS *Flandre*. As our small liner was hooting its intended departure, my brother Howard in his tiny motor boat came zipping about on the Hudson's waves far below the deck where Jack and I were standing with our kids and Anne and Brendan Gill, Jack's former Yale classmate and writer at *The New Yorker*, and their seven kids. We were all screaming at him when, with a final swoop, he headed back up to Riverdale.

Once we reached London, one of the first things I noticed was how improved the teeth of the people were on the street. The advent of socialized medicine following the war had clearly been of help.

Jack promptly got in touch with the three old Oxford chums of Phil Kaiser's whom Phil had notified about us. The list comprised Edward "Ted" Heath (later Britain's prime minister), Nigel Nicolson (later the biographer of his parents, Harold Nicolson and Vita Sackville-West), and Denis Healey (later the leader of the Labour Party). All three accepted a separate luncheon invitation to the Connaught Hotel, where we were staying. Ted Heath kindly reciprocated by inviting us with the children to the House of Commons for tea on the terrace. My second cousin, Philip

Goodhart, a Conservative member of Parliament, was startled to see us there. Later, we visited his parents, Arthur and Cecily Goodhart, at their country place outside of Oxford.

Back home in Loudonville, Jack and I hosted the birthday of Reinhold Niebuhr (June 21) and myself (June 20). On June 20th, Reinie and Ursula drove from Stockbridge, Massachusetts, and Averell and Marie came over from the mansion. I was nervous about how the two most famous men I knew would get along. When the conversation centered on politics, the exchanges were animated, but when religion was raised, Averell's eyes became hooded and Reinie stuck to politics.

The launching by the Russians of their *Sputnik* spurred Americans to be more patriotic. Exploded in that blast-off was our assumption that we could stay technologically far ahead indefinitely. Though Jack had enjoyed appointive office, he felt he could get more done as an elected official. When an opening occurred for a Democrat to run for the State Senate from the Bronx, Jack decided to try for it. It would be hard because the incumbent, Republican State Senator Joseph Periconi, was so popular. Jack received the nod from the Bronx boss, Charles Buckley. For us, this decision meant a move back to Riverdale at the end of the school year.

Whatever chances Jack might have had of winning, however, were dynamited two months later by a political disaster at the New York Democratic State Convention in Buffalo. Averell, who was running for reelection, thought that he should decide who the candidate for the U.S. Senate seat should be. Carmine De Sapio, boss of Tammany Hall, however, refused to cede this much power to Averell. An uneasy compromise was reached on having New York City's mayor, Robert Wagner, Jr., run for the Senate seat once held by his father, but at the last minute, Bob Wagner, a pleasant Yale man, withdrew his name. Jack and I were with Marie in the Harriman suite at the Statler Hilton Hotel in Buffalo when Averell emerged from the bedroom having just received this news. His face

Governor Averell Harriman (left) and Bronx Democratic boss Charles Buckley (center) with Jack in 1957, the year that Jack ran, unsuccessfully, for the New York State Senate from the Bronx.

was ashen. The other candidates whom Averell wanted, Carmine did not, and vice versa. Reporters picked up on the rift between the governor and the Tammany chieftain, and the groundwork for the subsequent charge of "bossism" against the Democrats was thereby established. Had Uncle Herbert been at the convention, the results might have been less disastrous, but, perhaps by design, he was far away in Switzerland at a World Brotherhood Seminar. In Rochester, the Republicans jubilantly nominated Nelson Rockefeller to run against Harriman for governor.

Jack became absorbed in his own State Senate campaign. The children and I worked the mimeograph machine that he had installed on our side porch. It took weeks to get all the purple ink off our hands. Every day that wasn't rainy, we visited the streets and parks to deliver Bingham brochures to the voters. The children liked being able to witness, for the first time, just what their father was doing during the day. Yet they also missed his being free enough in the evening to discuss what was of concern in their own lives. Our two phones rang nonstop and no meal was ever uninterrupted. At a thank-you party we threw for our hard-working volunteers and our contributors just before election, the kids sang the lyrics they had composed, based on an old melody:

> *Now the day is over,*
> *Daddy's drawing nigh,*
> *No more Bingham children.*
> *Fatherless do cry.*

> *No more on street corners,*
> *Cards he will be giving,*
> *No more speeches nightly,*
> *Soon we'll all be living.*

> *Whether he's the winner,*
> *Or the one who's sad,*
> *We rejoice in singing,*
> *"Welcome home to Dad."*

Meanwhile on the hustings, Nelson Rockefeller, whom Jack and I had met in Washington, was exhibiting an ebullience and charm that made Harriman appear gray and old. "Hiya fellah," Nelson would say to greet the men and clap them on the shoulder. To the ladies he offered a sexy wink. And he never forgot to mention the issue of "bossism" among the Democrats.

On Election Day, Rockefeller won by more than half a million votes. The Republican candidate for the senate, Kenneth Keating, also won. This meant that in New York both senators (the incumbent being Jacob Javits), as well as the new governor, would be Republican. Way down the ballot in the State Senate spot, twelve thousand voters in our district had split their vote, pulling down first the Rockefeller lever and then switching over to the Democratic side to support Bingham. But this was not enough to overcome the big margin by which Averell lost our district, and thus Bingham, too, was defeated.

I was even more desolated than Jack. In fact, for a few days, I experienced waves of paranoia. Of course, we were not in danger because of this public rejection, but I kept wanting to pull down the blinds. At the same time, I was also furious because so many of the factors that determine a candidate's failure or success are totally beyond his control.

Worst of all, I hated the way a political campaign can turn a considerate man into a single-minded machine dedicated only to success on Election Day.

The next week, Jack suggested that he and I go to Salem for a few days.

"No, thank you."

"Why not?

"November's too cold to be outdoors, and I don't want to be cooped up with you."

"What . . . ?"

"All you ever do is talk about yourself and your campaign."

"Have I really been that bad?"

"Yes. You haven't mentioned anything else for the last three months!"

"Well, wouldn't that be all the more reason for you and me to go up there and do some catching up?"

"Well . . ."

"Please."

We spent several days hiking through the bare, stark woods and tawny meadows. We wore bright yellow jackets so that the Connecticut hunters wouldn't think we were deer. In time, Jack, with his unusual capacity for objectivity even about himself, labeled his previous behavior "candidate-eye-tis" and compared it to the "invalid-itis" that hospital patients get, when all they can think about is whether their bowels have moved that day. As he returned to being his old warm-hearted, omnivorously interested self, with his finely tuned antennae for the reactions of other people, I recalled why I had fallen in love with him. We resolved to resist the erosion of our closeness, which could have been caused by the discrepancy between the position of the candidate who is daily invigorated by the adulation of him by staff and voters, and the spouse who is debilitated by being taken for granted and subjected to an exhausting number of demands.

Once home from Salem in mid-November, we still had a month of commuting to Albany to help Harriman finish out his gubernatorial term. Because we had sold our Loudonville house, we stayed at the Executive Mansion. Harriman was ferocious in his chagrin. He repeatedly lit into Jack for having been among those who had recommended Nelson Rockefeller as chairman of a State Commission to plan a convention to bring New York's 189-year-old constitution up to date. This post was then parlayed by Rockefeller into statewide publicity for himself. Ave also lambasted Marie for not having campaigned every instant. It was like living with a newly captured lion. Adding to Jack's and my discomfort was our feeling we should stay up, after Ave had stamped off to bed, to comfort Marie who, despite her surface toughness, was shattered by Ave's harshness.

It took several years before he, in his beguiling honesty, was able to say to Jack, "You know who lost that election of 1958? Me."

When Jack and I had originally moved to Albany, we rented our Riverdale house to the permanent representative of Liberia to the United Nations. The only object we left behind was our big Tiffany grandfather clock. Before the Liberian ambassador and his family moved in, they sent ahead only one object, namely, a tall, thin, African drum. These two beautiful representatives of our respective cultures stood side by side in our empty dining room. Our arrangement with the Liberians was that Jack and I, on occasion, could spend the night in one of their guest rooms. This we did only rarely, however, because it was more convenient to stay at the Harrimans' house on East 80th Street, with delicious breakfast included.

Riverdale at that time had almost no African American residents. Except for Ralph Bunche's daughter and her black husband, the few black people around were household help or in couples where the man was black and the woman white. One of the Riverdale neighbors I had thought might object to our black tenants was old Mrs. George Perkins, a classic grande dame who reminded me of Aunt Sissie, conversationally responsive about most subjects but with a rigid boundary between those that could be broached and those that could not even be hinted at.

It was therefore with a bit of trepidation after we moved back into our house that I walked over to Wave Hill for tea.

"Interesting," she said as she started to pour, "those tenants of yours." (Oh boy, I thought, here it comes.) "They were so very black."

"Yes."

"And their car was so big and black."

"Yes."

"And their chauffeur was so white." With a titter, she threw back her head, and I joined in her laughter.

In 1952, when we had bought our house, we were warned that the moment Mrs. Perkins died, the person most interested in buying the estate was a developer who wanted to build eleven-storey "garden apartments" between us and the Hudson. For that reason, our house was reasonably priced (an acre of land with an eleven-room house for $47,500). But a decade later when Mrs. Perkins did die, a group of local lawyers, led by Gilbert Kerlin, Robert Morgenthau, and Thomas Thacher (subsequently aided by Jack Bingham), went to work against the proposed rezoning. These lawyers organized local citizens to attend the city Board of Estimate's meeting that would vote on the rezoning. Several hundred Riverdalians went in buses to downtown Manhattan early in the morning and stayed on till late afternoon. Not a seat in the room was empty.

The result of this Board of Estimate meeting, presided over by Mayor Robert Wagner, Jr., was a unanimous vote to preserve Riverdale's residential character. In time, Robert Moses, among others, persuaded his friend George Perkins, Jr., Mrs. Perkins's son, to donate the twenty-eight acres to the city for a tidy tax deduction. The city built a wall around the property but did nothing for some five years. Fortunately, Newbold Morris, head of the Planning Commission, was an old friend of Gilbert Kerlin's and together they devised a joint private and public venture to turn Wave Hill into a cultural institution open to the public for a low fee, six days a week. By then Bob Wagner had been succeeded as mayor by another, younger, Yale graduate, John Lindsay. Lindsay appointed Jack's Yale friend, August Heckscher, as city commissioner of parks and cultural affairs. Augie was sympathetic to the Wave Hill idea, as was Gil Kerlin's wife, Sally, a long-time trustee of Bank Street College for training teachers in early childhood education. The two Kerlins made major gifts so that Wave Hill could enable the city's schoolchildren to learn firsthand about nature as well as enjoy cultural events both indoors and out. Now, half a century later, Wave Hill has become a public-private garden, with programs in environmental education and the performing arts. During the week, streams of youngsters, each proudly holding a small flowerpot with something green in it, emerge from the high Wave Hill gate to clamber back onto their yellow buses. On a fine Sunday, attendance was so huge that we could scarcely nose our car out of our own driveway into the stream of traffic on narrow Independence Avenue, which, in our area, was officially renamed by the city, "Bingham Road." But that minor vehicular inconvenience was well worth it, and we gloried in our small but unimpeded view of the Hudson. Because those apartments were never built, our property has soared in value.

By the late 1950s I had completed my research for the Niebuhr book and had to wrestle with how to organize the mountain of material I had compiled. Intellectually this was the hardest job I have ever faced, and if I had not been so enthralled by Reinie, I doubt if I could have summoned the stamina to keep at it. When the manuscript was finally finished, Diarmuid Russell offered it first to Scribner's, Reinie's own publisher. Their religion editor, William Savage, phoned Reinie to ask if it was all right if they published it. Apparently Reinie was so fearful of being guilty of the sin of pride, the worst of all sins, that he made confusing noises to Savage about not wanting to appear to be promoting himself. So Scribner, thinking Niebuhr didn't want it published, turned the book down. Plenty of other publishers, Savage predicted, would be glad to accept it. But the other publishers, as Diarmuid gradually discovered, felt that Scribner was so obviously the place for the book that they were reluctant to take it on. An impasse. Finally, I steamed into Reinie's office and said that here was his chance to prove what he had so often written about, namely, the importance of justice in day-to-day human affairs. In what way was it fair to me for the book to be blocked by his discomfort at appearing egocentric? He allowed that perhaps I was right. By the next mail, Diarmuid received an official acceptance from Scribner. Diarmuid's phone call to me was one of my life's happiest moments, and I ran out of the house because I couldn't contain my emotions.

After the typical nine-month gestation period that most publishers still adhere to, the book was out. The reviewers were kind, and ten years later it went to the printer again. The most important reader, from my point of view, was Reinie. He wrote me a letter in 1961, the main part of which follows:

Nov. 8th

Dear June:

I owe you a great debt of gratitude. You have with the greatest diligence and imagination pored over my record, put it in a dramatic whole (for biography is a form of art which imposes form on the formless stuff); and above all you have given a very fair and lucid account of my religious and political convictions and stances. Also you have traced my various polemical controversies, some of which I had forgotten. I was embarrassed only by your correspondence with Anthony West whom I never challenged, your publication of my letter about Larry Kubie and your mention of the fact that I made up to $2500 for an article (The Sat Eve Post paid me more than all my articles together in 20 years). All these things are peccadilloes which are fly specks on the work of art. I am truly grateful for the industry and imagination you have lavished on this work. I hope you will be rewarded beyond my capacity to reward you. If the subject were more inherently interesting you might have a sale for the book. But we can only hope. Much love to Jack and the children, who must have suffered from your devotion to this strange subject.

Affectionately yours,

Reinie

Later, in conversation, Reinie said he wished I hadn't made contact with the psychiatrist who had briefly treated him for post-stroke depression. What the psychiatrist had said was, "I really believe that Dr. Niebuhr's success was due to his very rare qualities and very rare strength. It is his own greatness that made him a success in this undertaking as it has in others. He has an extraordinary ability to face his own self objectively, with humility and lack of fear. He would not like my saying this, but I believe it to be true."

The psychiatrist was right: Reinie didn't like his saying this, and he liked even less my finding it out and including it in the book. But if these were the worst criticisms Reinie could make, I could live very happily with them.

Throughout the preparation of the book I had been torn between the biographer's duty to her subject, on the one hand, and to her readers, on the other. How much privacy is the biographee entitled to? Where does the reader's "need to know" begin and end? These specific decisions are difficult enough when the subject is dead; they are even more so when he is alive and his opinion matters deeply to the writer.

Reinie's health was deteriorating, and Ursula felt that they would be better off living in Stockbridge full-time. For the actual days of their move, she asked if "Reinhold" could come stay with us. This was wonderful for Jack as well as me, and we all talked non-stop. By that time Reinie's left hand had so stiffened from the stroke that he needed help in small things like buttoning his shirt cuffs. We were more than glad to oblige, and he was an appreciative houseguest (though of no more use in the kitchen than he ever had been).

By the end of the 1950s, the stodginess of the decade had begun to dissipate. One small example came in 1959 when a grown nephew of ours, blond and bewhiskered, arrived in Riverdale in his rattletrap car with an equally scruffy young woman. After welcoming them, I showed them to their respective rooms. He spoke right up. "Aunt June, we've been traveling together for weeks, and we like sharing a bed. If this is a problem for you, we'll be glad to go to a motel—and be back in the morning for breakfast."

Because I had several impressionable teenagers in the house, I agreed to his plan. In the morning, the couple returned, their previously unkempt hair freshly washed and their eyes puffy from sleep or, presumably, lovemaking. The following year, as it happened, the nephew married the young woman—later they divorced and still later they married again. But it took years for me to feel fully comfortable when assigning the same guestroom to an unmarried couple, whether in Riverdale or in Salem, even when the couple's relationship seemed to be one of mutual commitment. Even after my own children were grown and brought home their fiancés, I assigned them to separate rooms. What went on in the house after Jack and I had closed our bedroom door at night was, we felt, all right with us, but we were not yet ready to give it our official stamp of approval.

Nationally, there was little approval for the growing involvement of the United States in Vietnam. Following the defeat of the French at Dien Bien Phu in 1954, we were assured by President Eisenhower that the help he proposed for the beleaguered non-Communist South Vietnamese government would not lead us into a war. And, at first, it did not. But that would change in the decade to come.

PART FOUR

The Sixties

CHAPTER 10

The United Nations

IN NOVEMBER 1960, JACK AND I, together with millions of other Americans, exulted in the election of John F. Kennedy even though his margin over Richard M. Nixon was very narrow (and somewhat open to ethical question). At the same time, we had no idea of what unprecedented dangers and difficult decisions would soon confront not just us and our family but our nation.

Though of small scale, the Bay of Pigs was an embarrassing disaster for the White House. Jack and I were baffled by the way Kennedy and his top staff, later characterized by journalist David Halberstam as "the best and the brightest," could have perpetrated so egregious a blunder. The only explanation we could come up with was hubris. Certainly, arrogance was visible in some of the White House top advisers we knew.

In January 1961, Jack and I attended the White House party given by the Kennedys for the new "presidential appointees," the people like Jack who would need the Senate's approval before they could start their new jobs. This evening, which moved from cocktails in the East Room to a lavish buffet in the State Dining Room, exuded idealism and excitement. As our young president had made plain, a New Frontier was at hand, with altruism expected of its citizens.

Among the party's effervescent young people was now-gray Averell Harriman, about to take a lower position as a roving ambassador. (Behind his back we, along with Marie, referred to him as "Rover" though the first predecessor for that job as "ambassador at large" had been no less than Ben Franklin.) This appointment came about only as a result of a luncheon Averell gave in November 1960 at his 80th Street house for president-elect Kennedy. The other guest of honor was the British Labour leader, Hugh Gaitskell. Filling out the table were Jack Bingham and young Michael Forrestal, son of FDR's secretary of the Navy, James Forrestal, and a long-time friend of both Harrimans.

At one point, Gaitskell spoke a few words in disagreement with what Averell had just said. Ave, not hearing well, thought the speaker was Jack. Ave laced into him. Jack said, "Hey, Guv, I didn't say that," but Ave didn't hear. After lunch, Kennedy drew Mike Forrestal aside. "If your friend Averell wants a job in my administration, he has to get a hearing aid."

And so he did.

A year after the Bay of Pigs—when the Cuban Missile Crisis arose—Jack and I, like the rest of the world, held our breath and finally were able to exhale when Kennedy and Khrushchev exhibited calm and flexibility. Later, as a Washington hostess, I enjoyed hearing about the small Georgetown dinner that President Kennedy had asked his old friend, Joe Alsop, and Joe's new wife, Susan Mary, to give. Without attracting the attention of the news hawks, JFK wanted to pick the brains of two top experts on Krushchev, namely, Isaiah Berlin who was visiting from England and Charles (Chip) Bohlen of the State Department. Theirs was the kind of conversation that Washington hostesses dream of facilitating. Apparently, Isaiah and Chip agreed that Khrushchev would likely back down were a face-saving device to be provided.

The public moment that caused Jack and me to cheer out loud during those terrifying days of nuclear confrontation was Adlai Stevenson's challenge at the United Nations to his Soviet U.N. counterpart to deny the evidence of their missiles in Cuba—which Stevenson then unveiled through photographs. Arthur Schlesinger, a presidential assistant, had been sent from the White House because the Kennedy brothers feared that Adlai might need "stiffening" against the Russians—but, as Schlesinger believed at the time and forcefully stated in an interview forty-two years later, "Adlai needed no stiffening."

Jack's and my continued devotion to Stevenson had kept us supporting him at the Democratic National Convention in Los Angeles in August of 1960. This, of course, did not endear Jack Bingham to the Kennedy operatives. A New York delegate we knew was followed into the men's room by one of these operatives and not allowed to perform in peace until he said he'd support Kennedy against Adlai. At the time, we were also told that at Patricia and Peter Lawford's swimming pool, a former mistress of Jack Kennedy's—a Washington lady we knew—announced, "Jack Bingham will never get a job with the new administration! He's hung on with Adlai for too long."

Fortunately for Jack Bingham, JFK bore no grudge against capable Democrats who had remained loyal to Adlai in Los Angeles. Actually, Schlesinger himself had only switched from Adlai to JFK in the spring of 1960, in a joint announcement with Ken Galbraith, Henry Steele Commager, and other Harvard luminaries. Its timing, however, was other than ideal from Arthur and Marian's point of view, since Stevenson had just spent the weekend as their houseguest in Cambridge. Marian, in fact, remained loyal to the end to Stevenson; during that interval, Arthur received a letter from Bobby Kennedy, saying "For God's sake, can't you even control your own wife?" and then, "Of course, neither can I."

After the Democratic Convention, Jack worked for the New York State Kennedy campaign. Some position papers he wrote impressed George Ball, a close associate of Adlai's. When Adlai was handed the job as permanent representative to the United Nations (instead of secretary of state, which he had very much wanted), he sought advice from Ball and others about who his immediate underlings should be. He then appointed as his top three ambassadors, Francis T. P. Plimpton, Charles Yost, and Philip Klutznick. Fourth in the pecking order was Jack as U.S. representative to the U.N. Trusteeship Council, with the rank of minister. After two years, Klutznick resigned and Jack was promoted to his job and rank, as U.S. ambassador to the U.N. Economic and Social Council (ECOSOC).

For the next three years, Jack and, to a far less extent, I were immersed in U.N. diplomatic life. It was inspiring and exhausting and educational. I began referring to my formal evening clothes as my "uniform" because every weekday evening during the General Assembly session, I had to dress up and drive into town to attend a reception or dinner hosted by some member state of the United Nations—or, on rare occasions, by the U.S. Mission to the United Nations. There were also diplomatic luncheons that I did my best to avoid because they cut so thoroughly into my writing time.

Each morning at the mission, the incoming diplomatic invitations would be parceled out among the top delegates. Adlai, together with Francis and Pauline Plimpton, usually took the European dinners; Charlie Yost, a discreet, experienced foreign service officer, and his wife, Irena, were handed the hairiest diplomatic ones; and Jack was assigned to the African, Asian, Middle Eastern, and Latin American ones. If some official American did not show up at such functions, the host country, especially if it was one of the newly liberated colonies, would feel insulted and therefore less likely to vote along with the United States on upcoming issues. As a result, some nights Jack and I had to attend as many as three receptions. Adlai's private description of his job was that it comprised, in equal parts, protocol, Geritol, and alcohol.

When Jack was the U.S. representative to the U.N. Trusteeship Council, he became acquainted with leaders of many British, French, and Belgian colonies even before the colonies' nationhood was established. He and I, therefore, were able to celebrate with genuine elation the occasion when their own country's declaration of independence came into effect.

Jack's closest friend at the United Nations was his British counterpart on the Trusteeship Council, the beguiling Sir Hugh Foot. Later Hugh and his wife, Sylvia, were given the title of Lord and Lady Caradon, which meant that he relinquished his seat in the House of Commons and instead served in the House of Lords. Hugh, who had the bushiest eyebrows and seemingly the bluest eyes in the whole United Nations, also had a wide-ranging sense of humor.

Another U.N. delegate with a notable sense of humor was the permanent representative from Burma, a relaxed-appearing Buddhist who always had a nugget of news or gossip to impart, whether funny or serious. No one would have dreamed that within the year, after the plane of Secretary General Dag Hammarskjold crashed in the Congo in 1961, our Burmese friend, Ambassador U Thant, would become the one diplomat whom the Soviets and the United States, despite the Cold War, could agree on to take his place. Forty-two years later, in a phone call from U Thant's daughter, Aye Aye Myint U, I learned that the two events that would have most astounded her late father were the end of the Cold War and the dissolution of the Soviet Union. In the 1960s, of course, he, like everyone else assumed the continuance of both; what set him apart was the combination of his country's nonalignment and his own personal ability to attract a degree of trust from both sides of the Cold War.

When Secretary General U Thant was elevated to the 38th floor of the Secretariat Building, Jack and I saw much less of him. I missed him, and, after the publication of my Niebuhr book that year, I decided to explore the possibility of writing a biography of U Thant. He turned out to be just as reluctant a subject as Niebuhr had been, but fortunately he approved enough of *Courage to Change* to invite Jack and me to have lunch with him and C. V. Narasimhan, his chief of staff, at least to discuss the project. When Jack sent word that he was otherwise occupied, but his wife would still like to come, the message came back that the secretary general would be pleased

to welcome Mrs. Bingham and one of her daughters for lunch. At
the luncheon, C. V. and U Thant relentlessly entertained me with
diplomatic anecdotes until I realized that unless I introduced some
biographical shoptalk, I'd be out of there without any commitment
by U Thant to my starting the book. I interrupted our jolly back-
and-forth and asked which individuals I should start interviewing.
Reluctantly, U Thant gave me some names and addresses and finally
agreed to my coming to see C. V. once a month on a Saturday morning.
At the first such meeting, it became clear to C. V. that he couldn't
possibly handle the kinds of question I needed answered. I was,
therefore, ushered in to see U Thant. I had brought along a kitchen
timer, which I set for an hour. When it went "ding," U Thant burst
out laughing and asked, "What on earth is that?" I explained, and he
said I could turn it off. And we went on talking—at that time and for
more than a year of monthly Saturday mornings.

By far my best informant was the eldest of U Thant's three
younger brothers. U Khant lived in Rangoon and enjoyed writing
letters. He was wonderfully honest about their family, but he had to
be very careful in what he wrote about their country. Burma was
then ruled by General Ne Win, the leader of Burma's Revolutionary
Council, who had instituted strict censorship. (The world being smaller
than expected, General Ne Win had once played golf with my brother
Howard at the Century Country Club in Purchase, New York, in a
foursome arranged by their mutual friend, Richard Paw U.)

That autumn, Jack and I made a brief visit to Burma (most
Americans were allowed only a single day there, but thanks to a message from U Thant to General Ne Win, we were given three). I was
able to meet my pen pal, U Khant, and meet the two younger brothers,
as well as their mother and several old friends of U Thant's. One of
the friends took us on a day-trip by boat down the Irrawaddy River
from Rangoon to a town much like Pantanaw, where U Thant was
born and later taught school. U Khant, the most devout of the

brothers, took Jack and me to Rangoon's Shwedagon Pagoda, surely one of Buddhism's most impressive temples. After Jack and I left, U Khant and I continued to correspond about matters religious and personal, serious and amusing for many years, even after I had finished writing the book.

Just as the research for *The Inside Story* had forced me to learn something about psychiatry, and research for *Courage to Change* had forced me to learn something about Judaism and Christianity, so the U Thant book forced me to learn something about Buddhism (especially the Hinayana variety practiced in Burma) and meditation. My practice of meditation, however, was badly disrupted by our dog—who could sense when my brain waves were shifting over to the alpha state, thus causing total indifference to him and everything else in the room. He would therefore bark. This broke my meditative state so many times that I finally gave it up until Jack could get home and take care of the damn dog. But then I thought—this was silly. Jack was home and I wanted to be with him. Besides, I had sensed what the meditative state was like and I profited from it, but I had not grown to crave it the way some of my now-teenaged children did. (They got headaches if they didn't practice twice a day for twenty minutes.) When I asked U Thant what meditation was like for him, he said, "A good experience leaves me with Metta, a feeling of 'Give my love to everybody.'"

When I finally had the completed manuscript in hand, I walked down the road in Riverdale to the secretary general's estate where U Thant was living with his wife, Daw Thein Tin, who spoke no English. Also in their household was Aye Aye and her husband, Tyn Myint U. U Thant came to the door dressed in a Burmese *longyi*. He hefted the manuscript and then handed it back.

"I think I won't read it after all."

"Why not?"

"Because if I make even a small change, then I would be implicated in the writing of the book."

At the party honoring the 1966 publication of my biography of U Thant (left), both victims of my biographical pursuits met! In all the years that followed, I never met anyone again who inspired my interest and devotion enough to write a full-length biography.

"But no one would know."

His look, for a moment, was stern. "*I* would."

So, with manuscript in hand, I trudged back home, feeling like a chump.

When *U Thant: The Search For Peace* was published, the Burma Council of the Asia Society threw a party in its honor. On this festive occasion, I had the joy of introducing U Thant and Reinhold Niebuhr to each other. Reinie greeted U Thant: "Hello, fellow victim!" The three of us laughed, but their laughter was more spontaneous than mine.

Jack and I continued to see U Thant over the years, and were amused at how competitive he remained about our respective grandchildren. His first grandchild, by way of Aye Aye and Tin Myint U, was a boy, Koko. U Thant continued inquiring as to whether Edward could walk or talk or do the expected things as early in life as Koko was doing them. U Thant was inordinately pleased when we said no.

Another permanent representative to the United Nations with whom we became real friends was Ousmane Socé Diop of Senegal. A devout Muslim, a brilliant graduate of the Sorbonne who had won the Prix de France for one of his novels, and a veteran of the French Foreign Legion, Ousmane was a hefty, very dark man with a so-called "eye for the ladies." (In reality, he had serious problems with his vision.) Among the many ladies he flirted with were Marietta Tree and myself. What he did not know (as many non-Americans do not) is that a mutual loyalty among former female schoolmates leads them to compare notes about the fellows who flirt with them. Thus, when Ousmane sent Marietta and me identical postcards from Senegal and brought us identical bottles of Chanel Number 5 from Paris, she and I shared a good laugh and thought nothing of it. Whether she reported these gifts to her second husband, Ronald Tree, I don't know, but I automatically kept Jack up to date about mine. Jack, too, felt kindly toward Ousmane, especially after the Wednesday when we had invited him to dinner in Riverdale and he arrived a full week early. Claudia was at home and told him in her best French that we were out, but she knew we were planning a dinner party the following week. He departed and in the morning I phoned with an abject apology for the misunderstanding. *"Mais Madame,"* he answered consolingly, *"je faisai seulement la reconnaissance"* (I was only doing reconnaissance). He came back to our house on the appointed evening, and we all had a good time.

Subsequently, Ousmane phoned one morning at dawn to warn Jack of a hostile parliamentary maneuver that the French delegate

251

on the Trusteeship Council was planning for that day, together with some of Ousmane's Francophone African colleagues. Because of the warning, Jack had time to neutralize the maneuver, and the French delegate apparently never figured out why it failed. Ousmane, however, once went too far in friendly gestures toward me. I had been formally invited to his nation's Mission to the United Nations for a luncheon. I arrived on time and was startled to find no other guests. When Ousmane suggested that he and I take the little elevator upstairs to the dining room, I said that I loved climbing stairs. He said that because of his war wounds that would be "impossible." In the confines of the elevator, he made a lunge. *"Non, non, Excellence,"* I cried. *"Je suis mariée"* (I am married). His answer was, *"Mais moi, aussi"* (I, too). This made me shout with laughter, which fortunately turned out to be contagious. By the time he opened the elevator door, he understood that he and I would clearly remain "just friends."

In fact, I felt so at home with him that when he threw a fancy reception at the Plaza Hotel in honor of his visiting foreign minister, I asked him afterward whether it was appropriate for a country as poor as Senegal to be spending so much money in New York. I mentioned that many of us in the U.S. diplomatic service were trying to move in the opposite direction and simplify our entertaining. (Indeed, the State Department's allotment of funds for that kind of "representation" was so skimpy that Jack and I were always out-of-pocket after hosting a party for our U.N. colleagues.) "Ah," said Ousmane, "but yours is a huge rich country. You can afford to entertain with simplicity, but we small poor countries cannot."

Ousmane may have been a flirt, but his wisdom was what had the biggest impact on me.

One of Jack's and my most successful social endeavors involved our renting the whole of a Bronx ice-skating rink. Many of the delegates had never been on skates before. I remember a West African, with one upper arm firmly held by Jack and the other by a

Senegal's permanent representative to the United Nations, Ousmane Socé Diop, with whom we became real friends, greets Jack in 1961 at a formal diplomatic function.

sturdy male member of the British Mission, kicking up both feet in ecstasy. Afterward, everyone came back to our house for mulled wine and huge Dagwood sandwiches. One of the delegates, full of spirits (in both senses), told me it was the party of the year, but that next time we should please serve the hot wine *before* the skating.

Jack and I collapsed afterward, overcome not only by fatigue but also relief that no one had been physically injured or socially offended by so casual a form of hospitality. The best skater had turned out to be the Japanese ambassador. Impressed, but puzzled, we asked him whether there was much skating in Japan. He laughed. He had served for many years at his country's embassy in Norway.

On the other hand, one social custom that Americans take for granted was viewed as a serious gaffe by at least one delegate. At a dance at their big Westchester house given by an African Mission to the United Nations, complete with delicious chicken and irresistible music, I was dancing with a Nigerian when Jack cut in. As soon as the music stopped, Jack and I went over to my erstwhile partner who was glowering.

"What's the matter?"

"No one can take away my dance partner without my permission."

"But cutting-in is an old American custom."

"You are not in America. This house is a part of Ah-free-kah."

Jack apologized for what the man had seen as a form of rudeness. In due time, this African diplomat married an African American woman and learned more than he may have wanted to about American customs. She was a tall, elegant, bright lady but somewhat absentminded. The day I lent her our station wagon, she promptly drove it into a neighbor's hedge. Later on, Jack and I visited the couple in Nigeria. Her adopted country appeared to me to be full of drivers no more skilled than she, all at the wheel of buses and trucks, mammy-wagons and antediluvian cars, and all with their hand on the horn. She took me out in her husband's motorboat for a tour of the impressive Lagos harbor. Only after she and I were far out in its choppy waters did she take a look at the fuel gauge. Empty. Darkness had fallen by the time she managed to get us towed back to the dock. Jack was frantic, but her husband was more philosophical— or more accustomed to her insouciance.

The third permanent rep with whom we became good friends (as well as golfing companions) was Alex Quaison-Sackey of Ghana. Like Ousmane, he was very big, but unlike Ousmane, he was handsome, with the most dazzling smile I've ever seen. In the fall of 1962, Jack and I were scheduled to play golf with him at his country club in Mamaroneck, New York. At the last minute, Jack had to bow out, but Alex told me to come along. When Alex and the Malaysian ambassador and I arrived at the first tee at one-thirty, the starter nervously informed us that we could not drive off till two. Alex, enraged, said, "I'm due at the Security Council at six. I will not stand for this delay."

"I'm sorry, Your Excellency," the starter quavered. "It has nothing to do with you." Looking over at me, he said, "It's the ladies who are not allowed to tee off until two."

Alex shouted with laughter. Then he pointed at me and laughed again. I was so relieved that he and his country were not being insulted that I laughed along. With the women's movement still a decade in the future, I never thought to defend my gender. Even the starter found Alex's laughter so contagious that he giggled and let us tee off ahead of time.

"All's well that ends well," shouted Alex as he strode off down the fairway. (He, being an Oxford graduate, was fully at home with English literature.) Later, Alex was appointed Ghana's foreign minister. He was on the plane with his president, Kwame Nkrumah, when the pilot's radio reported that their government had been overthrown. Although Nkrumah refused to return to Ghana, Alex decided that he should; his wife and children were there. He was thrown for a time into prison. He became the headmaster of the fine private high school in Accra that he had once attended. Several years later, we paid him and his wife a visit. He was a bit less casual with voicing his political opinions but still effervescent. We had a hilarious golf game, partly because in Ghana, as in parts of the Arab world, the "greens" are "browns," not made of grass, but of sand covered with oil and rolled smooth. Jack and I had never encountered anything like them and our putting was thrown way off, much to Alex's delight. (In golf, we all agreed, there's no shot that doesn't give someone some pleasure.)

During our Washington years, Alex had been our guest at the Columbia Country Club across the D.C. border into Maryland. His blackness was a cause of visible surprise, not only by the member-golfers we met but also the caddies, most of whom were black. From that day on, the caddies vied to carry Jack's and my bags. At least with them, our stock had risen.

Other U.N. African delegates were not so lucky as Alex when adverse political changes occurred in their homeland. Our Riverdale neighbor, Guinea's Ambassador Ashkar Marouf, went back home only to find that his country's dictator, Sékou Touré, had been turned against him. Ashkar was imprisoned and was hanged. Several other African diplomats whom we knew felt forced, reluctantly, after leaving their U.N. post, to remain in exile from their native lands.

Diplomacy, I learned the hard way, should entail one's antennae being more sensitive than usual, even when dealing with one's fellow nationals. One winter Sunday, Marietta Tree and Jack's boss Adlai Stevenson came to Riverdale to play tennis and have lunch. Standing on our terrace in the sun, she and I brought each other up to date on Ousmane Socé Diop's latest move. (The locus of his pounce on her turned out to have been the backseat of his limousine as they approached the Holland Tunnel.) Hearing us laughing, Adlai came over and asked what was so funny. We quickly filled him in, and then, to the consternation of Marietta, Jack, and me, Adlai's face went rigid: "I will not permit the ladies of my embassy to be treated with disrespect."

Marietta and I did our best to soothe him, explaining that neither of us had been remotely upset and had no need to be protected from this friend of ours. Jack backed us up, but Adlai refused to listen. Instead, he ordered Jack to have Ousmane stricken from the U.S. Mission's official invitation list. Within a few months, I got a call from Ousmane asking why he seemed to be ostracized by Ambassador Stevenson. Would I please ask Jack to find out what, if anything, was wrong. I told Ousmane not to worry, that it was probably just the result of some inefficiency by a secretary. Jack and Marietta and I then decided that Jack should go to Adlai's social secretary—who was anything but inefficient—and ask her to reinstate the ambassador of Senegal for all of Adlai's big parties, but not for the small ones. Knowing how absentminded Adlai could be and how many black diplomats would be trooping through his receiving line, we were willing to take the chance that Adlai would never notice Ousmane's reappearance, and he never did.

My favorite anecdote about Ousmane is this: Jack and I had been privileged to meet the Rev. Martin Luther King, Jr., at an ADA Roosevelt Day dinner when Jack was newly at the United Nations. We were sitting at a table with Ousmane and several other African delegates. "The Star-Spangled Banner" was sung by a black female singer. Ousmane pointed to the only other black sitting on the dais.

"*Qui est ce noir?*"

I answered, with French intonation, "Martin Luther King."

"Ah." Ousmane looked vague. "*Va t'il chanter?*" (Will he sing?)

The discrimination I experienced as a Jew and a female was microscopic compared to the suffering by victims of the Nazis and Stalinists and by African and Asian victims of colonial powers. I now think, however, that the more years a person experiences prejudice, the greater its power to injure them over the long haul. In Africa, Ousmane Diop and Alex Quaison-Sackey, like the Sabras in Israel, had grown up not as members of a scorned minority but as offspring of leaders in their locally based majorities. By the time they experienced prejudice, Ousmane in France and Alex in Britain, they had a built-in confidence. At any hint of condescension, their immediate reaction was outrage at the perpetrator rather than doubt about themselves. In contrast to an American black or Jew, they had never in early childhood been confronted with a generalized hatred. They, therefore, did not internalize the pain. Though the natives of Senegal or Ghana had their outer freedoms curtailed by their country's colonial rulers, many, like Ousmane and Alex, were free during childhood from contact with these whites. One day Ousmane who was Senegal's ambassador to the United States as well as the United Nations, mentioned that there was no good restaurant on his commute between New York and Washington that would accept him as a customer. In deep chagrin, I apologized for my country, but he laughed and said that he needed to lose weight anyway.

In 1963, Martin Luther King, Jr., made his electrifying speech, "I Have a Dream." Our daughter Micki and our son Tim interrupted their studies in New England to drive to Washington to join the close to three hundred thousand people at the Lincoln Memorial. Tim later said, "What I particularly remember is that on the way back, in Maryland, a restaurant refused to serve us lunch because one of the people with us was a black girl. Mick and I were shocked."

The death of Mrs. Eleanor Roosevelt in November 1962 was a grievous loss to the world as well as to the large family to which she was devoted. Hated as perhaps no other first lady, including Mary Lincoln, she also was beloved by hundreds of millions of foreigners as well as Americans. At one of the U.N. parties we attended together,

Jack was startled when she mentioned that she'd wanted to see the new musical called *South Pacific* but had heard that it was sold out for at least six months. "Mrs. Roosevelt, please," he said. "Have your secretary phone the producer and tell him who it is who wants the tickets." She seemed amazed at this suggestion and said she would consider it. Later, he found out, it worked.

Jack then decided that he would follow his own advice and be personal in his application for tickets for ourselves. He told the box office what was true, that he needed two tickets for his wife's birthday in June. That enchanted evening, young Frank Roosevelt and his new bride, Sue Perrin, were also in the audience. Jack complained to them that I had broken his hand by holding it so tightly while Ezio Pinza sang "Some Enchanted Evening" to Mary Martin.

After seeing Frank and Sue, we sent them a wedding present. I was startled to receive from Eleanor Roosevelt a letter thanking us for the lovely little pitcher. I had to write her back and explain that the gift was intended for the newlyweds. She then wrote again, reporting that she had reluctantly handed it over.

Not long after that, her final illness began. Jack and I drove to Hyde Park for the funeral that was held in the Rose Garden where her body was laid to rest next to that of her husband. Both their valiant spirits seemed much alive in that peaceful green square.

Before the service, Jack and I were invited by Franklin, Jr., to a luncheon at Valkill, his mother's house. I don't imagine that a more dazzling group of political figures had gathered in the chintz-furnished rooms since the Declaration of Independence was first celebrated in Philadelphia. President-elect and Mrs. Jack Kennedy, Vice President–elect and Mrs. Lyndon Johnson, former presidents Harry Truman and Dwight Eisenhower, foreign dignitaries, and many others were there. On our way out, I preceded Jack as we walked past the chair where President Kennedy was sitting very straight. As my eyes met his, I noticed the hazel of his eyes seemed

259

practically on the surface—and their expression was one of straight-out lust. I was paralyzed. Finally, with dry mouth, I mumbled a good-bye and stumbled out, followed by Jack.

Two months later, Jack was invited to the White House for the swearing in of the presidential appointees like himself. Each appointee was allowed to bring one guest. I was still a'twitter from the impact of Kennedy's gaze. "I don't know if I should go," I said and told Jack what had transpired between Kenney and me.

"I saw it," he said.

For two long months neither of us had mentioned it.

"I think I'll invite Jim Bland," he said.

"Good idea."

Jim, the husband of our daughter Sherry, was then a student at Virginia Theological Seminary in Alexandria. Because she was teaching history at a public high school in nearby Arlington (where some of the seniors were scarcely younger than herself), she would not be free in the middle of the day to accompany Jack to the White House, but Jim would. Later, Jim said he was enthralled with shaking hands and exchanging a few words with President Kennedy. In fact, Jim was so affected that later, when Kennedy was assassinated, his faith in God was badly shaken. As a result, he decided not to train to be a preacher after all but instead to become a professor. The following year, he went back to Harvard to earn his Ph.D. It was, therefore, in Cambridge that his and Sherry's first child, Edward Bingham Bland, was born. I imagined the glass window through which I first saw my grandson shatter from the primal vibrations that were so powerful. (A similar intensity recurred after every birth of our nine grandchildren and thereafter, in a less diluted form than I had expected, when our fourteen great-grandchildren were born.)

In fact, gravitational fields seemed so palpable to me that I determined not to be pulled in too much by President Kennedy. The greatest of all aphrodisiacs, said Henry Kissinger, is power. Certainly

I was far from the only female to be bewitched by men who exuded it. A pretty sister-in-law of mine, who was standing on a New York sidewalk when President Kennedy, from his slowly moving car, caught her eye, reported that she had grabbed a lamppost in order not to fall.

Someone once defined happiness as "fulfillment of a childhood dream." Although Jack greatly enjoyed his work at the United Nations, he still craved elective office. In 1962, therefore, he went to the White House to ask a member of the top staff if the president would support—or at least remain neutral toward—a challenge by Jack to the by-now-infamous "Boss" of the Bronx, Charles Buckley. Buckley, a member of Congress for thirty years, was chairman of the House Public Works Committee. While this enabled him to wield financial power countrywide, he paid little attention to voters' problems in his home district, not even bothering to have a Bronx office where constituents could meet with him or his staff. The White House adviser, Kenny O'Donnell, whom Jack spoke with, answered his question brusquely: "Not a chance." The reason was that Buckley had helped JFK in 1960 to win New York state's hefty bloc of electoral votes. The White House would, therefore, remain loyal to Buckley no matter who challenged him.

During those years in Washington, Marian Schlesinger and I used to walk our poodles at least once a week along the Georgetown Canal. While Arthur was serving as special White House assistant to Kennedy, Marian had her own talents as a successful portrait painter, gifted writer, and warm and witty conversationalist. Even so, she was far from the only wife who spent much of the post-dinner interval in the White House ladies' room so as to avoid being seen as a wallflower or someone who goes home far earlier than her husband. The Camelot husbands were apparently so bedazzled by the gorgeous "young things" imported from New York, as well as the older, fashionably garbed ones like Marietta Tree and Fifi Fell, that they failed to dance with their own—or each other's—wives.

Marriage in Camelot was viewed cynically, and after Camelot's tragic end, all three of JFK's close associates whose names begin with "S," namely, Schlesinger, Sorenson, and Salinger, got divorced. I didn't know Pierre Salinger, but I did know the other two, and their subsequent marriages to much younger women turned out well, complete with new child.

Divorce, of course, is an absolute necessity at times. On the other hand, it seems incredibly unfair that the deserted partner is almost never treated with the attentiveness that a widowed one receives, although the divorced one's suffering may be even more acute. Especially in politics did Jack and I observe split-ups where the elected official remained cheerfully in office while the ex-wife slunk back to the home district or tried to brazen it out in Washington where women outnumber men three to one and the partner with the power is the partner with the invitations. We could often spot these new divorcées because their hair was brighter and their eye shadow was heavier and their décolletage was lower. Conversely, we also saw couples who remained miserable in double harness because the officeholder couldn't afford the bad publicity a divorce would entail, and the spouse was reluctant to destroy his career in addition to his marriage.

In November 1963, the unthinkable occurred: Kennedy was assassinated. We were all devastated, no matter what our individual politics were. There was no one quite like John F. Kennedy.

The new president, Lyndon Johnson, turned out to have no special tie to Charlie Buckley. The Johnson White House, therefore, would presumably not care which particular Democrat represented the Bronx's 23rd District. With the outcome of the general election in the 23rd being predictably Democratic, the only contest would be within the Democratic Party in its spring primary.

When Jack went to Adlai to tell him of his plan to challenge Buckley, Adlai said he was crazy. For one thing, Jack was taking a formidably long shot in trying to wrest the nomination from someone as entrenched as Buckley; for another, if Jack were to fail, Buckley's friends in the Senate would forever block any presidential appointment for Jack. Jack, in other words, could not return to the U.S. Mission to the United Nations or perhaps ever again serve his country in an appointive capacity.

My mother felt the way Adlai did, only more so.

"Don't tell me Jack is giving up being an ambassador in order to be just a *congressman*?"

"No, he's actually giving it up in order to try to get elected as a congressman."

As Jack began exploring ways to attract support in the primary scheduled for June 2, 1964, he discovered that, as usual in politics, the underlying situation was far more complex than it had originally appeared. Among the twenty-thousand "regular" Democrats, most would probably stay loyal to Boss Buckley no matter what. The few whom Jack could attract would probably be too scared of Buckley to admit this in public. Among the "reform" Democrats, there was a wide difference between the five local clubs. Some were, and some were not, closely affiliated with the New York State Reform organization that Mrs. Roosevelt, Herbert Lehman, and Thomas Finletter had founded after the 1958 Democratic debacle in Buffalo. Some Bronx Reform clubs disliked the ideology of their fellow clubs and said so publicly. In short, there was no way that Jack could please them all despite the fact that he desperately needed them all. He also needed the Reform-minded Democrats who had never joined a political club and didn't want to. How could we get all these names and addresses and phone numbers in order to enlist their aid? How could we also reach those independent voters who, if persuaded to care enough about a Bingham candidacy to vote in the primary, would first have to go register as Democrats?

The Reform clubs ranged from conservative to far left. Both within the clubs as well as between them, members disagreed about what kind of candidate could beat Buckley. Some wanted a pure idealist and were not concerned about his lack of previous political experience; others wanted a seasoned candidate with the ability to appeal to voters outside as well as inside the Reform movement. Analysis of voting patterns in previous Democratic primaries showed that about half the electorate was Jewish, a quarter was Irish Catholic, an eighth was Italian Catholic, and the final eighth was a mixture of blacks, Latinos, and WASPS (thus Jack was a member of a mini-minority). Buckley, of Irish descent, would predictably attract many Catholic voters; furthermore, over the years, he had done favors for several rabbis in the district, a few of whom were reputed to be swayable by financial contributions to their synagogues. Jack and I had dinner with one of these rabbis and his new bride who was a previous acquaintance of ours. At the end of the large meal, our host made it clear that a one thousand dollar ad in the next issue of the synagogue's journal would assure the rabbi's public support for Jack. The rabbi's wife appeared as embarrassed as we were by this offer.

Vying with Jack for the Reform clubs' endorsements were two Jewish candidates, plus, to our total surprise, the minister of our small Edgehill Congregational Church. Though Jack, a member there, had previously confided his political plans to its handsome young minister, Forrest Johnson, Forrest had not said a word about his own intention to enter the race. This put us in an extremely uncomfortable position. The five Reform clubs had already announced the dates for their debates between the candidates. Jack hated to make public attacks on his own minister who, in our opinion, was the kind of lofty idealist without political experience who would be shredded by Buckley. At the same time, we remained indebted to Forrest for the help he had previously given to our daughter, Claudia, when she was deeply upset by her confirmation teacher in another local church who told the class, "If there's anything God hates, it's a doubter." Jack and I had immediately removed her from that church. Instead, she went to Forrest for spiritual counseling and was enchanted by his big blue eyes as well as his tolerance for her own and other people's doubts. The last thing she needed was to be informed that her beloved minister, without a word of explanation to her father, had become his rival. Yet Jack was hardly about to bow out in Forrest's favor.

By this point, Uncle Herbert had died. At age eighty-five, he was shaving on the morning he was scheduled to go to Washington to be awarded the Presidential Medal of Freedom, when his brave heart suddenly and completely gave out. We would have liked his kind words of support for Jack's risky decision to go forward, but more, we would just miss him.

During Jack's campaign for the nomination, our immediate family was mobilized, including Yankee Poodle wearing a cardboard sandwich sign I had concocted that read on both sides, "Underdogs for Bingham."

Every non-rainy day several members of the family went forth to woo the Democratic voters on the sidewalks and in the parks. We carried brochures about Jack and answered questions as best we could. The most poignant was from a tiny lady on a park bench who looked searchingly up at me: "Can I trust him?" I told her that I'd been trusting him for twenty-five years and still did. She nodded, but whether she voted for him or not, of course, I never knew. The comment most difficult to respond to was, "I am Democrat. I vote Democrat." We would try to explain the difference between the primary among candidates within the same party, and the general election for candidates from several parties. But, in some instances, the voters' English was so limited that we weren't understood.

Jack sometimes accompanied us; other times he went off with staff or volunteers. Mornings and evenings he would be at one of the many subway stops to greet the voters as they went off to, or came

Jack and I campaigning in 1964 in the Bronx when Jack ran for the U.S. House representing the 23rd district.

back from, work. We also had our ancient, wooden-paneled Chevrolet station wagon adorned with two big "Bingham for Congress" signs. Named the "Bingham Bandwagon," it was driven around the district by two volunteers, one at the wheel and the other with a bullhorn begging the voters to vote on "June second, Primary Day, for Bingham."

At one of Jack's three campaign offices in the district, a stranger asked to see him in private. When shown into Jack's tiny office, the man reached into his briefcase and pulled out a thousand dollars in

266

small denominations. It was from the man's labor union. When Jack explained that he would have to declare the donation on the official government form, the man cursed him and left.

For me, the most onerous aspect of campaigning was the fund-raising. Yet we needed to hold a number of cocktail parties for that purpose both in Manhattan (where the major money was) and in the Bronx (where all the voters were). Hosts had to be recruited, lists of their and our friends and other prospects had to be drawn up and invitations sent, if possible, with a personal note from whomever it was who had suggested that person's name. If a host with an address convenient for guests did not wish to pay for the food and drink, a co-host had to be found. At the party itself, someone had to introduce Jack and then, after Jack's speech, make the pitch for funds. Because most wealthy people have no contact with the realities of elective politics, they have no inkling of the expenses for office rent, staff, and supplies, people to oversee the volunteers, mailings, posters, and, if possible, ads in local papers. In fact, radio and TV, which in New York City reached far beyond any single congressional district, were prohibitively expensive. One heavily bejewelled lady boasted to me that because Jack's speech was so wonderful, she had contributed twenty-five dollars!

Some of the parties were emotionally and financially rewarding; others were disasters. But whatever they were, I wrote thank you notes to the hosts, speakers, and volunteers. Not only did I cringe every time we begged for money, but I also hated some other by-products of fund-raising. One was being forced to rank our friends in financial terms. Another was to add so many political donors to our Christmas card list that the process of sending out cards ceased being either personal or satisfying. A major instance of "less is more."

Our children varied widely in their reactions to the campaign. One hated it and later accused us of having schooled her in hypocrisy because we expected her be pleasant to all voters regardless of how

The Bingham family proudly stepping out on the campaign trail during
Jack's campaign for the U.S. House of Representatives in 1964. From left to
right, Claudia, June, Micki with Yankee, Jack, Sherry, Jim Bland, and Tim.

she really felt. Another loved the opportunity, at last, to find out what
Dad was doing all day. But few of them enjoyed being dragooned into
publicly performing in our family orchestra, Sherry on the flute,
Micki on the viola, Claudia on the violin, Tim on the cello, me on
the recorder, and Jack on the violin. Our repertory shifted with the
locality where our sidewalk concerts took place. "When Irish Eyes
Are Smiling" was for the Irish areas, the "Hatikvah" for the Jewish
areas, "O Sole Mio" for the Italian areas, and "East Side, West Side"
for the indeterminate ones.

Our campaign manager was a brilliant, marvelously funny but
easily roiled young man named Steve Berger. He was full of ideas,

some great, some less than great. He and I headed into what I later discovered is the classic tug of war between campaign manager and candidate's spouse. The manager wants to win even if it kills the candidate, and the wife wants the candidate to survive even if that kills the campaign. When I tried to persuade Jack to skip some of the many stops that Steve had scheduled, Steve was enraged. When Steve phoned Jack at ungodly hours, I was enraged. Sometimes Steve would dispatch me in place of Jack to kaffeeklatsches or other small meetings — which was fine by me because it spared the candidate but dismaying because it cut into Jack's and my very little time together.

Jack's brother Alfred came from Salem to help in the campaign. He stressed to the voting public that Jack's grandfather, Charles Tiffany, had been a major force in establishing Van Cortlandt Park in the heart of our Bronx district.

One evening, Alf and I were on the living room sofa, he on one phone with WCBS, and I on the other phone with WNBC. Jack, of course, was unreachable because he was off in the Bandwagon. What the networks needed to know before six was Jack's response to yet another accusation by Buckley: Buckley actually dared to accuse Jack Bingham, of all people, of being an anti-Semite. Jack and I could deny this until we were hoarse, but how could we convince the multitude of voters who were hearing this calumny from an official whom they trusted, often a Jewish leader, many of whom were beholden to Buckley for past favors? Buckley had deliberately conflated two entirely different "America First Committees." The first was the long-defunct one formed to keep America out of war, which Jack and I had joined for a few months in 1941 and from which we promptly resigned in protest against Charles Lindbergh's Des Moines speech that August. The second was a recently formed, truly anti-Semitic organization that had co-opted the old one's title. Thus, we found ourselves in the miserable but not uncommon political dilemma of having to decide whether to try to refute a false accusation, thus giving it further publicity, or hope that the voters would forget about it. We decided that the New York media were trustworthy and sophisticated enough to tease out the complex truth from Buckley's big lie. As we became aware, unless the media are essentially free, smart, and honest, the kinds of elections essential for a country's democracy cannot take place.

Jack called a press conference for nine in the morning at a seedy, mid-Manhattan hotel convenient for the reporters. I busied myself passing doughnuts and danish. The reporters seemed to me to be blasé, if not totally bored, at the prospect of listening to yet one more candidate whine about yet one more insult from his opponent. Jack took the mike and laid out the facts about the two America First Committees (ho hum); he then pointed out that the accusation of anti-Semitism didn't fit very well with a man whose wife was Jewish (a brief flicker of interest but not much). Even the fact that Jack and I had both given blood to the Haganah fifteen years earlier stirred only a few reporters into taking notes. But then Jack introduced Irwin Echtman, a young, Jewish lawyer in the Bronx. Irwin had heard that Buckley was summoning the major Jewish leaders to a meeting about "a very important subject." Echtman was able to gain admittance although he had not personally been invited. At the meeting, Buckley asked for help in spreading the word about Bingham's anti-Semitism. The implication was that benefit would accrue to anyone doing so, as well as to his synagogue. Irwin was only too aware that by joining Jack in Manhattan that morning, he was jeopardizing his Bronx law practice. Understandably, he had been torn between idealism and self-interest. He finally decided, he said, that he would have to exhibit the kind of selfless courage that is only too rare in political campaigns or not be able to live comfortably with himself.

How much this step cost his career, I do not know. Politics is full of moments of deep intimacy followed by lifelong loss of contact. All

I know is that after a few years, Irwin and his young family moved away from the Bronx.

On that day in 1964, no sooner did Irwin start giving his firsthand evidence than TV cameras began whirring and reporters began writing. By evening the news was out, not just in the Bronx but throughout the city, that the Boss of the Bronx had felt so threatened by an upstart candidate named Bingham that he had collected local leaders in order to hurl a patently false accusation against this challenger. Thus did the media turn Buckley's potentially lethal weapon into a boomerang.

Another useful side effect of the whole hateful business was Buckley's enraging of Aunt Edith Lehman. Her public endorsement of Jack was something we'd hoped for because so many of our voters remembered Uncle Herbert with love and admiration. But Aunt Edith, though generous to the campaign in a quiet financial way, was reluctant to get ensnarled in the complications of public endorsement. "Herb," she kept reminding us, "never took sides in primaries." Because she was thus emulating her late husband, one of my jobs was to phone her almost every evening and drip poison about Buckley into her ear. But none of Jack's or my efforts bore visible fruit until Buckley made a further mistake. As a guest on the Barry Gray radio show, he boasted that he had known "Hoibitt Layman" a lot better than Jonathan Bingham ever did. Not only was this falsehood infuriating to Aunt Edith, so was his mispronunciation of the Lehman (Leeman) name. Shortly thereafter, she publicly endorsed Jack, and we mimeographed a pile of broadsides about it to be handed out to voters in the parks and at subway stops and to be pushed under apartment doors.

Buckley must have felt really desperate when he decided to impugn our dog, Yankee Poodle. Her name, Buckley claimed, proved that her owner, Jonathan Bingham, was not a true Bronxite despite having lived in the district for eleven years; instead, the name revealed him to be what he really was, a carpetbagging Connecticut Yankee. This accusation brought some guffaws, but when Buckley went after Bingham's own name, people stopped laughing. "Jonathan, Jonathan," Buckley said, "Who in the Bronx ever heard of the name, Jonathan?"

Well, many people, Jews and Christians, had and had given this biblical name to their sons.

Not content with ridiculing Jack's first name, Buckley then went after his middle name. "Brewster!" he said. "Brewster! Isn't that pathetic!" He also called Bingham "a big stiff." This caused my naughtiest brother to phone me to ask when Buckley had seen Jack in the shower.

Yet some of Buckley's comments did damage. Especially was this true with local Orthodox leaders. On the advice of our few contacts within this community, we hired a kosher caterer and invited the leaders of the Orthodox synagogues to our house for dinner. Our children were dressed up, our dog was brushed, our newly delivered kosher food was on paper plates on the table, together with plastic cutlery. (Orthodox people cannot be served on plates that have previously held both meat and milk products.)

Not one person came.

We were heartsick both at the time and for several days afterward as we and the children ate kosher pastrami and other tasty but humiliating leftovers.

Finally, an Orthodox rabbi in the central Bronx was persuaded to let Jack pay him a call. His name was Israel Miller; he later served as vice president of Yeshiva University in Manhattan. In time, he and his wife, Ruth, became our friends, as did our Riverdale neighbors, Rabbi Irving (Yitz) Greenberg and his wife, Blu. Shortly before the day of the primary, at a public meeting to which many Orthodox and other Jewish leaders came, Israel Miller, wearing his yarmulke, stepped forward on the stage, his right hand extended toward Jack: "The house of David welcomes the house of Jonathan."

Relief had me crying like a baby in my seat.

The most exhilarating parts of the campaign resulted from our taking the offensive. In those days, it was only in politics that a lady could publicly exhibit anger—or even outspokenness—and not be seriously censured. One evening, when I heard that Buckley was scheduled to visit a tavern in Riverdale, I volunteered to go nose-to-nose with him. Neither Jack nor Steve objected since I, as a mere female, and probably an unrecognized one at that, could get past the guardians at the door, which neither of them would be able to do. As escorts, I corralled my son Tim who was home from Yale, together with one of his classmates, Gordon Kerr. The three of us marched into the low-ceilinged tavern filled with cigar smoke. The two boys were nervously trailing me as I walked up to Buckley who was standing surrounded by some tough looking hombres. "Congressman," I said, "You and I met in Albany." He looked vague and nodded. "I'm June Bingham and I'm glad to see you again because I've been trying to reach you through the Bronx phone book, and I can't find a listing for any district office."

Boing! A strange sound from my left. Involuntarily I turned my head. Nothing there except a slit-eyed man who said, "Ya hadn't orter talk dat way to de Boss." By the time I turned back to Buckley, he was gone. Vanished. Nowhere to be seen. Tim, Gordon, and I were frustrated but felt that perhaps we had done Jack some good by bringing the battle into Buckley territory and undermining his local aura of omnipotence. He, after all, was the one who fled. And at least we had prevented him from doing himself any further good that evening with the people in the tavern.

Jack's most dramatic offensive, which made the evening TV and radio news and the next morning's front pages, cost a lot of money but was worth every penny. Buckley had long made a point of living, together with his wife, in a relatively modest house in the heart of our district, but he was also rumored to have a huge estate in the Catskills. Jack hired a helicopter and a photographer to get pictures of Buckley's private racetrack. That picture was worth a thousand words—and thousands of votes. People were stunned by the lavish lifestyle he had kept to himself. Meanwhile, Jack and Steve, our campaign manager, indulged in some shenanigans of their own, not in terms of money but of warm bodies. After Jack had presented himself at the five Reform clubs, he needed to make a splash at the Reform convention at which the members would finally choose their candidate. This was to be held at the Concourse Plaza, the only large hotel in the Bronx. Fortunately for our team, the leader of the biggest of the Reform clubs, Angelo Risi, was enthusiastic about Jack. When he was a Regular, Angelo had learned some of their tricks. We were never entirely clear as to how he did it, but somehow he got word out within his club's area that all new members would be welcome at his club even if they couldn't immediately pay their dues. Once these new members were registered, they were asked to vote for Jack. Not all of them lived within the confines of our 23rd Congressional District, but through their membership in the club, they were eligible to vote at the convention. When they all marched into the main hall with their Bingham banners and balloons, they were an impressive sight. In due time, the vote was taken and a virtual stampede resulted when Bingham was acclaimed the victor. Angelo had been smart enough to make sure that Jack did not know about any of these questionable machinations beforehand. As we left the hall, if looks could kill, Forrest Johnson would have done away with Jack and me.

I made peace with this when I thought about how all the major elected officials we knew—or knew about—had at least one politically savvy person on their team who was capable of doing things that the candidate would not do or perhaps even approve of. Franklin Roosevelt had Louis Howe, Herbert Lehman had Charlie Poletti, Averell Harriman had Carmine De Sapio, and Jack had Angelo Risi.

Despite the unremitting efforts by our team, the primary's results would depend more on elements over which we had no control than on those over which we had some. Prime among the former was the weather on June 2. Were the day to be rainy, the Regulars had enough buses and drivers to transport their twenty thousand members to the polls, while the Reformers didn't even have that many umbrellas. The day, thank the Lord, dawned clear. The polls were jammed. Not long after they closed, the result was announced on the radio and TV. Jack and our family were at his main headquarters. When the announcer said that Bingham had won, I was talking to a campaign worker. He and I simultaneously jumped straight up into the air, screaming. When we returned to earth we hugged each other and cried. It was an exultation that I had previously felt only on giving birth and on having a book of mine accepted by a publisher. And everyone in the room seemed to feel the same ecstasy.

CHAPTER 11

Rebellions

IMMEDIATELY FOLLOWING PRESIDENT KENNEDY'S DEATH in Dallas, Marie and Averell turned their house in Georgetown over to Jackie Kennedy and her two children. The Harrimans disliked living at the Georgetown Inn, not that their apartment wasn't large and attractive, but those two people needed a very big home for them to be at ease. The more weeks the stunned and grieving Jackie stayed on in the Harrimans' house, the more restless Marie and Ave became. There was much relief, therefore, when Jackie finally was able to pull her life together and move with the children first to another house in Washington and then to New York.

The new White House incumbent, Lyndon Johnson, retained several of the Kennedy staff, including Walt Rostow and "Mac" Bundy, and added people of his own. One was Bill Moyers, whom we met on several occasions and grew to admire. Eventually, even members of the Kennedy staff had to admit that Johnson, because of his previous experience as Democratic leader of the Senate, succeeded as perhaps no one else could have in promoting the cause of civil rights in America.

A bit more than a year after Johnson arrived at the White House, Jack, as part of an unusually large group of freshmen, arrived in Congress. Though the Voting Rights Act had already been passed, Jack and many of his new colleagues were able to support enthusiastically all the essential follow-up legislation.

This was the era when our Riverdale friend and neighbor, Bob Wylie, a chest surgeon, was called in to Harlem Hospital to help repair the stab wound Dr. Martin Luther King, Jr., suffered. On other occasions we got to know some of King's key associates, notably, Andrew Young, first a colleague of Jack's in Congress and then the U.S. permanent representative to the United Nations. John Lewis, also a congressman, and Roger Wilkins, a journalist, were with us on the trip to Lagos, Nigeria, sponsored by the Africa-America Institute in the course of which our traveling companion, Whitney Young, tragically drowned.

Jack and I were deeply impressed by the self-disciplined, non-violent sit-ins by blacks, women and men, in the South, as well as by the courageous black youngsters who sought admission, supported by federal troops, to formerly all-white institutions of learning. We and most of America were sickened by the viciousness of some local white segregationists and their attack dogs. Television coverage did much to open eyes all over the country to the overriding need for blacks, especially in the South but in the North as well, to register to vote in order to achieve the equality that the Constitution had declared their due after the Civil War.

We also branched out, on occasion, to some after-dinner parties. One was when we took our then older teenagers, Sherry and Jim Bland, Micki and Tim, to the Greenwich Village house of William and Edna Phillips. William was coeditor of *Partisan Review* and was trying to lure me to work for the magazine, more, I suspected, in a fund-raising than literary capacity. The party was intellectually glamorous, with James Baldwin zeroing happily in on Tim and Jim who, I had to admit to myself, were very handsome in an Ivy League way, and with Norman Podhoretz literally sitting at the feet of Diana Trilling, who was reigning in queenly fashion from the sofa. I was thrilled to meet Lionel Trilling whose novel, *The Middle of the Journey*, I had enjoyed and told him so. It had received less critical praise than his literary criticism did, so he seemed pleased to have someone be genuinely enthusiastic about it. We also discussed his friend and neighbor, Reinhold Niebuhr.

Following that evening, the Trillings invited Jack and me to their large Claremont Avenue apartment for an after-dinner party. The conversation, somewhat to my disappointment, centered far more on political power than literary matters. It seemed everybody had politics on their minds at that time.

Within our extended family, the most active member on behalf of civil rights was our nephew, Steve Bingham, youngest child of Alf and Sylvia. Steve was a Yale undergraduate and an editor on the *Yale Daily News* at the time that the Mississippi Summer Project was established under the auspices of the National Council of Churches. Summer sessions were held for six hundred young people in Oxford, Ohio, to prepare them for the Deep South and how best to aid people in registering to vote. Steve attended the first session; our daughter Micki, with her friend Penny Pinkham, oldest child of my friend Bunnie Struthers and Jack's Yale classmate, Dick Pinkham, attended the second. After the training, which included assuming the fetal position when attacked, Steve went off to Mississippi, but Micki and Penny, after much painful soul-searching, decided not to go. Steve assured them he didn't blame them for not coming along to Mississippi where three civil rights workers (one black, two white) whom he knew, Michael Schwerner, James Chaney, and Andrew Goodman, had recently disappeared and not long thereafter were found dead.

Needless to say, Jack and I, like Bunnie and Dick Pinkham, were hugely relieved at our daughters' decision. Alf and Sylvia Bingham applauded their son but remained in a state of constant anxiety, as events fully justified. Some of these are mentioned in a letter that Steve later wrote home:

> I gained a sense of our ability to . . . really fight for a
> cause. The Black communities . . . were patrolled by
> white policemen who at that time could arrest us, and

any Black people who were with us, simply because of our association. . . . I learned late that the thing which angered whites more than anything was not the work we were doing but the fact that we were living with Negroes . . . We realized . . . that there were many things we simply could not do, like drive at night, or travel alone. Once, the verbal assault became physical for me. Canvassing in Durant . . . I was accosted by two white men in a . . . Ford. After a lengthy discussion . . . a heavy-set man of about 30 got out of the car and began to hit me with his fists. I immediately fell into the nonviolent position, which is similar to a fetal position. . . . He hit me for perhaps a minute . . . and then speeded off. I managed to get his license plate and was even able to have him arrested. The trial was even more frightening than being beaten up. All the people in Durant who had harrassed us . . . were at that trial . . . . This town believed not in segregated seating in the courtroom but in an all-white courtroom. At the end of my testimony . . . the mayor suddenly declared him guilty and fined him $60. The man said he would appeal, at which point, I fairly ran to my waiting car and left town at about 100 miles an hour, fearing that part of the crowd in that courtroom would follow. I never did find out the outcome of his appeal. The whole trial seemed contrived to me, [yet] it is highly significant that the mayor thought it important at least to go through the legal motions. This never would have happened a year earlier.

Steve was also arrested and spent a night in jail for "loitering." Later, about to be physically beaten, he assumed the fetal position again but forgot to take off his glasses. They were broken, but, mercifully, his eyes were not injured.

When Alfred heard that Steve's next assignment was to the southwest section of Mississippi then ruled, in effect, not by the relatively moderate White Citizens Councils but by the extremist Ku Klux Klan, Alfred, counter to Steve's wishes, flew south. He wanted to make contact with an old law school classmate of his, a judge who disagreed with Alf on most political issues but nonetheless was a loyal friend. The judge, through his personal network, somehow managed to get Steve's assignment altered. Although this action may have saved Steve's life, Steve was far from grateful to his father. The irony is that while Steve considered his father insufficiently radical, at the same time Alf's own father, Hiram Bingham, refused to talk politics with Alf because Alf was far too radical in his view.

In the mid-sixties, Jack, now a congressman, and I became concerned that far more than politics was heating up in Vietnam. From the American point of view, democracy's enemy there was not the usual villain, Communist Russia. Instead, it was Communist China, which was aiding the Communist North Vietnamese under Ho Chi Minh against anti-Communist South Vietnam. Jack and I were suspicious but did not know enough to counter the prevalent domino theory, originated by Eisenhower pundits, who constantly reminded us that if only England and France had stepped up and halted Hitler in the Rhineland in 1936, there might have been no need in 1939 for World War II. But which lesson of history should be applied at which date and to which country? Just as Hitler learned nothing from Napoleon's defeat by Russia's bitterly cold winter plus its indomitable populace, so the American leadership seemed to have learned nothing from the defeat of the French colonialist rulers by the North Vietnamese in Dien Bien Phu in 1954.

The Sixties

Jack and I were particularly torn about what U.S. policy should be in Vietnam after our trip there in November 1967. American troops and civilians were doing so much good there as well as so much harm that when we got home I wrote an article for *Mademoiselle* warning American girls, "If your young man is assigned to the society-building rather than the destructive side of the Vietnam War it is no insult to you if he [re-enlists] . . . Life in Vietnam is a drug—a habit-forming one at that. The situation is so dramatic, so complex, so rapidly changing, that few Americans there, even when off duty (a rare event since many work a seven day week), speak of anything else."

Flying into Tan Son Nhut, by then the second biggest airport in the world, was an extraordinary experience. Its runways went east and west as well as south and north, with all of them constantly in use as military aircraft of every size and shape entered and exited, together with a few commercial planes such as ours.

Jack and I were impressed by the Point Four–type work Americans were doing in agriculture, health, and education, both through the International Voluntary Services and USAID, together with projects instituted by our military. Whether civilian or military, these Americans in South Vietnam had to remain on constant guard against the local undercover allies of the North, the Viet Cong. Jack and I flew over some dicey areas, once with Lieutenant General Lewis Walt, a humorous and much decorated Marine officer who took us up in a Marine chopper. He was visibly amused by the way I alternated between standing with both hands over my ears (a helicopter at 130 miles per hour is *loud*) and using both hands to cling to a pole midway between the gaping apertures on either side (a military chopper doesn't bother with doors).

Another bit of our flying was from Da Nang, the giant American base on the coast, to Hue, the ancient capital of the once-united Vietnam, with its historic temples and statues of Buddha. On the way, we helicoptered over a patchwork of paddies where people in conical straw hats and black pajamas were stooping and straightening

282

as they worked. Our chopper first headed in one direction, then in another. I shouted at Jack.

"Nice of the pilot to show us so much of the countryside."

"That's not why we're fishtailing."

"Oh?"

"Some of those farmers may be Viet Cong."

"You mean they'd shoot at us."

"Why not?"

"Hmmm."

On arrival at Hue we were amazed by the extensive preparations for our safety. All the way from the airport to the outskirts of town were South Vietnamese troops on the road facing not us but into the jungle whence the camouflaged enemy might strike. Once in the city, we were escorted by South Vietnamese soldiers with guns at the ready on all visits to local officials and to the famous sites. Later, I was told that I had been the last congressional wife to be allowed into Hue and for good reason. Within two months of our visit, the Tet Offensive exploded, with serious American as well as Vietnamese casualties, and Hue itself, for a brief time, was captured by the Viet Cong.

In Saigon, the official briefing I attended was held at the guarded residence of Ambassador Henry Cabot Lodge. The brass had all offered optimistic estimates about the progress of the war. But the questions from the reporters reflected a puzzlement similar to our own. While the enemy body counts were gruesomely high, the enemy dead were being more than replaced by troops moving down from the North and by local converts (voluntary or forced) to the Viet Cong. Ward Just, who we saw occasionally because he lived down the hall from the Brownells, had recently written in the *Washington Post*, "No one can understand the war . . . because the correspondents have not devised a calculus for measuring it as a continuum. The military is worse, professing to find significance in the corpse count and mistaking valor for progress."

Soon after we got home, the Tet Offensive destroyed American hopes for bringing the war to a successful conclusion in the near future, if, indeed, ever. Yet the White House cover-up of war costs continued, and more and more young Americans responded with peace marches. Tono Hixon, Adelaide and Alec's second son, came to stay with us in Georgetown while taking part in one of these marches. He and others were teargassed by local Washington police for shouting, "Hey, hey, LBJ, how many boys did you kill today?" Incongruously, perhaps, Tono later enlisted in the Navy and trained as a frogman, performing highly dangerous underwater demolition in the Vietnam waters.

Senator Eugene McCarthy served as a valuable focal point for the war's opponents when he ran for president in 1968 and came within three hundred votes of winning the New Hampshire Democratic primary. His former wife, Abigail, became a friend of mine through our joint membership in International Club II. These clubs combined diplomatic and congressional wives and had a four P rule for our bipartisan, bicameral meetings: no politics, no protocol, no projects (fund-raising), and no publicity. Our club's members included Barbara Bush, Bethine Church, Betty Ford, and Jane Gebhardt. Our most famous member, Lady Bird Johnson, was by then in the White House.

Much later, Betty Ford recalled that time in her life as one of depression and drink. I did notice that she always liked a couple of preluncheon cocktails, but she never got out of shape the way one of our leading Democratic wives did at a later White House luncheon given by First Lady Pat Nixon. I remember cringing as we Democrats watched one of our own lurching about in her chair next to the unmoving and impassive first lady. A part of Betty's problem was that her husband, Gerry, with his safe seat in Congress, no longer had need of her at campaign time, and the rest of the year he was off helping other Republican members of the House. Betty, therefore, like a number of other congressional wives, felt useless.

Abby McCarthy, on the other hand, had a burgeoning career of her own, contributing a regular column to *Commonweal Magazine* and the *One Woman's Voice* syndicate, as well as publishing excellent books. She was also much more fun to be with than Jack or I ever found her former husband Gene to be. Though Gene was a gifted poet and a courageous political leader, he became, in the phrase coined by our children, "too great of himself." In fact, the only time I ever had to yank Jack Bingham by the arm in order to remove him from what was fast developing into a shouting match was when he and Gene got to arguing at a party on Capitol Hill.

By 1968, Bobby Kennedy, also running for president, was more and more critical of the war in Vietnam. Jack had become acquainted with him when Bobby ran for the U.S. Senate from New York, and Jack was able to help him in small ways in the Bronx. Jack and I were also invited to Hickory Hill, Bobby and Ethel's big rambling white house in McLean, Virginia, for Averell's 75th birthday. The occasion was dressy and glamorous, with an elaborate montage of photos showing Averell at every age. But after the dinner with its hilarious toasts, Bobby seemed more interested in the tete-à-tete he was having with Candace Bergen than with anyone or anything else. Still, Jack's opinion of Bobby had changed from dislike for the young man's earlier hubris to respect for Bobby's ability to learn from experience and his greater depth following the assassination of his brother. We were enthusiastically supporting Bobby for president in 1968 when another, unbelievable, impossible to comprehend, event occurred: Bobby, like his brother, was gunned down.

Just as impossible to take in had been the sickening, ferocious assassination of the Rev. Martin Luther King, Jr., earlier that same year. While Jack and I were painfully mulling over catastrophic matters on the national scene, our children were forced to do far more than mull: they had to decide what to do with their lives in the light of the sixties turbulence. Although the four of them had been born within six years, their attitudes reflected three different "generations." The eldest tended to share the values of her parents, the youngest rebelled violently against these, and the middle two were in between. As Jack and I helplessly watched our youngest turn into a person unfamiliar to us, not only because of her white Sikh costume complete with turban, her brother was facing the potential life-and-death decision of what part he should take in regard to the Vietnam War. He disapproved of America's increasing military involvement there, but he was far from pacifist. He continued his studies at Yale, first at the college and then the law school, and volunteered for community service. He finally joined the Naval Reserve and served one summer on land, and the next at sea. Yale, meanwhile, was confronted with growing radicalism.

During the late sixties, the newly fierce disagreements within families were not restricted to the subject of Vietnam. A second hot issue was the rise of feminism or, as Thurber's cartoons had long labeled it, "The War between the Sexes." Just as Jews, together with blacks, Asians and Latinos, could now choose where they could live and study and work, so, increasingly, did women fight for greater equality in regard to where they could study and work. For my generation, volunteerism enabled many women, as well as some men, to achieve a satisfying, albeit unpaid, career. Ellen Sulzberger Straus coined the term "professional volunteer" for the people, like herself, who performed major such jobs. And Felice Schwartz, through Catalyst, the organization she founded and ran, helped women find good jobs in the paid sector as well as the volunteer one. Yet many volunteer jobs, even at lowly levels, had certain built-in demands that made them unavailable to people like myself who divided their time between two residences. When Jack and I first moved to Washington, I made an appointment with the director of volunteers for the District of Columbia. My hope was to become a tutor in English for inner city children. But when the director learned that Jack's schedule meant that we would frequently be back in New York for a week or more, she turned me down. The prerequisite for successful tutoring, she said, is regularity. When Jack and I first moved to Washington, I was asked by the *New York Post* to write a weekly column describing the life of a brand-new congressional wife. I confessed as amusingly as I could my numerous goofs in house hunting, getting acclimated, and keeping dinner both warm and edible when my husband repeatedly phoned from the Hill to say that he was being delayed by yet another vote, with probably more of them to follow.

In those days, the wife of a newly elected member of Congress was still expected to don hat and gloves and go "drop a card," i.e., an engraved visiting card with its top right-hand corner turned down to denote that it was she herself who was delivering it, on the wife of the speaker of the House and the wives of the chairmen of the committees to which her husband had just been assigned.

At this time, the decision about Jack's committees was delayed. Though Buckley was out of office, he had prevailed upon his friends in the House Democratic leadership to deny to Bingham whatever committee he requested. Jack had thought he would easily attain a place on the Foreign Affairs Committee because it was not a popular one as its members were not able to produce much in a visible way for their constituents. But the House speaker, John McCormack, refused to appoint him. Instead, he offered something that Jack refused to take. Finally, they compromised on the Interior Committee. Jack grew to like it but remained frustrated by having been delayed by at least one term in achieving seniority on Foreign Affairs, which was, after all, his chief area of expertise.

With Buckley still so active against Jack, Jack's political advisers in the Bronx began to worry lest Jack's reelection be undermined by my column's lack of awe about my role as congressional wife. The next primary, after all, was only a year and a half away and we had witnessed how Buckley had tried to use even our poor dog against Jack. On the other hand, I refused to write an "oh gee whiz" kind of column. It would have bored me as well as, I suspected, my readers. So I simply gave up the column. By then, I had milked most of the novelty from my situation as a new arrival anyway. And it went without saying that in any conflict between the needs of Jack's career and mine, his clearly took precedence.

Later, thanks to the recommendation by Abby McCarthy, I was asked to contribute any sort of a column I wanted, once a month, to the national syndicate, *One Woman's Voice*. I found myself writing biographical pieces about women whose lives intrigued me. These included Congresswoman Barbara Jordan, Alice Acheson, Iphigene Sulzberger, and, later, in London, Dame Cicely Saunders, founder of the hospice movement. I also wrote about the three men who had uprooted their own careers in order to accompany their congressional wives to Washington. They were the husbands of Representative Pat Schroeder of Colorado, Representative Yvonne Brathwaite Burke of California, and Representative Patsy Mink of Hawaii. The cheerful adaptability by these men was impressive. I liked and admired them all.

I was also trying to finish my biography of U Thant but this work became complicated. When Jack had moved our family to Albany, I was able to take along all my research material for the Niebuhr book. But now we were living in two cities at once ("I feel," said one congressional wife, "as if I had one foot on the dock and the other on a moving boat"). Even with matching typewriters in both houses, writing was hard for me because my manuscript grew heavier and my voluminous files could only be in one house. When we commuted by air on weekends, my big leather briefcase bulged so much that I could scarcely lug it aboard the Eastern Airlines shuttle. Also jammed into it, to Jack's amusement, would be a small container of milk for our breakfast the following morning and whatever flowers might survive the trip. Just as a flowerless house was an emotional impossibility for me, so was a dogless one. Poor Yankee Poodle, therefore, had to accompany us. At the very sight of her travel box, her ears and tail would droop. I told her I felt the same way.

Our children used to complain that they never knew which house we were in when they wanted to phone—and sometimes I didn't know which house we were in before I opened my eyes in the morning. If Jack was at my left, we were in Riverdale; if he was at my right, we were in D.C.

In New York I had plenty of friends, but they grew discouraged from receiving no answer when they phoned to include me in some daytime activity. In Washington, to begin with I had few friends, and my old ones, Kay Graham and Polly Fritchey, were so engrossed in their work that I could spend time with them only in the evening at dinner parties rather than during the day. Those two were especially close to each other because of having endured identical tragedies: husbands stricken with depression who, on weekend passes to their country houses from the mental hospitals, shot themselves to death.

I didn't mind spending most of my Washington days alone, but when Jack couldn't return in the evening, usually because of a hurried round-trip to the Bronx, I was sometimes lonely. No longer was my house alive with the sound of children—or even a domestic helper—and I had no nearby chums for a spontaneous last-minute date.

A new project that at first seemed promising was to write a book called *Patrician Politicians*. Jack was by no means the only member of Congress to rise from a long-established and well-regarded family. I had a good time interviewing Senator Stuart Symington from Missouri, a friend of Will Scarlett's, and Stuart's wife, Eve Wadsworth Symington, as well as their son, Congressman James Symington. I also talked to Senator Claiborne Pell of Rhode Island and his elegant wife, Nuala. Others who fit the category were Southern senators Bill Brock and Al Gore. But after a number of interviews, I realized that there was no book in this material because these people voted far more often as unique individuals

289

than as predictable members of their class. Karl Marx was wrong in this instance. These men were little more likely to agree on, say, the environment, than any other batch of people. Their main pattern was a lack of pattern.

In time, I grew close to several congressional wives. One was Lucy Moorhead, wife of Bill Moorhead, Democrat from Pittsburgh; another was Emily Preyer, wife of Judge Richardson Preyer, Democrat from North Carolina; and another was Edie Wilkie, wife of Don Edwards, Democrat from California. In spring, the Senate and House wives' tennis tournament provided an opportunity for us to become acquainted with wives from "The Other Body" (as the House and Senate refer to each other) as well as from the other party. I remember playing hard against Barbara Bush whose husband, George H. W. Bush, was still at that time a Republican member of the House. When Barbara had been a little girl in Rye, I had known her older sister, Martha Pierce; also, George Bush's uncle, Louis Walker, had been one of Jack's ushers. Jack and I got along cordially with George and Barbara and later, when George became Reagan's vice president, we were invited, together with other congressional couples, to the vice president's house. A high point of congressional wifehood for me was the evening in early 1965 when I sat in the jammed House Visitors' Gallery to listen to President Johnson addressing the joint session of Congress on the need for greater justice for our Negro citizens. "Ah feel this," he said, "in the marrah of my bones." I fully believed him.

For Jack and me, the Lyndon Johnsons' dinners for congressional couples were fun but stressful. We were invited for seven o'clock but sometimes didn't eat until ten. The president would summon the members to his study and harangue them about how well the war in Vietnam was going while Lady Bird was faced with a batch of wives, growing hungrier by the moment. After the first of these endurance contests, she had her secretary phone a couple of us wives who were known for a skill that might be put to use during the interminable cocktail hour. In 1965, I was asked to make a speech on what it's like to be a writer. It was the only occasion when I have ever been met at Washington's National Airport by a White House limousine (poor Jack, earlier in the day, had been saddled with Yankee Poodle in her box when he flew down from Riverdale). My speech went off nicely, and I was glad to be of use to Lady Bird whose equanimity appeared unshakeable and whose adaptability was impressive. Johnson himself was an overpowering, testosterone-exuding giant.

Jack, together with a few white and black colleagues, went on the civil rights march in Selma, Alabama. He got banged up, but not by white supremacists. He simply lost his balance while clambering over a stone wall as a shortcut to joining up with his congressional friends and ended up with a bleeding leg.

Though neither he nor I contributed in any important manner to the civil rights struggle other than financial donations, we tried in small ways to demonstrate our heartfelt solidarity with it. When all congressional families were asked by the black-led Welfare Rights Organization to live for a week on the dollar-allotment for food that welfare recipients receive, we volunteered. I later wrote an article called "Weak on Welfare." At the end of those seven long days, I truly felt weak on the few rations we could afford. Each working day I made Jack a big peanut butter and jelly sandwich and scraped two carrots for his lunch; my own lunch was even skimpier. For dinner, we couldn't afford our usual fresh fish or meat as a main course, but I did make a stew with chicken wings and a soup with lots of beans and rice and the stem-area of the tomatoes for our salad. Jack lost weight, but I gained some. During the final two days, I had a severe headache. My doctor later explained that a radical shift in diet makes some people retain fluid in their tissues. Probably my extra fluid had caused the weight gain while the swollen tissues inside my skull caused the headache (both symptoms promptly disappeared as soon as we went back to our ordinary diet).

For some reason that he didn't explain, Averell was furious at us for this experiment in poverty. Perhaps it was too quixotic; perhaps it triggered some guilt in him for having always had so much money. He was alerted to what we were doing because Jack's and my small rented house was only a block from his elegant mansion, and I often spent the torrid Washington afternoons in their swimming pool. Partly this was for the pleasure of being with Marie, and partly it was a form of therapy for my back, which was growing more and more painful.

Again, the orthopedic surgeon and the neurosurgeon wanted to remove the protruding disc and fuse my two lowest vertebrae. Again, I tried to postpone the operation. The statistics in regards to cure were not all that much better than they had been nineteen years before. But now our children were grown, so their need for me was no longer so compelling. Jack said this was to be my decision. If only we tolerated separation better, I could stay put in one or the other of our houses and see him part of the time, rather than straining my back by commuting virtually every weekend so we could be together. Yet how could I complain after our silver anniversary had passed that we still yearned for each other's company to such a degree? Basically, what I needed to decide was whether the opportunity to improve the quality of my life was worth the risk of losing it entirely, or, less awful but still frightening, of emerging from the operation a cripple? These were high stakes, and I continued to waffle for as long as I reasonably could. That whole experience helped to persuade me that making up one's mind can be sometimes just about the hardest work in the world.

CHAPTER 12

Disaffection

ONE WEEKEND IN 1965 as I was driving our station wagon from Washington to New York, a back spasm caused such agony that I had to use my right hand to lift my right leg from the gas pedal onto the brake pedal and back again. This was clearly a stupid and dangerous way to drive. I caught sight of a young soldier hitchhiking by the side of the road. I moved my foot to the brake.

"Hi," I called, "Do you know how to drive?"

"Of course."

"Well, please come take the wheel, and let me lie down in the back."

Thus he and I cruised along together until his turn-off for Fort Dix. Reluctantly, I had to take the wheel again and barely managed to get the car and myself home. Jack and I agreed that the spinal fusion could no longer be postponed. The surgeons fitted me into their schedules and the operation took five hours. My recovery was painful, especially the right hip from which the chief of orthopedic surgery at Presbyterian Hospital had removed the bone chips needed to "glue" the two vertebrae together. I also lost the top notes of my singing voice because a vocal chord was damaged by my having to lie for all those hours on my stomach with a tube down my throat.

Jack commuted every day from Riverdale to Washington, stopping off to see me at the hospital at seven in the morning and returning there in the evening whenever he could get back. I would try to time my painkillers so that I would be at least somewhat coherent when he came by. His visits were the high point of those very long days. My mother's visits were well-meant, but I found my muscles clenching up. I begged Frank, the surgeon, and Bud Wilcox, our family internist, to ask her to limit her time with me, but either they didn't dare confront her or she ignored their requests.

For six months, I was encased by day in a torso-length, steel-reinforced corset. Even with it on, I couldn't lift anything of weight. To be both helpless and in severe pain caused me for the first time to understand why people who do not have a whole lot to live for might consider putting an end to it.

A few months later, I managed to land myself in even worse trouble. Two years previously, at age forty-seven, I had discovered lumps in both breasts. The lumps turned out to be benign. (The program for breast self-examination was decades in the future, and mammograms were still at an experimental stage.) Suddenly I felt a golf ball-like object deep in my left breast. The next morning I phoned Bud Wilcox. His response was other than the standard professional one. What he said was, "Oh dear."

He sent me to Bob Wylie, the chest surgeon who worked on Martin Luther King, Jr., when he was shot. Bob wanted to operate right away, but the OR schedule had no opening for a month. I went back with Jack to Washington to wait. It never crossed our minds to hurry up and have the operation done there.

Three weeks later in Washington my phone rang. It was Bob Wylie.

"We've just had an OR cancellation. Can you get here by tomorrow afternoon?

"I'll ask Jack . . . "

"Don't ask. Just be here."

"Is it that urgent?"

"Yes."

This time Jack did the driving. With us were Yankee Poodle and also our domestic helper, Annie Price, who was as small and wizened as her cousin Roberta had been tall and full-figured. Annie

294

Price usually remained in Riverdale, but during that week I'd need her in Washington.

Jack dropped me off at Presbyterian Hospital. He then took Annie and Yankee to Riverdale and came back. That evening he was in my hospital room when Bob Wylie, accompanied by Bud, both white-coated and solemn-faced, appeared. What they had never even hinted to us before was the fact that when my benign lumps were removed two years earlier, the surrounding tissue in both breasts was found to have further deteriorated to a precancerous condition called lobular hyperplasia. Bob now asked me to decide whether, if they found that tissue had further deteriorated into carcinoma-in-situ, should he remove the second breast as well as the one with the lump? I looked at Jack and we both immediately nodded. What I wanted above all was to have cancer off my mind, as well as off my body, and what he wanted above all was to have my company, regardless of my body's appearance.

When the doctors departed, Jack and I were stunned. Why hadn't they warned us about the hyperplasia? Why hadn't they checked my tissue during the intervening two years? At that time, patients didn't talk back to doctors or even ask many questions, and malpractice suits were rare. Both Bud and Bob were at the top of their profession, teachers as well as practitioners, and pals of ours besides, yet Jack and I felt somewhat betrayed. Of course, in those days, there were none of the diagnostic tools like CTs or PET scans or MRIs.

After the operation when I came to, Bob Wylie was sitting by my bedside. From his expression, I assumed the worst.

"Both?"

"Yes. Actually the carcinoma in the second breast was worse than in the first."

"And the lump?"

"Benign."

So that golf ball had acted like a barking dog and saved my life. Because the cancer was caught at so early a stage, I did not have to undergo radiation or chemotherapy. But my two similarly stricken contemporaries, Martha Morgenthau and Nancy Blaine Harrison, did, and nonetheless soon died.

When I was finally wheeled back to my room, Jack was so relieved that I was safe that he paid little emotional heed to the loss of my breasts, much as he had appreciated them. He also had major news to impart. The night before, he had arrived home to find Annie Price unconscious on the dining room floor, with Yankee Poodle curled comfortably against her side. Jack phoned Bud Wilcox, our doctor, who lived nearby. Bud had just gotten his pants off and was looking forward to bed, but he put his pants back on and came over. He diagnosed Annie as having had a massive cerebral hemorrhage. He summoned an ambulance, which took her to the neurological section of Presbyterian Hospital. She had been just across the street from me. She died the next day.

How could we handle her funeral? Jack had to be in Washington and I was flat on my back with drains on both sides going into containers on the floor. We phoned Tim, then a student at Yale, and asked him to represent the family. This he did, apparently with great charm.

My friend, Adelaide sent a beautiful plant with a note that read, "No use crying over spilt milk." My brother Dick, too, managed to make me snicker when he first came to see me at home: "You just look the way you did when you were eleven."

My mother, however, berated me for referring to the surgery as an amputation. "Don't talk like that," she cried. "You can't imagine how dreadful it was for me to go to Bloomingdale's and buy you those padded bras; I nearly wept, right there in front of the sales-woman." So once again I was at fault. But dammit all, it *was* an amputation, and I felt the better for having found for it the mot juste.

In those days, body parts, especially those with sexual or elimi-native function, were never mentioned in public—nor, most of the

296

time, even in private. Only to my closest friends did I report on the loss of my breasts. Reinhold and Ursula knew because he, too, had simultaneously landed in Presbyterian Hospital for an operation. Fritz Redlich knew about me because he was a doctor as well as a pal. A year later, I drove to New Haven for a ceremony at the Yale Medical School at which a bronze bust of Fritz was unveiled. Afterward, I went back for a drink to the handsome modern house he shared with his second wife, the opera singer Herta Glatz. I was walking down the stairs to their living room as he and Herta stood near the bottom step.

"Hey, Redlich," I called. "Now you have a bust, and I don't."

He burst out laughing.

Then death did occur. I was brushing my teeth in our Riverdale bathroom when Jack, who had gone down for breakfast reappeared, looking odd.

"Your mother has died."

"What! You mean *your* mother. She's twenty years older . . . "

"I know, but it's your mother who died. Howard just phoned from the apartment. Dick's there, and they want you to come right away."

I was stunned, but I also felt some relief, partly for her, but also for me. She was seventy-two and during the past years her life had been reduced to visits to doctors for her arthritis, sinus, and colitis, as well as for her depression that was exacerbated by the neglect by her former beaus plus all the mistakes made by her children. Yet three days beforehand, she had enjoyed a visit from her first great-grandchild, Edward, aged one-and-a-half. "A chip off the old block," she told me on the phone. "He loved the caviar I gave him."

When the coroner arrived at her apartment, he asked Howard, Dick, and me if we thought she had killed herself. We simultaneously said, "No." He pointed out that her medicine cabinet held enough drugs for several suicides, but we continued in our denials. Her internist had reported that a fit of coughing in a lifelong smoker like her might well have arrested her heart or caused a massive stroke. The coroner asked if we wanted an autopsy. We did not.

Whereas my grief at my father's death had been the clean kind, my grief at my mother's death was a murky one. Intellectually, I realized that I had never been able make her life a happy one, but, in fact, I felt guilty for having failed to do so. I did not honestly want her alive again because her demands on me had grown progressively more onerous, but I still felt awful about her death. I had nightmares. I tried wearing black clothing but that depressed me; I tried wearing bright colors but that seemed disrespectful. Even after her death, I felt I wasn't doing enough.

To my surprise, the condolence letters from her few old friends reported how proud of me she had always been. Saying nice things behind people's backs turns out to be a terrible waste. If only she had said a few of them to my face.

Our children's lives were mostly centered well beyond the family home. Three of them were falling in love and getting married, with the adorable Will Scarlett loyally traveling down from Maine to perform each wedding. Sherry and Jim Bland's was in 1962 in the Rosemary Chapel, with the reception held at Thirlsmere; Micki and Erik Esselstyn's was in 1967 in the Congregational Church in Old Lyme, Connecticut, with the reception at the Salem Camp; Tim Bingham and Sue Hulsman's wedding and reception were in 1968 in the Boston area.

Micki's wedding at the Camp was unbelievably complicated because two days earlier, Jack's mother, aged ninety-two, died there. I suspect the UPS truck bearing presents for the bride almost ran into the hearse conveying the bride's grandmother to the funeral parlor. We couldn't cancel the wedding; some people, like Steve Bingham who lived in California, were already en route by car and thus unreachable. We simply went ahead with our plans. We even chose the new dress my mother-in-law had been pleased to buy for the wedding to be her burial garment.

Disaffection

The surreal aspect of the weekend was symbolized by two vases of white peonies and gladioli that I had ordered to grace the rehearsal dinner. The following day they were moved to the altar of the church for the wedding and on to the Camp for the reception under the marquee. On Sunday, they were moved to the main room of the Camp for my mother-in-law's funeral and when last seen were fading peacefully at her grave in the family cemetery. The headstones of Mothe's parents, Alfred and Annie Olivia Tiffany Mitchell, face south because she so loved her places in Florida and Jamaica, but Mothe's and Henry's, like most of the rest, starting in the late 18th century, face east.

Around this time in Georgetown, when Jack was up in the Bronx wooing the voters, I was sitting in the sunny kitchen of our small house when the mail was shoved in through the brass slot in the front door. Oh hurray, I thought as I picked it up: a letter from Claudia who had transferred after two years at Vassar to the University of Chicago, which she loved.

The large paper contained an "I love you" in tiny wiggly letters on the right-hand bottom corner but otherwise was totally covered with yellow and orange, blue and green, psychedelic designs.

With barely any forethought I ran out of the house and rang the doorbell of a neighbor who was a psychiatrist. He opened his front door and I shoved the paper at him.

"Is this LSD?"

"Clearly."

This led to a trip to Claudia's dormitory at the University of Chicago. She didn't look well and was clearly getting involved with drugs and the wrong people. I was torn by guilt, anger, and utter frustration. When I told my brother Howard what Claudia was up to, he said, "Well, I remember one time when she was little, she clung to your leg and you pushed her away." My face must have registered such despair that Howard's wife, Ellie, spoke up. "Oh Howard, everyone pushes off a clinging toddler at some stage."

299

Jack and I tried to decide how to handle our financial contribution to Claudia. She was receiving an allowance to cover education, room and board, clothing, and travel. Should we continue to subsidize her immersion in hippie excess? We decided to continue enough money for her room and board, but not for tuition since she had announced her refusal to finish college (which she could have done, since she had somehow managed to pass her final junior year exams). The following year, at age twenty-one, she would gain control of the fund we had been building for her since the day of her birth (three thousand dollars a year from each was the maximum we could give on a tax-free basis to each child).

I set myself to learn as much as I could about the counterculture. For me, the radical divide in values between the two generations was epitomized by the Beatles' music and lyrics. Indeed, the first time I heard them, I had to sit down abruptly; these gifted and articulate young men made me think I might faint. "Lucy in the Sky With Diamonds" had as subtext "LSD"; "She's Leaving Home" was so close to our experience with Claudia that I could bear to listen to it only one time.

The spitting on treasured values forced Jack and me, like many others in our generation, to question our own convictions. After some painful self-examination, we concluded that we fully intended to remain "square" in regard to our marriage and our careers, while opening our minds to the important suggestions by the young about such indisputable values as taking care of the environment. We consequently cut back, as we had during World War II, on personal consumption of meat and gasoline, and had solar panels installed in the south-facing roof of the Riverdale house.

Claudia, pregnant, and her boyfriend went to the south of France where they bought an isolated place near Collobrières. In the process of a home birth, the baby tore the mother's birth canal. Claudia was rushed to a general practitioner who sewed her up and gave her a tetanus shot. Taiki turned out to be a boy with big brown eyes and blond hair and an infectious laugh. After the Vietnam War began to wind down, Claudia and her little family settled in Colorado. Becoming a parent was for her a sobering experience, but not for the man. He continued with drugs; she refused to. Claudia started going to meetings of spiritual leaders, many of them from India.

Jack and I heard about Claudia's change of heart through a letter from her announcing that she and Taiki, then a year-and-a-half old, would be separating from her man and coming to stay in Washington where a Sikh spiritual leader, Yogi Bhajan, had opened an ashram. Around that time, I wrote an article about the set-breaking values espoused by the hippie revolution, both those I agreed with and those I didn't. The *New York Times* used it as the lead article in the *Sunday Magazine*, with a photo of a wistful male hippie on the cover. They entitled the piece, "The Intelligent Square's Guide to Hippiedom." It elicited letters of all kinds from all parts of the country. What an irony for me to have a literary success distilled from all that pain.

In August 1968, a number of her fellow rebels, including some militant Yippies, traveled to Chicago in time for the Democratic National Convention. They wished, understandably, to register their abhorrence of the Vietnam War. Jack and I had checked into the Fairmont Hotel, which was across from Lincoln Park where the disaffected young were gathering. In the afternoon, I wandered out among them, feeling almost invisible because of my advanced age of forty-nine. Some of these latter day "raggles-taggle gypsies" made eye contact with me and a few actually smiled. To me, they appeared like a bunch of male and female Claudias, middle- or upper-class kids, gently nurtured and reasonably well educated. There was a clear likelihood that violence would erupt between them and the sturdy, clean-cut young males of the National Guard stationed in front of the hotel, who appeared to stem mostly from blue-collar backgrounds. Before these fellows pulled down their visors, some of their faces seemed to me to be perplexed, as if they wished that they, too, could have had the chance to go to college, yet they were repelled by the sight and smell of the hairy ones sprawled on the grass, some smoking dope, some tossing food around, and some making out.

Not long after I returned to the hotel, the brewing hostility between the two groups exploded, and the nation was horrified to watch on TV as one batch of American kids hurled teargas at another batch of American kids. After the pandemonium subsided, the injured were removed and the park was cleared, but the cost was a further dividing of an already torn nation.

To Jack's and my relief, LBJ decided to retire in favor of his vice president, Hubert Humphrey. Unfortunately, however, starting at the convention, LBJ was incapable of keeping his heavy hand out of the campaign. He kept hogging the limelight and demanding that Hubert not differ substantially with him on Vietnam, thus making Hubert appear little better than a puppet. For that and other reasons, Nixon won the election. The only good thing about that, from Jack's and my point of view, was that Dick Moore was appointed a presidential assistant. Thus, he and Janie would be moving from California to Washington.

When Jack and I attended the first Nixon reception for congressional couples, President Nixon and the first lady greeted the group in a formal receiving line. Jack preceded me (none of the usual "ladies first" at such protocol-driven events). What on earth, I asked myself, was I going to say to this man whom I had loathed for decades since his vicious and unwarranted attacks on Helen Gahagan Douglas when they were rivals for the same California seat in Congress that he then won? As he greeted me and shook my hand, I said, "You know, Mr. President, Dick Moore was best man at our wedding." Nixon's impassive face broke into a flash of sweetness. "Isn't he wonderful," he said.

Disaffection

That nosey Jack Bingham couldn't wait to hear what I had said to elicit that momentary unbending of the president's expression. After I told him, he said we must be sure and report it to Dick. Over the next several years, Jack and I kept up our enjoyable evenings with the Moores and played an occasional golf game with Dick, but Jack and I deliberately avoided bringing up the subject of Moore's boss. Friendship is one thing; politics is another. Had we met Moore for the first time after he became a Nixonite, we would probably not have become friends. But because our friendship long preceded any connection with Nixon, it survived. Only once, after the Watergate scandal erupted, did Moore raise the issue with us. His feeling was that H. R. Haldeman and John Ehrlichman, whom he personally avoided whenever possible, had done the president grievous harm. Later on, Moore was called to testify before the Senate Judiciary Committee deciding on impeachment for Nixon.

I went over to the Moores' that morning to be with Janie and their daughter Kate as, struck dumb, we watched the hearings on television. Dick Moore's performance was dreadful. He kept saying, "I can't remember" or "I don't know" in response to almost every question. One would have assumed that he was either lying or stupid. Afterward Jane, Kate, and I ruefully agreed that he couldn't have done worse if he'd tried. In time, events proved that he had never been in the main White House loop. When Nixon's tapes were finally released, the president was heard saying something like, "For God's sake, don't tell Moore."

Jack's enjoyment of old friends like Moore was matched by his delight in new friends in Congress. Some were men, like Don Edwards (D-CA), Father Robert Drinan (D-MA), and Morris Udall (D-AZ); others were women, like Bella Abzug (D- NY) and Millicent Fenwick (R-NJ). Those women were always unhesitant about making their opinions known, but in other ways they were very different. Bella was brash and loud, fat, liberal, and Jewish;

Millicent was slim, aristocratic, WASP, and in some ways conservative. Both had trademarks that made them identifiable to the voters, Bella's being her broad-brimmed hat, Millicent's, her tiny pipe. Both also sported a fair amount of jewelry. Both also adored Jack and repeatedly turned to him for advice about how to vote, especially in foreign affairs.

I further grew to like Bella's husband, Martin Abzug, and to salute his and Bella's ability to keep a good marriage going despite her constant absences from New York where his career pinned him down. His relaxed, unthreatened attitude toward her successes was like Jack's comfort with my own (albeit far, far less impressive) ones. Millicent was long divorced, though she must have had many beaus along the way. In her single-minded focus on the issues she cared about, she might have appeared too powerful for some suitors. As it was, on one congressional trip, she nearly got Jack and me, as well as herself, thrown out of the dining room at the ultra-fashionable Brown's Hotel in London because she insisted on lighting up her pipe.

Jack's and my original move from Riverdale to Washington in January 1965 had been relatively easy because, by that time, our children were off at college or beyond it. Also our furniture could remain in place because we planned to be back in the Bronx almost every weekend to permit Jack to court the voters. Buckley's top assistant, Patrick Cunningham, was readying his own challenge to Jack which took place in 1968. Strangers on the streets near the Cathedral of St. Nicholas of Tollantine greeted Jack with shouts of "Baby Killer." This appellation, we assumed, referred to the fact that Jack (as well as I) had long contributed to Planned Parenthood even when contraception (in neighboring Connecticut) was still being prosecuted as illegal, with jail sentences for both doctor and patient. Yet Jack, with Steve Berger's help, won handily.

Buckley persuaded his cronies in the New York State Legislature to alter the borders of Jack's then-23rd Congressional District so that it would include fewer Jewish and Protestant voters and more Irish and Italian. This, in turn, would make it harder for Jack to remain in Congress, a job he relished more and more as he picked up its finer points. Not surprising to me were the comments from some of his colleagues about how useful his legal and wordsmith skills were when compromise language was needed to bring two warring factions into agreement. I cheered when Jack finally reached the Foreign Affairs Committee and, in time, was given his own subcommittee on exports. As a result, we took many official trips, either just us or as part of a congressional delegation.

Fortunately, by the late 1960s, both my back and my front had healed well enough for me to take trips abroad with Jack. When we flew into West Berlin, we were reminded of an earlier trip by our friends, Telford and Mary Taylor. He was a top litigator at the Nuremburg trials, and Mary was eight months pregnant. This was when the Soviets had blocked all roads and railroads to Berlin from the rest of West Germany. Something went wrong with the Taylors' plane, and they were ordered to parachute out onto the Tempelhof tarmac. Mary had no choice but to jump. She survived, and so did her son.

Jack and I spoke in German and English with a number of West Berlin students and government officials as well as ordinary folk on the street. We visited the stark, heavily guarded Wall the Soviet Union had built in 1961. We were given permission to go through the Wall's Checkpoint Charlie into East Berlin. I don't know which was more depressing to us, the drab exteriors of the Soviet-style buildings or the furtive expressions of the people hurrying past them. In contrast to West Berliners, these people did not stop and exchange a few words with Americans.

Another trip was to South Korea. Seoul was a thriving modern city where the fast-walking pedestrians startled Jack and me with the pinkness of their cheeks. We were granted an interview with the prominent opposition leader, Kim Dae Jung, who had formerly been imprisoned—and tortured—by his political enemies. But he appeared not to be embittered, he was even cheerful. After what seemed to me to be a remarkably open discussion between him and Jack, he handed me a thin necklace at the end of which was a small square amethyst-colored stone. From the PR point of view, Kim Dae Jung was impressive in his hopes for his country's growth in democracy. Many years later, in 1997, he was finally elected president of South Korea in his fourth bid for the office.

Jack and I were also driven to the DMZ (demilitarized zone). From the porch of the shack that contained the South Korean command post, we looked through telescopes across at the North Korean guards who were standing on their porch looking back at us through telescopes. The DMZ itself was a wild grass- and shrub-filled area that appeared innocent on the surface but was, we were told, riddled with mines and also tunnels built by the other side.

Claudia soon moved herself and Taiki to the ashram, but he was allowed to spend Wednesdays with me. Teresa Heinz, wife of Senator John Heinz (R-PA), had three little boys about the same age as Taiki; on rainy afternoons, he and I sometimes went over to her large Georgetown house so that he could play with them in their well-equipped playroom. Most of the time I sat companionably with their nanny, but on some occasions Teresa was home and claimed me for tea.

By the time Claudia remarried, to a fellow member of the ashram, Gurunum Singh, Jack and I had moved to a slightly bigger and much more modern house on Reservoir Road in Georgetown. It faced south, with a tiny upstairs view of the Potomac River. On their wedding day, our living room was flooded with sunshine. There, with his back to the wall-sized window, seated in the lotus position on our big yellow pouf, was the yogi. Music was by ashram members playing Indian instruments. Claudia wore a pretty Mexican-embroidered long white gown and, in traditional fashion, was escorted by her father.

Gurunam Singh, like his colleagues, was dressed all in white, including the turban. He had previously come to Jack and me, not to ask permission to marry our daughter, but simply to inform us that he loved her very much. We found this statement touching-- and very welcome.

Later that year, Claudia gave birth to her and Gurunam Singh's first child. I was invited to the birthing. I, with Harbhajan (the name their yogi gave Taiki) on my lap, was in the bedroom where Claudia and Gurunam, were on the double bed together with a midwife who was coaching Claudia and rubbing her shoulders and back. Seated in the lotus position on the floor near the bed were twelve ashramites of both genders, chanting.

I had begged Claudia to go to a hospital, but she insisted on a home birth, and, be it said, the midwife had the name of a doctor whom she could call if unexpected complications arose. The night and the labor continued. So did the chanting and Claudia's hard breathing, and the kindly gestures from her husband and the instructions from the midwife. At last, the head was said to be crowning. Everyone went over to the side of the bed to view this event. I tried to keep Harbhajan on my lap, but he insisted on taking my hand and joining the crowd. Thus, I witnessed birth for the first time. The baby was wet and peaceful. We could see a little Inca-like face before the rest of the body was born. A boy. His father laughed with joy. Yogi had told the parents that the child's name was to be Gurubhajan Singh Khalsa.

I wrote an article about this experience that was published in the *Vassar Alumnae Magazine*. When Kay Graham read it, she asked the *Washington Post* to republish it. On the morning that it re-appeared, I received a phone call from a woman I had never heard of named Mary Z. Gray. She said that before nine in the morning she had received two phone calls from friends asking why she had published the article in the *Washington Post* under the pen name of Bingham. For Mary, too, had a daughter who had had a home birth under similar circumstances. The main difference was that when Claudia's midwife had requested the placenta to take home and someone asked why, she said, "for my garden," whereas Mary Gray's daughter's midwife wanted to eat it. I screamed with laughter: "Cooked or raw?"

Apparently it was cooked—and the placenta, I am informed, is full of minerals and vitamins good for gardens when raw and for adventurous diners when cooked. Mary Gray and I, having been introduced under such unusual circumstances, remained good friends, and she showed a special interest in Gurubhajan.

Because we had been living in New York, not Washington, during the Camelot era, Jack and I had never run into Ethel Kennedy. But after Jack was elected to Congress, we would see her on rare occasions at a Washington party. I decided to write a magazine article about her and the courageous no-nonsense attitude she exhibited toward widowhood and single parenthood.

In the course of my research, I arranged to have a tennis game with her and her sister-in-law, Eunice Shriver. My partner was my Vassar roommate, Sue Bontecou DuVal, who lived not far from Hickory Hill in McLean, Virginia. Our match was extremely competitive. For one point I raced to the back of the court to retrieve a lob and slammed my left hand into the wire backstop. When the point had concluded, I noticed that my hand was bleeding. The fence I had encountered was covered with rambler roses with thorns. After the match I showed my wound to Ethel. She said the roses were pretty and players just have to take their chances. In spite of her tough attitude, I liked her and admired the warm but casual way she handled her many children. Her attitude was not unlike that of my prolific sister-in-law, Rose Bingham.

The national magazine that had commissioned the article on Ethel wanted me to add some material that I thought was too gossipy. When I objected, they said they would pay full price for the piece but insist on their own additions. I said that in that case they could not use my name. I rather suspect that they didn't care a whit. So the article appeared with some material I would not have used and under someone else's name. At least I could look Ethel in the face and at myself in the mirror.

After my well-received article on hippies in the *New York Times Magazine*, I was asked to speak on that subject at New York's Colony Club. Outfitted in a long gown covered with psychedelic images and wearing a headband around my long-haired wig, I started out by saying, "You squares are all wet." After voicing the hippies' chief complaints against people like myself and my audience, I suddenly pulled off my wig and plaintively cried, "What are we going to do about these kids of ours?"

But before I could reach that point in the speech, three perfectly coiffed and elegantly garbed older ladies marched out of the auditorium. I didn't know how to respond but decided just to continue with my tirade. I was happy to be told later that the three had been mercilessly teased by their friends for having missed the rest of the speech and the probing questions it elicited. Adlai Stevenson's statement, "No generation can predict the weapons the next will use against it," was especially applicable to us squares during the 1960s when our idealistic but extremist progeny turned away from us in unconcealed disgust.

PART FIVE

The Seventies

CHAPTER 13

Challenge

JACK BINGHAM WAS SHOCKED IN 1972 when the New York legislature redrew the state's congressional lines. He was deprived of about one-third of his district, and our neighboring liberal Democratic congressman, James Scheuer, was deprived of two-thirds of his. Before the new lines were definite, Jack and I had attended a fund-raiser for Jim Scheuer and gladly contributed to his upcoming campaign. After the lines were definite, we were told that Jim was planning to run against Jack in the new district—which was mostly Jack's. Jack was distressed but philosophical; I was furious and wrote to Jim asking for our money back. It promptly arrived.

Politically, this was a hard fight for Jack because of Jim being Jewish and very rich, while the new district was heavily Jewish and quite poor. Jim had made and continued to make major financial contributions to local synagogues and other worthy organizations. During the ensuing campaign, he dedicated a thirty thousand dollar swimming pool in honor of his mother at a local YMHA. If most of the district's Jews were to vote along ethnic lines, Jack would lose badly, especially if the Regular (Buckley) Democratic clubs, with their Irish and Italian Catholic membership, continued to bad-mouth Bingham for having dared to defeat first their long-term leader and then his successor, their current leader, Pat Cunningham. On the other hand, the Regulars had no great love for Scheuer. As for the Protestants in the new district, these were a mere 10 percent and included many blacks who, characteristically at that time, did not bother to register for or vote in primaries.

Once again Steve Berger became Jack's campaign manager and once again part of my role was to drip poison into Aunt Edith Lehman's ear. In the middle of the campaign, a bright, sexy young woman on Jack's Washington staff confided to him that she had been offered a fancy apartment in a nearby Scheuer-owned building if she would secretly cooperate with Jim's campaign. This was the kind of thing Aunt Edith was not happy to hear, especially as the young woman had been with Jack since his first day in Congress and had proved herself thoroughly loyal to him. By the latter part of the campaign, Aunt Edith became so incensed over statements by Scheuer and his campaign manager, Dick Brown, that she finally agreed to come to the Bronx and publicly endorse Bingham. We invited her to Co-op City for an afternoon concert by our family orchestra. The jam-packed audience was so responsive that Aunt Edith got swept up in their enthusiasm and ended up dancing the hora, much to the amazement of her family members and, I strongly suspect, herself. I kept having trouble blowing into my recorder because of the laughter welling up within me at the thought of what my grandmother, even my mother, would be saying. But Uncle Herbert and Uncle Irving, I was certain, would have been delighted with her.

Another good break for Jack was that Scheuer happened to be in the Bronx campaigning on the day the House of Representatives voted an appropriation of thirty million dollars for aid to Israel. Although Jim's vote was not needed for passage of the bill, our team was out the next day at the subway stops, parks, and streets handing to voters a one-page broadside asking why Jack's opponent had missed this crucial vote. There followed, needless to say, a similar mailing by us to registered Democrats.

But mass mailings are expensive, as is much else in a campaign, and again we had to devote a huge amount of time and energy to fund-raising. This I found more than usually galling because Jim was rich enough not to have to do much of it and was outspending us by more than two to one. Again we were forced to drum up publicity for Jack, and again we were grateful to those reporters who came to his press conferences and lent at least half an ear.

The primary, for Jack and me, was difficult because we often felt that this seemingly endless expenditure of time, effort, and dollars was likely to be in vain. When I first went out into the Jewish areas and said to people, "I hope you'll vote for my husband," the typical answer was a shrug and "I hope so." Midway through the campaign, when I said, "I hope you'll vote for my husband," the answer became, "Good luck." At the end of the campaign when I said, "I hope you'll vote for my husband," the answer was "Why not!" That was the day I came home and told Jack I thought he was going to make it after all.

And indeed, on Primary Day, it was clear that the Jewish voters, contrary to prediction, did not vote as an ethnic bloc. In the section of the new district that had been Jim's former area, he won, but not by much, and in the part that was Jack's former area, Jack won decisively. Again, Jack and I felt an inexpressible elation, together with an almost tearful gratitude to the voters, the indefatigable campaign workers, and the generous contributors who had made Jack's victory possible.

Why did the voters act as they did? One theory is that they felt that Jack could do the most good, both on behalf of the Bronx and also Israel, precisely because he was not Jewish and would therefore not be dismissed as a special pleader. Steve Berger's hypothesis was that people enjoy having their representative appear higher in social status than themselves. In any event, two years later, Jim Scheuer moved to Brooklyn and ran for Congress, with Steve Berger as his campaign manager. That time Jim won. I had always remained on cordial terms with Jim's wife, Emily Malino, a gifted decorator, and Jack and Jim proceeded to work comfortably together on liberal legislation. Underneath, the relationship between our two families was probably best symbolized by one of their young children who, on the day after the Bronx campaign, stuck out her tongue at Jack.

Back in Washington, Jack went for a routine physical at the Naval Hospital in Bethesda. For reasons lost in the mists of time, the Navy takes care of House members, while the Army at Walter Reed Hospital takes care of the senators. To our shock, Jack was diagnosed as having prostate cancer.

We were both so stunned that we could hardly think what to do. The only thing Jack was sure of was that no one, aside from the doctors and myself, was to find out about it, lest the word get out and the political piranhas start circling his congressional seat. This meant that not a single one of our children, or our close friends, or his devoted staff should be given the slightest reason to suspect that all was not well with him. This rule of silence was a realistic safeguard for his career, but it also meant that I would have no one except him to talk to about my feelings — which varied between terror and hope. In fact, I was reluctant to bring up the subject with him unless he mentioned it first. If he could momentarily be free from worry about it, I didn't want to reduce that freedom. For him and me, it was a time of great closeness, yet also of unprecedented loneliness.

The Navy captain who served as chief surgeon of urology at Bethesda Hospital summoned Jack and me for a conference. He said that we had three options: surgery, radiation, or female hormones. Jack, with my total agreement, opted to start out with radiation. Every morning for six weeks, he presented himself at George Washington University Hospital, which was on his way to the Capitol. There he was bombarded with the requisite number of localized rads. I cancelled all the social engagements I could so he could rest in the evenings. He became fatigued, a bit pale and a bit thin, but none of the children or anyone at his offices in Washington or the Bronx suspected anything.

No sooner did he recover his strength than a routine bone scan revealed that the cancer had metastasized from the prostate into the bone. When I was asked if I wanted to see the film, I said yes. Jack's upper spine and rib cage looked like the night sky, with many sizes and shapes of stars, each denoting a new cancerous lesion. He was given the choice of surgery or the daily taking of a female hormone (DES). Some men refuse the hormone or agree to it and then "forget" to take it because it is far from an enhancer of virility. But Jack, a realist, named the pills his "Life-Savers," and swallowed one every morning without fail. Six months later his bone scan, to my eyes, was an incredible miracle, with the former night sky totally dark except for one remaining "star," which the doctor thought was probably just scar tissue. How lucky we were that Jack's prostate cancer fit into the 50 percent that do respond to hormone treatment. A reprieve had been granted, of perhaps a year, perhaps five, perhaps even ten, perhaps, unbelievably, more. That was when he coined the term "enjoyer" for the human capacity to revel in the moment without allowing worry about the future to interfere. He insisted that it was up to me, too, to keep my own "enjoyer" well-honed.

I agreed with him. When I was very young, I had lived in terror of being cheated by death before I'd had a chance fully to live. Even in early middle age, I was terrified that Jack or I might be killed before we'd had a chance to bring our children safely into adult independence. But by the 1970s, with all the kids married, I realized that for Jack and me our quality of life was more important than its quantity. As long as he felt well enough to live in normal fashion, I would not allow the present to be undermined by fears for the future. Hawthorne wrote, "All persons chronically diseased are egotists, whether the disease be of the mind or the body." Jack was "chronically diseased" but did not become an egotist; I, therefore, had no excuse to allow myself to become one either.

At the same time, at age fifty-five, I had to face not only what his illness might do to him but also what his death might do to me. I started keeping a diary. Before then, I'd been so absorbed in the process of living that I could rarely summon the requisite energy at night to write down the day's doings. (I did, however, keep annotated date books.) Also, I figured that crucial events would indelibly etch themselves into my mind while much of the rest would conveniently slip into oblivion. Thus, I'd avoid saddling myself with a shelf of notebooks that I was sure I'd be reluctant to read. On the other hand, to write about what is churning inside me is second nature. Most striking, as I now read it, is the frankness with which I weighed suicide for myself as an escape from what I foresaw as the overwhelming anguish of bereavement. I had been married for twice as long as I'd been single — and to continue life without Jack simply didn't seem worth the trouble. Besides, what could the final decades of life provide that would be worth the immense and painful effort to keep myself going from day to day with appropriate grace? As I wrote at the time, "Do I owe a duty to grandchildren not to take an overdose the same time J. goes? Probably not. My impact on them is marginal . . . and certainly my children do not need me."

Right?

Wrong.

Our children clearly still needed us. For example, shortly after the birth of our first granddaughter, Katherine Ellis Bingham, Jack and I were in Riverdale when her father phoned from New Haven early in the morning:

"Hey, Mom, what are you doing today?"

"Nothing special. Why?"

"Well, Sue has a breast engorgement and high fever."

"No!"

"Nothing to worry about. She's on antibiotics.

"Thank God."

"But she's feeling kind of weak and I have to go to work. and Katherine needs . . . "

"I'll be there."

I gathered up some necessities, whistled for Yankee Poodle, and drove off. My day was nonstop but immensely gratifying. My ordinarily independent and bustling daughter-in-law lay in bed and had meals provided; my newborn granddaughter was tolerant about being bathed and cuddled by a stranger. (Sue had been encouraged to keep up the nursing.) I was able to venture forth to procure groceries and then fix supper for when Tim got home. Feeling essential to young people whom one loves is surely one of the major elations of one's middle years. It was particularly rewarding that day because by evening Sue's fever had dropped. I left their dinner in the oven with instructions for Tim and departed for Riverdale to fix our own.

Three months later, I again served as amateur nurse for our second granddaughter, June (Jody) Eriksson Esselstyn, born to Micki and Erik in Cambridge, Massachusetts, where Erik was working at Harvard for his doctorate of education and Micki, for her Boston University master of social work. Both mother and daughter were doing so well that my main job, besides shopping and cooking, was to fend off the multitude of visitors who arrived at their doorstep with baby clothes and demands to see Micki "just for a minute." I did let them peer down at newborn Jody in our family bassinet that had once held my brothers and me, my own children, and then, more recently, Jody's first cousins, but I insisted that Micki be left to sleep. This did not go over well with some of the guests, but Micki was relieved. My nickname became "Cerberus," though what I was guarding was not the gates of hell but those of an earthly heaven.

Just as Katherine and Jody were born within a three-month interval, so were their brothers, two years later. Jonathan Brewster Bingham II arrived in New Haven in December, and Blakeman Bingham Esselstyn arrived in March in Charlotte, North Carolina, where Erik was working as assistant to the president of a large community college. Again, I had to play Cerberus toward Micki's even more attentive new Southern friends. When Blake was just a week old, I received a phone call from Sherry in Brunswick, Maine, announcing, that her and Jim's third son, Richard Franklin Bland, had just been born.

I barely had time to stop off in Washington, embrace my neglected husband, and collect another clean white blouse before flying off to Brunswick to take care of Sherry and Rich. Jack joined me there over the weekend, and we had a happy time with Sherry and Jim, their three lively boys and two lively huskies. They lived in a beautiful 19th-century house in the middle of that picture-book New England town. Jim had recently received tenure as associate professor of American history at Bowdoin College and was very popular with the students. "I feel I am doing," he said, "what I was put on earth to do."

He was also able to keep his elegant sloop in a nearby marina; in good weather, he often took his family for a sail. Or he would go off by himself to explore the waters around the small offshore islands that caught his fancy. In sum, he appeared to have everything in the world that anyone could possibly want—except, as it turned out, an enjoyer.

Jim's depression grew, and in the end, he overdosed on pills. In Jim's farewell note, found in his wallet, he had told Sherry she was the finest person he had ever known.

As with the suicide of Louis Stone, her godfather, twenty years before, I kept wishing I believed in an afterlife just so when I died I could go up to the one who killed himself and kick him in the shins. Jim—like Lou—has missed so incredibly much by not being around to help his three children grow up, and the children have missed their father in such profound ways that I still get upset when I think about it.

Sherry decided she would not stay in Brunswick for the winter but would move to Washington where she could be near not only us but also her many friends from Potomac School days.

One day when her son Edward was around eight, I pulled out a cigarette and started to light it.

"Ahmee," he said, using the name all my grandchildren and, later, great-grandchildren, called me. "What are you doing?"

"What does it look like? I'm lighting a cigarette."
"Don't you know it's bad for you?"
"Um, well, yes."
"Then why are you doing it?"

Oops, I thought; whatever answer I give is likely to be thrown back in my face when this child becomes a teenager and perhaps experiments with drugs. I decided that until I could think up a suitable explanation, I had better not smoke. I, therefore, put away the cigarette and never smoked again. For the next ten years I missed it, and for ten years after that, I still enjoyed secondhand smoke; now, smoke revolts me. All that time Edward has been Mr. Smugs about having saved his grandmother's life.

Some two years after Jim's death, Micki's husband, Erik Esselstyn, began feeling odd. Finally, after an extensive endoscopy, the doctors discovered a cancer in the duct that drains bile from the liver into the intestinal tract. For almost a decade afterward, Micki was the breadwinner while Erik was repeatedly subject to wild fevers caused by bacteria that invaded the bile duct and reproduced with great speed.

Micki and Erik left Charlotte and went to live in Blue Hill, Maine. After a decade, Erik was well enough for a full-time job, and they moved to New Haven where he worked for the Gesell Institute. Micki earned a master of divinity degree at New York Theological Seminary. We proudly attended her ordination as a minister in the Congregational Church in New Haven, the one from which her Bingham ancestors had gone forth to the Pacific as missionaries.

Around this time, Jack came home with a wrapped box, too big to be a jewel, but too small to be a dress. He couldn't wait for me to open it. I did so and cried out, "Oh no!" It was a clarinet.

"You've always said how much you love its sound."
"But that doesn't mean I want to play it."
"It comes complete with a batch of lessons."
"I don't—"

Here I am, right, in the family orchestra, in the late 1950s, playing the recorder. Jack urged me to graduate to a clarinet, which he wrapped up as a present and offered me with great enthusiasm, in the 1970s. He was imagining a fuller and truer sound for our impromptu chamber music concerts.

"You know that the recorder doesn't play true enough for family orchestra . . ."

"But still—"

"Just think! Once you learn it, you can play the slow movement of the Mozart clarinet quintet with our string quartet . . ."

"Well . . ."

Jack's Washington string quartet comprised Justice Abe Fortas, John Wolf, and Gordon Stott; his far more informal Riverdale one was improvised with our neighbor, Joe Ford, and visiting violists like Micki, and cellists like Tim. That wicked Jack Bingham knew that my favorite piece of music, up in the stratosphere with the "Liebestod," was the Mozart clarinet quintet.

I took the clarinet lessons and had sore cheeks as I developed the necessary embouchure (maintaining flatness of cheek while blowing into the instrument). In time, I was able to play the quintet with him and his Riverdale friends. For me it was ecstasy.

On another occasion, too, the clarinet came in handy. Yankee Poodle had been growing lamer and deafer and more reluctant to travel in her box by air between Washington and New York. One Saturday in Riverdale, after the trip, she was lying in the sun in the dining room. Jack and I were in the kitchen. Yankee must have made some sound, because I found myself hurrying to her side. I picked her up, instinctively holding her like a baby against my heart, with my hand up against her chest. I could feel her heart beating heavily, and then it simply stopped. She must have waited for me to be with her at her death. I carried her to the kitchen. Jack swallowed hard, went to the garage for a spade and dug a hole big enough for a St. Bernard. I wrapped Yankee in the waterproof cover of her plaid pillow-bed. When I could gather my strength, Jack placed Yankee in the hole, and while he was shoveling the dirt back in, I played "Taps" on my clarinet.

Eventually our children abandoned their instruments in favor of that lovely one, the human voice. Sherry sang in the church choir, Micki interspersed songs in some of her sermons, Tim sang in all of Sue's chancel operas, and Claudia did a great deal of chanting, both solo and with other devotees.

Around this time, I met Alice Roosevelt Longworth, daughter of President Teddy Roosevelt, and widow of Speaker of the House Nicholas Longworth, whose own granddaughter, Joanna Sturm, a teenager, was still living at home with her.

"Mrs. L," as her younger friends addressed her, was someone I had come to know by way of Marie Harriman (one of the few people who addressed her as "Alice"). At that time, I was writing my syndicated column and thought that one describing Washington's famous grande dame, the former "Princess Alice," would be of general interest.

Actually the article expanded and instead ended up as a full-length feature in *American Heritage* magazine.

Marie took me to tea at Mrs. Longworth's old townhouse on Massachusetts Avenue just above Dupont Circle. The groundcover on the rectangle adjacent to her front walk was riddled with poison ivy. When Stewart Alsop, the journalist who was Mrs. L's nephew, suggested that she might wish to have the ivy eradicated, she snorted dismissively, "I like it there."

Apparently, she had decided that our teatime together should start off with a bit of shock treatment. No sooner had Marie introduced us than Mrs. Longworth said, "Your mother-in-law, Suzanne Bingham, is a dreadful woman."

I burst out laughing. "She certainly is."

My response surprised her, and we had a fine time comparing notes on Suzanne. Mrs. L hooted at the story of Suzanne's behavior toward me at Woodbridge's luncheon. "I hate snobs," Mrs. L said, "They're always snobbish for the wrong reasons."

She and I agreed, however, that my father-in-law was as handsome as the day is long but sometimes stuffy in his viewpoint. Mrs. L, by birth a Republican, was far from stuffy in most of hers. Later, when I brought Claudia along to tea, Claudia said approvingly, "Mrs. L is just like someone who has dropped acid: her associations are so free."

When I reported this to Mrs. L, she was delighted. She had recently had a second mastectomy. "Now I'm on LSD as well as being the topless wonder of Massachusetts Avenue."

Claudia and Joanna Sturm liked each other although their paths rarely crossed. Joanna looked eerily like her "Grammy," Mrs. L: the same cool, light-blue eyes; the same quick intelligence. But Joanna had been brought up to be religious (Roman Catholic) and Mrs. L had jettisoned such religion as she had been brought up with (Protestantism). Mrs. L was not a maternal sort, but she took devoted care of Joanna who at age eleven had suddenly been sent to live with her.

The reason was that Joanna's mother, Mrs. L's only child, Paulina, newly widowed, had just killed herself. Up to then, Joanna had heard nothing good about "Grammy." Nonetheless, the two of them were confronted with the need to get along in the same house for more than a decade. They solved this problem magnificently. Mrs. L sent Joanna to Catholic schools and at home continued to disagree with the pope. Joanna laughed.

Mrs. L's approach to tragedy was like that of her stiff-upper-lip father and included a flat refusal to allow personally painful subjects to be raised in her presence. She accepted life's lumps as its price of admission, and when bad things happened, as they not infrequently did, she went right ahead with whatever was next on the agenda. In her eighties, she was slim, almost too thin, and still able to stand on her head—which she did with pleasure at the slightest encouragement.

She could also assume the lotus position, often doing so on the backseat of her big black Cadillac sedan driven by her black chauffeur, Turner, with whom she was great friends. She always wore a wide-brimmed hat—straw in summer, felt in winter.

"Alice," LBJ had once said on her arrival at the White House, "I don't like your hat. It stops me from giving you a kiss."

"That's why I wear it," she said.

During most of the many years when her cousins, Franklin and Eleanor Roosevelt, occupied the White House, Mrs. L had been ostracized because she did such a cruel imitation of her contemporary, Eleanor, and also because she complained all over town that the White House food was awful. Everyone who dined with the FDRs, including FDR himself, agreed about the food, and Mrs. L continued to do her imitations of Eleanor into her own nineties. I could see that they were accurate, but because I admired Eleanor Roosevelt, I was not as amused by them as other people were. This, of course, did not stop Mrs. L from doing them in my presence— rather, it probably encouraged her. Following the FDRs, neither the

Trumans nor the Eisenhowers saw cause to add Mrs. L to their guest list, but the Kennedys adored her. She told Jack and Bobby Kennedy to their faces that they were like the Bonaparte sons, enjoying the chance to rule their respective fiefdoms but still dominated by their terrible old father.

In the political sphere, Mrs. L and I had a number of subjects we disagreed strongly about, such as the United Nations, which I loved and she spurned, but I can only remember one argument in the personal sphere. That concerned fidelity in marriage, something I felt to be valuable and she did not. Indeed, Washington gossips were still a'tingle over her reputed long-ago affair with Senator William Borah of Idaho during the many years when Nick Longworth, still speaker of the House, was, in the phrase of the day, "drowning his sorrows."

Mrs. L herself had no interest in alcohol, but she served vintage wines and gourmet food at her large and formal dinner parties. The menu was usually the same: a homemade soup, often lobster bisque; a filet of beef sliced thin and rare; with potato and vegetable; and an ice cream dessert. She enjoyed seating people next to someone they would fight with (while she observed, smirking, from the head of the table). I, therefore, found myself more than once next to Joe Alsop, Stewart's brilliant but snobbish older brother, who was a fierce hawk about Vietnam. Although Jack was a fellow Grotonian with Joe, and a member of Congress besides, Joe barely deigned to recognize his presence, probably because Jack was doveish about Vietnam. As for myself, to Joe, I was merely an appendage to Jack. The fact that I had written books was of no interest. Yet, he must have had a better side, for Kay Graham and Polly Fritchey were devoted and referred to him as "Old Black Joe." The three of them sometimes went off together to The Homestead Hotel in Hot Springs, Virginia, for R&R.

On only one occasion did Jack and I glimpse a more human aspect of Joe. It was in Paris after a ribald evening with him and Arthur and

Marian Schlesinger, and Chester and Edith Kerr. Joe insisted on all of us coming to a garish, white-tiled diner for a nightcap dish of something like oysters, but we three couples, all traveling with young children who would be up in only a few hours, demurred. As Jack and I walked off, I looked back. Joe was sitting at the counter with an expression of profound loneliness, bordering, I felt, on panic. His homosexuality was still unknown to us and most people. At that time, Jack and I had no idea why this brilliant, successful man seemed so tortured.

After our children grew up and married, Jack and I continued to take great joy in their unions. Though all had chosen someone whom none of their siblings could have lived with, they seemed content with their choice and got along with their siblings' choices at weddings or funerals or family reunions. The four in-laws named themselves the "outlaws" and would occasionally gather in a room from which shouts of (doubtless disloyal) laughter could be heard. I believe the family expression, "controlled disloyalty," stemmed from that time.

During 1976's bright, beautiful Indian summer, Jack and I were having lunch with a British diplomatic couple in the House of Representatives dining room. One of Jack's staff members arrived breathless at our table:

"Your house is on fire."

"Which house?"

"Riverdale."

"What's happening?"

"The firemen are there."

"How did you find out?"

"Ellie Rossbach phoned. From your house. She had a key and let them in."

Our guests rose in mid-meal to let us figure out what to do. Jack asked them to please sit back down. He and I both insisted that there was nothing on earth we could do about our house, so we all should finish our meal. No use receiving more bad news on an empty stomach.

They were astounded at our apparent cool, but Jack and I felt we had no alternative. The four of us concluded our lunch in fine style and British American good relations remained undiminished.

In Riverdale, as we soon found out, two lucky events had been triggered by one unlucky one. The unlucky cause of the fire was our housesitters, who lived on the third floor and had gone out, leaving their propane lamp in full sunlight, which somehow ignited it. The first of the lucky events was that our immediate neighbor, Dr. Douglas Smiley, happened on that lovely day to have gone home to have lunch on his porch. He was drinking iced tea when he heard a crackling sound like leaves burning. Knowing that this had recently been forbidden because of air pollution, he ventured forth, glass in hand, to investigate. Flames were roaring from our third-storey windows. He raced home and phoned the new system called 911.

The second of the lucky events was that our sister-in-law, Ellie Rossbach, was at home in Riverdale and, because the day was so sunny, had only a screen door between her and the sound of fire engines passing by her house. She ran outside and inquired of one driver where they were headed. When he said, "5000 Independence Avenue," she hurried back in, grabbed her key to our house, ran across the neighbors' yards and arrived at our front door in time to prevent it from being broken down by a fireman's axe. Other firemen already had hoses trained on our third floor. She was allowed to enter the first floor and pull our antique dining table out from under the water that was pouring down through the chandelier from two floors above.

Jack and I went back to Riverdale for the weekend and were appalled at the damage, not so much from fire as from smoke and water. The whole house stank and every bit of stuffed furniture plus all curtains had to be sent out to be cleaned. The third floor was a charcoal ruin, but because the firemen had arrived so quickly, the direct destruction did not extend below it. We asked the housesitters to leave, which they were glad to do. Renovation ended up costing one hundred thousand dollars. The insurance company paid every cent.

My New Year's resolution that year was to simplify wherever possible. Americans are so bombarded with appeals to spend on things, whether food or clothes, cars or gadgets, that I now consciously resist these appeals and suggest to the youngsters that they do the same. One of the benefits to me of the women's movement is that, because it honors my career, I do not feel I have to maintain a perfectly appointed home with the latest kind of furnishing or shininess except for special occasions.

Also following that evening, in 1971, Jack and I went to Stockbridge for Reinhold Niebuhr's funeral. It was a Friday afternoon, and the eulogist was Rabbi Abraham Joshua Heschel. His words and manner were deeply touching, but everything had to be hurried along because the rabbi needed to be driven back to the city before sundown preceding the Sabbath. I had the feeling that we were all talking faster than usual, almost as fast as Reinie himself was in the habit of doing. Later we heard that that the fellow who drove Rabbi Heschel back to the city reported on their having had to run several red lights. Reinie would have laughed.

I was so pleased when, twenty years later, on the 100th anniversary of Reinie's birth in 1892, my book was republished by University Press of America in paperback.

In the early 1970s, I was honored to become one of my alma mater's trustees. Although the commute from Washington for the Barnard meetings was often a strain, it was worth it. This was at the time of expansion to coeducation. Even Yale, to the disgust of my brother Dick, started admitting women after its proposition that Vassar join with Yale had been turned down; indeed, Vassar itself soon began admitting male students.

Barnard was proud to remain one of the few colleges solely for women. The major decisions the Barnard board had to make during the time I served on it concerned our relationship with neighboring Columbia College for men. They wanted to swallow us up, as Harvard had swallowed Radcliffe, and Brown had swallowed Pembroke. This we refused. In too many instances, we had been told, the admission of men to formerly female institutions of learning had resulted in most classroom discussions being dominated by males, as were the extracurricular organizations, whether of self-government, campus newspaper, or volunteer good works.

Our board, over all, was rather conservative, containing such senior statesmen as Francis Plimpton, Jack's former colleague at the United States Mission to the United Nations, and my friend and North Street neighbor, the late Eleanor Thomas Elliott, a lifelong Republican (until 2004 when her revulsion at George W. Bush led her to the Democratic Party).

A diverting moment came when the first-ever student representative to the board arrived, bursting with ideas for change. We listened politely and then asked where in the budget she would make the cuts necessary to fund these changes.

"You mean I can see the budget?"

"Of course."

She was given a copy and duly returned the next month somewhat less bursting. She had made careful annotations, some of which we were glad to accept. She went on to law school and then became president of Barnard. Her name is Ellen Futter, and she is currently President of the American Museum of Natural History.

Meanwhile, Columbia College, far larger, richer, and older, was appalled at our stand against being absorbed by it. Instead of wooing, Columbia turned to threats. Barnard students would have to pay even more than they did to use the Columbia library. (The Barnard library was negligible because of lack of space and money.) Finally,

Columbia played its trump card: if we didn't agree, it would accept women as students. After much internal debate, our board told them to go right ahead. Although secretly we feared that the number of applications by top-rank young women to Barnard would decrease, that has not really happened. In the decades following Columbia College's opening of its doors to women, the applications to Barnard, both in quantity as well as quality, increased and continue to rise.

Among the many faces of feminism, in this instance ours was a broad grin.

CHAPTER 14

Remember the Ladies

FROM THE BEGINNING OF THE 1970s, all over North America the women's movement jolted people into reevaluating their lives, some in a mild way, others in a revolutionary one. Said a character in a novel by the late Canadian writer Carol Shields, "Feminism sailed in . . . like a dazzling ocean liner, powered by injustice and steaming with indignation."

Even happily married women, myself included, began asking more of our spouses within the home. From the beginning of Jack's and my time together, he had, when necessary, been an adequate washer of dishes and lugger of garbage.

Yet, a decade later when he was considering retirement from Congress and I suggested that one day a week he be in charge of our lunch together, he reacted with amazement: "Are you crazy?" Similarly, later on, when I suggested to our son that he share a bit of the menu-planning for our Salem reunions, he laughed out loud. "We'd have nothing to eat but peanut butter," he predicted (doubtless with accuracy).

This attitude of theirs has been termed "learned helplessness," and my father, who never fathomed how to boil water, was a prime example. But then I must confess to a similar helplessness when I read a tax return, and I can rarely recall what make of car we have. After ten years with the same car, I told a grandchild we got a new one.

"Oh great! What kind?"

"Um, er—a green one!"

Jack not only believed that women should have equality and dignity; he did his bit to promote these aims by introducing a bill in

Congress mandating that federal employees address all female correspondents as "Ms." rather than continuing, in sexist fashion, to make
a distinction between "Miss" and "Mrs." A further small step he took
was described thirty years later by one of his legislative assistants,
Michael J. Rosenberg:

> The proudest thing I ever worked on for JBB was
> establishing Eleanor Roosevelt's Valkill as the first
> national historic site dedicated to a woman. That house
> would be a medical park if JBB hadn't stepped in. I
> even got to tell President Clinton about JBB at the
> White House and he seemed to know all about him. In
> the same conversation he talked about Eleanor
> Roosevelt and said he had just gotten back from his
> first visit to Hyde Park. I said, "You never made it
> there until you were President yourself?" And he said,
> "I think that's the best way to go, don't you?"

An unexpected event regarding my career occurred when I sold
my article on Mrs. L to *American Heritage Magazine*. The editor in
chief, Oliver Jensen, who had been a Yale classmate of Jack's, asked
if a thousand dollars would be satisfactory.

"Sure, but how about another thousand for Mrs. Longworth?
Her stair carpet is dangerously worn and the animal heads on the
wall are molting."

He thought for a moment. "Okay."

I had to wait till two o'clock to phone her with the news because
she slept late. She cried out with pleasure: "All that lovely money!
Let's have caviar for tea." So we did, just she and I, on triangles of
thin white toast.

Feminism, however, was of zero interest to Mrs. L. All her life
she'd been able to do pretty much as she wanted, including the earning

of some money when she needed it after Nicholas Longworth's death. She wrote a surprisingly tame memoir that nonetheless sold reasonably well. But she had never been remotely interested in a career for herself other than that of influencing influential men. She did a lot of that, starting with her father and continuing with her husband. (He, like his friend, Senator Henry Cabot Lodge and her reputed lover, Senator William Borah, were as dead set as she was against the United States joining the League of Nations.) She also tried to do a bit of latter-day influencing with the Kennedy brothers and presidents Johnson, Nixon, and Ford.

I, too, felt that I had been able to do most of what I wanted to in life, but my consciousness was raised by the new *Ms. Magazine*, which described the discrimination suffered by blue-collar women, especially black women and Latinas. My consciousness was further raised by the brown bag lunch group in Washington started by Arvonne Fraser, wife and (unpaid) administrative assistant of Representative Don Fraser (D-MN).

Some fifteen of us met once a month to exchange reports not only about our home lives but our many different kinds of work. I resonated particularly to the problems of a Foreign Service wife whose husband had recently been posted back to Washington. Bert Hartry had served with her husband Ted in many foreign countries, had learned several languages, was bringing up four daughters, and had had no time or opportunity for a separate career. Now she was in Washington, with all her children off to school and no foreigners to entertain, yet she doubted if she and her husband would remain in the United States long enough for her to get a career going.

So much depends on a partner's work. If he—or she—is a lab scientist, there is no need for input unless the spouse, too, is a scientist. If the partner is a diplomat or a clergyperson, a politician or a high school or college president, however, often considerable team-playing is required of the spouse. Furthermore, people like Bert Hartry and myself thoroughly enjoyed watching our husbands in the limelight while we worked behind the scenes. Surely it wasn't fair for us to be reviled by some ambitious young feminists. Just as the hippie shift in values had been upsetting, so was the feminist revolution, even though its effects were far more constructive for the country. "Equal pay for equal work" is a far more pragmatic slogan than "Make love, not war."

I felt embroiled enough to write some articles for *The Foreign Service Journal*, one called "Unsung Heroines" and another called "Diplomats in Striped Pantsuits." By then, the chasm between the old-fashioned and new-fashioned diplomatic wives was having a visible effect on America's embassies abroad. Some young wives were refusing to accompany their husbands overseas because of their own careers at home; some were refusing because they didn't want their children to suffer in a hardship post. Even in the top echelons of the Foreign Service, this kind of conflict was visible. For the first time, in four West African countries where the climate is fiercely damp and hot, not one U.S. ambassador had been accompanied by his wife. The hospitality formerly dispensed by her was now handled by a lower-ranking officer who, in turn, was forced to borrow time from regular duties.

Destructive as male chauvinism and racism are in themselves, they're far worse when combined. I learned about this, not through my upper-middle-class white consciousness-raising group, but in the alley behind our house in Georgetown. There, as I was walking the dog one afternoon, I saw a tall, impressive-looking black woman hanging laundry in a nearby backyard. Her name was Bettie Davidson and in time she and I became friends and co-conspirators. She was the cook for a socially eminent white couple whom Jack and I knew. Although she and their other black female helper had worked there for more than twenty years, they were forbidden to eat from the same dishes or drink from the same glasses as "the family." The two women were not beaten, as our maid, Millie, once had been, but their employers' constant discrimination hurt their feelings almost as much as a beating might have. Moreover, the family never arranged for any kind of pension or annuity for either of them. I was outraged when I heard this and suggested that Bettie seek more congenial employment, but she said she was too old to change.

She did, however, begin moonlighting for us. Because she was willing to devote her day off to cooking for a dinner party of ours, our social life became dependent on the convenience, not of our honored guests, but of Bettie. And, during her summer vacation, she came to Salem. She would never have addressed me as "June," so I called her "Miss Bettie" (she scorned "Ms."), and my descendants did the same. After she retired from her full-time job, Jack and I provided her with an annuity, but her employers never even gave her a farewell bonus. She always came to Riverdale to help me with Christmas.

I was slower than some to support the full feminist agenda because my career had been so relatively free from male chauvinism. Freelance writers had been able to peddle their wares with some success in the 20th century. Even when I got into science writing, as I did first with the Mental Hygiene Association of Westchester County and then with the book with Redlich, my gender was never a disadvantage. As for the writing of biography, whether as books or articles, my gender appeared, if anything, to be an advantage, since many males find it easier to talk to a woman than a man.

In ever-growing numbers, graduate schools in law and medicine, diplomacy and theology, accepted female students. Before long, many new presidents of universities were women, including some in the Ivy League. Interestingly, just as *Gentleman's Agreement*, promoting rights for Jews, had preceded *The Feminine Mystique*, promoting equal rights for women, so, too, Harold Shapiro, the first Jew to be president of Princeton (as was happening also at Harvard, Yale, and Dartmouth), preceded the first woman, Shirley Tilghman, as its president.

When Shirley Chisholm, a black member of Congress from New York whom Jack admired, was asked whether she had suffered more discrimination as a woman or a black, she promptly answered, "As a woman." When I interviewed for one of my columns Congresswoman Barbara Jordan from Texas, who had made a national name by her brilliant service on the Judiciary Committee at the time of Watergate, she agreed that being a woman was harder than being African American. (I remember how shocked I was when told that Stokely Carmichael, the influential black civil rights leader, had said that the appropriate position for women in the social revolution was on their backs.)

Even for highly placed white women some covert chauvinism remained, as it does to this day. Carolyn Heilbrun was the first female to achieve tenure as a full professor of literature at Columbia (one of her role models was Lionel Trilling who, a quarter century earlier, had been the first Jew to achieve tenure as a full professor of literature at Columbia). In *Honest Doubt*, one of the successful novels Heilbrun wrote under her pen name, Amanda Cross, the heroine says about academe: "Women are constantly slighted, ignored, and blocked for promotion, grants and important University work . . . The odd part . . . is that the higher you rise, the more the male networks and individuals fear you, and the more marginalized and hated you become. This isn't universal, but it's prevalent."

I enjoyed *Honest Doubt* so much that I wrote Heilbrun a fan letter, mentioning that Jack and I had spent an evening at Lionel and Diana Trilling's and were somewhat disappointed because they seemed so focused on power and its accoutrements.

Soon thereafter I received a thank you note from Heilbrun. I wrote back and suggested tea or drinks. The result was lunch at the Cosmopolitan Club to which she had once belonged and I still did. We talked and talked, seemingly on the same wavelength, but then I mentioned the title of this book. Her expression became hooded. She was clearly too much of a feminist to be happy with the concept two lives so braided together that they function beautifully as a whole. Our budding friendship was thus frostbitten.

As for the progress of feminism, I revel in the fact that, with our grandchildren now adults and many of them married, our family includes a female Episcopal priest, a female physician, a female bassist in a band, as well as those who have chosen traditionally female jobs such as teacher and nurse.

I also credit the women's movement, to some degree, for the incredibly close and funny relationship my daughter-in-law and I enjoy. When I was young, the word "mother-in-law" was a synonym for "Wicked Witch of the West." But with women now working in hordes, mothers-in-law no longer have the time or energy to worry about their daughters-in-law and vice versa.

On the other hand, because the years when a young woman is building her career are also those best suited for childbearing, the choices a young mother must make can be excruciating. She needs every bit of reinforcement she can get from her partner, not to mention her parents, siblings, friends, and grandparents. President Shirley Tilghman of Princeton said about herself at the time when she was simultaneously a newly divorced mother and a rising young molecular geneticist, "It sounds ridiculous, but I think I jettisoned everything except family and work. I had this mindset: I was not going to feel guilty when I was at work, and I was not going to feel guilty when I was with the children."

When Jack and I used to run into Joe and Madeleine Albright at Georgetown parties, she was studying for her doctorate. Later, not entirely to Jack's and my surprise, we heard that the couple had gotten divorced. Of course, Albright went on to serve with distinction as Clinton's secretary of state, the first American woman to achieve so high a post. When invited by Wellesley to speak on whether her career had caused her divorce, she refused, saying, "I do not know the answer." But in her autobiography, she admits that if her husband had been willing to stay with her, she "would have given up any thought of a career."

There, encapsulated in the life of one woman, is the problem writ large: If a husband is not willing to braid his life with that of his highly placed wife, which one, career or marriage, is going to be least painful for her to shortchange?

The time I had the best sense of what that kind of decision could involve was when a few Bronx politicos came to me and asked if I would run for Congress in the district adjoining Jack's. They said all kinds of nice things about the natural political abilities I had shown while campaigning for him. When I asked Jack about it, his face fell. "Do you want to?"

When I honestly said I'd rather be dead, he embraced me. Our braided lives would stay wound around each other, but neither merge nor disappear.

I had not the slightest intention of returning to the arduous work of writing another book with another psychiatrist. This, however, was precisely what was proposed by a young man I met, thanks to Jack Bingham and, of all people, Claudia's yogi.

Yogi Bhajan, a talented promoter of his ideas and himself, had requested Jack to arrange a luncheon on Capitol Hill so that Bhajan could make a pitch for yoga as a method of weaning young people from psychedelic and other drugs. (Later he assigned Gurunam Singh, Claudia's husband, and other male disciples to teach yoga to male inmates of Washington prisons.) Jack agreed to invite some congressional colleagues from the House who dealt with such matters. Also included was the psychiatrist in charge of fighting drug addiction at the local Veterans Administration hospital. This blond if balding, blue-eyed man, Norman Tamarkin, M.D., and I were seated across from each other at the lunch. We got to talking about tennis. He was just learning, and I offered to be his human backboard. At the time he and I started playing, I could beat him easily, but because he was male and not much older than my children, he was soon the winner. After our games, we would discuss those aspects of human health over which an individual might exert far more control than is usually the case. He wanted to write a book on not just mental but general health, but he was not a writer. The next thing we knew, he and I were collaborating on the joint book that was later published as *The Pursuit of Health: Your Mind, Your Body, Your Relationships and Your Environments.*

Its "Relationships" dimension came to include not just obvious ones like those between two individuals, but also those between an individual and the small group(s) of which he or she is a member. The "Environments" section included not just obvious ones like air and water, but also the large groups, whether social, economic, or national, of which the individual is a part. Norman read widely in systems theory; I just read widely. We ended up with far more material than any single book could encompass. Eventually, our book included, in addition to the four dimensions of health, the central organizing principle that continually coordinates these. This force, whether referred to as soul or spirit or, as we named it, "The Intimate Connector," may need to be harnessed by the individual to improve the health of the four dimensions. As in systems theory, if you change one part, you change the whole. We also used five case histories (well-disguised) from Norman's files to illustrate the way a change in one dimension can alter one or more of the others in ways that can turn a toxic situation into a healthful one.

I was deep into writing chapters and giving them to Norman for comment when I went off on a trip to Russia and Eastern Europe with Jack. He and I were in Moscow, walking across the Red Square by moonlight with Ken Galbraith, when a terrible pain shot down my right leg. Ken, at 6'6", and Jack at 6'2", were taking much longer strides than I was comfortable with, but that could hardly have initiated my pain. The next day Jack and I were scheduled to go to Czechoslovakia. I got there but was unable to move from my bed in the embassy residence. Fortunately, the American ambassador, Bud Scherer, was a tennis player whose regular opponent was a Czech neurosurgeon. Although the Communist government forbade Czech doctors to treat private patients, the surgeon (in tennis clothes) came to examine me. He said that the disc in the spinal joint above the one that had been fused was protruding and pressing on the sciatic nerve leading down into the leg. I should, therefore, get home for expert surgery as fast as possible. He administered a shot of painkiller and off we went. Though forbidden by the Czech government to pay the doctor, we were able, via the diplomatic pouch, to send him two cases of tennis balls.

By the time I got back to Washington, I was in terrible pain. The neurosurgeon I went to ordered total bed rest; I stayed at home in a hospital bed for a month. But after the month was up, the pain was no better; it was worse. He operated and the leg pain was magically and totally relieved, but my back hurt so agonizingly and my recovery was so slow that he and I and probably Jack, too, became deeply discouraged.

During all those months, I didn't hear one word from Norman. Not a phone call, not a get-well card, not a posy. Much later, when I was well enough to work on the book again, I inquired about this inattentiveness. He ducked his head:

"I was so scared you were going to die that I couldn't get myself to do anything."

"Thanks a lot."

We laughed ruefully together at how difficult ill health can be for everyone concerned.

Years later, after the book was out and we had done our requisite television and radio appearances (which Norman enjoyed more than

I did), he had a swimming accident that led to a prolonged lung infection. Now the doctor was the patient, and he was kept in the hospital for almost a year. Although he had never before been able to settle on one woman he wanted to marry, now at last he found one and she was equally devoted to him. Jack and I were back in New York when she phoned with the news that Norman had died suddenly. She and I wept together.

Around this time came the candidacy of Jimmy Carter. We first encountered Carter during preprimary time in 1976 at an ADA winter meeting in Washington. (We were told that Carter had invited himself there.) He got up on a chair and addressed us in a folksy way. Yet, by the time the Iowa primary came around, he had managed to convey concern and sharpness of intellect that caused American voters unexpectedly to bet their future on "the peanut farmer" from Plains, Georgia.

After the primaries, Carter appeared on Capitol Hill for a visit. Jack and I had been delighted to discover through the media how impressed Carter was with Reinhold Niebuhr. When Jack shook hands with Carter, Jack mentioned that I had written Niebuhr's biography. Carter said, "Send me a copy and I'll read it before election." Jack felt that any such promise was impossible to fulfill, but he sent the book anyway.

In August, at a Democratic fund-raiser in Washington, Jack took me over to Carter's table to introduce me. Carter rose. "I not only read your book," he said, "but I underlined it."

I was flabbergasted.

On election night, 1976, in New York, Jack and I invited Cy and Gay Vance and Zbigniew and Moushka Brzezinski to have dinner with us at the Century. Cy and Zbigniew were cordial with each other but likely to be rivals for top positions in Carter's administration if he were to win. The wives were as pleasant as any two could be under such circumstances. (Cy Vance became secretary of state and Zbig became the national security adviser. The rivalry between the men did not abate, however, and ultimately, Cy resigned on a matter of principle.) Afterwards, we went off to separate bashes and when the election results came through, celebrated *con gusto*.

The following spring the Carters' first White House party for the Congress was an informal barbecue on the South Lawn. It was there that we met the slightly formidable Rosalynn Carter and also Jimmy's cheerful young blonde secretary, Susan Clough. In my brief conversation with the president, we spoke of Niebuhr and tennis and how tickled Jack and I were when Carter appointed Bob Weaver, the first African American to serve in a Cabinet, as secretary of housing.

A year later, I was invited by the Miller Center at the University of Virginia to give a speech about Niebuhr to its graduate students. What on earth could I say that they didn't already know? Then I remembered Carter's having underlined my book. I, therefore, wrote to him and asked to borrow his copy. The answer came right back, via Susan Clough. It was "No!" I phoned her and still asked for her help. Luckily, photocopying had recently been invented, so she was able to make copies of the forty-eight pages that contained his under-linings. Jack came home from the Hill one night with a big manila envelope. "I don't know what the White House is sending you, but it weighs a ton." In it were copies of the underlined pages. As I looked them over, I cried out with joy. Carter had chosen quotes from Niebuhr and statements about Niebuhr's ideas that would have been exactly what I believe Reinie would most have wanted a president to emphasize. One was "Most evil . . . is done by people who do not know they are not good"; still others concerned the relationships between love and justice, justice and freedom, and the vitally needed curbs, inner and outer, private and public, on the uses of power.

Over the years, Jack and I met a number of dictators, including Romania's Nicolae Ceausescu. Ceausescu was furious at the United States for barring Romania from its "most favored nation" category in regard to tariffs, and he took out his rage on Jack. Jack was anything but meek in return. One dictator considered by many, though not all, of his compatriots to be corrupt was Somalia's General Muhammed Siad Barre. Ruthless, I have no doubt, but at least he demonstrated toward us not merely politeness but also a bit of humor. Jack and I had had no intention of visiting Somalia when we headed for Africa on a fact-finding trip. But after our visits to Ghana, Nigeria, and Senegal on the west coast, Jack received a message from the State Department. It said that the Somalis were complaining that they had not had a visit from an American member of Congress in a decade. Would Jack therefore reroute our trip home to include a few days in Mogadishu? Flying from West Africa to East Africa in those days was virtually impossible. Nor was there a train. We had to fly to Rome to go back to Africa.

The Somalis are among the most beautiful people in the world, with perfectly shaped heads, delicate ears, big brown eyes, little snub noses, and rosebud mouths. Jack and I enjoyed visiting community development projects in the capital and agricultural installations in the countryside. Jack had asked for an interview with the General, as Siad Barre was referred to, but we had no idea when this would be. Weary from a day of exposure to abject poverty, Jack and I collapsed in our hotel room that evening. "I'm going to wash my hair," I announced and started getting undressed. The phone rang. The General was willing to see us. Right now. I told Jack to go ahead, that I'd rather have a clean scalp than meet another dictator anyway.

Jack departed and I collapsed on our bed, too weary even to start fighting with the sporadic shower. After all, I had a whole evening free for the first time in weeks. The phone rang. My highly amused husband told me that when he had arrived at the General's headquarters, the first thing Siad Barre said, was *"Mais ou est Madame?"* Apparently word had reached him that I had been accompanying

Jack everywhere. The result was that I was expected to be at our hotel entrance fully dressed in five minutes to be picked up by an official vehicle. I put my clothes back on and was driven to the tightly guarded military compound where the General lived. I found him to be jovial and visibly pleased that Jack and I spoke French. Of course, many years later, a number of Somali leaders rose up against him and he was deposed.

The most memorable interview with a dictator was with Fidel Castro on a mini-congressional fact-finding trip in February 1977. Jack and I were accompanied by Roger Majak, the top staff person on the Foreign Affairs' Subcommittee on Exports, a committee that Jack chaired. On arrival in Havana, with Roger taking notes, we had a few days of meetings with the ministers for agriculture, education, and health, and were escorted to model farms, schools, and clinics. I had been to Cuba as a fifteen-year-old with my parents forty years before, and the difference in Havana was extraordinary. Outwardly, it looked more drab and our hotel was badly run-down, but no longer were we importuned by beggars on the street. We were further assured that literacy had climbed to 97 percent and health care, although more primitive than in the United States, was free and available to all. We were scheduled for a meeting with Castro, but he had not made up his mind as to when or where. It was thought that, for security reasons, he never slept in the same place two nights running. On our one weekend there, Jack and I planned to make a trip to Varadero where we had honeymooned thirty-eight years before.

That Saturday morning, however, we were told that Castro expected to see us at his Havana office at two p.m. Jack, Roger, and I were driven to the imposing presidential building and escorted past armed guards into a barn-like room where Castro, bearded, and without a smile, sat behind a big formal desk. An attractive, slim female interpreter sat nearby. Castro rose to shake hands with us. We have a photo of Jack looking astounded and amused as I showed off my one

Spanish word, *"Encantada"*—I am charmed to meet you. Castro and Jack proceeded to have a substantive, rapidly interpreted conversation about how to increase trade between our two countries, a move that Jack had publicly endorsed. After an hour, Castro stood up, then reached into a top drawer and pulled out a gun belt (with a gun in it) that he strapped around his waist. He patted his stomach: "I'm too fat," he said in English. He then announced that he was escorting us to Varadero. In a state of mild shock, I asked Roger to race back to our hotel, pack a suitcase for Jack and me, and meet us in Varadero. And off the two of us went with Castro and the interpreter.

Fidel, huge and very masculine, sat in the right-hand corner of the sedan's backseat. Next to him was the interpreter and next to her was Jack. I was in the front next to the driver. A rifle was lying readily available on a shelf between driver and passengers. Behind our black sedan was a jeep with two soldiers on each side, facing outward, with their guns at the ready. Behind them was another black car carrying who knows whom. Off went our little cavalcade and several times along the way, Castro would be reminded of something he wanted to show us, like the nursing school where his sister had studied or the roadway leading to his brother Raúl's *estancia*. Each time he would instruct our chauffeur to change direction, the vehicles behind us, like ice-skaters in a "crack the whip," would be forced to make a similar rapid turn. Tires squealed but no harm resulted.

"What kind of car is this?" Jack asked.

"Russian," said Fidel. "I need two. One is always in the shop." We all laughed.

Castro showed boundless curiosity about American life, ranging from which pitcher for the Yankees was hottest at the moment to what kind of food our grandchildren ate for supper. He gave us the impression of being a lonely man, starved for intimate information. (We were later informed that he had had several mistresses over the years, one of whom was still with him.) He and we talked a bit about what an ideal

347

Our congressional fact-finding trip to Cuba in February 1977 introduced us to Castro, one of the most interesting leaders we had come into contact with. In this picture, Jack looks on in amazement as I produced the single word of Spanish I knew—encantada meaning "charmed to meet you."

form of government would be. It was in that connection that I quoted Niebuhr's words, "Man's capacity for justice makes democracy possible; man's capacity for injustice makes democracy necessary."

Fidel sat forward: "Who is it who said that?" Jack explained that Niebuhr was an American theologian and political thinker whose biography I had written. Fidel replied that his own early education had been in the hands of the clergy, both priests and nuns. He would like to read my book. I said I'd be more than happy to send him a copy. He wanted to know how to spell Reinhold's name and wrote it down.

Every so often, abruptly, Fidel would order the driver to stop in the middle of a town. *Screech!* came the sound of the brakes of the cars following us. Fidel would leap out of his car, shake the hands of the startled passersby, exchange a few words with them, and get back into the car.

With all these detours and stops, the trip that should have taken two hours took three and a half. Even after we arrived in Varadero, Castro seemed loathe to say goodbye. We were taken to a restaurant where a group of local leaders had gathered in a private room. We drank margaritas and ate steaks and continued to exchange a few jokes and also speak substantively with him. When Jack told him that he thought his recent sending of Cuban troops to Africa was a mistake, Fidel shrugged. Half kidding and half not, he said that too many people were living on his small island and he had to send some of them somewhere. I had difficulty believing how relaxed Jack and I could feel while talking with a dictator, whether or not he was a full-fledged Communist. (Opinions about that differed at the time.)

Finally, Castro said he had to depart because he had an early Sunday morning date to go fishing. He asked someone to fetch him a baseball. He carefully inscribed it to our eldest grandson, Edward Bland. I was genuinely sorry to tell Castro good-bye. On a human level, I couldn't help but like him. Roger Majak, by then, had caught up with us and handed over our suitcases. The three of us went out to the same golf course that Jack and I had played on thirty-eight years before. Built by the du Ponts, it used to restrict guests to those at the Kawama Beach Club where we were staying. Now, it was open to the public and adequately maintained but nowhere near its former manicured condition. On Monday, we and Roger, with Castro's permission, visited a prison near Havana. We talked to some of the jailed dissidents who clearly had to be circumspect about what they said to us, but they appeared to be in good health.

Many years later, in response to a request by the class secretary for Yale '36, Jack presented the rest of our Cuban trip by way of a dialogue with me. Jack told the group:

349

It was 10 o'clock on a Monday night in Havana. Our official escorts had taken us to dinner at one of Ernest Hemingway's favorite bistros and then back to our hotel to pack for an early morning departure. I was in my pajamas and June in the tub, when there was a knock on the door. I opened it and there, looming large, was Fidel, once more.

At the sound of the knock, June leaped from the water and draped a large towel around her torso. When I opened the door, I heard his burst of laughter. I peeked around the corner, and there was not only Castro but behind him the usual expressionless military guard with submachine gun.

"My staff—Didn't they tell you I was coming?" Castro asked.

"No, Mr. President, it's quite clear from our clothing that we didn't expect you," I said.

He dropped his head. "I'm so embarrassed."

"Well, don't be embarrassed," I said. "Come on in."

So he did. He took the armchair, I took the straight chair, and June, after unpacking her wrapper and putting it on, sat on the bed. (She never did find her slippers.) For some twenty minutes, until Castro's perennially surprised staff caught up with him, we had a comfortable conversation in English. He had been mulling several things we had said . . . and followed them up with probing questions. His is a mind and personality, we felt, that would have made him a leader, no matter what his country. Cuba seems too small for him; hence, at least in part, his adventures in Africa.

350

As I recall that evening in the hotel bedroom, Castro asked me to write down again the name of my book on Niebuhr. He pulled from his pocket a crumpled, smeared bit of paper. It was the note I had given him on Saturday. He admitted that on his fishing venture he had fallen out of the boat and soaked the contents of his pockets. The three of us had a good laugh at his expense. He was as charming as could be. He asked for the baseball he had autographed for Edward; he wanted to make a correction. He also said he'd been worrying about how our vegetarian grandchildren got enough protein.

When Jack and I returned to Washington, we were both invited to report to President Carter in the Oval Office. The only other person there was his chief of national security affairs, Zbigniew Brzezinski. Whether Cyrus Vance, the secretary of state, was invited or not, we did not ask. Carter seemed more receptive to the idea of expanding trade with Cuba than Zbig was. We had the feeling that Zbig would likely undercut Jack's arguments as soon as we left.

ABC-TV got wind of our trip and asked me if I would go back to Cuba for them and try to get an on-camera interview with Castro. I was enchanted by the offer, but Jack was against it. I honestly think he wasn't comfortable putting me in the hands of an absolute dictator. Not long thereafter, Sally Quinn went to Havana to visit Castro, but, as a recognized media person, she would presumably have been protected by her colleagues. Yet, for a short while, I couldn't help thinking about what that adventure for me might have entailed.

Two years later we went back to Cuba, this time as part of an official congressional delegation. By then Castro was discouraged about the prospects of any real improvements in U.S.-Cuban relations, and he resumed the role of hard-nosed Communist. Tough dictator he most certainly is, but long-time observers in Cuba argue over whether he is primarily Communist or primarily opportunist.

Jack and I briefing President Carter on the official congressional trip to Cuba we were part of in 1977.

During this later trip, Fidel was formal and chilly with our group, though one of his intimates made a point of telling me that Fidel had had parts of my Niebuhr book read aloud to him and, when necessary, translated into Spanish. But as Fidel and I shook hands, it was clear that his mind was on something far more important than me.

The next time we encountered the fallout from a dictatorship was in Washington a few years later, after the historic Nixon-Kissinger opening to China. At diplomatic dinners, we kept running into the new ambassador to the United States from China, Han Xu, a man of wit and charm, whose nation, understandably, was interested in what export policy the United States would establish in relationship to it. Jack and I decided to invite him to our little house for dinner.

In one sense, Ambassador Han reminded us of the way Ambassador Thant had been before the burdens laid on him as U.N. secretary general caused his manner to become more serious. In all events, Han clearly wanted to accept our invitation. But no definite date could be set until, first, he got permission from the Foreign Office in Beijing to visit an American private home and, second, until a second Chinese official we agreed to as his fellow guest.

Since the Chinese opted for an evening that was not Bettie Davidson's night off at her regular job, I had to try to find another cook. But the night before the party, the cook I had engaged phoned in sick. This had happened so often in the past that I had learned to choose menus that I could fix myself, when necessary, and that would not be ruined if Jack, as also frequently happened, was delayed by votes on the Hill. I was, therefore, marinating a pot roast in red wine the night before the dinner when I discovered we lacked the pimento-stuffed olives the recipe called for. I asked Jack to scoot up to the supermarket and get some, which he obligingly did.

The next evening we all helped ourselves at the buffet and sat down at our protocol-appropriate places. (I always phoned the State Department ahead of time to be sure that my seating plan was on target.) We took our first bite of the main dish and *Woof*, was it hot! I apologized for its spiciness and went to look for the bottle of olives. Instead of their having been stuffed with pimento, as I had requested, they were stuffed with red peppers.

I feared that U.S. relations with China had been seriously damaged, but Ambassador Han was convulsed with delighted laughter. He had never dreamed, he told us, that in the United States members of Congress got sent to market or that congressional wives did their own cooking. He drank a lot of water and assured us that Chinese people love hot food. Even the official "chaperone" got the giggles and asked for a second portion. A few years later when Jack and I visited China, Ambassador Han was back in the Foreign Office. He was wonderfully hospitable to us in Beijing and when we went to meet Prime Minister Deng Xiaoping, we discovered that the tale of our hot peppers had preceded us.

One of the few officials from a Communist country who did not have to be chaperoned when visiting an American home was Jerzy (George) Michalowski, Poland's ambassador to the United States. At diplomatic parties, his wife, Mira, a fellow writer, and I had often gravitated to each other. She was always dressed in the latest fashion and because "George" had previously served as his country's permanent representative at the United Nations, we had lots of New York friends in common. Yet when Mira confided to me that their Washington phone was tapped and their car was followed by an unmarked car each time they left the confines of Washington, I thought she was just using her fertile imagination. Later, however, we were told by a CIA friend that this, indeed, had been the custom in regard to Communist country officials. Paranoia, as they say, is occasionally accurate.

One evening the Michalowskis invited us to their apartment for dinner with Anatoly Dobrynin, the Soviet ambassador to the United States. I had assumed that our customarily uninhibited conversation with the Michalowskis would continue, but I was mistaken. Both George and Mira were extremely cautious in their comments, and the atmosphere crackled with unfamiliar tension.

When Jack and I visited Warsaw a few years later, the Michalowskis, by then back in private life, were comfortably outspoken again. Mira took me to a meeting of the Polish Writers' Group, but some of its members whispered to me that they had to look over their shoulders, so to speak, when talking or writing, and they feared that the Michalowskis were too rash. Perhaps the freedom the Michalowskis allowed themselves was based on their two sons' having decided to remain in the United States and develop their careers in a place where the Polish Communist dictatorship would have no power over them.

Our trips to India in the 1970s provided several instances of déjà vu. On the first one, Chet and Steb Bowles were back in their ambassadorial role, and our official call was to a member of the Nehru family. This time it was Jawaharlal Nehru's daughter, Indira Gandhi. Like her father, she emanated dignity and, also like him, she was bored by yet another official visit. Again the answers to Jack were monosyllabic. Finally, I took a deep breath and said, "So many American women would like to know how you have handled the conflict between the needs of your children and those of your job."

Her eyes lit up and she began to talk about how difficult it had been when her two boys were young, how she tried to keep her afternoon and evening official engagements to a minimum. After that, her conversation about current substantive matters flowed in a more comfortable fashion.

Most glamorous, of course, were the White House state dinners. Because of our friendship with the German ambassador, Berndt von Staden, and his writer wife, Wendi, we were included in the state dinner for Germany's prime minister, Helmut Schmidt. It was exactly as portrayed in the movies, with tables of ten, too big for general conversation, and more forks and glasses per setting than anyone needs. You were therefore stuck talking to whoever your two protocol-dictated dinner partners might be. In my case, these were officials in the Prime Minister's entourage. Because over the past several years I had become fond of Wendi, whose Christian, anti-Nazi family had remained in Germany throughout the war, I no longer felt the hairs on the back of my neck bristle when I heard a German accent. I even trotted out my own rusty German, which the two men were polite about (although their own English was perfect).

The most exciting White House dinner was the impromptu one that the Carters gave in 1979 to celebrate the signing of the Camp

Jack and I greeting Menachem Begin, Israeli prime minister, after the signing of the Camp David accords in 1979. Our later meetings with him in Jerusalem were not to be so relaxed and friendly, as the serious issue of settlements in the West Bank came between us.

David accords. Their elation, as well as that of Menachem Begin and Anwar Sadat, was palpable. People who would never have dreamed of hugging each other were doing so, many with tears in their eyes. Peace in the Middle East had become a possibility.

The number of guests had grown too big for even the White House to hold, so a marquee was set up in the Rose Garden. The only problem was that rain had fallen the previous day and the ground was soggy.

Prime Minister Begin had clearly been well-briefed on Jack and me. He knew that Jack had been nicknamed their "Shabbos goy" by members of the informal Jewish caucus on the Hill. (This term refers to the Christian who does chores on the Sabbath that

Orthodox Jews are forbidden to do, such as turning lights on and off.) Begin also knew that I was the great-niece of Herbert Lehman.

A few years later, we renewed our acquaintance with him in Jerusalem. This time instead of being jovial, his attitude reminded me that he had once been a ruthless Irgun fighter against the British troops who were then occupying the Holy Land. He was tense and tough and used a pointer the way teachers do when indicating to us where on the big map of the West Bank the proposed new Jewish settlements would go: "Here in Judea, here in Samaria."

My stomach turned over, and Jack was looking sick. Many of those settlements were not close to the boundary between the West Bank and Jerusalem, where their existence could enhance Israeli security, but were deep into the West Bank. This, we felt, would surely breed trouble for the future. Jack tried to press Begin about reducing the number of this second group, but Begin cut him off. Jack and I left his office worried. Later, in Washington, we had dinner at the Israeli embassy and found Ambassador Yitzak Rabin not much more open-minded on the subject than his boss.

We went on to Egypt and met with Anwar Sadat and his wife, Jihan, at their airy summer house in Aswan. Sadat's frizzy hair and dark skin contrasted with Jihan's delicate European chic. Jihan pleasantly recalled the luncheon for three where she and I had originally met. It was given by Gay Vance, not at the State Department but at her house. It was great fun for me because Jihan, like Gay, has an iconoclastic sense of humor. Actually, as I had noticed during Jack's and my years at the United Nations, there is little difference between cultured persons from no matter what country, while a wide gap may remain between the privileged and the poor members of the same nation. This was brought to our attention dramatically in Egypt where poverty-stricken people from the countryside were crowding desperately into Cairo to beg on the streets by day and sleep in the mausoleums of the city's huge cemetery by night. "More dead than alive" was true of

After visiting Israel, we moved on to Egypt where we met President Anwar Sadat at his home in Aswan. Here I am greeting him, with Bob Meyner (on my right), former governor of New Jersey, and his wife Helen Stevenson Meyner (on my left), who represented New Jersey in the House of Representatives. Clement Zablocki, chairman of the House Foreign Affairs Committee is in the foreground, on the right.

some of these skinny people. We were also able to meet a female Cairo doctor because of her valiant undercover work to prevent ignorant local mothers from having their daughters' clitorises excised—and without anesthetic. What a disappointment twenty-five years since Point Four had gone into Egypt, and USAID had been pouring in millions of dollars a year, to find that these dire situations still prevailed. But the doctor had to be very careful in what she said in public.

At home, Jack and I were slightly unnerved to realize that many of the top jobs in Washington were now held by friends or acquaintances who were younger than ourselves. This had begun with Mac and Bill Bundy during the Kennedy administration, and it mounted through the Johnson and Nixon years into the Carter ones. Yet, even if these people were younger than us, it was sometimes an advantage to have friends in high places. One example was when Cy Vance (who was two years behind Jack at Yale) had to fly to Paris for a weekend and invited Jack and me along on the official plane. For me it was hardly credible to find myself marching across the tarmac at Andrews Air Force Base to climb the steps into an "Air Force One" with the American flag painted on its tail. Sunday night, on the plane flying home, Cy used a small bedroom where he could lie on his back, which was in pain. Everyone else was expected to sit up on the seats that reclined somewhat, but, for my back, not enough. Halfway through the night, I decided that Cy wouldn't mind if I lay down on the floor outside his bedroom—which I proceeded to do, causing a bit of inconvenience to the nice young Air Force stewards as they tiptoed back and forth on their duties.

Adequate as Jack's and my French was, the best accent in the Bingham family became that of our nephew Steve Bingham. After his Mississippi Summer, followed by a stint as a Peace Corps volunteer in Sierra Leone with his wife, Gretchen, Steve got divorced and started working as a lawyer in California. In 1971, he apparently was the last person to visit Black Panther leader George Jackson in San Quentin Prison before the shoot-out that killed Jackson and two guards.

California's governor at the time was Ronald Reagan; the state's attorney general was Edwin Meese. After Steve's visit with Jackson, he zoomed off from the prison on his motorcycle in order to have Sunday lunch with his Uncle Woodbridge and Aunt Ursula in Berkeley. They noted that he had his usual excellent appetite. But while they were all watching a post-lunch game on TV, an announcer interrupted to report the shooting at San Quentin. One of the suspects was Stephen Bingham. Steve's immediate assumption was that he could not possibly be given a fair trial in California at that time. He climbed back onto his motorcycle, and, in effect, disappeared. His bearded face was promptly featured on the government's "Most Wanted" placards in post offices around the country. His parents were frantic.

As we found out thirteen years later, Alf and Sylvia did manage one brief meeting with Steve, highly secret and dangerous for him, during his years in hiding. He eventually decided that the government of California had improved sufficiently for a left-winger like him to take the chance of returning to face trial. The government is said to have spent a million dollars on the trial, and Steve's family and friends raised at least five hundred thousand dollars for his defense. Steve went through a jury trial and was acquitted.

For years afterward, he refused to say where he had been, but his French was notably more fluent and he was accompanied by a charming, bright young Frenchwoman, Françoise Blusseau. The day after his acquittal, they married. They now have a daughter named Sylvia after Steve's mother. They live in California where Steve practices public service law. They always come back to Salem for Christmas.

Steve was one of several of our thirty nephews and nieces to become a close adult friend. We have also been lucky in our children-in-law. By the year 2000, Sherry had been married to Richard Downes (most people called him by his last name) for longer than she was married to Jim, and Downes's strong male presence was of inestimable value to her three boys. His job before retiring from the ministry at age sixty-five was as rector of a large church outside Boston. Sherry, whom he sometimes teased by calling her "the rectorine," has braided her life successfully with his, hosting large and small gatherings for their parishioners and for fellow clergy, and chauffeuring Downes, whose eye problems preclude a driver's license, to hospitals to make sick calls and to parishioners' homes to make the kind of pastoral call he once made on her.

My family would sometimes fall apart but always pull itself back together.

PART SIX

The Eighties

CHAPTER 15

Disaster

JIMMY AND ROSALYNN CARTER HAD an unusually close political marriage, though, in contrast to Pat and Jim Schroeder's, it was in the traditional mold of the officeholder being the man rather than the woman.

Even so, as first lady, Rosalynn Carter found herself violently criticized by some voters for sitting in on those Cabinet meetings that concerned her special interest, mental health, and for having a "working lunch" once a week with her husband.

Not only did I admire her, but I felt that she would be a fine subject for my "One Woman's Voice" column. I, therefore, requested an interview and in time was instructed to come to her office in the East Wing. While waiting there I became conscious, for the first time, of its considerable physical distance from the West Wing. Later I heard resentment voiced by some of her staff about that distance. Those I talked to felt that their side of the White House was not taken seriously by the West Wing, which made the big decisions. But lots of small decisions can also add up to something big, and even small mistakes can be damaging to the president. Because the East Wing people considered themselves just as bright and public-spirited as their counterparts, they resented being viewed by the other side as involved only in tangential matters.

This was surprising to me because the Carter marriage appeared to be unusually egalitarian. Was the natural competition between their two staffs similar to the natural competition between the campaign manager and the candidate's spouse? Or was Jimmy Carter's public and sincere espousal of women's rights occasionally undermined by his own, self-admitted, proclivity to make some decisions entirely on his own? Certainly his previous resignation from the Navy to try his luck as a peanut farmer and future politician had forced a distressed Rosalynn to adjust to a radical alteration in their joint lives, one that she would likely have fought against if given the chance beforehand.

Or was it simply the fact that the president is elected and the first lady is not that makes many voters feel that the spouse should not be entrusted with substantive responsibilities? Certainly, it was true that the president could not fire her if she were to mishandle her job.

Nor was it only male voters who voiced disapproval of the Carters' steps toward gender equality in the White House; many female voters did the same. Thus, in a sense, the White House appears to be a place where major strands of the couple's lives need to be kept separate, at least in the public view, no matter how tightly intertwined they may be in private. Biographer Phyllis Levin's portrayal of Woodrow Wilson's wife, Edith Galt Wilson, provides a frightening example of a first lady's private power impinging on public policy at home and abroad. On the other hand, a 21st-century version of the old doormat kind of presidential wife no longer sits well with many female voters, as well as some males. Neither Mrs. Calvin Coolidge nor Mamie Eisenhower was criticized for lacking a cause of her own.

During the Carter years, Joan Mondale, wife of Walter "Fritz" Mondale, Carter's vice president, became known for her interest in art and was nicknamed "Joan of Art." Jack and I had originally met the Mondales through Americans for Democratic Action (ADA), where Joan's chief characteristic was a quiet adaptability to the demands of politics. I wrote an article about her, but nothing in it was dramatic enough to cause a magazine editor to sit up.

After Jimmy Carter was defeated in 1980 for his second term, he and Rosalynn wrote books admitting that the following year had put unprecedented strains on their marriage: there were too many things they wished that they themselves and their partner had done differently. Nonetheless, they remained together and built what appeared to many people as the most graceful joint postpresidential endeavor since John and Abigail Adams retired together to Quincy, Massachusetts. Jimmy Carter's Nobel Prize for Peace did not make explicit reference to Rosalynn, but much of the world must be aware of how thoroughly her work has been braided into his.

In 1982, based on the census of 1980, Jack's congressional district was again carved up by the state legislature. It now incorporated both a conservative section of Yonkers in Westchester, then represented by the rather right-leaning Democratic congressman, Mario Biaggi, and also a long narrow stretch along the Hudson in Manhattan, then represented by the liberal, relatively young congressman, Ted Weiss. If Jack were to retire, Weiss could win the new district's primary, whereas if Jack battled the two of them for it, he and Weiss would split the liberal vote and thus perhaps hand the nomination to Biaggi. (Subsequently, Biaggi was convicted of corrupt practices and went to jail for a short time.)

The main factor in my mind was Jack's health. Up to that time, his prostate cancer was what the doctors called "indolent," but the strain of another hard campaign might undermine his immune system and thus permit the cancer to flourish. I hoped that he would decide to retire.

But it was hard for him to give up his seat after eighteen years. He loved much of the work and many of his colleagues, and he cared passionately about issues such as nuclear nonproliferation on which his subcommittee on exports was having a small but clear impact. He had also played a role in the internal politics of the House by way of the new rules that diminished the power wielded through seniority by conservative Southern committee chairmen. Up front, Jack had fun with several proposed bills, one of which was to initiate a constitutional amendment that would allow non-native-born Americans to run for president. The person Jack had in mind was Franklin Roosevelt, Jr., who had been born in Campobello, Canada. Jack received a wildly enthusiastic letter about his proposal from the German-born Henry Kissinger. The proposal did not pass the House, but a special bill by Jack did.

Probably his most important accomplishment was the way he, virtually single-handedly, undermined the power of the Joint Committee on Atomic Energy. That unique House-Senate entity had basically been established to promote the nuclear power industry. All legislation regulating nuclear energy went to the joint committee where it would predictably die. Jack, deeply worried about the impact of atomic waste on the environment, plus the possibility of nuclear accidents, devised a quiet way to abolish the joint committee by a vote in the House Democratic Caucus. This somewhat sneaky effort succeeded and suddenly such pronuclear panjandrums as Senator Henry (Scoop) Jackson lost their ability to ram through pronuclear-industry legislation. Instead, it would be routed through the normal committee structure where environmentalists and other nuclear skeptics could block proposals that put the industry's concerns ahead of those of the public. Jack's reform, combined with the Three Mile Island disaster, helped to ensure that nuclear power would remain a highly regulated segment of the nation's energy mix. Thus, behind the scenes, though not in the national media, Jack was able to put his thumbprint on history. This form of gratification is one that I don't suppose anyone in seemingly good health easily surrenders.

In addition, Jack basked in various honors that came his way, both from local organizations and those further afield, like a Chubb Fellowship at Yale that enabled him to live briefly in one of the colleges and teach as well as learn from the students there.

Later on, Jack was appointed by the chairman of the House Foreign Affairs Committee to lead a congressional trip to China. An

Air Force plane was assigned to the group. I was amazed, on a walk to the plane's lavatory, to notice on a galley shelf several large boxes of cheesecake from the Bronx. These were with us, not in honor of the delegation's chairman, but simply as standard fare on Air Force planes. The stewards were amused to hear that the bakery was in the chairman's home district, and the chairman was delighted that the Air Force considered our Bronx product the best.

Jack, as chairman, decided that our group would be less jet-lagged and readier to talk policy with our Chinese hosts if we stopped off for a night's sleep in Anchorage, Alaska, rather than fly straight through. This did not suit some members of the delegation, but Jack stood firm. It was the one place where he permitted us to go easy on ourselves. He was hard-nosed about refusing to permit the plane to detour to Hong Kong so that members and their wives could go shopping. To even my chagrin, he later refused to authorize our plane to ferry us on a day trip from Beijing to Xi'an so that we could see its life-sized statues. The Chinese officials we met referred to their former leader as "Ch'manMao." By the end of the trip some of our group, not without edginess, were referring to Jack as "Ch'manBingham."

I was actually the person least surprised by Jack's sticking to our mandate. He and I had visited India three times for at least a week, and he always refused to allow sightseeing to interfere with business. I have never seen the Taj Mahal in the moonlight or any other way. Our congressional group, he felt, was using taxpayer money to get to China to work, and the work, by and large, got done.

The members met daily with officials of the Chinese government, culminating in a half-hour for all of us with Prime Minister Deng Xiaoping at his vast reception room, its huge square armchairs further separated by large square end tables. We were also fed delicious food at official dinners, complete with bottoms-up toasts between each of the very many courses. We did finally get escorted by our Chinese hosts to the Great Wall and to the Forbidden City on our way back. That's where Jack and I discovered the famous two large trees whose trunks had early in life been braided.

On the drives to our various destinations, we traversed the impressive Tiananmen Square, which later became the scene of the terrible slaughter of dissidents by the government. One day, I escaped from our group and took a walk by myself along one of Beijing's wide avenues. We had been told to bring little keepsakes from America to hand out to Chinese people. I, therefore, had in my pocket some small balloons with the American flag on them. Walking toward me was a young Chinese mother with a baby in a stroller and a young boy holding her hand. It seemed innocent enough for them to respond to my smile by stopping. I pulled out a balloon and blew it up for the baby. The little boy was furious that he had not received the first one, so I quickly blew up another balloon. Encouraged by the children's pleasure and the mother's smile, I tried out my very few words of Chinese. *"Mei guo ren nai-nai,"* I said. At first she looked baffled, and then, with a different pronunciation, she repeated the words to the children who smiled. What I had said was that I was an "American granny."

Back in Washington, a congressional evening was hosted at the White House by the Reagans. We felt rebuffed when they didn't deign to come downstairs to join their guests until the party was half over. The following year, 1982, we figured that if the Reagans cared so little about our group, this freed Jack and me from needing to accept the president's usually mandatory invitation; we, therefore, stayed happily—and a tad smugly—at home.

We could afford to break some rules because Jack had finally made the difficult decision to retire from Congress. I was delighted at the prospect of no longer having to commute between Washington and New York. But which city would become our permanent home? We dearly loved our sunny little modern house in Georgetown within walking distance of many friends, but we finally concluded that

Disaster

Washington was too much of a company town. Once you retire from government, you're continually reminded of your has-been status. Foreign embassies, for example, have to drop you from their invitation list to make room for your successor, and if you are still included in private parties subject to protocol, you are seated well below the salt. The immediate loss of people you thought were lifetime friends can come as a shock.

New York, on the other hand, is not limited to just one main pyramid, but has dozens in different forms, whether in the realms of theatre or art, fashion or banking, finance or other. Few New Yorkers on one pyramid know or give much of a hoot about where on your own pyramid your niche may be. As a result, when you retire, your nose isn't constantly rubbed in your diminishment. Having been recognized, if not as a personage, then at least as a person whom other people have heard of, that status remains and to some extent still provides access to those in power. For Jack and me, moreover, the roominess of our Riverdale house where all ages of family members could gather was a major incentive for returning to New York.

On the Sunday in January 1983 that we drove away from our Georgetown house for the last time, the *Washington Post* published an article of mine called "Home Free." It was illustrated by a drawing of a blithe Mary Poppins–type with bag in hand, flying off from the Capitol, with some thirty men and women sadly waving good-bye. The article reflected an insouciance I hadn't experienced since Jack had first entered the political arena. I even dared to mention my relief that the ever-ringing telephone in our home would no longer serve as a form of "coitus interruptus."

By the following week, our friend Bill Walton had sent the article to his friend Jackie Kennedy, by now a publisher. The first I knew, the phone rang and a husky female voice said slowly, "This is Jacqueline Onassis. Bill Walton showed me your *Post* article and I wondered if you'd like to expand it into a book."

369

She and I made a lunch date at the Polo restaurant on upper Madison Avenue near where she lived. She appeared wearing a simple black pantsuit and little make-up. We talked excitedly about political marriage. She fully understood my reluctance to make a book out of other people's domestic disasters, but as a publisher she made it clear that a book that was too discreet was unlikely to have big sales, or even to be bought at all. We left it that I would send her an outline — which I did — but apparently it was insufficiently revealing.

When I called Bill Walton to thank him for the reference, he suggested that he bring Jackie to dinner some night at our house. I knew that although I would have hostess-worry to the highest degree, Jack would be charmed by such an occasion. He and I decided to include one further couple, Brian Urquhart who was still at the United Nations and his attractive new young wife, Sidney. I hired a local Irish helper to serve the meal and clean up afterward but didn't mention the guest list. Her expression of disbelief when she caught sight of Jackie was a delight to me, although, doubtless, old hat to Jackie.

Bill and Brian had us helpless with laughter as they compared their World War II experiences, Bill from the American side, Brian, from the British side; Brian went on to describe some similarly dangerous and funny occasions from his recent trip to the war-torn Congo. Jack, at the head of the table, was the picture of contentment. The evening, in a way, was the last social gift I was able to provide for him, and that made me contented also. At the time, by the end of his day, he was often too weary to want to do much, and gradually we had been cutting back our attendance, first at big dinners and then at small ones.

One of the last big dinners we attended was at the United Nations under the auspices of the Africa-America Institute, whose board I had been invited to join in place of Jack. Jimmy Carter was the dinner's guest of honor. As I, followed by Jack ("ladies first," in contrast to the White House protocol), went through the receiving line, Jimmy stepped forth and enveloped me in a huge hug. "Rosalynn and I just loved your article about leaving Washington! We agreed with every word."

I blushed scarlet. Jack laughed out loud.

Another pleasure the Africa-America Institute, like the ADA, provided was the opportunity to meet more American blacks than we would otherwise have been likely to. These included New Yorkers like Randolph Nugent, Charles Rangel, Percy Sutton, and Clarence Jones, Washingtonians like Roger Wilkins, and Georgians like Andrew Young and Julian Bond.

Partly by having to do research in order to introduce him at an institute dinner, I became friendly with my seatmate on the dais, the Nigerian general, Olusegun Obasanjo. Some years later he was elected president of Nigeria.

One day I was honored to be included in a tiny luncheon at a restaurant hosted by the institute's Frank Ferrari. The only other guests were Bishop Desmond Tutu and his two adult daughters. These lively women had clearly been brought up to speak their minds. "Aren't they terrible?" Tutu would ask, beaming with pride. "No respect for their elders!" The daughters would laugh and tell him he didn't know what he was talking about. The bishop's spiritual grounding didn't need to be expressed in words; he emanated it. Many years later, the younger daughter was ordained an Episcopal priest by her father, the bishop. The first person she blessed was him.

Oddly enough, Bishop Tutu's home-away-from-home on America's West Coast was Adelaide and Alec Hixon's beach house in Santa Barbara. They lent it to him and his family for weeks when he needed a hideaway in which to become refreshed.

During the five hours of our final commute by car from Washington to New York, Jack and I felt a bit like newlyweds, debating what kind of career we each should engage in. He wanted to teach a course at the Columbia Law School, to practice some law, and to serve on boards of private institutions concerned with public affairs. Before long he joined People For the American Way, where he worked closely with Norman Lear and Andrew Heiskell, the Population Crisis Committee, and the U.S. Committee for UNICEF.

For myself, I realized that because New York is the theatre capital of the nation, I could go back to my first love (and college major), playwriting. Jack was taken with this idea, and said he hoped I'd write about not just imaginary characters but also some of the historic ones whom the country needs to understand in greater depth. A result of this discussion was the biographical play I wrote called *Triangles*.

In addition to writing plays, I also contributed articles to a few national publications and the alumni magazines of Vassar, Barnard, and Choate-Rosemary Hall. Although the national magazines paid much more money and reached many more people, the alumnae journals reached more of my friends and acquaintances. Having an impact on strangers is gratifying but receiving feedback from pals is far more fun. Best in this regard were my occasional op eds, letters to the editor, and articles that were published in the *New York Times*. I had never gotten there as a youthful reporter, but I did end up as an occasional essayist.

In addition to the Africa-America Institute, I also joined the board of a few good-works organizations. One was a Manhattan-based Carnegie group, then called the Council on Religion and International Affairs; another was Bronx-based Lehman College; and the third was the Woodrow Wilson Foundation, which I rejoined. The last held most meetings in New York but some in Princeton. All along, I had remained a board member of the Riverdale Mental Health Association, which had published several of my pamphlets. Even in my mid-80s, when I tried to resign from it, they told me I couldn't because I was their "institutional memory."

Jack very much enjoyed his teaching one day a week at the Columbia Law School, especially his contact with the students. He also joined a midtown, medium-sized law firm, Pryor, Cashman, Sherman and Flynn, in the "of counsel" capacity. From his office at 410 Park Avenue, he could walk to the Century for lunch, often joining the long table with Arthur Schlesinger, Augie Heckscher, Brendan Gill, and Ved Mehta, thus gaining access to literary *and* political doings.

At first, Jack badly missed being in Congress. An early chore he had assumed was to replace our official license plates with ordinary ones. After waiting interminably in line at the Bronx Bureau of Motor Vehicles, he finally reached a grumpy official. "What district?" she asked as she took his old plates. When he told her, she said, "Well, you didn't do much for me." He slunk out with our new plates.

I could revert to my natural informality; no longer did I need to worry that I would lose voters for Jack if my shoes were not shined or my hair not coiffed. To sink back into anonymity, as Jack's political position faded from the voters' memory, felt like liberation. Some people yearn for celebrity—and enjoy being recognized on the street by strangers; I personally felt that even the small amount of reflected celebrity I had been granted was as much a burden as a joy. I always get a rush of adrenaline when something I write is published or a play of mine is produced, but a small taste of ego nourishment now goes a long way. As Adlai used to say, "Flattery is all very well, as long as you don't inhale."

The summer following Jack's 1983 retirement, he and I, with our children and their spouses, were sitting around the dining room table in Salem after supper. Indoors, the candles were guttering, and outdoors the cicadas were singing. Jack happened to pull from his wallet a card to show someone who had asked about his post-Congress health coverage. The card was passed around the table. Micki's husband, Erik, who had gone through a year of medical school, studied it with unusual care. "Bapu, how come you're taking diethylstilbestrol?"

At some level, Jack must have wanted the children to know about his anticancer battle, and now he had no choice but to reveal what had been going on for more than a decade. I was immensely relieved that I could now talk to the kids about it—but when Jack and I went to our bedroom that night, I did gently tease him for having been, in effect, a blabbermouth.

The next day I also had to explain the situation to Miss Bettie, our itinerant cook who had gotten wind that there was a new problem in "her" family. She unceremoniously shooed the late breakfasters out of the kitchen so that she and I could talk in our usual open fashion. Jack's and my children and grandchildren adored her, though her scolding could sometimes alarm them. One of the young men courting Sherry after Jim's death had been invited to Salem with his two young children. When the younger child was impertinent to Bettie, she went straight to Sherry, who told her guest. He, in turn, told his child to apologize—but the harm was done. The man and his children departed the next day. "We sure put the rollers under him," Bettie said with relish. Among the continuing advantages of our family reunions, with and without Bettie, is the informal screening they provide for candidates trying to woo some family member.

Jack and I were lucky, he in his early seventies, I in my late sixties, to be able still to play tennis with the children and grandchildren, as well as to enjoy occasional golf. Thanks to the improvement in the metal of both tennis racquets and golf clubs, based on discoveries originated in the space program, Jack's and my game was no worse than it had been earlier, and many a fierce competitive battle took place on the Camp's two tennis courts between members of three, and eventually four, generations.

All our problems were dwarfed for me when the family gathered in Riverdale for Christmas 1985. The day before everyone arrived, the phone rang. It was Jack's doctor. "His PSA has gone off the chart," the doctor told me. "Have him phone me right after the holidays."

I took our dog Pepsi, an even-smaller edition of Yankee, for a very long walk. By the time I got home, I had decided to let Jack and the visiting children and grandchildren have a carefree, doubtless final, Christmas together. No need for me to spread the bad news until afterward, since nothing could be done during the holiday anyway. When Jack got home, I mentioned that his doctor had phoned to report that the PSA wasn't too marvelous. Jack, uncharacteristically, did not ask for details and agreed to phone the doctor right after New Year's.

We had a memorably good time, and on Christmas night, as was our custom, Jack and I took the grown children to Manhattan for dinner and theatre, leaving the grandchildren with Miss Bettie. By that time the elder grandchildren were asking when they could be included in the theatre party, but we held them off (after all, there is a limit to the number of people who can enjoy a general conversation around a restaurant table, and, besides, the original purpose of the party was to allow our exhausted adult children to have an evening free from their own darlings—who had likely awakened them at dawn in search of their stockings).

When we got home from Neil Simon's *Brighton Beach Memoirs*, which made us laugh and cry, Jack thought he might be coming down with a cold (an unintentional Christmas present from the younger grandchildren: my rule of thumb has become, the smaller the child, the more virulent the germ he or she transmits). Jack and I therefore went promptly to bed. But no sooner did we turn the light out then my heart began to act like a caged bird, flying wildly about the inside of my ribcage. I turned the light back on.

"Sorry, but I may have to go to the hospital. My heart has suddenly gone bananas," I said.

"I'll drive you."

"No, you won't. Not with a cold. Erik's in the next room. I can hear him and Micki."

I shouted to Erik and he came and took my pulse. His eyes grew enormous. "Hey, Ahmee, let's go."

He drove me to the emergency room of Presbyterian Hospital, where I was placed on a gurney with intravenous digoxin dripping into my vein. Erik was given my clothes to take home. Later, I was moved to a cardiac monitoring floor where I almost froze to death. I rang and asked for more blankets, but they had not a one. The December winds off the Hudson were hurling themselves at the leaky windows of Harkness Pavilion, and I thought how ironic it would be if my heart were corrected but I died of pneumonia. About five hours later, just as suddenly as it had begun, the heart arrhythmia ceased. I rang my bell. I needn't have bothered, for the bleating monitor above my head had alerted several doctors and nurses who rushed into the room.

"My heart's fine again!"

One of the doctors looked down at me, who, because the monitor was over my head, couldn't see it. "How would *you* know?"

By late in the afternoon, I was sprung from the hospital, having declined to eat the good-smelling meal that had been brought to my bedside. Instead, I was looking forward to the chicken dinner I'd asked Miss Bettie to fix for us that evening. Jack appeared with my clothes, but in his hurry to pick me up he had forgotten to bring my overcoat. Again I hoped that pneumonia would not result. When I got home, I discovered that one of my vegetarian children had countermanded my menu and instead of the chicken I expected, we were served some variety of tofu. I was tempted to sneak back to the hospital for my earlier tray.

The following day all the young departed, and I was able to brief Jack about his PSA. He phoned his doctor. What appeared to have happened was that the female hormone that Jack had been taking for fourteen years had lost its power against the cancer cells. The doctor wanted Jack to come right into the hospital for chemotherapy. After ascertaining that the chemo most likely would not do much good, Jack said, "I'd rather go to Mexico and play golf."

That had long been our plan for January, to meet Adelaide and Alec Hixon in Cancún, sightseeing one day and golfing the next. So off Jack and I went to Cancún, and the four of us had a lovely time. Jack and I did not mention our problem, and the sole member of our group to be stricken with illness was myself.

When Jack and I returned home, he was still able to play his violin and for another month or so, we played a bit of tennis indoors. Then he developed a cough accompanied by wild chills and fever every afternoon. I would cover him with blankets and comforters and one time I even wrapped my body on top of his in an attempt to quiet the heavy jerking of his shivering limbs. That day we agreed that the problem had become too much to handle at home. The next day he went into Presbyterian Hospital for intravenous antibiotics. When his chills and fever still continued, a specialist performed a bronchoscopy to see what was going on in his lungs. I was sitting by Jack's bedside after he was wheeled back from that procedure. Though he had an oxygen cannula in each nostril, I thought he was growing paler. I rang for the nurse and asked if she could increase his oxygen.

"He's getting just what the doctor ordered," she said, and flounced off. Fortunately, before long, the bedside phone rang. It was our doctor's secretary.

"How's the Congressman?"

"Looking a bit green, but the nurse won't give him any more oxygen."

"Just wait."

Within a minute, our door was flung open and in came doctors, nurses, and a technician who measured Jack's blood gases. When he announced the numbers, Jack was moved onto a gurney and wheeled off toward the intensive care unit. With me pushing his intravenous "tree" and a man at the gurney's head and another at its foot, we literally ran through the halls. Jack was laughing at the drama of it, and I laughed with him. But nothing was funny in the ICU where he was put on a respirator. I never heard his voice again.

The next day, when I approached Jack's bed, a very young nurse was saying, "Say, Johnny, it's time to turn over."

I could see by Jack's expression that he would prefer some other form of address. He hated being called Johnny. I therefore said to her, "Would you please call him Mr. Bingham or Congressman or, if you prefer, Mr. Ambassador?"

The nurse was about to give a sharp retort when a handsome young resident spoke up. "Nurse, please do what Mrs. Bingham says. Here, I'll put his form of address right in the chart."

The nurse huffed off, and I looked at the young man's nametag: "Dr. Henry Cabot Lodge, II."

"Are you the Senator's grandson?"

"Great-grandson."

"Well, your patient's father, Hiram Bingham, was in the Senate with your great-grandfather during the twenties."

Dr. Lodge took especially good care of Jack, but, alas for us, the doctor was soon rotated to another specialty. He is now a very successful internist in Manhattan with a couple of best-sellers on health to his name.

For six weeks, Jack lay in the intensive care unit, getting thinner and paler and more beautiful as the bony structure of his brow and nose, cheekbones and chin, revealed itself. His eyes were even more eloquent than usual, and he was able to communicate both non-verbally and by way of a yellow pad. One day when I entered the unit, a nurse pulled me aside.

"He's lost his mind."

"What makes you think so?"

"No one can read a thing he scribbles on that pad."

"No one has ever been able to read his handwriting," I said.

I marched into Jack's cubicle. He looked about the same to me. "What's going on?"

He wrote something. I quickly tore it up. What he had written was, "That nurse is stupid."

But each week some other complication arose. He managed to develop clots on the lung, holes in the lung, viral pneumonia, bacterial pneumonia, and an infection called pseudomonas. The only lung problems he avoided were the emphysema that had killed his father and the lung cancer that the pulmonologist expected Jack might have as a result of his prostate problem. The doctors jointly decided that a lung biopsy was needed and a chest surgeon was summoned. He informed Jack that he would make an incision in his side, pull apart the ribs and take a sample of lung tissue. Jack would wake up to find a drain in place. I stepped up to this man: "What can you find by this test that will be treatable?"

The surgeon was tall and clearly furious at the interruption. If looks could kill, I would have been on my way to the morgue. He didn't answer me or say another word. Later, I was told that the medical conference concerning my question was the longest that the ICU had ever held.

Their decision was to let Jack be.

The next day when I arrived, Jack wrote, "Where is the drain?"

"Dummy!" I shouted with relief. "You didn't have to have the operation."

He gave me a big smile as a thank you.

I spent all day, every day in his cubicle, starting at noon when visitors were first allowed into the ICU. By about seven o'clock, he was ready to drift off, and I was ready to go home. I purposely kept the kitchen table decorated with flowers and candles and forced myself to sit down and eat a proper dinner, but with only one glass of wine. After dinner, I had a multitude of phone calls from family members and friends who were checking in or had left word on our answering machine. (My brother Dick and brother-in-law Alf called daily.) These calls were both invigorating and exhausting, but I felt it a duty to keep up with them.

I never gave up hope that Jack would return to 5000 Independence Avenue nor, as I found out later, did the ICU's chief doctor, the late Glenda Garvey. Because Jack kept losing weight while being fed through a nasogastric tube, the doctors agreed to remove it and also to attach his respirator through the front of his neck rather than down through his nose. These steps enabled him to eat in a normal fashion, but his appetite was tiny. Still, it was a thrill for me to see his face again without all the tubing. But because of the respirator, he was still not able to speak. I brought from home some heavy cream that he enjoyed on sliced banana, and the nurses let me keep it in their refrigerator. I was able to feed him a bit every day, thus supplementing the Ensure the hospital was providing.

The children all came for visits and he was delighted to see them, but it was clear to the nurses and me how fatigued he was afterward — no matter how beloved the visitor. One day our daughter-in-law appeared from New Haven without an appointment. Because Jack was already scheduled to see Augie Heckscher that day, I unceremoniously backed her out of the cubicle. To conserve my patient's energy — which would aid in the healing process — was my first priority. She told me later that I had been very rude in my single-mindedness. I have no doubt that she was correct. But even as it was, later in the day because Jack was feeling too weak, I had to phone Augie and ask him to come another time.

One guest whose trans-Atlantic visit gave Jack a visible lift was our senior grandson, Edward Bland, who flew back for a few days from Italy where he was studying. Jack excitedly wrote on his yellow pad, *"Parla Italiano."* And Edward did, at least for a moment. Anyway, I left them to their own devices.

But soon afterward, when Doug Auchincloss arrived as planned, Jack signaled to me that he wasn't up to the effort of communicating. Instead, Doug and I went out to lunch in the neighborhood.

The machine that measured the percent of oxygen that Jack's lungs could absorb kept revealing a number below the minimum necessary to permit him to go off the respirator. If the number was up a few points, I would congratulate Jack; if it was down, I'd say, "Better luck tomorrow."

After he'd been in the ICU for a month, I was so hopeful about his coming home that I lined up a local pulmonary technician to handle Jack's oxygen supply, and I rented a hospital bed for our bedroom. I mentioned to Jack the next morning that in the night, when I went to the bathroom, I had bumped into his big new bed and barked my shin. He thought this was funnier than I did, perhaps because he was so relieved that actual plans were being made for his return. He wrote "5000" on his pad quite often, and I would say he could be there just as soon as his stupid oxygen absorption rate would climb to an acceptable level.

What he didn't know, and I saw no need to burden him about, were the agonies I sometimes suffered in the ICU visitors' waiting room. It was a dark, narrow chamber with a "No Smoking" sign at one end, and a "Smoking Permitted" sign at the other. How the smoke was expected to stop in the middle, I had no idea. The worst moments came when I phoned the ICU for permission to visit and either no one picked up the intercom or the ward clerk said, "No, you can't come in" and hung up. Sometimes I was told, "Call back in thirty minutes," but when I did, no one told me anything; they just said I could not yet visit Jack. My imagination was soaring into the worst possible scenarios: Why couldn't I visit? Was my patient alive or dead? Helplessness is not a perfect adjunct to fear, and I was subject to large amounts of both.

Gradually, after I made friends with some of the nurses, I was told that the reasons for forbidding a visitor to enter the unit were usually simple enough to have been communicated if anyone had taken the time. They included a clean up of the patient or the administering of some treatment or a problem with one of the patients in nearby cubicles. Actually, I had noticed that opposite the foot of Jack's bed were three young men who never had a visitor, except once when an older woman appeared, but she didn't return. I assumed that the patients, pitiful as they lay in the fetal position, were probably dying of AIDS, and I would have liked to try to comfort them, but I was wholly absorbed with my own patient.

As it happened, Jack's and my acquaintanceship was relatively free of AIDS. Except for one friend whose son died of it, and one young man whose partner died of it, we escaped involvement in that particular form of tragedy. It was, however, decimating the worlds of theatre, art, music, fashion, and other arenas of creativity to which New York, perhaps more than any other part of the country, was host.

Furthermore, our personal world was shrinking as we focused on what was happening in one cubicle of one intensive care unit. Still, I read the *Times* to him, at least in part, every day.

One morning Tip O'Neill, speaker of the House of Representatives, phoned the unit to inquire about his erstwhile colleague. Three of the nurses were named Mary and they separately came to Jack to say how impressed they were by Tip's call.

The oxygen level on the machine by Jack's bed began inching downward. His internist took me aside and told me to summon the children to say farewell. But I thought the doctor was alarmist. I did, of course, report to the children what he had said, and some of them made a special trip to see their Dad that week.

Then, once again, Jack rallied and once again my spirits soared. I even went out to dinner a few times with friends. My June 20 birthday came and went. I found on Jack's desk a tiny stainless steel saucepan that matched those of ordinary size in our kitchen. He must have bought it for me and forgotten about it. I thanked him profusely in person. Two Sundays later, he was well enough for me to read him the fat *New York Times*. I remember it taking the entire afternoon. But two days after that I came in to find him comatose—not fully unconscious because he was able to move his arms and legs, but thoroughly unreachable. Apparently his kidneys were failing. Did I want dialysis for him? How much time would it give him? Probably only a few days. I knew that its installation would make his arm hurt. My primary aim at that point was to prevent him from any more suffering. I said "No," and this time I phoned all the kids.

The next day when I entered the cubicle, Jack was back in full consciousness. I said, "Hey, you were out to lunch yesterday." He shrugged as if to say, "I don't remember, so who cares?" His oxygen machine was turned up as high as it could go, enough to burn out his lung tissue in a week, but also enough to give him a day of being himself. During that day, Sherry and Tim appeared and sat together at the foot of his bed. They were swapping stories and behaving as if they were at home, their voices natural, interspersed with audible chuckles. Jack smiled. We had not been able to get him back to 5000, but we had managed to bring to him the sounds of home.

We had been warned that his pulse rate would slow during the afternoon until he slipped painlessly into a coma and then into death from uremic poisoning. As the monitor showed his pulse dropping, I went up to where his face was, took his hand, and said, "You have nothing to worry about. We have lived our love, and loved our life." His eyes met mine and he nodded hard. Each of the children went up to bid him a separate good-bye. I heard Sherry say, "Don't worry about Ahmee. We'll take good care of her." An expression of anguish passed over his features, as if to say, "No, that's *my* job." But it soon passed and he looked peaceful again. I don't know what Tim said because by then I had retired to the foot of the bed in order to hide my tears from Jack.

Everything went as predicted. He slipped into a coma around seven o'clock, and I clipped a lock of his beautiful white hair to keep.

I also signed the form permitting an autopsy. We sat with him for several more hours, but I began feeling woozy. Tim wanted to stay to the very end. I felt that Jack was already gone—and with him the very center of my life. Around eleven, Sherry drove me home, and at midnight the doctor phoned to report the exact time of death. By an hour, Jack had missed dying on July Fourth.

The next day I was belabored by decisions about arrangements for the memorial service that Downes, Sherry's husband, arrived to take charge of. He did a fine job, but I still had to be consulted about where it should be held and how many programs should be printed and what music should be played and by whom, what food and drink should be served at the reception afterward, which newspapers should be provided with what announcement (the *New York Times* published a wonderful obituary, as, a few days later, did the *Riverdale Press*), and who would deliver the eulogy. Pat Moynihan's office phoned to notify me that the senator would be glad to oblige, but I said no. Instead, Augie Heckscher flew down from Maine and spoke with his trademark intimacy and eloquence about the "Bing" he remembered from their college years at Yale. Augie was not tall, but in the pulpit he became a giant. Jack had composed, among other pieces, a sonatina for violin and piano that we decided should start off the service. Sue Bingham corralled a skilled Israeli violinist whom she accompanied on the piano. Most of the three hundred people in Manhattan's Riverside Church had had no idea of the importance of music to Jack, and several of them later reported they had been stunned by the sonatina's passion, its soaring melodies, and its disciplined development of theme. Woodbridge Bingham had recently died, also of lung problems, but Jack's other five brothers were there with their wives, as were my two brothers and their wives, and many of our thirty nephews and nieces plus their spouses. Some old friends made a big effort to get to New York (Kay Graham and Clayton and Polly Fritchey chartered a plane from Martha's Vineyard) but others, like Averell Harriman, were too frail to attend.

With me in the front pew were my four children and their spouses. Directly behind us sat the grandchildren. Much snuffling and frequent requests for tissues. Fortunately, I had brought along a pile for myself but, as it happened, I had no need for them. The service was exactly as Jack would have liked, and I was so grateful for it that I felt no need to cry.

As the final hymn was ending, Downes stepped quickly from the pulpit, took my arm, and marched me out through the center aisle. Row after row of people I knew and loved were there—family, friends, political colleagues, staff members, supporters and constituents, all with the most sorrowful faces. I was able to do the last thing on earth that I would ever be able to do for Jack. And so, I smiled.

At the memorial service, seated amid the Yale '36 gang were Dick Moore from Washington, Louis and Grace Walker from Maine, Brendan and Anne Gill, and Dick and Bunnie Pinkham from Westchester. As sad as the day was, there was an emotional relief just to see them gathered together.

I then got on with what Freud called "the work of grief." (And work it certainly is, both when one is awake and asleep.) Yet although my anguish at times was so severe that I would drop to my knees on the back lawn and bang my forehead against the crabgrass, it never precluded the blessed occasional eruption of laughter. In fact, on the very night of Jack's memorial service, while my children and grandchildren were still under my roof, I decided to give away Jack's clothes. What would have made him, too, burst out laughing was the avidity with which two fifteen-year-old granddaughters grabbed for his well-worn oxford-cloth underwear. What for? To wear to school as outer garments, of course—the newest fashion. They tried to reassure me: "Don't worry, Ahmee. We'll sew up the fly."

For myself, I kept only the silk paisley dressing gown that I had once given him. It was soft and comforting, and I wore it every morning at breakfast.

Though consciously I felt no anger at anyone, my irritability kept mounting during the first months. Let the phone stop ringing just as I reached it, and I would shout a four-letter word. Or burst into tears. My fuse was short; my tolerance for frustration, infinitesimal. After a few weeks of paralyzing lethargy, I felt a surge of agitation. Our front hedge needed trimming—one of Jack's chores. I finally figured out how to use his big electric clipper. But the hedge was recalcitrant and the clipper needed oiling. As it screeched, I began screaming.

Generally, though, I was useless for the practicalities of life. During the first week, I wasn't even fit to drive a car. Fortunately, Sherry stayed on for several days, and Tim took over the will and tax documents. The phone never stopped ringing, and huge amounts of mail were delivered. The dining room table was soon totally covered with papers. Flowers arrived, casseroles were brought by friends; and all such attentions needed to be recorded so that in time I could convey my genuine gratitude.

Having signed permissions for an autopsy, organ donation, and cremation, I still had to fill out the death certificate. Jack's social security number needed to be announced over the phone, it seemed, every hour. For me to take over the ownership of his car meant four trips to the motor vehicle office; to apply for his veterans' benefits meant locating his Army discharge papers—where, oh where, could they be? And my credit card, which was an adjunct to his, was not renewed when I applied under my own name.

For the first time, I felt I had to watch my pennies. Overnight, I was deprived of Jack, of the institution of marriage, of his sizeable congressional pension, and of my coverage under his health insurance. Within the first week, Sherry and I were in the kitchen when the doorbell rang. She came back with a small, square cardboard box. "Here's Dad."

I don't know how I expected his ashes to arrive, but this was not it. Inside the box was a metal container, which I kept on the mantel in his study. The container would be buried in Salem when we gathered there in about a month. Meanwhile, I got in touch with some Connecticut gravestone cutters. I decided to include just his name and the dates of his birth, marriage, and death, and, above the name, a carved facsimile of the congressional seal. I was asked if space should be left below Jack's name for my own, but I found myself saying with some vehemence that I wanted a stone of my own, thank you. (To take the gallow's humor of this further, an anecdote: a nephew whose wife has predeceased him has a stone in the family cemetery with his name at the top but no death date, followed by her name and death date. Since he is very much alive and now happily remarried, a problem will arise as to where the death of the second wife will be recorded.)

Though bereavement, as expected, was a form of agony, it was a sort of salty one: even at my most miserable, I had to be grateful for the underlying cause of the pain, which was Jack's and my deep love for each other. At least he had died long before our love had. That would have been even worse. This way, no matter how physically diminished he had become, I had still passionately wanted to have him home. And he knew that, and I knew that he knew it.

A few weeks after his death, Dick Moore came up from Washington to spend the day with me. His wife, Jane, had died several years before, so he was particularly sympathetic. We had a fine game of golf. At one point, when I took the seven iron out of my bag, I could just hear Jack's voice: "No, Dummy, use the six: you'll never reach the green with a seven." Obediently, I replaced the seven with the six and hit, what was for me, a good shot. It landed on the green. Dick was most impressed—as was I. I didn't tell him about my invisible caddy.

A week after that, Adelaide Hixon flew in from California. Her taxi appeared at my doorstep. "I was scared to see you," she called out as she alighted with paper bags from Zabar's. "But you look just like you. What a relief." We played golf by day and two-handed bridge by night. She helped with the seemingly endless task of addressing and stamping some three hundred envelopes so that I could insert a printed thank-you card with a brief handwritten message on each, making mention of the flowers or food or letter that the person had sent. She and I laughed and cried as we reminisced. When she left she said that she felt newly appreciative of *her* husband.

Jack's colleagues in Congress scheduled a memorial meeting on the floor of the House. I flew to Washington to sit in the Visitors' Gallery and listen to their eulogies. These were very moving. This time, it was Jack's staff rather than our grandchildren who were sitting behind me. The snuffling was the same, but at least these adults had brought along their own tissues. One of the speakers said that Jack's rectitude was so evident that he, the congressman, "never dared commit an unworthy act in his presence." I could just hear a ghostly whisper, "Where do you suppose he went to commit it?"

I lost twenty pounds, mostly, I suspect, because I found it so difficult to sleep. Jack used to tease me by saying that the only activity for which I could ever receive a Nobel Prize was as a sleeper. No longer. Sherry advised me, on the basis of her own widowhood, that I could take sleeping pills every night because after a few months the need for them would disappear. She was right. But even when I began sleeping better, I still couldn't dream about him. And when finally he appeared in a dream, it woke me right up. "But you're not here any more," I shouted. Gradually his dream appearances stopped waking me, and I started looking forward to them. There was no telling what age he would be: sometimes a young man, sometimes old; sometimes ripsnorting with energy, sometimes weary unto death. But the dreams were always in bright color. In a sense, I was a widow by day and a wife by night. Not long thereafter, I put away the pills.

Even in the daytime, I found my internal life returning to the years before I met him. Tunes from the 1930s drummed in my ears, complete with lyrics I hadn't thought of in half a century. I was nineteen again, wondering if that dashing young fellow (and big man on campus) would pay attention to me. I so deeply hoped that he would. "Wait a minute," I told myself. "He did."

Still, there were days as well as nights when I wasn't sure I wanted to go on living. My own death appeared a welcome respite from prolonged pain. In the mail came the standard notice from my gynecologist that I was due for a Pap test. As I phoned to make the appointment, I realized that I must, at some level, be planning to go on with life. (Fifteen years later that very test, given routinely, with no symptoms preceding it, saved my life.)

Aside from his gravestone, we had no tangible memorial for Jack. One day, I delighted myself by thinking up one. On the golf course at St. Andrews Club, in Hastings-on-Hudson, the fourth hole demanded a straight long drive from a tee elevated by several hundred feet from the fairway. In between was a steep hill covered by brush. Why not have a memorial tee built halfway down the hill? That way many women and older men would not need to spend time on the hillside looking for their ball but would have a sporting chance of its reaching the fairway. Inquiries made it clear that for three thousand dollars such a tee could be built. The powers-that-be at the club were pleased because play would be speeded up for the good players as well. No longer would they be delayed by duffers on the hillside searching for their ball or hacking it out in slow stages.

So, across the cart path from the new teardrop-shaped tee is a brass plaque affixed to a boulder announcing that this is the Jonathan Bingham Memorial Tee. In the same-sized lettering, it mentions that Jack was a member of the House of Representatives from 1965 to 1983 and a member of St. Andrews Golf Club from 1979 to 1986.

The dedication was on Thanksgiving Day. My children and grandchildren were there plus Lex Hixon and his son, Dylan, both top golfers. Lex asked if he could hit off the first ball, and I agreed. He teed it up, took a mammoth swing, and— but no one had seen the ball fly off. Where was it? We finally looked on the tee. Lex had hit under the ball which had lifted into the air, and then landed slightly behind where he was standing. We laughed until we cried. Lex handed his driver over to Dylan. Dyl took a mighty swing and hit the ball so far that when we went to look for it, we couldn't find it. I felt Jack Bingham's amusement as well as my own.

Two other memorials came later. At Yale, a bas-relief was installed in Sheffield-Sterling-Strathcona Hall to honor him for having started the Liberal Party of the Yale Political Union, and in Riverdale the section of Independence Avenue that goes by our house was officially renamed by New York City, "Bingham Road."

One morning, Sue Bingham drove down from New Haven and swept me up to visit a computer store. Totally bemused, I emerged from it several thousand dollars poorer, and the ignorant owner of a word processor and printer. But, in time, and with a huge amount of patient coaching by Sue, I managed to learn the basics and use the new machinery for my plays and articles. Once again, as with the radio in the 1920s, the commercial airplane in the 1930s, the television in the late 1940s, and the car without a clutch in the 1950s, a new form of luxury came to feel like an instant necessity. I would now suffer real deprivation if my computer weren't there to enable me to "find" a particular reference within a lengthy document or enable me instantaneously to move a passage from one page to another. As I threw away my outdated boxes of carbon paper and bottles of White-out, I realized that the acquiring of a new skill is also a partial antidote to grief, perhaps because it uses a part of the brain that is not associated with the missing person.

Disaster

The day after Jack's death, Sherry had gone to the ICU and retrieved the baby pillow and the light, handwoven blanket that Jack had used during that incredibly long month and a half. At that moment I couldn't possibly have set foot in the hospital. Although most of my anguish connected with it was not preventable, too much of it was, especially during the first weeks when I was ignorant of the ICU's routines. Doctors and nurses in a big city hospital are often seriously overworked, and I had no complaint against any individual, but the system of communication between the ICU staff and the anxious visitors in the waiting room was on occasion a disaster. Since doctors and nurses usually don't have time to answer the visitors' many questions, then perhaps someone else could be trained to? What if a group of volunteers was just there in the waiting room to interact with the visitors, not at a professional level but a simple, human one? The volunteer could then enter the unit and find out why the visitor was being kept out. The volunteer could also alert the visitor to the various services that the hospital offers that had taken me weeks to discover. Surely there had to be a way to prevent other people with an ICU patient from having to go through all that I had recently suffered. I found that I was still angry enough about it to decide to take action. But not just yet. For even more burdensome than my anger was my lassitude. Sometimes putting one foot ahead of the other was almost more than I could summon the will or energy to do.

CHAPTER 16

Renewal

JACK'S DEATH WAS ON THE third of July 1986. At the end of that month, I drove with Pepsi Poodle to Salem for five weeks. Grateful as I was to my children and grandchildren for coming, for me the visit was a repeated pryer-off of scabs: too many memories of Jack at all ages, too many knife-like reminders of his absence. When my brother-in-law Alf had gotten remarried to Kitty Dunn, Jack and I had given them tennis racquets as a wedding present. Almost daily, they came up to the Camp from their house in the valley to play doubles with me and one of my descendants. Again, as I had found with Adelaide and golf, exercise is the best medicine, but one afternoon, as Alf and Kitty drove off, one of my children asked, "Isn't it hard for you to see how happy they are together?"

All of Jack's and my descendants gathered in mid-August for the placement of Jack's ashes in the family cemetery. We sang a beautiful blessing composed by Sue, and each of us placed some earth on the grave. The headstone was in place, stark and simple, but when we trooped back to the Camp, I found that I missed the ashes terribly. As a result, I walked down to the graveyard daily, sometimes accompanied by dogs or grandchildren or both, sometimes as alone as a person can feel. I wondered how I could bring myself to leave the ashes and go back to New York when the time arrived.

Among the condolence letters that both tore my heart and also offered consolation was one from Louis Walker containing an anonymous poem:

> I am glad, not that my friend has gone
> But that the earth he lived and laughed upon

Was my earth too, and that my love I'd shown.
Tears at his departure? Nay, a smile,
That I had walked with him a little while.

My old friend Marian Heiskell invited me to break the trip from Salem to Riverdale by spending a night with her and Andrew in Darien. Pepsi and I, therefore, had a pleasant evening with them, but the next day my return to my big empty house could no longer be postponed.

The dog ran ahead into the house. I was grateful for that kind of protection as well as for her company. After unpacking, I went to listen to the accumulated phone messages. One was from Bob Birge. He left a number, but when I called it, there was only an answering machine. I left word that I had returned his call.

Bob was at Jack's memorial service and he, too, as it happened, had been married for forty-six-plus years when his spouse had died a few months previously. He later claimed that my smile at the memorial service was his undoing—that at that moment he fell in love. I later remembered that my first love, Walter Birge, shared the same last name as my last love.

I remember when Bob came through the receiving line, and my brother Dick introduced us. After Yale, Bob Birge had graduated from Union Theological Seminary where, ironically, one of his favorite teachers was Reinhold Niebuhr. Jack and Bob used to have lunch together every ten years or so. In the course of a fairly recent lunch, Bob had asked Jack if he could borrow my biography of Reinie. When Bob eventually mailed it back to Jack, he enclosed a polite fan letter. I had answered it briefly and forgot about it.

Because of his own recent experience with bereavement, he knew enough to leave me alone initially so that I could grieve first. That evening I went to Jack's study and pulled down his Yale '36 books, starting the year they graduated, and including their 25th and

50th reunions. Bob's resumes were quite impressive. He, like Jack, had been one of eleven boys to have achieved Phi Beta Kappa during their junior year. He had gone on to graduate from Union Theological Seminary and planned a career in the Protestant ministry, but after serving in World War II, he went into business, first with the Hudson's Bay Company and then in the field of mergers and acquisitions. He and his late wife had one son who went to Yale a year after our son Tim. (It turned out that the two boys had met when Tim was trying to recruit young Bobby for his singing group.) Bob senior listed cooking and gardening as his avocations.

The next day he phoned. His voice was deep and somehow soothing. He said he had "a project" he wished to discuss with me. Could I meet him for lunch in the city? I said I could. (My writing had been stalled ever since Jack's final illness.) He named a Portuguese restaurant on Eighth Avenue and 29th Street; he would be coming in by train from Long Island to Penn Station. He chose noon, which struck me as about as unfashionable as the address.

On the appointed day, I took my car to a nearby parking lot. The attendant was unwelcoming:

"We close at three."

"I'll be back by 1:30," I said.

"Okay, lady, just so you know the fence will be locked."

As I walked up 29th Street, each foot felt heavier and heavier. What was I doing here? How would I recognize this fellow? What did I care about his "project"? Bob was standing outside the restaurant. When he spotted me, he dashed across Eighth Avenue to escort me back. In the restaurant, we both ordered the shrimp with ginger. It was remarkably tasty. He talked about Dorothy, his wife; I talked about Jack. Tears ran down our cheeks, but we didn't care. At one point, I asked if he would take his glasses off. I wanted to see what color eyes he had. They were blue and emitted an extraordinary kindliness. His "project" was to start a new journal for preachers that would, in effect, make their sermons less boring. Each issue of the journal would cover a particular theme, such as love or anger, faith or evil, and would include the latest in scholarship and biblical interpretation. There would be no printed sermons, only a series of profound or arresting articles by experts to enrich the minds of the ministers or priests or rabbis who had a sermon to prepare.

I told Bob it was a fine idea but didn't see what I could do to help. He said that my knowledge of literature as well as of Niebuhr's thought would enable me to write for them. He also filled me in a bit about his family, especially his mother, who had died in a Connecticut hospital at the age of thirty-seven from "blood poisoning" following the Caesarian birth of her fourth child and only daughter. Bob's face glowed when he recalled her bravery at the time when he, his two younger brothers, and their parents had to lay down their luncheon forks and immediately abandon their home in Turkey. He said these words, in effect:

> In 1922 my father, John Kingsley Birge, a Congregational missionary, was teaching at the American International College near Smyrna. We were forced to flee from our house because the Turkish Army was rapidly approaching in pursuit of Greek troops. The commander in chief of the Turkish Army was Kemal Ataturk who, fortunately for us, looked up to the U.S. as a model democracy. He had given his officers strict instructions not to harm Americans.
>
> A few days after we had left, orders came from the American Consulate requiring all Americans to gather in a theatre in Smyrna prior to being taken aboard an American destroyer. My mother was very concerned about the fate of my father's Armenian students. She told them that if they were willing to risk their lives, she would get them to the United States. Seventeen

Armenian boys accepted the challenge. The Armenian
boys were packed like sardines in the truck she drove
and blankets were spread over them. We drove to
Smyrna along a road with dead bodies on both sides.

When we pulled up in front of the theatre, my two
little brothers and I scampered inside. An American
Naval officer said that only Americans were being
allowed in. My mother reached for the nearest boy
and called out his name, "Haritoun Casparian Birge,"
and shoved him through the door. Then his brother,
"Haig Casparian Birge." One by one she gave our
name to each of the boys. The Naval Officer did not
stop her. Once inside the theatre, my mother hurriedly
went from family to family and succeeded in persuading
sixteen of the women to adopt a boy until we reached
Athens. I should say that my father remained in the
area to help refugees escape by ship.

By the time the seventeen Armenian boys followed us to America, my mother had raised enough
money to cover their expenses at the American
International College in Springfield, Massachusetts.

In 1924 a letter arrived at our home in Northampton,
Massachusetts, informing my mother that the Armenian
boys would have to return to Turkey because their one-
year visas had expired. My mother took the next train
to D.C. Once there, she went to the White House and
met with one of President Calvin Coolidge's assistants.
He told her there was nothing the president could do.
"There must be someone in Washington who can do
something," she said. "Who?"

He said the chairman of the Senate Committee on
Immigration. My mother pleaded with the committee

to allow the boys to remain in the United States, saying that if they were forced to return they would be imprisoned or killed. The chairman said there was nothing they could do because the Armenian quota was full. My mother looked him in the eye and said, "Senator, when you die and appear at the Gates of Heaven, St. Peter is going to say to you, 'No admittance, the American quota is full.'"

The stunned chairman asked her to withdraw for a few minutes. When she returned, he said, "Our committee has considered your plea and we have decided to introduce a special bill in the Senate permitting the Armenian boys to stay."

The special bill was introduced and passed by both houses and signed by the president. The boys finished college and went on to professional careers.

As Bob talked, I heard a strange humming sound from behind me. It was like a vacuum cleaner. I turned around. My God! It was a vacuum cleaner! And we were the last two people in the restaurant. I glanced at my watch. Three o'clock!

We left at a run. The light on Ninth Avenue was against us. As we waited impatiently at the curb, he asked what my feelings were toward Dick Moore. I said, "Dick was our best man, but politically he's to the right of Thutmose the Third." Bob's shout of mirth reflected both his great talent for laughing and also what seemed to me to be considerable relief. But it also caused us to miss the traffic light. Breathless, we finally reached the parking lot, to find the fence about to be locked. I was lucky to be able to extricate my car.

Bob Birge was planning to be away for ten days, escorting an elderly female cousin to Cape Cod to visit yet another cousin. It was clear that he cared about family. He said that on his return he would phone and perhaps we could go to a movie.

The appointed evening finally arrived and a pale blue Cadillac rolled slowly into our gravel driveway. He came inside, and we sat on my living room sofa. Pepsi planted herself firmly between us.

We never got to the movie.

Ten years earlier I had feared that the loss of my breasts would finish off my days as a love-object. From Jack's point of view, after a quarter-century of marriage, this was a lot of malarkey. But what about another man whom I had not been married to? Might he not be repelled? When Bob first took me in his arms, I whispered that a funny thing had happened on the way to the operating room. His answer was immediate and unequivocal: "Love is not love that alters when it alteration finds."

I could not, in a million years, have asked for a better answer. Nor was he, as became abundantly and repeatedly clear, in the least repelled. Indeed, as we began spending every evening together, we sometimes didn't even get the dinner dishes done.

A few months later when he said he thought we'd better get married, I reminded him that he was in a sellers' market. (At our ages, there are five women for each man.) He laughed.

He hadn't exactly moved into my Riverdale house, but he was there much more than in Manhasset, Long Island, where he and Dorothy had lived for forty years. Bob's golf game and mine were similar enough for enjoyable competition, though he usually won. Then he suggested tennis. The fact was that he rather prided himself on having won a tournament in Turkey as a boy. But he hadn't played much over the years, so I managed to win. Some men can't stand losing to a female, but Bob, a passionate feminist, was, first startled, and then contentedly amused.

In so many ways, he was reminiscent of Jack: outwardly, both sported full heads of beautiful white hair; inwardly, both remained bright, warm, sensitive, and interested in just about everything and everyone. Also their "take" on people was almost eerily like my own. Like Jack, Bob is musical, though his instrument was the piano rather than the violin. Bob and I tried playing some Mozart duets, with him at the piano and me on the clarinet, but the impact of the music was too shattering for us at our stage of grieving, and we didn't try again. Similarly, we weren't able to listen to concerts or opera or even music on the hi-fi or radio or TV. I found myself immersed in writing again. After many drafts, the result was a play, *Triangles*, which explored the three main emotional triangles that Eleanor and Franklin Roosevelt formed, one with his demanding and possessive mother, another with his ladylove, Lucy Mercer, and the third with their cousin, that beguiling mischief maker, Alice Longworth. We had several dramatic readings of the show, the most notable being at the American Academy of Dramatic Arts when the part of Eleanor was taken by Kitty Carlisle Hart and that of Franklin by former mayor John Lindsay (who admitted that he had always wanted to be an actor). After each reading, I would make major revisions in the script. As someone has said, "Plays are not written, only rewritten."

These readings also offered an opportunity for people who might be interested in becoming "angels" to see the play and for potential producers to come or send an emissary. I was honored when Robert Whitehead, a major Broadway producer, came to the off-Broadway production of *Triangles*.

Before Jack's final illness, I had managed to raise the requisite sixty thousand dollars from four donors. (If your angels are limited to four, you qualify for a special tax benefit.) My contributors of fifteen thousand dollars each were two friends, Iphigene Sulzberger and Barry Bingham, Sr., one cousin, Frances Lehman Loeb, and one person, Ruth Lord, I had never met but who loved the script when it was sent to her at the recommendation of our mutual friend, the producer

Alfred de Liagre. I met with Ruth and I became friends with her. In fact, her summer place is near Salem.

I found an enthusiastic director for the show. As I later discovered, theatre directors run the gamut from sublime to ridiculous, with some self-appointed Napoleons in between. The most sublime director was Jack Alter in Dallas, Texas, where my musical about the Roosevelts was later produced. The director of *Triangles* was the opposite. First, he tried to discourage me from attending rehearsals, then he gave me a later hour than the rehearsal was actually scheduled to begin. We got into an argument about historical accuracy, and he said he didn't give a damn about it. "The actors will never do their job right if the playwright keeps interfering."

The actors, on the other hand, were a wonderful group of young men and women, and the show ran for its allotted six weeks. The *New York Times* gave it a full-length review but criticized it for too much melodrama. Iphigene Sulzberger, as grand dame of the *Times* and one of the play's four angels, was enraged at the reviewer's ignorance of history. The audiences dwindled, and the show closed but was later resuscitated as the musical I wrote with a composer and a lyricist. This was briefly presented in Dallas, Texas, as well as in New York and Washington.

One night Bob drove down from Riverdale to pick me up after the show. For reasons known best to himself, he had brought Pepsi along. He was walking her on the sidewalk outside the theatre as I emerged with Ellie Rossbach, my sister-in-law, who had come to the show that evening. "There's a dog that looks like Pepsi," she said. As the dog plunged ecstatically toward me, I had to explain that it was, indeed, Pepsi and then introduce Bob.

Over the course of the next several months, I arranged for Bob to meet each of my children in a casual-seeming way. They all enjoyed his company but had no idea how serious he and I were becoming. To our amazement, we found ourselves sharing the depths of grief and the heights of love. Death had deprived us both of the person we had loved above all others and also of the institution of marriage. The person could never be brought back into our lives, but the institution could. We didn't stop grieving, but we have continued to be blessed with times of great happiness, coziness, laughter, and agreement about people and priorities. We enjoy going out, but we also enjoy staying home.

After Bettie's retirement, we did the cooking ourselves. This was not easy because of the family's increased size and polarization of diets. We had to cater to the vegetarians and the carnivores, the teetotalers and the winebibbers, the three-meal-a-day eaters and the constant snackers. At times, an old sibling issue would resurface, especially if a power vacuum had arisen, such as who was in charge of cooking the veggies that evening (we have since learned to post a sign-up sheet for chores, which keeps such vacuums to a minimum). One year, voices were raised over whether the delicious local corn should be boiled or steamed or, if boiled, whether the water should contain some salt and/or sugar. By and large, I have concluded that for me, "Happiness is having children in their fifties," with enough time having passed for them to have resolved many of their childhood emotional issues, whether with their parents or their sibs. We now know that some regression is to be expected at family reunions and also some competitiveness regarding the ways our children are bringing up their own children. Often Jack and I, and then Bob and I, found ourselves instinctively acting as a balance wheel. We were indulgent with the strictly brought up and strict with the indulgently raised. Alec Hixon was heard to say that the hardest thing in life is to watch one's children making mistakes with their children.

After I had finished introducing Bob to my four offspring, he and I drove to Pittsburgh to visit his married son, Bobby, and his wife, Joanne, and their two young sons, Jonathan and David. Bob and I were assigned separate bedrooms, which was appropriate given the age of his grandsons. While in Pittsburgh, we also visited his former

402

sister-in-law, the widow of his youngest brother, Bill, who, like their mother, had died at age thirty-seven.

Bob had been only eleven when his mother died. She had taken him aside and told him that she would not be returning from the hospital. She was completely calm, he remembers, and seemingly ready for what appeared to be God's will. But this family tragedy, in effect, ended his childhood. From then on, he felt responsible for his two younger brothers, Kingsley and Bill, and their baby sister, Kathy. In time, their father married again, and a daughter, Dee, was born when Bob was twenty.

When Miss Bettie was scheduled to arrive in Riverdale to help me with Christmas (twenty-one people scheduled for seated dinner one night), I asked Bob to be fully dressed, as if he had just driven over from Manhasset for breakfast. But Miss Bettie arrived earlier than expected. I, still in a negligee, ran down the stairs to let her in. She and I embraced, but then I felt her stiffen. She was looking up the stairs. There, on the landing stood Bob in his bathrobe. "Hello, Miss Bettie," he called. "I've heard so much about you."

"Well, I ain't heard nothin' about you!" she said and stamped off to the kitchen.

In time they became fast friends, but it took awhile.

After Bob's and my visit to Pittsburgh, he drove me to see his sister-in-law, Kingsley's widow, and also his first cousin, Jack Harlow, both of whom lived in Maine. In time, Jack Harlow's sister, Ruth, came to visit us in Riverdale with her husband Harold Berman. Hal is a legal scholar and gifted writer who continues to teach law at Emory University in Atlanta *and* in Russia.

Bob and I remain amused to realize that if we had met when he was still at Yale—or even at Union Theological Seminary—we would not have had the slightest interest in each other. To him, I would have appeared as a worldly flibbertigibbet, while to me he would have appeared, in Yale parlance, as a "Christer." He neither drank nor smoked, he didn't go to dances, while I knew virtually nothing about religion. He was a scholarship student who had to watch his marks and his pennies; I was lucky enough to be insouciant about both.

Nor would either set of parents have approved a match between us at that time. Mine would have been shocked at his comparative impecuniousness and plans to go into the ministry; his family would have been shocked, not so much at my being Jewish as being secular.

Because circumstances postponed the time of our meeting until I was sixty-seven and he was seventy-two, we found innumerable points of agreement. Foremost was our high admiration for Jack Bingham, FDR, and Reinhold Niebuhr. By then, our styles of life were not noticeably different, since Bob had amassed plenty of money during his years in business. My brother Dick who, in 1939, had suspected Jack Bingham's motives in wooing me proceeded in 1986 to suspect Bob's. When I assured Dick that Bob had more than enough money of his own, Dick relaxed. I then asked Dick if he would "give me away" at my forthcoming wedding. He said, "I've been trying to give you away for sixty-seven years." But actually he didn't do it; my son, Tim, did. At some level I don't think Dick wanted me to marry again or at least not so soon. He adored Jack, and like a few of my grandchildren, would, in a sense, have preferred to see me symbolically, like a traditional Hindu widow, commit suttee by throwing myself onto my first husband's funeral pyre.

One of several differences between Bob and me is that my speech is unbuttoned. When something goes wrong, I'm quite capable of swearing at top voice, while he, by nature and training, is calmer and quieter. Still, he can't help laughing when a funny off-color remark is exchanged between me and either Dick or Adelaide or those of my offspring who enjoy such things. Part of his hearty laughter may result from the contrast between this kind of rascality and the proper behavior expected of a missionary family's eldest child. When he was small, his grandmother nicknamed him "Little Martin Luther" because he was so solemn, and his father, the Rev. Kingsley Birge, was known for averting his eyes from any pregnant woman on the street lest he be reminded of how she got to be that way.

Bob's joie de vivre is infectious and his affection unlimited. He has made friends not only with my four children and their four spouses but all ten grandchildren and the spouses of more than half of them, not to mention the fourteen great-grands. Recently, a photo from Salem was sent to me by Blake Esselstyn, a fine photographer, showing Bob reaching out to Blake's young niece, Edie Aten, who is reciprocating. "Typical of Bob's outreach to all of his step-relatives and in-laws," Blake wrote on the back of the photo.

A mild problem for me early in our relationship arose because of one of Bob's own ancestors. I had written a musical about the Pilgrims called *Squanto and Love*. It centers on a little boy, Love-of-God Brewster, who, on the one hand, is devoted to his father, the Pilgrim leader, Elder William Brewster, and, on the other hand, grows to love and admire the Indian chief, Squanto. Both of Jack Bingham's parents were descended from William and Mary Brewster by way of the Brewsters' eldest son, Jonathan. (That Jonathan was smart enough to avoid coming over on the *Mayflower*; instead, he hung around London and kept supplies flowing to the Pilgrims; by the time he arrived in Plymouth, all the hardest work of clearing the wilderness had been done.) Bob, I discovered, was descended from the *Mayflower*'s William Bradford, the diarist of the Pilgrim years, who, however, was needed in my play to be a strait-laced foil to the versatile Brewster and therefore someone whom Love-of-God avoided.

Bob wasn't happy with my portrayal of his ancestor. He pointed out with justification that we today would know a lot less about 17th-century America if Bradford had not been so articulate a writer. Besides, Bradford had gone on to become governor of the Plymouth Colony. Nonetheless, I couldn't change the play to make Bradford into someone my confused, young hero would have turned to.

A few years before Bob and I met, he had had major surgery for colon cancer. The doctors said they "got it all," but he still had to go back for a colonoscopy every three years.

When I drove him to his doctor's office for this procedure and sweated out the hours of waiting, I was forced to ask myself if I was ready for the possibility of yet another ICU and another very sick husband. Part of me never wanted to see the inside of a hospital again, yet the major part of me knew that marriage entails loyalty "in sickness and in health." Loving someone deeply and thoroughly is the biggest—and I believe the most important—gamble in life. If I were to forgo love's culmination by way of marriage just because I was frightened of an illness in my mate, I'd not only be a coward but an idiot. He, himself, had recalled Shakespeare's "Love is not love that alters when it alteration finds." By the time Bob emerged from the anesthetic, I knew I loved him enough to face whatever lay ahead.

Thanks to God and the medical profession, the test findings continued to be negative—but we went through the ordeal on a regular basis. In fact, the awareness of his problem forced me to realize that I was of an age to have such a test for myself. Not on the first occasion but three years later, my life was saved by the excision of a precancerous polyp. The doctor said that for some reason as yet unknown, more colonic polyps appear in people aged seventy to seventy-four than at any other stage of life. My brother Howard, only in his late fifties, however, had died from a colonic cancer that spread to the liver. He put up a brave front and insisted, as he grew thinner and weaker, that he had "the cancer answer." But the walks he and I took with our dogs that started with half a mile, dwindled gradually to a half block, and then to no walk at all. He died in his beloved Adirondacks.

In the 1980s, Dick's cancer, lymphoma, recurred after a thirty-year remission. But he continued to fight against it, even when it was joined by leukemia. He was truly stunned when I went to see him to tell him I planned to marry Bob, but well enough to attend our wedding at the little local Congregational Church. At the altar stood, in effect, not two principals but four, two of them visible and two, not. For Bob was as certain of Dorothy's enthusiastic approval of our marriage as I was of Jack's.

At the end of the service, Tim's sisters and he sang the musical blessing composed by Sue, "The Lord bless you and keep you." I doubt that there were many dry eyes among the hundred guests. We all went on to the small Riverdale Yacht Club, right on the Hudson River. The heavens smiled and the temperature was so unseasonably warm that we were able to have drinks outside on the terrace. Howard's widow, Ellie, together with Dick and Sue, was there, as were my brothers-in-law Alf and Charlie and Brewster and their wives. Previously, during one of our phone talks, Alf had said, "You know, you're not my sister-in-law any more." For an instant I thought, "Oh no, now that Jack's dead, I don't count as part of the Bingham family."

"How come?" I asked.

"Because you're my sister."

After the reception, Bob and I spent the night at a JFK Airport motel and flew off the next morning to London. As his son Bobby had warned me, "It's easy enough to get Pop into a museum, but it's impossible to get him out." Yet there were several times when, with Bob as with Jack, I couldn't keep up with my husband.

One day I suggested that we go for lunch to the Connaught Hotel where Jack and I had stayed, both with and without our children. I ordered a chump chop, mostly because the name struck me as so funny. But when it came, I couldn't eat. Waves of nostalgia were causing waves of faintness. I ended up going to the ladies' room and lying down on the carpet lest I black out completely. My "work of grief" was still far from completed.

When we got back to Riverdale, Bob immersed himself in *The Living Pulpit*, which published its first issue in January 1992.

Topping its masthead were two distinguished clerics, David H. C. Read, then known as the best Protestant preacher in New York, and Walter J. Burghardt, S. J., often described as the best Catholic preacher in America. Because David and his wife, Pat, lived in New York City, we saw a great deal of them for business and for pleasure.

Among the many devout Protestants, Catholics, and Jews with whom Bob stayed in touch about the magazine is his former Yale roommate, Bill Lovell, a Presbyterian minister in Chicago who had come east to perform our wedding. When Bob and Bill were at Union Theological Seminary in 1940, Bill, together with a few others, had refused to register for the draft and was sentenced to a year in jail. David Dellinger, who became the group's best-known member, ultimately wrote a book titled *From Yale to Jail*. He was given a book party in New York by Peter Yarrow of Peter, Paul and Mary. At Peter's apartment, Bob and I also saw Noel Paul Stookey, the Paul of the group who had become a friend of Micki and Erik's in Maine. I soon learned Dellinger remained a pacifist, but Bill Lovell, once he understood the depth of evil in the Nazis, forcefully did not.

With Jack, my house was not a home because it was a campaign headquarters; now it was a publishing office. Papers, articles, letters, and religious journals littered the front hall, the dining room, the laundry room, the kitchen, the porch, and our bedroom. I compared them to the driftwood, shells, and seaweed that cover beaches no matter how often these are swept clean. (Yet my own home office, be it admitted, was also a scene of "creative chaos.")

As I continued writing plays, I realized that theatre is prime territory for "hurry up and wait." When a play is in production, the playwright may scarcely have time to eat, but between productions, delays may proliferate. I, therefore, started writing short essays, some of which were published in the *New York Times* Op Ed section, and many of which were published in the *Riverdale Press*. But still, being a writer didn't feel like quite enough, and I thought I should also give back something to the world that had continued to be so generous to me. Yet the only volunteer jobs I knew about were either full-time or not quite my calling. Because I was still haunted by my frustrations as a visitor at Presbyterian Hospital's ICU, I wondered if there was some way that family members could be spared some of the anguish.

What I devised was a plan for a corps of volunteers who would take turns in the ICU waiting room to help the visitors. We could provide a shoulder to cry on and a voice to provide information about their patient; we could also direct them to the many services, like pastoral care or social work, that are offered by the hospital.

Such a program would cost the hospital nothing, except for a tiny office in which the volunteers could hang their uniforms, use a telephone-intercom, and keep a log of what happened on their watch. Nonetheless, it took me a year to get the then-head of patient relations to allot me five minutes to describe this project. But once we had crossed that hurdle, she called together an interdisciplinary committee that included the head of the medical ICU, the late Dr. Glenda Garvey; the liaison psychiatrist, Dr. Philip Muskin; and the head of social work, Esther Chachkes.

The group agreed that family members need a new brochure, one that demystifies the unit's procedures even before the visitor goes in for the first time. I got to work on the writing of it and, in time, with the help of Phil Muskin and the professional photographer, Libby Wilcox (wife of Jack's and my retired doctor, Bud Wilcox), a pamphlet emerged called *You and the ICU*. Ralph Andrew prepared a grant proposal for the United Hospital Fund, and Phil Muskin and I went to call on this institution with begging bowl in hand. The result was a grant for twenty thousand dollars to the Auxiliary of Presbyterian Hospital to cover the cost of a professional layout of the pamphlet, plus its translation into Spanish and the printing of fifty thousand copies in English and ten thousand in Spanish. Requests for it came from hospitals all over the country and Canada. A similar grant, several years later, from the New York Community Trust, paid for the reprinting of the pamphlet and the preparation of a video version, which went out to six thousand hospitals. The national organization of critical care nurses invited me to address their national convention in San Francisco in 1996, not only paying my way but also giving me a stipend of five hundred dollars. For many years, they handled the nationwide distribution of the pamphlet.

The volunteer program I named TLC refers both to "tender loving care" and "Trained Liaison Comforters." Our volunteers are a few men but mostly women, and we have discovered that it's best if they are quite mature. The imminence of death is too hard on young people unless they have had some professional training. One young potential male volunteer literally fled. At one moment, he was standing with me in the hall outside the ICU visitors' waiting room, the next moment, he was in the elevator headed down. There had been a death in the unit that day.

Most volunteers, including Bob and me, have found the work rewarding. At first some of the ICU nurses were edgy with us; they apparently didn't like the idea of laypeople snooping on their turf and perhaps tattling about their slip-ups. But, after time had passed with no such problem, I was asked to give a short talk explaining the program to the nurses. I pointed out that we were their allies rather than their potential antagonists, and that if we could keep the visitors happy and willing to return, then the nurses' patients would benefit. Also, we could act as gatekeepers when the nurses did not want a particular visitor coming in at a particular moment, and we could keep the visitor number down to two at a time.

One day a nurse pulled me aside when I was fishing for the keys to our office in a drawer in the ICU. "Would you please pay special attention to Mrs. Doakes? She's been begging to come in, but her husband is in real trouble."

I had noticed the patient being given cardiac resuscitation, so I assumed it was he. In any event, I went out to the waiting room and identified Mrs. Doakes. I escorted her into our little TLC office where she told me about her life and her husband. It turned out that they, too, lived in the Bronx. After an hour, her husband's doctor appeared. I immediately rose to make my exit, but Mrs. Doakes clung to me. "Don't go!" So I sat down again. Dr. Joseph Tenenbaum (who happened also to be my own cardiologist) knelt on one knee so that his face was no higher than Mrs. Doakes's. "I'm so sorry to have bad news," he said. "We did everything we could, but it wasn't enough. Your husband died." All three of us got teary. After the doctor had gone, I helped her phone some family members and then took her into the unit for a final farewell to her husband's body.

Once into my eighties, I resigned as administrative head of TLC and turned its management over to my capable friend and neighbor, Frances Dennison. Six days a week, a TLC volunteer is posted in the ICU waiting room. The very first, who claims he went originally with the tines of a pitchfork in his back, was Bob Birge. He sees the work as a form of ministry, and he and I continued to do it once a week for a few hours, often finding, as many volunteers do, that we receive far more than we give. One grateful family member tried to tip me a dollar; another said, "You volunteers have the touch of an angel." Actually, a lift comes from feeling so clearly useful, and the expressed gratitude by visitors is a welcome reinforcement.

Around this time, the new wealth of the so-called Me Generation was making itself visible in New York City, with chicly coiffed young women in ankle-length mink coats (despite well-publicized objections by the new animal rights activists), stretch limousines cluttering the traffic, and skyrocketing prices in top restaurants. Bob and I were grateful for the rise in the value of our stocks and their dividends, and I began talking to my kids about how best to reduce my estate so that they would not be faced by a whopping tax when I die. I discovered

411

that, in addition to giving to each of them and their combined ten children the maximum tax-free gift each year, I could also, over a seven-year period, turn over to them my ownership of the Riverdale house by way of a qualified personal residential trust. I also decided to sell the piece of beautiful river-view property that Jack and I had bought with the hope of building a one-storey house in which, some day, we would chase each other around in wheelchairs. I discussed with Bob whether he would want to build there, but we agreed that we were too busy to spend the necessary hours over blueprints and discussions with architects and contractors. Our remaining time on earth was too limited and precious for us to give up what we were doing. I, therefore, handed over the money from that property to the grandchildren—most of whom needed it for higher education, which I consider about the best investment that can possibly be made.

As I continued in this way to deplete my capital, my children commented that few, if any, of their friends' parents were doing the same. One set of parents, for example, left an estate of several million, without having ever handed over to their children or grandchildren the now-legal tax-free gift of ten thousand dollars a year. More than half their estate, therefore, went for federal and state taxes. Perhaps my well-off contemporaries feel uncomfortable talking to their descendants about money; perhaps they don't wish to reduce the funds that fuel their sense of security; or perhaps they think it foolish to give up the power that accompanies being the richest person in the family. Certainly, many novels and plays would be less riveting without the climactic scene in which the dominant elder's last will is revealed. In real life, my children will have no such drama. They know what's in my will and have even offered suggestions for making it more equitable.

Bob kindly assumed the overseeing of my account and began to make the kind of noises that Dick did when I gave away too much stock. Over the years, I became ever more grateful for the money that kept me financially secure but not elevated to the realm of mega-bucks. For, as I watched those few people I know in that category, I noted how much less free they were than I was from having to think about money. Emotionally, too, it seemed to force some of them, like doctors, to develop a self-protective detachment in regard to the suffering of those who come to them in painful need.

A small instance of the insulation that desensitizes the very rich occurred after I had treated myself to a wildly expensive but lovely blouse at a fancy boutique. The first day I wore it, I ran into Tod Rockefeller, Nelson's former wife. She exclaimed over the blouse and said that she, too, had bought it. "I hope you also have the matching skirt," she said. I shook my head, unwilling to explain that the blouse alone had taken my self-set clothing allowance for the year.

Jack used to tell me, every ten years or so, that he'd had lunch that day with Bob Birge. None of the three of us, in our wildest dreams, could have imagined that I would be having lunch with Bob Birge every day. Sometimes we discuss his problems, sometimes mine. As with Jack, the meal is often interrupted by a business-connected phone call for him. In any event, we never run out of topics for conversation.

What neither Bob nor I had expected, either in regard to his work on *The Living Pulpit* or mine in the theatre, is the frequency with which an ethical dilemma can arise. Jack had found the same to be true in law practice, as does our son Tim. Tim's son, Jack's namesake, Jonathan Bingham, M.D., says the same is true in medicine.

A moral dilemma for me arose when the producer of a musical of mine, together with its director, drew me aside and said that if I would agree to replace the show's lyricist, they would move to the next step in producing the show. I said that I couldn't do anything that cruel to a fellow human being who had worked so hard on the project. They shrugged and dropped our show.

Had I been younger, with a long life of playwriting ahead, I might have been tempted. As it was, the singer playing the hero came up to me after a performance at which the audience had shouted and stamped and applauded.

"June, you've got a big future in the theatre."

"No, my dear, you've got a future; I have a present."

PART SEVEN

The Nineties

CHAPTER 17

A Century Turns

IF I COULD TURN BACK TO the year of my birth and flip my eighty-plus subsequent years backward, I would land at the Age of Jackson, with its horse-drawn vehicles and gaslit streets, and death in childbirth by women in a sparsely populated America with very few Jews. That earlier time is as difficult for me to identify with as my youth must be to my great-grandchildren. Yet, in regard to the basic values by which Americans have been living, I suspect that fewer changes occurred during the earlier period of time than the subsequent one. Perhaps this was because Queen Victoria was firmly planted on her throne and her stable influence was widespread. Or perhaps it was because the second half of the 20th century included a degree of change unprecedented in history.

Some older people observe the world around them and take note mostly of its truly terrifying aspects. Said Einstein, "I know not with what weapons World War III will be fought; I only know that World War IV will be fought with sticks and stones." More recently, ecologists warn that we may already have passed the point at which "sustainable" development on our planet is possible.

Other older people emphasize the miraculous genetic and other new medical procedures that are in the pipeline. Because I see both sides, I probably fit into the category defined by late biologist René Dubos for himself, as "a despairing optimist."

Sometimes I am relieved not to be young any longer. Bob feels the same way, as did Alf even after he was declared legally blind. "There were lots of things I hated looking at," he said cheerfully, "and now I don't have to see them." Another brother-in-law,

417

Bob Birge, my second husband, and I at the beginning of the decade at a bene-
fit for Wave Hill, the arboretum and garden hugging the cliffs of the Hudson
in our Riverdale neighborhood in the Bronx.

Brewster, at eighty-six, with his upper spine bent to a right angle, said, "I look like a question-mark, but I feel like an exclamation point." In short, whatever it is that we elders have become, many of us have grown relatively comfortable with it.

Oddly, too, many of us are far less bothered by fear of death than earlier. I know it because in 1993 I ended up as "clinically dead" in the cardiac ICU of Presbyterian Hospital and wasn't afraid at all.

The problem had started on a Monday night when I dreamed that I was fainting. I woke up and I *was* fainting. On Tuesday, for the first time in my life, I forgot a lunch date. That night I again dreamed that I was fainting and woke up to find that I was. On Wednesday, I wondered whether to engage in my usual tennis game. I decided, when in doubt, exercise. So I played tennis and felt better afterward than I had in days. But on Thursday, while walking the dog, I had to sit down on a rock and drop my head between my knees in order not to faint.

When I got home, I phoned my internist and described the symptoms. In addition to the black scrim that had descended in front of my eyes, I felt as if a cape of stone had been laid across my shoulders, with a chill descending to both elbows. The internist said the problem sounded neurological to him, and he gave me the name of specialist to call. I called. But he could not see me until Monday.

On Friday, the frequency of the attacks increased; on Saturday, they were worse. For the first time in all the years that my internist and I have been together, I phoned him at home. His teenager took the message. I needed to know whether to try to play tennis on Sunday or whether that would actually be dangerous. He never called back.

By Saturday afternoon, I was miserable and talked to Calvin Plimpton, friend and internist. He told me to phone my cardiologist. I did, but the cardiologist was out of town. One of his colleagues, however, finally got in touch with me and told me to go immediately to the emergency room. Once there, I was attached to machines and eventually sent to a heart-monitoring floor. By then it was half past one in the morning. Around seven the two young residents who had cared for me the night before burst into my room, their faces alight.

"We've got it!"

"Got what?

"What's wrong with you."

"What?"

"Your heart stops."

"Really! "

Later that day, I was moved to the cardiac intensive care unit because the staff there had more experience with the machine called an external pacemaker. I was lying in my cubicle, with Bob sitting by my bed, when I said I felt another episode coming on. He looked up at the heart monitor and his face went pale. He raced from the room. I turned toward the monitor. The recorded heart action was absolutely flat. No peak, no valley, no ripple. Wait a minute, I thought, I'm dead, but I'm also watching it. Something is crazy around here.

Bob had a much worse time. At the central section of the unit he grabbed the first doctor he saw. "Help! My wife's in trouble." The doctor looked at the number of my cubicle: "Not my patient," he said. Then, taking pity on Bob, he said, "Look behind you." Out from the nurses' station, at a run, came a nurse, a technician, and a young doctor. They switched on the current in my external pacemaker that was already in place. It hurt.

"Knock it off," I shouted, "I'd rather have the episodes."

"No, you wouldn't!" They zapped me again.

The next day, my cardiologist surfaced and suggested that I stay in the ICU until Monday morning when one of the surgical specialists could install an internal pacemaker in my chest.

The physician-wife of my internist happened by. She explained that the reason I had felt so much better after tennis was that it provided fresh blood to my oxygen-starved brain. She said that her husband had figured since I'd played tennis, nothing was serious.

Several months later, I went to the pacemaker surgeon for a check-up. He gave me a circular magnet to hold to my left chest while he fiddled with his big computer.

"What were you doing yesterday morning at eleven?"

I thought for a moment. "Tennis."

"Good."

"Why?"

"Your pulse went up to 150."

As I was lying in the ICU, I had asked myself what omission in my life could, if I were to survive, be corrected. Time with old friends

420

was the item I had skimped most on, while absorbed in spousehood, parenthood, and career-building. After I got home from the hospital, therefore, I phoned three women with whom I had gone to grade school: Marian Sulzberger Heiskell, by now a civic leader involved in national parks, the Audubon Society, and the rebuilding of Times Square; Marjorie Lewisohn, M.D., a practicing internist and professor of medicine at New York Hospital; and Hilda Reis Bijur, a successful photographer. (An old friend who would have belonged with us was Joan Untermyer Erdman, but she had taken her own life by hanging during a weekend leave from a first-rate hospital in Boston where she was being treated for depression. Recent studies reveal that close to thirty thousand Americans annually commit suicide, some not in the depths of depression—when they would not even have the energy for it—but as they begin to feel better.)

We four had lunch and laughed at our past selves and the way we had blithely eaten eggs every morning and sunburned with reflector-collars to magnify the rays. We recalled how helpless we had felt at the threat of polio for ourselves and our children, somewhat the way today's parents fear AIDS. Overall, we agreed that while we used to have great hopes for our future, we now have great memories of our past.

As for the wartime or subsequent tragedies in our lives, we recognized that these had served to forge such strength as we now can summon, but agreed that we would never, ever, want to go through the process again. We also indulged in a bit of cattiness about some of our mutual acquaintances. As the restaurant emptied, one woman said, "Our next lunch will be at my place." Another said, "I'll take the following one." We had formed an instant tradition. It was a relief to all of us to notice the major differences between our wartime selves and now. In those early days, we had been terrified of losing out on life, and now, how could we be? We had lived it—in abundance.

Like many elders, I gain satisfaction from the thought that after my death someone else will have a turn with my corneas and slivers of bone or pieces of skin or whatever else from my body that can be of use. Yet not everyone agrees with me. One senior, a highly decorated military man, could not bear the prospect of having his eyes removed following his death, so instead, he went to his grave with corneas intact. His widow went a step further, though still not all the way. She willed her corneas to be removed and frozen, but solely for use by her own children.

I signed a document willing my corpse to Presbyterian Hospital. The hospital will send someone to fetch it if I'm lucky enough to do my dying at home, ferry it to the hospital, use it for research or teaching, and after some months, cremate what's left. The ashes will then be delivered to my family, all paid for by the hospital. It gives me the kind of satisfaction I used to get from creating a casserole (or soup or salad) out of leftovers that would otherwise be thrown away.

I mentioned the corpse-donation in front of a grandson who was about to start medical school at Presbyterian Hospital. His face altered.

"What's the matter?" I asked.

"When I start my class in anatomy, I don't want to pull back the sheet and find *you*."

He and I laughed so explosively that the other family members wanted to know what the joke was. When we told them, some of them did not think it was all that funny.

One of the greatest shocks both to my children and me was the death of Lex Hixon in middle age from cancer. Adelaide Hixon and Alec were devastated, and the world was deprived of a creative and charismatic spiritual leader. I phoned Adelaide every day for weeks, yet it was hard for me to take in the enormity of her child predeceasing her—in peacetime. At least in wartime other parents were going through the same thing. It never occurred to me that I, too, would have to go through something similar.

On the 7th of January 1999, Micki phoned me from Gainesville, Florida. Aged fifty-six, she was now the minister of a nearby Congregational church (United Church of Christ) and had been married for thirty-two years to Erik. Her two children, Jody and Blake, were now grown.

"Hey, Mom! Do we have any history of migraine in the family?"

"Certainly not. It's not allowed. Why do you ask?"

"Well, I was just doing my aerobics and suddenly I saw flashing lights and my head really hurts."

"Doesn't sound like migraine to me. Anyway, we don't have it in the family. Why don't you go to your doctor?"

The doctor sent her for an MRI, which showed a golf-ball-sized tumor in the center of her brain, inoperable because of its location. A painful biopsy revealed it as a fourth-stage glioblastoma.

Micki and Erik had been vegetarians for twenty-five years. "Wouldn't you know," Micki said with aplomb, "I'd have to get a kind of cancer that's *not* diet-related." She then took herself to McDonald's and had a Big Mac. For breakfast, she began enjoying boiled eggs and for lunch and supper, ice cream.

Our family and doctor friends fanned out to do research by way of the medical grapevine, the Internet, the Brain Tumor Society. The consensus was that without radiation Micki would have two to four months to live; with radiation, six to nine months. She opted for the radiation and during the following six weeks received a lifetime's worth, administered twice a day, five days a week, yet she managed to give sermons that were stunning through the power of her faith and the naturalness with which she explained why she was wearing a hat.

After another test, we learned that despite the radiation, the tumor had actually *grown*. At that point Micki was still strong enough to travel. She went to the Florida Keys to swim with the dolphins; she went to California to visit her godmother, Adelaide Hixon, and to consult an expert on former lives; and she went to Arizona to visit a Christian healer. She and Erik also took a trip to New York, New Haven, and Boston to see family members and some of their many friends. First stop was Riverdale. I shooed Bob and Erik off to whatever lunch dates they cared to make, and laid on an elegant ladies' luncheon for Micki and three of her close old friends. After the meal, they went out on the front terrace underneath my bedroom window. After I had washed up, I went upstairs to take what Micki called, "a little lie-down." When I awakened, I heard a chorus of giggles. For a second I thought, Oh, good, Micki's home from school with some of her classmates.

Many people also flew to Florida to visit her, some of her nieces and nephews bringing their small offspring. She called being around the little ones "Baby Power" and said she felt the stronger for it. Her brother, Tim, also came. Apparently when they were little, she had pummeled him more than I realized. "Your patient," he said to Micki's nurse, "used to beat up on me something awful." The woman chuckled: "I bet you deserved it!" and from their three-way mirth came a burst of better feeling.

Micki's son, Blake, set up a webpage that enabled people to stay in touch with what was happening and also to convey their love. This made a huge difference to her and to us all. Some messages were like mini-eulogies with humor that Micki could enjoy. Others were straight compliments for her singing, her ministry, and her joyous gift for friendship.

When the headaches became too painful, Micki was given a shunt in the arm that enabled her to administer her own morphine. She was exultant at no longer needing to ask or wait for it; this small return of control over at least one aspect of her life gave us all a lift. Her sister who visited shortly after the shunt's installation reported, half in fun and half in agony, "Mick's being her old bossy self."

For Micki's birthday, I sent her a jacket in autumn colors, composed of squares of chenille and decorated on the pockets and around the neck with boa feathers. It was the silliest garment I had

A Century Turns

ever seen and it cost a small fortune. When I questioned the price, the sales lady bridled. "But Madam, it's *vintage* chenille" (translation: from old bedspreads). Anyway, Micki adored it and kept it hung around the back of a straight chair next to her bed. She called it her joy jacket, and it fitted in with her deliberate attempt to turn her dying into what she called "a ministry of joy."

She was offered chemotherapy, but with only a microscopic chance of any success. She turned it down. Quality of living, not quantity, was her aim, and the hospice people did wonders in helping her achieve a seamless transition from ordinary life to its gradual reduction to its ultimate cessation.

She slept more and more and finally slipped into a coma. Death came nine and a half months after diagnosis. She asked that no one wear black to her song-filled memorial services, one in Gainesville, and one in New Haven. Her daughter, Jody, looked beautiful in the joy jacket.

At the end of the service in the church in New Haven, a middle-aged man in the audience stood up and sang "The Irish Blessing." He was Micki and Erik's friend, Noel Paul Stookey of Peter, Paul and Mary. His glorious voice repeated the last line, "And may He hold you in the palm of his hand," but in the final version he acquiesced to his friend Micki's preference, and sang, "May *She* hold you in the palm of her hand."

It was impossible not to cry. Actually, so many people, maybe three hundred, had come to the church that the reception afterward ran out of sandwiches. Micki would have laughed. "Serves you right for serving meat," she would have said.

At the reception, three of her former Rosemary Hall classmates came up to me. They had decided to raise money in Micki's memory to install at the school a bronze statue of an angel that one of them, Sterrett Kelsey, had sculpted. They showed me its photo. I was reminded of Micki's definition of coincidence: "Coincidence is God's way of staying anonymous." For that angel clearly resembles the young Micki and is smiling in her similarly contagious way. A coincidence? Or was it meant to be, as Micki would have said?

In addition to the Micki's illness, my family had a good deal of experience with cancer: my loss of my breasts, and Erik's loss of part of his digestive tract, my brother Howard's colon cancer, and my brother Dick's lymphoma. From a genetic point of view, it was odd that our parents never had cancer nor did three of our grandparents.

Two years after Micki's death, her first grandchild, June Edith (Edie) Aten, was born. The rejoicing by Edie's parents, Jody and Jeff Aten, was shared by Erik, the beaming grandfather, and Blake, the enthralled uncle. In time, Erik found a new wife, a professional soprano who had sung at his and Micki's wedding. Micki had instructed him to marry again, but to be sure that the new wife could sing to the grandchildren.

Bob and I greatly enjoy the role of great-grandparent. Nor are we alone in this. Never in history has there been such a cohort of buoyant elders as flourishes now in all the developed countries. With the reduced birthrate that coexists with this phenomenon, it's ironic that young parents today are likely to have more grandparents in the family than children.

To our surprise, Bob and I find that some of the rules we learned (the hard way) as grandparents can be ignored by the great-grandparents. For example, the chief rule, to keep one's mouth shut around one's grown children in regard to the way they are bringing up their children no longer applies as frequently. The new parents not only appear remarkably receptive to an "old one" reporting on how things used to be done in the quaint mid-20th century, but they sometimes actually ask for our advice. When I give it, I sometimes have no idea whether I am dispensing wisdom or malarkey.

A three-word phrase I often use is a plaintive, "It all depends." What this does is place the person's problem within a broader historical or sociological or psychological frame. Another irony is that just as I was once blamed by my teenage children for events over which I had had little control, now I am credited with helping to solve problems over which I have little control. The selectiveness of memory, both bad and good, never ceases to startle me. In a recent note, a grown grandson said that I was the first woman he can remember who took tender loving care of him. "Utter nonsense," I replied. Although, of course, I cherished him when he came to visit, he had a perfectly good mother at home. I even fished out an old photo of her cuddling him. He went off with it and eventually became more polite to her.

Also gratifying to me has been the growing interest on the part of some of my children and grandchildren in our Jewish heritage. In one sense, this interest is an individual thing; in another sense, it reflects a major change in American society. My own largest charitable donation each year is to the United Jewish Appeal/Federation of Jewish Philanthropies. My cousin, Robert Lehman Bernhard, is president of Temple Emmanu-El; my cousin, Manhattan District Attorney Robert Morgenthau, is chairman of the board of the Museum of Jewish Heritage in lower Manhattan; and my son, Tim, a devout Episcopalian, was the lawyer who drafted the 1998 statement at the national convention of the Episcopal Church that apologized to the Jews for the church's previous tolerance of atrocities committed against them, including the Holocaust.

Tim's passionate insistence on this apology stemmed from the time when, as a young teenager, his Episcopal Sunday School class was told that all non-Christians would be consigned to hell when they died. He adored his Jewish grandfather and couldn't bear the thought that Max Rossbach would ever have to suffer. Even though Jack and I assured Tim that his Sunday School teacher was a total idiot, the effect of that early fright stayed with him.

When Tim was invited by the Holocaust Survivors' Group in Riverdale to address a Sunday morning meeting, Bob and I accompanied him. Tim took the mike and explained that he didn't expect this group to accept the apology by the Episcopal Church, but he did hope that they would take note of its having been offered. After the applause for his sincerity and eloquence died down, the elderly female German refugee who was running the meeting announced, "Und now vee vill hear from de Mudder."

What? Who? Me?

But she was smiling in so welcoming a manner that I rose and went to the podium.

I now have no recollection whatsoever of what I said.

When Micki had been ordained in the United Church of Christ, I asked what she would like as a present. She asked for a pendant that would combine the Star of David and the Cross. I found a jewelry designer who created a beautiful combination of the two.

A major irony is how the anti-Semitism that so bedeviled my youth prevented me from making the worst mistake of my life, namely, to marry Fred rather than Jack. Anti-Semitism was also a source of irony for Jack. When Buckley tried to portray him as anti-Semitic, this boomeranged so badly that it alone may have cost Buckley the election.

As it was with Jack, Bob and I, too, have braided our lives together, our spiritual lives included. In *The Living Pulpit*'s first year, I read submissions, edited articles, suggested topics for future issues, and did some writing. Bob does similar editing in regard to my work. The short pieces now have a webpage set up by Blake called www.binghamlitbits.com.

As for my literary reputation, I was honored to be included in *Who's Who In America*; I also received an honorary doctor of humane letters from Lehman College in the Bronx. At last, I was no longer the only member of the Birge clan not to have something beyond the B.A. On December 31, 1999, the prospect of a new millennium caused Bob and me to bestir our homebody selves. Ordinarily, we spend New Year's Eve with Riverdale friends at the house of one or another of us, starting with drinks and an elegant potluck supper and ending with the clock having been moved forward an hour. We thus can sing "Auld Lang Syne" at "virtual midnight" and still be home asleep by the time the real witching hour comes around.

But this millennial night demanded something more. Fortunately, we had been invited to not just one dance but two. We, therefore, in our eighties, put on our fanciest regalia and ferried forth. We were twirling on the dance floor when the 21st century arrived.

The imminence of the millennium accented the need I was feeling to take stock of my life. Although I've suffered some failures, I'm relieved to note that, at least to a degree, I have "had it all." To be sure, the "all" was not at the same time, nor was it accompanied by any assurance that what I most craved for the future would ever come about. But on an ad hoc basis, I did manage to balance marriage and parenthood as well as my contributions to Jack's career and my own. As my father once cheerfully commented when he entered my house where four small children and two large dogs were gamboling about a messy living room, "Now I know how you do as much as you do; you don't do any of it very well."

In a sense, he was on target. To the annoyance of my young children who were scouts, I never baked cookies from scratch, and I took every other shortcut I could to make time for my writing. I learned to "do" my own hair and nails, and buy clothes that were classic rather than fashionable so as to preclude having to shop again the following year(s). Also, I was fortunate much of the time to have domestic helpers who, though far from perfect, were genuinely fond of children.

What Jack and the children and I most went after got accomplished and that, in itself, is a source of latter-day satisfaction.

My mother was rarely, if ever, satisfied with the best I could offer, and this aroused painful anxiety and guilt. It may be un-American to admit it, but I now suspect that some interpersonal problems are not soluble, and one may simply have to learn to live with them.

I learned even more about myself when the play I had been writing and rewriting with composer/lyricist Carmel Owen was accepted for production by an off-Broadway theatre. Not only did changes in the script of *ASYLUM: The Strange Case of Mary Lincoln* need to be made, we had to raise close to two hundred thousand dollars.

Through huge efforts, it worked. Most gifts were from generous relatives and friends, but a few came from foundations. The theatre itself contributed fifty thousand dollars. Fund-raising for a play, I found, uses the same muscles as fund-raising for politics. In addition to all the hand-written letters and phone appeals, we also organized cocktail parties at which some songs and dialogue from the show were presented.

The play ran for its planned duration and was a success both financially and critically. It received a long, respectful review from the *New York Times* and a rave from the very tough critic John Simon. The full-length review in *The New Yorker* was a startling one, and we got wonderful attention from other print and on-line sources. At intermission one evening, a woman came up to Carmel and me.

"Would you like to see some letters between Mary Lincoln and her lawyer-friend, Myra Bradwell?"

Would we like to see them? The next day we presented ourselves at her elegant Central Park West apartment. In an old flat trunk were many letters dating from 1875, the year Mary was incarcerated in the asylum (the hospital's name being, of all things, Bellevue). This trunk had recently surfaced in the attic of the woman's brother who was moving from Washington to Maine. She had gone to D.C. to help him pack. When she caught sight of the trunk labeled Lincoln she asked what it was. "Oh, just some old papers," he said.

The "old papers" turned out to be handwritten copies of letters dating back 130 years. In 1927, our new friend's father had signed an agreement with Robert Lincoln's widow to burn her letters, and he did so, but not until after he had had them copied. Also in the trunk was a carbon copy of a typescript by a granddaughter of Myra Bradwell telling more about the letters and what was going on at the time between both her grandparents and their friend Mary Lincoln.

As I read the letters, I could feel the hair on my arms rising. How spooky to see exactly what Mary was saying, particularly about Robert whom, as it became more and more evident, neither she nor Abraham Lincoln had much liked. Robert's feeling of rejection, which Carmel and I had intuited, was eminently justified. Said Mary in a letter shortly after she left the asylum: "I remember the contrast between RTL (she always thus referred to Robert, the eldest of her four sons) and my other blessed boys, the latter so lovely, gentle and noble. . . . " At that time, she was living in Springfield with her sister and, in effect, had stopped speaking to Robert.

Mary also quoted Lincoln as comparing Robert to a flower that blooms prematurely and never develops further. According to Lincoln, the height of Robert's development was at the age of six. For whatever reasons, both parents infinitely preferred their third son, Willie, and, after Willie's death, the youngest, Tad (the second son, Eddie, having died at age three). Not surprisingly, in time, at least in his relationship with his mother, Robert's behavior became dramatically unlikable.

About the production of the play, for the first time in my life, I fought "down and dirty." Early on, I was shocked to hear myself making tough threats, but I soon grew to relish it, especially when it worked. The little old lady in tennis shoes was morphing into a storm trooper with hobnailed boots. When the frustrated director told the show's producer, namely, the theatre's artistic director, that he, the director, would quit if I got my way, I said, "Let him."

But he didn't.

With proof and back-up from the historian, Jean Baker, who has written a definitive biography of Mary Lincoln, I tried to talk things out with the director and producer. Eventually, I became so frustrated with the director's refusal to listen that I threatened to turn to The Dramatists Guild. The guild is the playwrights' labor union and has explicitly declared that a director may not change so much as a comma without permission of the author. Fortunately, I didn't have to make good on my threat because the producer has the last word and he sided with me. But if I had had to tattle to the guild, I would have done so. The ferocity felt by a playwright protecting her work can be much like that of a parent guarding her child.

Another form of immortality emerged through Presbyterian Hospital's decision to take over the running of TLC. The Trained Liaison Comforters program will still supply volunteers to help visitors in the waiting rooms for the intensive care units, but its management will be by the hospital's Volunteer Department. Thus TLC, too, will long outlast me, as will the pamphlet I wrote for it.

Certainly few professions have improved as radically during my lifetime as medicine and surgery. In the early 1940s, I had gone into childbirth with what turns out to have been far too few worries. Statistics now show that delivering a child when Sherry was born in 1941 was likely to be the single most dangerous event in a woman's life. After the latter 1940s, when antibiotics became available, the risk fell more than 90 percent.

Not long ago, I learned that the estrogen I had been given for three decades by doctors in New York and Washington was a possible contributing factor to the pelvic cancer I developed. I came to need a hysterectomy with radiation and megace, a sort of chemotherapy that has no effect on the brain. As I told the oncologist, I need every neuron I've got left for the production of the musical and the finishing of this book.

PART EIGHT

A New Century

CHAPTER 18

Growing Older Without Growing Old

NOW THAT THE FORMERLY UNSPOKEN WORDS, s-e-x and c-a-n-c-e-r are freely trumpeted, the remaining forbidden word seems to be d-y-i-n-g. Euphemisms abound and many people refuse to face its inevitability for themselves or the people they love. One lady in her nineties kept phoning her daughter and saying, "If I die . . ."

In fact, a large percentage of people never get around to making their will.

I risked losing a friend recently when we met on the street, and I asked after her husband.

"He has Alzheimer's."

"Oh, that's the worst! Do any of the new drugs help?"

"He can't be given them. They might cause liver damage."

"Well, what if they do?"

Like the prince in the fairy-tale who had a frog jump out of his mouth, I'm sometimes startled at what emerges from mine. My friend was startled, too. She shook her head. "I guess we'll have to think about health in a new way," she said.

Next, I ran into someone who reported that the father of a mutual friend had just died at ninety-two. "Such a tragedy!" she said.

"It's not a tragedy! It's entirely appropriate."

Probably I'll end up entirely friendless, since the number of old friends I've shocked in this way is almost as large as the number who have already died.

I've been asked by four very different people, two men and two women, one very religious and all with clear minds and deteriorating bodies, to help them commit suicide in the forseeable future by way of an overdose of sleeping pills. I agreed to do so. But when the time actually came, they either had a fatal heart attack or sank into a coma or became so confused that they couldn't have swallowed the medicine. So they died in their own time, and I, for one, was immensely relieved. But I would have helped them, and I remain grateful for Derek Humphrey's *Final Exit* and other how-to books.

What my fate will be, of course I have no idea, and I spend little time worrying about it. My hope is that my offspring will not suffer any guilt if I give the dying process what we in the Bronx call a "noodge." Some of my children agree with me that a suffering, severely incapacitated elder has every right to kiss the world good-bye; some do not. I respect the distinction made by my grandson, a doctor, that there is a substantive difference between, say, requesting that my pacemaker be turned off and actually swallowing a batch of sleeping pills (plus an emetic not to throw them up while unconcious).

As for those religious people who insist that the timing of our death is up to God, not to ourselves, my view is that during the past fifty years our deaths have been postponed so often by medical science that God's role in it is no longer clear. To cut short medical science's further postponement of our deaths, therefore, is not a sign of irreverence toward God but simply a refusal to permit human agencies to further prolong the process of dying.

In the meantime, one of the advantages of senior status is the capacity to mull the past and discern connections between events that one could not possibly have known at the time. I wonder if the pleasure this affords is a reason why less depression occurs among people in their eighties than people in their twenties.

As I became advanced in age, I took stock of the people in my life who have died.

After Kay Graham morphed into being a national figure, I was delighted at how gracefully she handled her new power. In an odd way she became the mirror opposite of Shakespeare's "Kate." While Kate the "Shrew" started out as a power-wielder and then became a cozy adoring wife, Kay started out as a cozy, adoring wife and later became a power-wielder. At her 70th birthday in 1987 at a rose-decorated auditorium in Washington, she sat between her old friend President Reagan and his secretary of state, George Shultz. Bob and I were happy to be among the six hundred guests. The toast I remember best was given by the late Art Buchwald who peered about nervously and then said, "The fantastic turnout tonight can be attributed to one thing: fear."

Among the most elegantly attired guests was Pamela Harriman. Averell (who married Pamela soon after Marie passed away) had died the previous year. His funeral at Saint Thomas's Episcopal Church on Fifth Avenue was a splendid one, attended by nine hundred people. Afterward, as I was descending the outer stairs, Bill Walton caught up with me. "It doesn't seem right for you to be here without Jack," he said. I had to blink hard: "It isn't!"

Kay Graham had a classy death. She was walking along between two fascinating men (one being her pal and adviser Warren Buffett) when she fell forward. She probably had a sudden stroke or heart attack because her palms bore no abrasions. In other words, she had not instinctively put them up to block her fall as she would have had she been conscious. I had seen her only a month earlier when she gave a luncheon following a fine short memorial service for her older sister, Elizabeth Meyer Lorenz. At that time, Kay proudly introduced me to her granddaughter who was working at the *Post*. The two clearly had a loving mutual respect.

Arthur Schlesinger had a bang-up 85th birthday party at the Century, with all four of his and Marian's adult children present as well as his second wife, Alexandra Emmet, and their grown sons. Arthur and I had lunch to compare notes about all the things we want to include, he, in his volumes about the second half of the 20th century, and I in this far more modest work. He had concluded that the two most impressive social changes were improvements in the lives of blacks and women. I suggested a third, namely, the improvements in health. He died at age eighty-nine while dining at a fashionable restaurant. Hard on Alexandra, but perfect for him.

The only one of my bridesmaids still alive is Marian Heiskell. She, like myself, was blessed in having found a wonderful man with whom to enjoy a happy second marriage. She and I still laugh about many events of the past. In their 1999 book, *The Trust: The Private and Powerful Family Behind The New York Times*, Susan E. Tifft and Alex S. Jones said about Marian's father, the handsome and debonair Arthur Hays Sulzberger, that in the 1930s "there was speculation that he had had his eye on Mabel Rossbach, the thin, chic wife of his [White Plains] neighbor Max Rossbach and the mother of Marian's close friend June. As teenagers, the two girls openly wondered whether their parents were sexually involved."

When I read this, I phoned Marian to see if she thought I should write to the authors and correct their misapprehension about her and me in an era when we were far too naïve even to have had the vocabulary, let alone the lack of inhibition, to raise such a subject. "Heavens," she said, "you and I were in our seventies before we mentioned it!"

Her mother, Iphigene, in her old age, made it clear to my brothers and me that she bore no love for our mother. Marian and I could well understand her resentment. Yet my own view of my mother was greatly softened by the book, *Children of Alcoholism: A Survivor's Manual*.

It wasn't until my much later years that I could picture what a hard time my mother must have had as a little girl, as little Mabel. Her father nursed the bottle and her mother came to his defense, seeing his urge to drink as simply a "lack of willpower." The birth of Mabel had been followed by the birth of two younger brothers who, in the fashion of the day, were clearly preferred by their mother to the girl. Luckily, or perhaps not so luckily, Mabel was a beauty. She, therefore, soon garnered admiration from grown-ups, especially males. This also, though, let her down when she grew old and her looks fell away, as did her chief admirers. Lacking close female friends, to whom could she turn? She herself began to drink, never earlier than five in the afternoon, but after that, quite a lot. She was lonely, and the bottle and the phone were her chief companions.

Some things I had thought were virtuous (like trying to provide my mother with happiness) were so hopeless that I would have done better to spend some of that energy elsewhere. Yet my mother's psychiatrist once told me that my mother's relationship with me was the only one she considered satisfactory, and that statement remains a cherished reward. Also, as the years—and the writing of this book—have progressed, I've become more aware of how many good things she modeled for me, such as her athletic endeavors. She rode horses, played tennis and golf, gardened and swam, and her immersion in literature, theatre, art, and music also influenced me. As Doris Lessing wrote, "You have to be grown up, really grown up, not merely in years, to understand your parents." Again, as with a palimpsest, our parents simultaneously appear to us as both the towering archetypal figures who dominated our childhood and also the confused young adults they must have been at that very time, so much younger than we are now.

As I came to feel sympathy for my mother, and not just for myself in relationship with her, I found that Iphigene Sulzberger's frequent criticism of her was painful to hear, but I did not argue. For it was also clear that Iphigene herself had been hurt by Mabel's flirtatiousness. As the daughter of Mabel, I'd been hurt too, but it brought me peace to arrive at a greater understanding of Mabel's own lot in life.

Iphigene, however, refused to allow her resentment about the past to interfere with her current enjoyment of Mabel's offspring and their spouses. First Jack Bingham and subsequently Bob Birge were entranced by her, and we three shared many lively meals at her Fifth

Avenue apartment or her second "Hillandale" in Stamford, Connecticut. She remained my female role model. My male one was Alf Bingham. The last time Bob and I drove to Clinton, New York, to see him and Kitty, his mood was chipper despite the congestive heart failure that forced him to have an oxygen canula in his nose day and night. At the end of the visit when I leaned over to kiss him, he caught hold of my hand:

"You know this is good-bye?"

"Yes."

"Will you do me a favor?"

"Of course."

"Take part in my memorial service?"

"You know I'll do anything in this world for you."

"I love you."

"I love you, too. Always will."

He died peacefully not long thereafter.

Still alive and engaged in new adventures in 2007 was Adelaide Hixon, with two new hips. She was forced, however, to undergo the agonies of bereavement when Alec one morning neglected to wake up. She manages her widowhood with panache and is actively engaged with California Public Radio, Yale's new Hixon Center for Urban Ecology, and its Lex Hixon Professorship in experiential religion. We talked weekly on the phone for years.

Her and Alec's marriage was similar in durability to Jack's and mine and also to Bob's and mine, but very different in that both of mine have been peaceful while hers and Alec's was tempestuous. I disagree with Tolstoy's opening of *Anna Karenina*: "Happy families are all alike; every unhappy family is unhappy in its own way." In my experience, happy families are far from all alike.

A word I enjoy utilizing is the term for the reduced mental and physical health that bedevils elders, namely, "The Dwindles." Dwindles or no, Bob and I often voice gratitude when we awake in the morning relatively pain-free and with energy enough to attend to some work and play. At our vintage, the litany became, "If you wake in the morning and something isn't hurting, you probably died in the night."

Bob and I continued to communicate a lot with each other during the day but often by our two telephones rather than using the stairs. A new pleasure for both of us was answering mail, email or regular postal, the day it arrived, for I was no longer receiving so much that I couldn't keep up.

Knowing that around the next bend of life's river may be Niagara Falls was very different from knowing exactly when Bob and I would have to confront it. The value of this vagueness was brought home to me when a sister-in-law phoned to say, in her characteristically gutsy, matter-of-fact fashion, "I've just been handed my death sentence."

She was diagnosed with a rare, quick-acting cancer (mesothelioma) that doesn't respond to traditional chemotherapy—or radiation, which could destroy healthy lung tissue. She was told she had nine months to live.

After that, I phoned her much more frequently. One day she admitted feeling depressed because of her doctor's latest prediction. I found myself reminding her of how she and I, over the years, had agreed that often "the doctor doesn't know his ass from his elbow." At this she laughed. "And you," I said, "may fool him by outliving us all."

Before we hung up, she was more cheerful. Later, I figured that I had not, of course, postponed her death by a nanosecond, but unwittingly I had returned it to the realm of vagueness in which our own death feels most familiar. Now, like Scarlett O'Hara, she could decide—as she always had—to think about it, not today, but tomorrow.

Because we elders are existentially aware that our time is short, some of us have become defensive when asked to waste a minute of it. A daughter came to visit.

"How about selling off some of these oversized antiques that none of us has room for?"

"Nope. I don't want to spend even one of my remaining days negotiating with antique dealers. This stuff was handed down to me, and I am handing it down to all of you. Do what you wish with it, in as fair a way as possible. All I know is that material objects, no matter how valuable, are not worth my energy. And if you guys ultimately allow them to cause rifts between you, I'll come back to haunt you."

When disagreements arise between me and one of my adult children or grandchildren or in-laws, I find that I no longer fear their anger as once I did. I air my opinion, and if they don't like it, well, then, they don't like it. Similarly, although I often ask for their views, I no longer paper over such real differences as persist. Agreeing to disagree works out all right as long as the people's emotions are under control or some humor can be enlisted.

When I am directly or indirectly engaged in an intra-family disagreement, I try to avoid pointing the finger. Instead I try to recognize how each person was trying to do his or her best. The trouble, I suggest, is that the human condition is such that our best is often far from good enough. For devout people this is one reason to rely on God's forgiveness; for non-devout people it is one reason to summon the memory of those times in our own life when our best was nothing to boast about.

One of the unexpected pleasures of being old is that we feel less need to load guilt onto other people. In part this may derive from our having become less defensive over the years. As old Popeye used to say, "I yam what I yam." My parents' marriage, perhaps because of the potent social taboo against divorce, survived—yet remained troubled to the end. Still, I remain grateful for it. It provided me with nurture, but, given my open-eyed view of it, it also provided me with an impetus to act in ways different from theirs, including two braided marriages that were rewarding beyond my dreams. Jack, too, decided to treat his wife differently from the way his father had treated his mother, with equally gratifying results. A benign cycle can build as easily as a vicious one—having a braided life with another person is what has deeply mattered to me—as, I believe, it did to Jack and does to Bob. Yet, as Heraclitus proposed, change is the one constant in life. How can this kind of loving, career-intertwined relationship be maintained for the sixty or seventy years? The capricious quality of luck is one aspect of it, yet some people seem to attract more good luck than the average. When given the name of a putative new general, Napoleon asked, "Does he have luck?"

I sometimes peer back with curiosity at the famous people I was privileged to view up close. So many memoirs, letters, and biographies have been published since I first met these people that I have changed my mind in some respects about some of them.

Harry Truman struck me at the time as a person fully comfortable in his skin. Later, I was shocked to learn how meekly he bore the loneliness caused by the long absences of his wife, Bess. Yet I also had to be sympathetic with her because she, like me, had a fiercely demanding mother.

Dean Acheson had originally charmed me with his good looks and brilliance and occasional mordant opinions. Later, I went to interview him at his law office after he'd left the State Department.

"How do you like the practice of the law?"

"Not much."

"Why?"

"Because I really don't care which son of a bitch wins the case."

As Dean grew older, he continued to write beautifully but his arteries and convictions became more rigid. He even ended up pro–South Africa at the time when apartheid was still in force. One day when I was lunching with his wife, Alice, she asked if dinner for just the four of us would be a good idea. I sadly shook my head because I feared that Jack would either explode—or feel hopelessly frustrated. So why, in the name of pleasure, should we attempt what might become an ordeal? With an understanding smile, she nodded.

Dean died soon thereafter; she survived him for decades. As long I was in Washington, I continued happily to see her.

As for Adlai Stevenson, I still—and always shall—miss him for his warmth and eloquence and humor. On one occasion, President Kennedy asked Clayton Fritchey, Adlai's press secretary at the United Nations, why it was that Adlai continued to be so attractive to women even after he became overweight and almost bald. "You love women," Clayton told JFK, "but Adlai likes them."

Mysterious as the self is, the beyond-self seems even more so. As someone has said, the more we expand the circumference of our knowledge, the greater is our contact with the unknown.

For my own part, I conjecture that deep within the unknown the granite of that peak is identical to the stardust on the bed of the river of life. As a result, when our individual time comes to die, we may be returning to what is familiar. I confess that I also look on that prospect less as a cause for fear than a chance at nosiness. Of course, there may be nothing in the hereafter, but that too will feel familiar— since that is the condition in which the creature whom I call "I" used to be during the eons before my birth.

Bob, in contrast, is convinced, as was Micki, that there will be an afterlife. Jack had no idea and didn't much care. Even Reinhold Niebuhr was uncharacteristically vague: "No use," he said, "in conjecturing about the furniture of heaven or the temperature of hell." In truth, all we know for sure is the adage, "We shall see what we shall see."

Meanwhile, what I do feel certain about, to my surprise, unwittingly formed itself into pentameter:

What I know is that love, in all its forms,
Matters, and that a timely death does not.

Acknowledgments

WITH LOVING GRATITUDE TO Sherry Bingham Downes for her skilled editing, to Tim and Sue Bingham and Claudia Bingham Meyers for their enthusiastic comments, to Adelaide Hixon and Joanne Birge for their careful overview, to Stephen Berger for his political memories, to Mary Z. Gray, Claude Heckscher, Helen Lang, Kenneth Libo, Michael J. Rosenberg, Sandy Shalleck, and Pennell Whitney for asking probing questions. I also want to thank those consummate pros, Mitchell Waters, my agent, and John Oakes, editor. Bob Birge, too, deserves gratitude for conquering his reluctance to be written about. All mistakes can be blamed on the author, although a few might be sloughed off on that exhilarating but devastating and, in retrospect, somewhat unbelievable 20th century.

Index

Index

Index

Index

Index

Index

Index

Index

461